THE GIGANTIC ADULT JOKE BOOK

THE GIGANTIC ADULT JOKE BOOK

JOHNNY SHARPE

ARCTURUS

ARCTURUS

This edition published in 2009 by Arcturus Publishing Limited
26/27 Bickels Yard, 151–153 Bermondsey Street,
London SE1 3HA

ISBN: 978-1-84837-300-6
AD001191EN

Printed in the UK

CONTENTS

★ CONTENTS ★

QUICK COMEDY

WHY CHOCOLATE IS BETTER THAN SEX

1. You can GET chocolate whenever you want.

2. "If you love me, you'll swallow that" has real meaning with chocolate.

3. Chocolate satisfies even when it has gone soft.

4. Two people of the same sex can have chocolate without being called nasty names.

5. You can make chocolate last as long as you want it to.

6. You can have chocolate in front of your mother.

7. If you bite nuts too hard, the chocolate won't mind.

8. You can safely have chocolate while you are driving.

9. The word "commitment" doesn't scare off chocolate.

10. You can have chocolate on top of your workbench/desk during working hours without upsetting your co-workers.

11. You can have chocolate any time of the month.

12. You don't get hairs in your mouth when eating chocolate.

13. When you have chocolate it does not keep the neighbors awake.

14. You can ask a stranger for chocolate without getting your face slapped.

15. You can have as many kinds of chocolate that you can handle.

16. You are never too young or too old for chocolate.

17. With chocolate there's no need to fake it.

18, Chocolate doesn't make you pregnant.

19. Good chocolate is easy to find.

20. With chocolate, size doesn't matter.

★ ★ ★

GOOD, BAD & UGLY

Good: Your husband is not talking to you.
Bad: He wants a divorce.
Ugly: He's a lawyer.

★ ★ ★

Good: Your son is finally maturing.
Bad: He's involved with the woman next door.
Ugly: So are you.

★ ★ ★

Good: Your son studies a lot in his room.
Bad: You find several pornographic movies hidden there.
Ugly: You're in them.

★ ★ ★

Good: Your husband understands fashion.
Bad: He's a cross-dresser.
Ugly: He looks better than you.

★ ★ ★

Good: You give "the birds and the bees' talk to your 14-year-old daughter.
Bad: She keeps interrupting.
Ugly: With corrections.

★ ★ ★

Good: Your daughter got a new job.
Bad: As a hooker.
Ugly: Your co-workers are her best clients.
Way Ugly: She makes more money than you do!

★ ★ ★

A MAN'S GUIDE TO FEMALE ENGLISH

- We need = I want

- It's your decision = The correct decision should be obvious by now

- Do what you want = You'll pay for this later

- We need to talk = I need to complain

- Sure... Go ahead = I don't want you to

- I'm not upset = Of course I'm upset, you moron!

- You're... so manly = You need a shave and you sweat a lot

- You're certainly attentive tonight = Is sex all you ever think about?

- I'm not emotional! And I'm not over-reacting! = I've got my period

- Be romantic, turn out the lights = I have flabby thighs

- This kitchen is so inconvenient = I want a new house

- I want new curtains = and carpeting, and furniture, and wallpaper...

- I need wedding shoes = the other 40 pairs are the wrong shade of white

- Hang the picture there = NO, I mean hang it there!

- I heard a noise = I noticed you were almost asleep

- Do you love me? = I'm going to ask for something expensive

- How much do you love me? = I did something today you're really not going to like

- I'll be ready in a minute = Kick off your shoes and find a good game on TV

- Is my butt fat? = Tell me I'm beautiful

- You have to learn to communicate = Just agree with me

- Are you listening to me!? = [Too late, you're dead.]

- Yes = No

- No = No

- Maybe = No

- I'm sorry = You'll be sorry

- Do you like this recipe? = It's easy to fix, so you'd better get used to it

- Was that the baby? = Why don't you get out of bed and walk him until he goes to sleep

- I'm not yelling! = Yes, I am yelling because I think this is important

- All we're going to buy is a soap dish = It goes without saying that we're stopping at the cosmetics department and the shoe department. I need to look at a few new purses, and those pink sheets would look great in the bedroom and did you bring your cheque book?

- The Answer To a Female Saying "What's Wrong?":

- The same old thing = Nothing

- Nothing = Everything

- Everything = My PMS is acting up

- Nothing, really = It's just that you're such a pain in the butt

- I don't want to talk about it = Go away, I'm still building up steam!

★ ★ ★

HOW TO SHOWER LIKE A MAN

1. Take off clothes while sitting on the edge of the bed and leave them in a pile on the floor.

2. Walk to bathroom wearing a towel. If you see your girlfriend/wife along the way, flash her.

3. Look at your manly physique in the mirror and suck in your gut to see if you have pecs and abs.

4. Turn on the water.

5. Check for pecs and abs again. (no)

6. Get in the shower.

7. Don't bother to look for a washcloth. (you don't use one)

8. Wash your face, then armpits.

9. Crack up at how loud fart sounds in the shower.

10. Wash your penis and surrounding area.

11. Wash your ass.

12. Shampoo your hair (do not use conditioner).

13. Make a shampoo Mohawk (if possible).

14. Open the door and look at yourself in the mirror (but avoid eye contact with penis as you know about shrinkage).

15. Pee (in the shower).

16. Rinse off and get out of the shower.

17. Return to the bedroom wearing a towel, if you pass your girlfriend/wife, pull off the towel, grab your wiener, go, "Yeah, Baby," and thrust your pelvis at her.

★ ★ ★

TEN HUSBANDS

A lawyer married a woman who had previously been divorced ten times. On their wedding night, she told her new husband, "Please be gentle; I'm still a virgin."

★ ★ ★

"What?" said the puzzled groom. "How can that be if you've been married ten times?"

★ ★ ★

"Well, husband #1 was a Sales Representative;
he kept telling me how great it was going to be.

★ ★ ★

"Husband #2 was in Software Services;
he was never really sure how it was supposed to function, but he said he'd look into it and get back to me.

★ ★ ★

"Husband #3 was from Field Services;
he said everything checked out diagnostically but he just couldn't get the system up.

★ ★ ★

"Husband #4 was in Telemarketing;
even though he knew he had the order, he didn't know when he would be able to deliver.

★ ★ ★

"Husband #5 was an Engineer;
he understood the basic process but wanted three years to research,

implement, and design a new state-of-the-art method.

★ ★ ★

"Husband #6 was from Finance and Administration;
he thought he knew how, but he wasn't sure whether it was his job
or not.

★ ★ ★

"Husband #7 was in Marketing;
although he had a product, he was never sure how to position it.

★ ★ ★

"Husband #8 was a psychiatrist;
all he ever did was talk about it.

★ ★ ★

"Husband #9 was a gynaecologist;
all he did was look at it.

★ ★ ★

"Husband #10 was a stamp collector;
all he ever did was... God, I miss him!"

★ ★ ★

"But now that I've married you, I'm really excited!"
"Good," said the husband, "but, why?"
"Duh; you're a LAWYER. This time I KNOW I'm gonna get screwed!"

★ ★ ★

KIDS BOOKS THAT DIDN'T MAKE IT

1. You're Different – And That's Bad

2. The Boy Who Died from Eating All His Vegetables

3. Robert: Dad's New Wife

4. Fun Four-Letter Words to Know and Share

5. The Kids' Guide to Hitchhiking

6. Kathy Was So Bad That her Mom Stopped Loving Her

7. Curious George and the High-Voltage Fence

8. All Cats Go to Hell

9. The Little Sissy That Snitched

10. Why Can't Mr Fork and Mrs Electrical Outlet be Friends?

11. That's It, I'm Putting You Up for Adoption.

12. Grandpa Gets a Casket

13. 101 Things You Can Do at the Bottom of the Pool

14. The Magic World Inside the Abandoned Refrigerator

15. Controlling the Playground: Respect Through Fear

16. The Pop-Up Book of Human Anatomy

17. Strangers Have the Best Candy

18. Whining, Kicking and Crying to Get Your Way

19. You Were an Accident

20. Things Rich Kids Have, But You Never Will

21. Daddy Drinks Because You Cry

22. Your Nightmares Are Real

23. Where Would You Like to be Buried?

24. You've Got Hepatitis B, Charlie Brown

25. Valuable Protein and Other Nutritional Benefits of Things from Your Nose

★ ★ ★

THE INTERNET IS LIKE A PENIS...

It can be up or down. It's more fun when it's up, but hard to get any real work done.

★ ★ ★

If you don't apply protective measures, it can spread viruses.

★ ★ ★

It has no brain of its own. Instead, it uses – and confuses – yours.

★ ★ ★

We attach an importance to it that is far greater than its actual size and influence warrant.

★ ★ ★

If you're not careful, it can get you in big trouble.

★ ★ ★

Some people have it, some don't

★ ★ ★

People who have it would be devastated if it were cut off – and they think those who don't have it want it.

★ ★ ★

People who don't have it may agree that it's a nifty toy but think it's not worth the fuss made about it.

★ ★ ★

Once you've started playing with it, it's hard to stop.

★ ★ ★

Some people would play with it all day if they didn't have to work. Of course, some people do anyway!

★ ★ ★

THE PERFECT MAN AND WOMAN

Once upon a time, a perfect man and a perfect woman met. After a perfect courtship, they had a perfect wedding. Their life together was, of course, perfect. One snowy, stormy Christmas Eve, they driving their perfect car (a Grand Caravan) along a winding road, when they noticed someone at the side of the road in distress.

Being the perfect couple, they stopped to help. There stood Santa Claus with a huge bundle of toys. Not wanting to disappoint any children on the eve of Christmas, the perfect couple loaded Santa and his toys into their vehicle. Soon they were driving along delivering the toys.

Unfortunately, the driving conditions deteriorated and the perfect couple and Santa Claus had an accident.

Only one of them survived the accident.

Who was the survivor?

The perfect woman survived.

She's the only one who really existed in the first place.

Everyone knows there is no Santa Claus and there is no such thing as a perfect man.

Women stop reading here, that is the end of the joke for you.

Men keep reading.

So, if there is no perfect man and no Santa Claus, the perfect woman must have been driving.

This explains why there was a car accident.

By the way, if you're a woman and you're reading this, this illustrates another point: women never listen either!

★ ★ ★

THE PERFECT DAY

The Perfect Day According To HER:

8:45   Wake up to hugs and kisses

9:00   5 pounds lighter on the scale

9:30   Light breakfast

11:00   Sunbathe

12:30   Lunch with best friend at outdoor cafe

1:45   Shopping

2:30   Run into boyfriend's/husband's ex – noticed she's gained 30 lbs.

3:00   Facial, Manicure, Pedicure, Massage, Nap

7:30   Candlelight dinner for two and dancing

10:00   Make love

11:30   Pillow talk in his big strong arms

★ ★ ★

The Perfect Day According To HIM:

10:00   Wake up

10:02   Oral Sex

10:10   Big breakfast

11:30   Drive up coast in Ferrari with gorgeous babe with big hooters

2:15   Enormous lunch

3:15   Oral Sex

3:25   Play sports with the guys

4:30   Drink beer with the guys

6:30   Meet Tyra Banks

6:40   Oral Sex

6:50   Huge Dinner, served by topless waitress

11:00   Gorilla Sex

11:20   Sleep (naked)

★ ★ ★

GENTLEMEN'S QUIZ

1. In the company of feminists, coitus should be referred to as:
   a) Lovemaking
   b) Screwing
   c) The pigskin bus pulling into tuna town

2. You should make love to a woman for the first time only after you've both shared:
   a) Your views about what you expect from a sexual relationship
   b) Your blood-test results
   c) Five tequila slammers

3. You time your orgasm so that:
   a) Your partner climaxes first
   b) You both climax simultaneously
   c) You don't miss *Sports Center* (Sky)

4. Passionate, spontaneous sex on the kitchen floor is:
   a) Healthy, creative love-play
   b) Not the sort of thing your wife/girlfriend would ever agree to
   c) Not the sort of thing your wife/girlfriend need ever find out about

5. Spending the whole night cuddling a woman you've just had sex with is:
   a) The best part of the experience
   b) The second best part of the experience
   c) $100 extra

6. Your girlfriend says she's gained five pounds in weight in the last month. You tell her that it is:
   a) Not a concern of yours
   b) Not a problem – she can join your gym
   c) A conservative estimate

7. You think today's sensitive, caring man is:
   a) A myth
   b) An oxymoron
   c) A moron

8. Foreplay is to sex as:
   a) Appetizer is to entree
   b) Priming is to painting
   c) A queue is to an amusement park ride

9. Which of the following are you most likely to find yourself saying at the end of a relationship?
   a) "I hope we can still be friends."

b) "I'm not in right now. Please leave a message after the tone..."
c) "Welcome to Dumpsville. Population: You."

10. A woman who is uncomfortable watching you masturbate:
    a) Probably needs a little more time before she can cope with that sort of intimacy
    b) Is uptight and a waste of time
    c) Shouldn't have sat next to you on the bus in the first place

If you answered 'A' more than 7 times, check your pants to make sure you really are a man.

If you answered 'B' more than 7 times, check into therapy, you're still a little confused.
If you answered 'C' more than 7 times, call me up. Let's go drinking.

★ ★ ★

BLONDES

Q: Why do blondes get confused in the ladies room?
A: Because they have to pull their own pants down.

Q: Why do blondes wear panties ?
A: To keep their ankles warm.

Q: What do blonde virgins eat ?
A: Baby food.

Q: What's the difference between a blonde and a walrus?
A: One has whiskers and fishy flaps, and the other is a walrus.

Q: What is foreplay for a blonde?
A: Thirty minutes of begging.

Q: What is a blonde's idea of dental floss?
A: Pubic hair.

Q: What does a blonde put behind her ears to make her more attractive?
A: Her ankles.

Q: What do you say to a blonde that won't give up?
A: Have another beer.

Q: What do you call a zit on a blonde's ass?
A: A brain tumor.

Q: How do you get a blonde pregnant?
A: Cum in her shoes and let the flies do the rest.

Q: How does a blonde try to kill a fish?
A: She tries to drown it.

Q: How does a blonde hold her liquor?
A: By the ears.

Q: How do you know if a blonde likes you?
A: She screws you two nights in a row.

Q: How do you know a blonde's just lost her virginity?
A: Her crayons are still sticky.

Q: Why can't blondes water ski?
A: Because when they get their crotch wet they think they have to lie down.

Q: What do you do if a blonde throws a pin at you?
A: Run like hell as they still have the grenade in their mouth.

Q: Why are blondes coffins Y-shaped?
A: When they lie on their backs their legs open.

Q: What did the blonde's mum say before the blonde's date?
A: If you're not in bed by 12, come home.

Q: Why did the blonde tiptoe past the medicine cabinet?
A: So she didn't wake the sleeping pills.

Q: Why did the blonde stop using the pill?
A: Because it kept falling out.

Q: Why aren't there many blonde gymnasts?
A: Because when they did the splits they stuck to the floor.

Q: What's the difference between a fridge and a blonde?
A: A fridge doesn't fart when you take the meat out.

Q: What have a blonde and a moped got in common?
A: They are both fun to ride until a friend sees you on one.

Q: What does a blonde and a lottery scratch card have in common?
A: All you have to do is scratch the box to win.

Q: What's the difference between a blonde and an inflatable doll?
A: About two cans of hairspray.

Q: What's the quickest way to get into a blonde's pants?
A: Pick them up off the floor.

Q: What do you say to a blonde with no arms and no legs?
A: Nice tits!

★ ★ ★

There are more important things in life than money – but they won't go out with you if you are broke.

★ ★ ★

I told the doctor I broke my leg in two places. He told me to quit going to those two places.

★ ★ ★

How can you be over the hill if you never got to the top?

★ ★ ★

Have you ever stopped to think, then forgotten to start again?

★ ★ ★

I have been happily married for four years – three different times.

★ ★ ★

Sure you can't take it with you, but you can stash it where no other bastard can find it.

★ ★ ★

If a motorist cuts you up, just turn the other cheek. Nothing gets the message across like a good mooning.

★ ★ ★

Why is it when you talk to God you are praying, but when he talks to you, you're crazy?

★ ★ ★

Old age is inevitable, growing up is optional.

★ ★ ★

My wife and I always compromise. I admit I'm wrong, and she agrees with me.

★ ★ ★

The reason men lie is because women ask so many questions.

★ ★ ★

Rome did not create a great empire by having meetings, they did it by killing everybody that opposed them.

★ ★ ★

If you can stay calm, while all around you is in chaos... then you probably haven't understood the whole situation.

★ ★ ★

Doing the job right the first time gets the job done. Doing the job wrong fourteen times gives you job security.

★ ★ ★

Never put off until tomorrow what you can avoid altogether.

★ ★ ★

Teamwork means never having to take the blame yourself.

★ ★ ★

Aim low, reach your goals, avoid disappointment.

★ ★ ★

You cannot make someone fall in love with you – all you can do is stalk them and hope they panic and give in.

★ ★ ★

Life not only begins at forty, but it begins to show.

★ ★ ★

Don't you hate it when you are in court and the low life scum who beat you up and robbed you is referred to as a gentleman?

★ ★ ★

Clones are people two.

★ ★ ★

As I said before I never repeat myself.

★ ★ ★

Depression is merely anger without enthusiasm.

★ ★ ★

Eagles may soar, but weasels don't get stuck in jet engines.

★ ★ ★

Don't hit a man with glasses – use your fist.

★ ★ ★

I intend to live forever – so far so good.

★ ★ ★

If Barbie is so popular, why do you have to buy her friends?

★ ★ ★

The only substitute for good manners is fast reflexes.

★ ★ ★

Give a man a free hand and he will run it all over you.

★ ★ ★

When I'm not in my right mind – my left mind gets pretty crowded.

★ ★ ★

If you choke a smurf, what colour does it turn?

★ ★ ★

What happens if you get scared half to death twice?

★ ★ ★

I poured spot remover on my dog – now he's gone.

★ ★ ★

I used to have an open mind, but my brains kept falling out.

★ ★ ★

How can you tell when you run out of invisible ink?

★ ★ ★

Join the army, meet interesting people, kill them.

★ ★ ★

Laughing stock – cattle with a sense of humour.

★ ★ ★

Why do psychics have to ask you your name?

★ ★ ★

So what's the speed of dark?

★ ★ ★

What's got two legs and bleeds?
Half a dog.

★ ★ ★

What's the last thing to go through a bug's mind when it hits the windscreen?
Its arse.

★ ★ ★

How do you define marriage?
A very expensive way to get the laundry done.

★ ★ ★

Why do policeman have bigger balls than firemen?
They sell more tickets.

★ ★ ★

How do you make a bunch of old ladies shout, "Fuck"?
Shout, "BINGO"

★ ★ ★

Why does a prostitute earn more money than a drug dealer?
Because she can wash her crack and sell it again.

★ ★ ★

How can you turn a duck into a soul singer?
Put it in the microwave till its bill withers.

★ ★ ★

How do you reunite The Beatles?
Two more bullets.

★ ★ ★

What's the difference between Hitler and Alex Ferguson?
Both wasted millions, but Hitler won more times in Europe.

★ ★ ★

What's invisible and smells of dog food?
A pensioner's fart.

★ ★ ★

What do you get if you cross a Pit Bull Terrier with Lassie?
A dog that will rip off both your arms then run for help.

★ ★ ★

Why do seagulls have wings?
So they can beat New-Age Travellers to the rubbish tips.

★ ★ ★

Why don't blind people ski jump?

Because it scares the shit out of the guide dogs.

★ ★ ★

Isn't it a pity that the only people that know how to run the country are either cutting hair or driving taxis!!!

★ ★ ★

Did you hear about the Irish fox that caught its paw in a trap?
It gnawed off three of its feet before it freed itself.

★ ★ ★

What's got a big stomach and lives in the Himalayas?
The Abdominal Snowman.

★ ★ ★

What's the difference between cheese and men?
Cheese matures.

★ ★ ★

Why do farts smell?
So deaf people can enjoy them too.

★ ★ ★

Dolphins really are intelligent. After only two weeks in captivity they can teach Americans to stand on the edge of their pools and throw them fish.

★ ★ ★

A man walks into a chip shop and orders fish and chips twice. The shop owner says, "I heard you the first time."

★ ★ ★

What's brown and smells of pine?

A turd in a radox bath.

★ ★ ★

Why are elephants large, grey and wrinkled?
If they were small, round and white they'd be aspirins.

★ ★ ★

What is a clunt?
A man who runs out of a Chinese takeaway without paying.

★ ★ ★

How do you know you've passed an elephant?
You can't close the toilet lid.

★ ★ ★

A down and out approached a well-dressed bloke. "Ten pence for a cup of tea, guv?" he asked.
The bloke gave him the money and after waiting for five minutes said, "So where's my cup of tea then?"

★ ★ ★

A highly excited man rang up for an ambulance. "Quickly, come quickly," he shouted, "my wife's about to have a baby."
"Is this her first baby?" asked the operator.
"No, you fool," came the reply, "it's her husband."

★ ★ ★

What is there in common between a passionate kiss and a spider?
Both lead to the undoing of the fly.

★ ★ ★

"I can't find a cause for your illness," the doctor said. "Frankly, I think it's due to drinking."

"In that case," replied his blonde patient, "I'll come back when you are sober."

★ ★ ★

What is a woman with sperm on her glasses most likely to say?
I saw that one coming.

★ ★ ★

Why do gay men wear ribbed condoms?
To get better traction in the mud.

★ ★ ★

THINGS NOT TO SAY TO POLICEMEN

- Sorry, officer, I didn't realize my radar detector wasn't plugged in.

- And that hooker I met said you were a nice guy.

- Hey, you must've been doin' about 125mph to keep up with me! Good job!

- That uniform makes your ass look really big.

- Excuse me. Is "stick up" hyphenated?

- I thought you had to be in relatively good physical condition to be a police officer.

- You don't happen to have any beer in your car?

- I was going to be a cop, but I decided to finish high school instead.

- Bad Cop! No Donut!

- You're not gonna check the trunk, are you?

- Gee, that gut sure doesn't inspire confidence.

- Lets do it differently this time... I will give you the breathalyzer test, now stick this in your mouth and blow.

- Didn't I see you get your ass kicked on *Cops*?

- I can't reach my licence unless you hold my beer.

- Wow, you look just like the guy in the picture on my girlfriend's nightstand.

- When you smack the crap outta me, make sure you smile pretty for the camcorder.

- I bet I could grab that gun before you finish writing my ticket.

- Is it true that people become cops because they are too dumb to work at McDonalds?

- I pay your salary!

- So, uh, you on the take, or what?

- Those sirens are hurting my ears, turn them off or I am not speaking to you.

- So what if I was speeding, whatcha gonna do about it, Mr Hotshot?

- Gee, officer! That's terrific. The last officer only gave me a warning, too!

- Aren't you the guy from the village people?

- Do you know why you pulled me over? Okay, just so one of us does.

- I was trying to keep up with traffic. Yes, I know there is no other car around, that's how far they are ahead of me.

- So, are you still crabby because your mamma didn't let you play with your gun when you were little?

- Sorry, I can't hear you over the radio. No, I am not turning it down, I love this song.
- Either speak up or just leave me alone.

- What do you mean have I been drinking? You're the trained specialist.

- Well, when I reached down to pick up my bag of crack, my gun fell off my lap and got lodged between the brake pedal and gas pedal, forcing me to speed out of control.

- Hey, man, you want a hit?

- Hey is that a 9 mm? That's nothing compared to this .44 magnum.

- Hey, can you give me another one of those full-cavity searches?

★ ★ ★

EXCUSES TO GET OUT OF A BAD DATE OR OTHER SOCIAL CATASTROPHES

1. At dinner, guard your plate with fork and steak knife, so as to give the impression that you'll stab anyone, including the waiter, who reaches for it.

2. Collect the salt shakers from all of the tables in the restaurant, and balance them in a tower on your table.

3. Wipe your nose on your date's sleeve. Twice.

4. Make funny faces at other patrons, then sneer at their reactions.

5. Repeat every third third word you say say.

6. Give your claim to fame as being voted "Most Festerous" for your high school yearbook.

7. Read a newspaper or book during the meal. Ignore your date.

8. Stare at your date's neck, and grind your teeth audibly.

9. Twitch continually. If asked about it, pretend you don't know what they are talking about.

10. Stand up every five minutes, circle your table with your arms outstretched, and make airplane sounds.

11. Order a bucket of lard.

12. Ask for crayons to colour the place mat. This works very well in fancier venues that use linen tablecloths.

13. Howl and whistle at women's legs, especially if you are female.

14. Recite your dating history. Improvise. Include pets.

15. Pull out a harmonica and play blues songs when your date begins talking about themself.

16. Sacrifice french fries to the great deity, Pomme.

17. When ordering, inquire whether the restaurant has any live food.

18. Without asking, eat off your date's plate. Eat more from their plate than they do.

19. Drool.

20. Chew with your mouth open, talk with your mouth full and spray crumbs.

21. Eat everything on your plate within 30 seconds of it being placed in front of you.

22. Excuse yourself to use the restroom. Go back to the head waiter/hostess and ask for another table in a different part of the restaurant. Order another meal. When your date finally finds you, ask him/her, "What took you so long in the restroom?!?"

23. Recite graphic limericks to the people at the table next to you.

24. Ask the people at the neighbouring table for food from their plates.

25. Beg your date to tattoo your name on their derriere. Keep bringing the subject up.

26. Ask your date how much money they have with them.

27. Order for your date. Order something nasty.

28. Communicate in mime the entire evening.

29. Upon entering the restaurant, ask for a seat away from the windows, where you have a good view of all exits, and where you can keep your back to the wall. Act nervous.

30. Lick your plate. Offer to lick theirs.

31. Hum. Loudly. In monotone.

32. Fill your pockets with sugar packets, as well as salt and pepper shakers, silverware, floral arrangements, i.e. anything on the table that isn't bolted down.

33. Hold a debate. Take both sides.

34. Undress your date verbally. Use a bullhorn.

35. Auction your date off for silverware.

36. Slide under the table. Take your plate with you.

37. Order a baked potato for a side dish. When the waiter brings your food, hide the potato, wait a few minutes, and ask the waiter for the potato you "never got". When the waiter returns with another potato for you, have the first one back up on the plate. Repeat later in the meal.

38. Order beef tongue. Make lewd comparisons or comments.

39. Get your date drunk. Talk about their philosophy. Get it on tape, and use good judgment in editing to twist their words around.

40. Discuss boils and lesions, as if from personal experience.

41. Speak in pig latin throughout the meal (or ubber-dubber language, or just nonsense).

42. Take a break, and go into the restroom. When you return to the

table, throw a spare pair of underpants on the back of one of the chairs. Insist that they just need airing out.

43. If they are paying, order the most expensive thing on the menu. Take one bite.

44. Bring 20 or so candles with you, and during the meal get up and arrange them around the table in a circle. Chant.

45. Save the bones from your meal, and explain that you're taking them home to your invalid, senile old mother, because it's a lot cheaper than actually feeding her.

46. Order your food by colours and textures. Sculpt.

47. Take a thermos along, and hide it under the table. Order coffee, and fill the thermos one cup at a time, taking advantage of the free refills.

48. Insist that the waiter cuts your food into little pieces. In a similar vein, insist that he take a bite out of everything on the plate, to make sure no one poisoned it.

49. Accuse your date of espionage.

50. Make odd allusions to dangerous religious cults.

51. Don't use any verbs during the entire meal.

52. Pass the hat in the restaurant. Use the proceeds (if any) to pay the bill.

53. Break wind loudly. Add colour commentary. Bow.

54. Feed imaginary friends, or toy dolls you've brought along.

55. Bring a bucket along. Explain that you frequently get ill.

★ ★ ★

OXYMORONS

45. Act naturally
44. Found missing
43. Resident alien
42. Advanced BASIC
41. Genuine imitation
40. Airline food
39. Good grief
38. Same difference
37. Almost exactly
36. Government organization
35. Sanitary landfill
34. Alone together
33. Legally drunk
32. Silent scream
31. Living dead
30. Small crowd
29. Business ethics
28. Soft rock
27. Butt Head
26. Military Intelligence
25. Software documentation
24. New classic
23. Sweet sorrow
22. Childproof
21. "Now, then..."
20. Synthetic natural gas
19. Passive aggression
18. Taped live
17. Clearly misunderstood
16. Peace force
15. Extinct life
14. Temporary tax increase
13. Computer jock
12. Plastic glasses

11. Terribly pleased
10. Computer security
9. Political science
8. Tight slacks
7. Definite maybe
6. Pretty ugly
5. Twelve-ounce pound cake
4. Diet ice cream
3. Working vacation
2. Exact estimate
1. Microsoft Works

★ ★ ★

BAD TO WORSE

Good: The teacher thinks your son's great.
Bad: In bed.

Bad: Your children are sexually active.
Worse: With each other.

Good: You go to see a strip show.
Bad: Your daughter's the headliner.

Bad: Your wife wants a divorce.
Worse: She's a lawyer.

Bad: Your wife's leaving you.
Worse: For another woman.

Bad: You can't find your vibrator.
Worse: Your daughter "borrowed" it.

Bad: Your wife's arrested for soliciting.
Worse: She implicates you.

Good: Hot outdoor sex.
Bad: You're arrested.
Worse: By your husband.

Good: You came home for a quickie.
Bad: Your wife walks in.

Good: Your boyfriend's exercising.
Bad: So he'll fit in your clothes.

Good: Your daughter's on the Pill.
Bad: She's eleven.

Good: Your wife likes outdoor sex.
Bad: You live downtown.

Good: Your wife's kinky.
Bad: With the neighbours.
Worse: All of them.

★ ★ ★

Q&A

Q: What is the definition of "making love"?
A: Something a woman does while a guy is shagging her!

Q: How can you tell when a man is well-hung?
A: When you can barely slip your finger in between his neck and the noose!

Q: What do you call the useless piece of skin on the end of a man's penis?
A: His body!

Q: Why do little boys whine?
A: Because they're practising to be men!

Q: How many men does it take to screw in a light bulb?
A: One – he just holds it up there and waits for the world to revolve around him!

Q: How many men does it take to screw in a light bulb?
A: Three – one to screw in the bulb, and two to listen to him brag about the screwing part!

Q: What do you call a handcuffed man?
A: Trustworthy!

Q: What does it mean when a man is in your bed gasping for breath and calling your name?
A: You didn't hold the pillow down long enough!

Q: Why do doctors slap babies' butts right after they're born?
A: To knock the penises off the smart ones!

Q: Why do men name their penises?
A: Because they don't like the idea of having a stranger make 90% of their decisions!

Q: Why does it take 100,000,000 sperm to fertilize one egg?
A: Because not one will stop and ask directions!

Q: Why do female black widow spiders kill their males after mating?
A: To stop the snoring before it starts!

Q: How do you keep your husband from reading your e-mail?
A: Rename the mail folder to "instruction manuals"!

Q: What's the best way to kill a man?
A: Put a naked woman and a six-pack in front of him – then tell him to pick only one!

Q: What do men and pantyhose have in common?
A: They either cling, run or don't fit right in the crotch!

Q: Why do men whistle when they're sitting on the toilet?
A: Because it helps them remember exactly which end they need to wipe!

Q: How does a man keep his youth?
A: By giving her money, furs and diamonds!

Q: How do you know when it's time to wash the dishes?
A: Look inside your pants. If you have a penis, it's not time!

Q: What's the definition of mixed emotions?
A: When you see your mother-in-law backing off a cliff in your car!

Q: Did you hear about the constipated mathematician?
A: He sat down and worked it out with a pencil!

Q: What have Kodak and a condom got in common?
A: Thay are both there to capture that special moment!

Q: What's the difference between erotic and kinky?
A: Erotic is when you use a feather, kinky is when you use the whole chicken!

Q: How many sexists does it take to change a lightbulb?
A: None, let the old girl cook in the dark!

Q: If the dove is the bird of peace, what's the bird of true love?
A: The swallow!

Q: How do you annoy your girlfriend during sex?
A: Phone her!

Q: What should you do if your girlfriend starts smoking?
A: Slow down and use a lubricant!

Q: What's the difference between oral sex and anal sex?
A: Oral sex makes your day, anal sex makes your hole weak!

Q: What's the difference between pre-menstrual tension and BSE?
A: One's mad cow disease, the other's an agricultural problem!

Q: Why does the bride always wear white?
A: Cos it's good for the dishwasher to match the stove and fridge!

Q: How many men does it take to open a beer?
A: None. It should be opened by the time she brings it in!

Q: If your wife keeps coming out of the kitchen to nag at you, what have you done wrong?
A: Made her chain too long!

Q: Why do women fake orgasms?
A: Because they think men give a damn!

★ ★ ★

LITTLE JOHNNY

A new teacher was trying to make use of her psychology courses. She started her class by saying, "Everyone who thinks you're stupid, stand up!"
After a few seconds, Little Johnny stood up. The teacher said, "Do you think you're stupid, Little Johnny?"
"No, ma'am, but I hate to see you standing there all by yourself!"

★ ★ ★

Little Johnny is passing his parents' bedroom in the middle of the night, in search of a glass of water. Hearing a lot of moaning and thumping, he peeks in and catches his folks in The Act. Before dad can even react, Little Johnny exclaims, "Oh, boy! Horsie ride! Daddy, can I ride on your back?" Daddy, relieved that Johnny's not asking more uncomfortable questions, and seeing the opportunity not to break his stride, agrees.

Johnny hops on and daddy starts going to town. Pretty soon mommy starts moaning and gasping. Johnny cries out, "Hang on tight, Daddy! This is the part where me and the milkman usually get bucked off!"

★ ★ ★

Little Johnny woke up in the middle of the night and went to the bathroom. On the way back to bed, he passed his parents' room. When he looked in, he noticed the covers bouncing. He called to his dad, "Hey, Dad, what are you doing?" The dad answered, "Playing Cards." Little Johnny asked, "Who's your partner?" The dad answered, "Your mom."

Little Johnny then passed by his older sister's room. Again, he noticed the covers bouncing. He called to his sister, "Hey, Sis, what are you doing?" The sister answered, "Playing Cards." Little Johnny asked, "Who's your partner?" She answered, "My boyfriend."

A little later, the Dad got up and went to the bathroom. As he passed Little Johnny's room, he noticed the covers bouncing.

He called to his son, "What are you doing?" Little Johnny answered, "Playing Cards." The Dad asked, "Really? Who's your partner?" Little Johnny answered, "You don't need a partner if you have a good hand!"

★ ★ ★

Little Johnny was sitting in class doing maths problems when his teacher picked him to answer a question. "Johnny, if there were five birds sitting on a fence and you shot one with your gun, how many would be left?"

"None," replied Johnny, "cos the rest would fly away."

"Well, the answer is four," said the teacher. "But I like the way you are thinking."

Little Johnny said, "I have a question for you now. If there were three women eating ice cream cones in a shop, one licking her cone, the

44

second biting her cone, and the third sucking the cone, which one is married?"

"Well," said the teacher nervously, "I guess the one sucking the cone?"

"No," said Little Johnny, "the one with the wedding ring on her finger, but I like the way you are thinking."

★ ★ ★

Little Johnny's class was on a field trip to their local police station where they saw pictures, tacked to a bulletin board, of the 10 most wanted men.

One of the youngsters pointed to a picture and asked if it really was the photo of a wanted person. "Yes," said the policeman. "The detectives want him very badly." So Little Johnny asked, "Why the fuck didn't you keep him when you took his picture?"

★ ★ ★

Little Johnny is taking a shower with his mother and says, "Mom, what are those things on your chest!?" Unsure of how to reply, she tells Johnny to ask his dad at breakfast tomorrow, quite certain the matter would be forgotten.

Johnny didn't forget. The following morning he asked his father the same question. His father, always quick with the answers, says, "Why, Johnny, those are balloons. When your mommy dies, we can blow them up and she'll float to heaven."

Johnny thinks that's neat and asks no more questions. A few weeks later, Johnny's dad comes home from work a few hours early. Johnny runs out of the house crying hysterically, "Daddy! Daddy! Mommy's dying!!"

His father says, "Calm down son! Why do you think Mommy's dying?"

"Uncle Harry is blowing up Mommy's balloons and she's screaming, 'Oh God, I'm coming!'"

★ ★ ★

Little Johnny had become a real nuisance while his father tried to concentrate on his Saturday afternoon poker game with friends and relatives. His father tried every way possible to get Johnny to occupy himself – television, ice cream, homework, video games – but the youngster insisted on running back and forth behind the players and calling out the cards they held.

The other players became so annoyed that they threatened to quit the game and all go home. At this point, the boy's uncle stood up, took Johnny by the hand and led him out of the room. The uncle soon returned to the poker table without Johnny, and without comment the game resumed. For the rest of the afternoon, Little Johnny was nowhere to be seen and the card players continued without any further interruptions.

After the poker game ended, the father asked Johnny's uncle, "What in the world did you say to Johnny? I haven't heard a peep from him all day!"

"Not much," the boy's uncle replied. "I just showed him how to masturbate."

★ ★ ★

Little Johnny was talking to a couple of boys in the schoolyard. Each was bragging about how great their fathers were.

The first one said, "Well, my father runs the fastest. He can fire an arrow, and start to run; I tell you, he gets there before the arrow!"

The second one said, "Ha! You think that's fast! My father is a hunter. He can shoot his gun and be there before the bullet!"

Little Johnny listened to the other two boys and shook his head. He promptly said, "You two know nothing about fast. My father is a civil servant. He stops working at 4:30... and he's home by 3:45!"

★ ★ ★

Little Johnny was in church with his mom for Sunday Mass when he felt a sudden barf attack impending. "Mom, I think I'm going to throw up!"

She told him, "I want you to run outside as fast as you can. Run across the lawn and go behind the bushes. You can throw up behind the bushes and nobody will see you."

So Little Johnny hauled ass for the door. Less than a minute later, he returned to his seat next to his mom. He had the look of obvious relief on his young face.

"Did you make it all the way to the bushes, Johnny?"

"I didn't have to go that far, mom. Just as I got to the front door, I found a box that had a sign on it: FOR THE SICK."

★ ★ ★

A police officer had a perfect hiding place for catching speeders. But one day, everyone was under the speed limit. The officer found the problem: a 10 year old boy was standing on the side of the road with a huge hand-painted sign which said "RADAR TRAP AHEAD". A little more investigative work led the officer to the boy's accomplice... Little Johnny, about 100 yards beyond the radar trap with a sign reading: "TIPS" and a bucket at his feet... full of change.

★ ★ ★

Little Johnny comes in to school one morning wearing a brand-new watch. Obviously, his best friend little Benny wants to know where the watch is from, so Johnny tells his story: "I was coming from the bathroom to my bedroom when I heard a strange noise from my parents' bedroom. I walked in and saw them bouncing up and down. Dad said I could have anything I wanted as long as I didn't tell the family. I asked for a new watch and here it is."

Benny decides he wants one too, so night after night he listens outside his parents' bedroom for any strange noises and, sure enough, eventually he hears some banging and groaning from the other side of the door. He walks in and catches his parents in the act, so his dad offers him anything he wants to keep quiet about the whole affair. Benny immediately says, "I want a watch." The dad sighs and says: "All right, but go and stand in the corner and don't make a noise."

★ ★ ★

Little Johnny walked into his classroom one sunny morning, wearing only one glove. The teacher, a little confused, asked him what it was all about. Little Johnny explained, "Well, ma'am, I was watching the weather programme on the TV this morning and the Weatherman said that it was going to be sunny today, but on the other hand it could get quite cold."

★ ★ ★

Little Johnny was in school one day when the teacher brought around cookies for snack time. "Here, Little Johnny, have a cookie."

"I don't fucking want one!" declared Johnny. The teacher was shocked. She called Little Johnny's mother and scheduled her to come in for a meeting the next day. When Little Johnny's mother arrived, the teacher had her hide behind the curtain until snack time came around. As she came to Little Johnny, she again told him, "Here, Little Johnny. It's time for your cookie."

"I don't fucking want one!" stated Little Johnny again. The teacher pulled aside the curtain and said to his mother, "See? Did you hear what he said?"

"So? Don't fucking give him one!" said Little Johnny's mother.

★ ★ ★

One day, Little Johnny wanders into the local brothel, dragging a dead frog on a piece of string along behind him (thud, thud, thud). He goes up to the woman at the front and says, "Please, Miss, I'd like a girl please."

"Go home, sonny," replies the proprietor, not unkindly, "you're too young yet for this."

Johnny reaches into his pocket and drags out a £50 note which he slaps on the desk and beams brightly.

"Up the stairs, third door on the right," comes the reply as the £50 vanishes. Johnny starts to climb the stairs, (thud, thud, thud) when he runs back again. "I forgot, this girl has got to have active herpes!" he cries.

"No way, kid, all our girls are clean!" Johnny reaches into the other pocket and another £50 appears.

"Ahh, last door on the left..." he is told. Johnny climbs the stairs, still dragging the dead frog on the string (thud thud thud), and some time later reappears. He waves to the woman at the front desk and is about to go out (with frog) when she calls him back.

"I can understand curiosity at your age," she says, "but why the active herpes?"

"Well," says Johnny, "when I go home, the babysitter will be there. I'll screw her before she goes home and she'll get the herpes. Later on, dad'll take her home and have her in the back of the Mercedes, and he'll get the herpes. Later on, he'll get back and jump on mummy and she will get the herpes too. In the morning, daddy'll go to work, the milkman will come and get in bed with mummy and he'll get the herpes and HE'S THE BASTARD WHO RAN OVER MY FROG!"

★ ★ ★

Little Johnny goes to school, and the teacher says, "Today we are going to learn multi-syllable words, class. Does anybody have an example of a multi-syllable word?" Little Johnny waves his hand, "Me, Miss, me, me!" Teacher says, "All right, little Johnny, what is your multi-syllable word?" Little Johnny says, "Mas-tur-bate." Teacher smiles and says, "Wow, Little Johnny, that's a mouthful." Little Johnny says, "No, Miss, you're thinking of a blowjob. I'm talking about a wank."

★ ★ ★

A man was walking on the sidewalk and noticed up ahead that Little Johnny was wearing a red fireman's hat and sitting in a red wagon. It appeared that the wagon was being pulled slowly by a large Labrador Retriever. When he got closer to the lad, he noticed that Johnny had a rope tied around the dog's testicles, which probably accounted for why the dog was walking so gingerly. Smiling, he spoke to the little boy, "That's really a nice fire engine you have there, son. But I'll bet

the dog would pull you faster if you tied that rope around his neck."
"Yeah," Johnny replied, "but then I wouldn't have a siren."

★ ★ ★

Ten-year-old Johnny rushes home from school. He invades the fridge and is scooping out some cherry vanilla ice cream when his mother enters the kitchen. She says, "Put that away, Johnny. You can't have ice cream now. It's too close to supper time. Go outside and play." Johnny whimpers and says, "There's no one to play with." Trying to placate him, she says, "OK. I'll play with you. What do you want to play?" He says, "I wanna play Mommie and Daddy." Trying not to register surprise, and to further appease him, she says, "Fine, I'll play. What do I do?" Johnny says, "You go up to the bedroom and lie down." Figuring that she can easily control the situation Mom goes upstairs. Johnny, feeling a bit cocky, swaggers down the hall and opens the utility closet. He dons his father's old fishing hat. As he starts up the stairs he notices a cigarette butt in the ashtray on the end table. He picks it up and slips it in the corner of his mouth. At the top of the stairs he moves to the bedroom doorway. His mother raises her head and says, "What do I do now?" In a gruff manner, Johnny says, "Get your ass downstairs and get that kid some ice cream!"

★ ★ ★

Little Johnny was left to fix lunch. When his mother returned with a friend, she noticed that Johnny had already strained the tea. So the two women sipped their tea happily while having lunch and chit-chatted. Afterwards, when her friend had left, Little Johnny's mother talked to him. "Was it hard finding the tea strainer in the kitchen?" his mother asked.
"Ma, I couldn't find it, so I used the fly swatter." replied Johnny.
His mother nearly fainted, so Johnny hastily added, "Don't get excited, ma, I used the old one!"

★ ★ ★

Little Johnny was at school and his teacher was lecturing on the four basic food groups. Johnny asks, "What food group does light bulbs fall into?" His teacher replies, "Light bulbs are not edible and they don't fall into any food group." Little Johnny insists that light bulbs are food because his Dad eats light bulbs. The teacher tries to get Little Johnny to drop the subject, but he just won't let it go. He says, "I know that light bulbs are edible because I heard my Dad tell my Mom that if she would turn off the light, he would eat it!"

★ ★ ★

One day a teacher was asking her class to use 'absolutely' in a sentence.
So Janet raised her hand and said, "The sky is absolutely blue." The teacher said, "No, it is not; sometimes it's black or has different colours." Another little boy raised his hand and said, "The leaves on the trees are absolutely green."
The teacher said, "No, they could be different colours at different times of the year."
Little Johnny raised his hand and asked if there were lumps in farts, the teacher said, "No, I don't believe so."
And Little Johnny said, "Well then, I absolutely just shit in my pants!!!!"

★ ★ ★

Little Johnny walks into school one day to find a substitute in place of his regular teacher.
She says, "Hello, class, I'm Mrs Prussy. When you say my name class remember it has an 'r' after the first letter."
The entire class says, "Hello, Mrs Prussy."
A few days later the regular teacher is still sick. When Little Johnny gets to his desk, the teacher asks what her name is.
Johnny thinks hard and then says to the teacher, "I remember it has an 'r' after the first letter." "That's right!" she coaxes.
Then after a few seconds Little Johnny says, "Mrs Crunt?"

★ ★ ★

MORE Q&A

Q: How do you turn a fox into an elephant?
A: Marry it!

Q: What is the difference between a battery and a woman?
A: A battery has a positive side!

Q: What are the three fastest means of communication?
A: 1) Internet
   2) Telephone
   3) Telewoman

Q: Why do hunters make the best lovers?
A: Because they go deep in the bush, shoot more than once and they eat what they shoot!

Q: How are fat girls and mopeds alike?
A: They're both fun to ride until your friends find out!

Q: How is a woman like a condom?
A: Both of them spend more time in your wallet than on your willy!

Q: What should you give a woman who has everything?
A: A man to show her how to work it!

Q: How are twisters (tornadoes) and marriage alike?
A: They both begin with a lot of blowing and sucking, and in the end you lose your house!

Q: Why does a bride smile when she walks up the aisle?
A: She knows she's given her last blow job!

Q: What's the difference between a bitch and a whore?
A: A whore sleeps with everyone at the party and a bitch sleeps with everyone at the party except you!

Q: What's the difference between your wife and your job?
A: After 10 years the job still sucks!

Q: What's the difference between love, true love, and showing off?

A: Spitting, swallowing, and gargling!

Q: Do you know why they call it the Wonder Bra?
A: When you take it off you wonder where her tits went!

Q: How do you make five pounds of fat look good?
A: Put a nipple on it!

Q: Why did the woman cross the road?
A: What's she doing out of the kitchen in the first place?!

Q: Why are there no female astronauts on the moon?
A: Because it doesn't need cleaning yet!

Q: Why is the space between a women's breasts and her hips called a waist?
A: Because you could easily fit another pair of tits in there!

Q: How is the card game Bridge and sex alike?
A: If you don't have a good partner you better have a good hand!

Q: What do you call a cow with no legs?
A: Ground beef!

★ ★ ★

MORE BLONDES

Q: Why did the blonde go around the block eight times?
A: Because her signal light got stuck.

Q: How can you tell a blonde is being unfaithful?
A: Everybody in the neighbourhood is going to the pharmacy for penicillin.

Q: Why did the blonde jump off the cliff?
A: She thought her maxi pad had wings

Q: Why did God give blondes two more brain cells than he gave cows?
A: So they wouldn't shit all over when you played with their tits.

Q: Why do blondes like tilt steering?
A: More head room...

Q: What do you call a skeleton in a closet with blonde hair?
A: Last year's hide and seek winner!

Q: What is the difference between a 747 jumbo jet and a blonde?
A: Not everyone has been in a 747.

★ ★ ★

WHAT MY BLONDE FRIEND DID

- She called me to get my phone number.

- She spent 20 minutes looking at the orange juice box because it said "concentrate".

- She put lipstick on her forehead because she wanted to make up her mind.

- She got stabbed in a shoot-out.

- She told me to meet her at the corner of "WALK" and "DON'T WALK".

- She tried to put M&Ms in alphabetical order.

- She sat on the TV and watched the couch.

- She sent me a fax with a stamp on it.

- She tried to drown a fish.

- She thought a quarterback was a refund.

- She got locked in a grocery store and starved to death.

- If you gave her a penny for her thoughts, you'd get change back.

- They had to burn the school down to get her out of third grade.

- Under "education" on her job application, she put "Hooked On Phonics".

- She tripped over a cordless phone.

- She took a ruler to bed to see how long she slept.

- At the bottom of the application where it says, "Sign here," she put "Sagittarius".

- She asked for a price check at the Dollar Store.

- It takes her two hours to watch *60 Minutes*.

- If she spoke her mind, she'd probably be speechless.

- She studied for a blood test.

- She thought Boyz II Men was a daycare centre.

- She thought Meow Mix was a record for cats.

- She thought she needed a token to get on *Soul Train*.

- She sold the car for gas money.

- When she saw the "NC-17" (under 17 not admitted), she went home and got 16 friends.

- When she heard that 90% of all crimes occur around the home, she moved.

- She thinks Taco Bell is where you pay your phone bill.

- When she missed the 44 bus, she took the 22 bus twice instead.

- When she took you to the airport and saw a sign that said "Airport Left" she turned around and went home.

★ ★ ★

Two vultures board an airplane, each carrying two dead raccoons. The stewardess looks at them and says, "I'm sorry, gentlemen, only one carrion allowed per passenger."

★ ★ ★

Two boll weevils grew up in South Carolina. One went to Hollywood and became a famous actor. The other stayed behind in the cotton fields and never amounted to much. The second one, naturally, became known as the lesser of two weevils.

★ ★ ★

Two Eskimos sitting in a kayak were chilly, but when they lit a fire in the craft, it sank, proving once again that you can't have your kayak and heat it.

★ ★ ★

A three-legged dog walks into a saloon in the Old West. He slides up to the bar and announces: "I'm looking for the man who shot my paw."

★ ★ ★

Did you hear about the Buddhist who refused Novocain during a root canal? He wanted to transcend dental medication.

★ ★ ★

IN YOUR ANIMAL KINGDOM

This man loved his pet ferret so much he never went anywhere without it. One night he went to the cinema but was told that ferrets were not allowed in. Unperturbed, he went round the corner and stuffed the ferret down his trousers, then bought his ticket and sat down to enjoy the film. However, after half an hour the ferret became very restless, so the man opened his flies to give the animal some air.

Two girls were sitting next to him and suddenly one turned to the other and whispered urgently, "Tracy, that man next to me has got his willy out."

"Never mind, just ignore him," replied the friend.

"I can't," she gasped, "it's nibbling my knee."

★ ★ ★

What's the difference between a sheep and a Lada?

You don't feel quite so embarrassed being seen getting out of the back of a sheep.

★ ★ ★

An elephant and a monkey were strolling through the jungle when suddenly the elephant fell down a large hole.

Immediately the monkey ran for help and flagged down a Rolls-Royce on a nearby road. Hearing of his friend's plight, the people in the car hurried over, dropped a rope down the hole and pulled the elephant out. Some months later the monkey fell down a steep hole, but was rescued quite easily when the elephant dropped his donger down for the monkey to climb up.

So it just goes to show that you don't need a Rolls-Royce if you've got a big dick.

★ ★ ★

A rabbit and a mouse found themselves squatting down side by side in the woods. The rabbit turned to the mouse and asked, "Do you have trouble with crap sticking to your fur?"

"No," said the mouse.

"Oh good." And with that the rabbit picked up the mouse and wiped his arse with him.

★ ★ ★

It was the monthly meeting of the Paranormal Society and the subject of the evening's discussion was ghosts. The speaker got up and asked the audience whether any of them had had an intimate relationship with a ghost and a man at the back put his hand up, but said he didn't really want to talk about it.

"Oh come now, don't be shy," said the organizer and after much coaxing the man approached the platform.

"Now, Ladies and Gentlemen, I'm delighted to say we have someone with us tonight who has had an intimate relationship with a ghost."

"What?" gasped the man, stopping dead in his tracks. "I thought you said goats."

★ ★ ★

"Now listen, sons" said daddy hedgehog. "You're old enough to leave home and there are many dangers out there, the worst one being that busy road. If you ever need to cross it, but a car comes along before you get to the other side, just make sure you're standing in the middle of the lane and it will go over you without causing harm. Look, I'll show you."

The hedgehog went out to the middle of the lane and waited for an on-coming car.

"Here comes one!" he shouted. "Now watch how its..." But that was all he had time to say before there was a sickening crunchy sound and poor dad was flattened.

"Oh dear," said one of the sons, "I meant to ask him about three-wheelers."

★ ★ ★

Two visiting athletes took time off to go on safari but they got separated from the rest of the party and soon found themselves face to face with a very angry lion. One of them immediately bent down to put his running shoes on and the other said, puzzled, "It's no good doing that, you'll never outrun the beast."

"I know," replied the first, "but if I can outrun you, that's all I have to do."

★ ★ ★

A motorist was having trouble with his car and stopped to see what the problem was. He'd been peering under the bonnet for a few minutes when a voice behind him said, "It'll be the carburettor."

Startled, the motorist looked around but all he could see was an old cow in the nearby field. He felt spooked out by the whole episode so jumped quickly back in the car and headed for the nearest garage. Later, as the mechanic was inspecting the car, the motorist recounted his experience.

"Was it a black and white cow with a crooked horn?"

"Yes, it was," he replied.

"Oh don't listen to her, she'll never make a good mechanic."

★ ★ ★

Why are there no aspirins in the jungle?

Because the parrots eat 'em all (paracetamol).

★ ★ ★

A deadly germ is chasing an arsehole through the park when the arsehole bumps into a wandering genie.

"Oh, please help me get away from this deadly germ," he pleads.

"OK," says the genie, "I've got nothing on this afternoon. I'll disguise you as a cat, just sit quietly in that tree over there."

A moment later the deadly germ appears and goes up to the cat.

"Have you seen an arsehole around here?"

The cat shakes his head and the germ is about to leave when he notices the cat is hanging on like grim death.

"You're an odd cat, why are you shaking so much? I thought cats were at home up trees."

The cat doesn't answer.

"Come on," says the germ," have you got nothing to say for yourself?"
By this time the cat is so terrified he opens his mouth to speak and out
comes a particularly noxious fart.

★ ★ ★

Two parrots are sitting on a perch and one says to the other, "Can you
smell fish?"

★ ★ ★

What do you call a flock of sheep tied to a West Country lamp post?
A Leisure Centre.

★ ★ ★

"What have you got there, Bob?" asks his mate.
"It's an elephant that fucks cats."
"Get away, that's got to be impossible!"
"Listen, I'll show you. See that cat over there?" And as he looks up, the
elephant goes over and squashes it with his foot. "See, I told you."

★ ★ ★

What do you call a lion with a loaf of bread in each ear?
Anything you like: it can't hear you.

★ ★ ★

A man went to the pet shop to buy a parrot but the only one on offer
cost £500.
"Why is it so expensive?" he asked.
"Ah well, it's a very special parrot, it lays square eggs," said the
petshop owner.
"How very odd. OK, I'll take it, but just one thing – does it talk?"
"Well, it's got the ability to talk, but up to now all I've heard is 'Aagh,
oooh, bugger...'"

★ ★ ★

A man walked into a club with a pet snake under his arm.
"Hey, you can't bring that snake in here, he might bite one of our members," said the Manager.
"Oh that's no problem, you just get a friend to suck the poison out."
"But what if he bites someone up the backside?"
"Well, then you really find out who your friends are."

★ ★ ★

It's Christmas Eve and there's a knock on the door, but when Jack opens it he can't see anyone until he looks down and notices a snail.
"Go on, piss off!" he says and kicks it away.
Easter comes round and there's a knock at the door and, when Jack opens it, he sees the same snail on the doorstep.
"What's wrong with you then? Got the hump or something?"

★ ★ ★

A man goes into the vet's.
"Say aaah...." says the vet.
"Why?" asks the man.
"Because your dog died half an hour ago."

★ ★ ★

A man, a parrot and a budgie were standing on the edge of Beachy Head. Suddenly the man jumped off and hit the rocks below with a mighty thud, dying instantly.
"Fuck that," said the parrot, "I don't think much of this parrot-gliding."
"And I'm not into budgie jumping, either," said his companion.

★ ★ ★

Pause for thought:
should mountain goats be illegal?

★ ★ ★

A randy old gorilla was walking through the wildlife park when he saw a lion bending over, drinking from the water hole. Unable to restrain himself, he came up quietly behind the animal, grabbed him by the front paws and gave him a good rogering. Once free, the lion went berserk, determined to take revenge on his attacker. Meanwhile, the gorilla had raced back into the undergrowth where he came across a lone hunter. He got rid of the man, took off his clothes and put them on himself, covering up his fur with a long coat and pulling a hat low down over his forehead. Among the man's belongings there was also a newspaper which he held up in front of his face and started to read. A moment later, the lion came along, saw the 'would be' hunter and asked him if he'd seen a gorilla.

"You mean the gorilla that molested a lion down by the watering hole?" he said.

"Bloody hell!" said the astonished lion. "Don't tell me it's in the papers already."

★ ★ ★

A woman was given a parrot for her birthday, but the bird had grown up with a "bad attitude" and some of the foulest language she had ever heard. Try as hard as she could – teaching it new words, soothing it with music – she could not get the parrot to change. One day, he was even worse than usual. She got so angry that she put him in the freezer and closed the door. The bird could be heard squawking, kicking and screaming, and then all went quiet. Frightened that she may have harmed him, she quickly opened the door and the parrot calmly stepped out.

"I am very sorry that I might have offended you with my bad language and beg for your forgiveness. I will try as hard as I can to change my ways," he said.

Astonished at the change in the bird's attitude, she was just about to ask him why, when he said, "By the way, may I humbly ask what the chicken did?"

★ ★ ★

What do you call a man with 14 rabbits up his arse?
Warren.

★ ★ ★

Once there was a small private zoo that was dependent on public contributions to pay for its upkeep. However, times were tough and the zoo was losing money hand over fist. Somehow the owner had to raise some cash. He came up with a brilliant idea. The next day, notices went up that anyone who could make the most ferocious lion jump straight up in the air would win £1,000. The entry fee would be £50. Many people tried, but no-one succeeded and much to the owner's delight, a lot of money was raised. Then, two days later, a small rather insipid man arrived at the zoo and offered his £50 to take up the bet. Feeling quite safe, the owner took him over to the lion's cage and called for witnesses. When a crowd had gathered, the man produced a wooden truncheon from within his coat, swung it around in the air and hit the lion's balls as hard as possible. With an almighty growl, the lion jumped three foot into the air. Very dispirited, the man handed over the £1,000 prize. A couple of months passed and the owner was forced to think up another bet. This time he decided to challenge people to make the lion shake his head from side to side within 15 seconds of meeting it. It was a roaring success and the financial situation started to improve. Alas, to his horror, the insipid man appeared one week later and handed over his entry fee. He went over to the lion and whispered, "Do you remember me?" The lion nodded apprehensively.
"Do you want me to do the same as I did last time?"
And the lion shook his head vigorously.

★ ★ ★

Two men on safari were cooling down by dangling their feet in the river. Suddenly, one of them screams. "Aggh, an alligator has just bitten off my foot."
"Which one?"
"I don't bloody know. When you've seen one, you've seen them all."

★ ★ ★

A man buys two dogs from the pet shop and no matter what he does he can't stop them from shagging. He tries throwing cold water over them, putting pepper on their backsides, and then changing their diet – but nothing works. In desperation he rings the vet in the middle of the night to tell him the problem.

"Here's a good idea," says the vet. "Why don't you take the telephone over to the dogs and give each of them a ring."

"Will that really work?" replies the astonished man.

"Well, it damn well worked on me," says the vet as he slams down the phone.

★ ★ ★

Out in the middle of the jungle a hunter spots a gorilla standing in a clearing. He takes aim and fires, but when he goes to collect his prize, there's no sign of the animal. Suddenly there's a voice behind him. "I'm fed up being target practice for you lot. Now get down on your knees and give me a blow job."

The hunter has no choice but to comply, thankful he has got off with his life. However, the next day he returns with a bigger and better gun, spies the gorilla and fires. Again he misses and again he is forced to see to the big brute.

Determined to succeed, the man returns on a third day, this time with telescopic sight, and tries again. Once more he fails and, as he gets down on his knees to give the gorilla another blow job, the animal says to him, "You know, I'm beginning to think it's more than the hunting you're after."

★ ★ ★

A man goes hunting with his two dogs and a monkey and his fellow hunters ask him what the monkey is for. He replies "When the dogs have cornered the animal up a tree the monkey goes in and shoots it at close range." Later in the day they hear the dogs barking so a gun is handed to the monkey and he shins up the tree only to return a few seconds later. He jumps to the ground and immediately shoots the dog dead. "Bloody hell" exclaims one of the hunters. "Why did he do that?" The man replied, "If there's one thing he can't stand, it's liars."

★ ★ ★

Two old ladies visiting the zoo land up at the giraffe enclosure and are amazed to find the giraffe's testicles just inches from their faces. One of the old ladies can't help herself and leans through the fence squeezing one of the testicles in her hand. All at once the animal jumps into the air, clears the fencing and gallops off into the distance. The zookeeper rushes out to find out what has happened and when he hears the two old ladies explain, he immediately drops his pants.
"Here, you'd better do the same to me, I've got to catch that son of a bitch!"

★ ★ ★

A man goes to buy some rat poison. The shopkeeper gives him a bottle of powder and tells him to sprinkle it round his hole.
Exasperated, the man replies, "If I could get that close I'd step on him!"

★ ★ ★

A rather shy girl is visiting the zoo when suddenly, as she passes the monkey house, a huge ape grabs her, pulls her over the moat and gives her a good seeing to. Afterwards she is taken to hospital in a state of shock and it is almost a week before she is allowed any visitors. When she does eventually have friends to see her and they ask how she is, she replies, "Terrible, he hasn't phoned, sent a letter..."

★ ★ ★

A woman is left a pair of parrots in her aunt's will and immediately rings the vet to ask him how she can tell which was the male and which the female.
The vet tells her to creep down first thing in the morning and if she

catches them mating, then the one on top is the male and she should mark him with some tape. This the woman does and on catching them in the act she puts a white tape around the male bird's neck. A couple of days later the vicar comes to tea and on seeing him the male parrot says, "Ah ha, I see you've been caught mounting a woman as well."

★ ★ ★

A man and a parrot find themselves sitting next to each other on a plane. As the stewardess comes along, the man asks for a coffee, at which point the parrot shouts, "Get me a brandy and be quick about it!"

A little upset by his attitude, the stewardess goes off and returns with the brandy but not the coffee.

"Excuse me, Miss, you've forgotten my coffee," he tells her.

"Oh sorry," she replies and is just about to go when the parrot shouts even louder, "And get me another brandy, you incompetent cow!"

This time she's very upset, but returns quickly with the brandy, having forgotten once again to get the man's coffee. Maybe if I take the same attitude as this parrot I might get results, he thinks to himself.

"Hey, get me my coffee quick or you'll be sorry, you silly bitch."

In no time at all the stewardess returns with two male colleagues who drag both the man and the parrot from their seats and throw them out of the emergency hatch. As the man passes the parrot on the way down, the bird turns to him and says, "For someone who can't fly, you've sure got a foul mouth on you."

★ ★ ★

In another part of the parish a woman has a parrot who uses such foul language she has to keep him covered up when visitors call round. One day the vicar comes to tea and on hearing about her problem suggests he take the parrot back to his house where he has a female parrot who is forever on her knees praying. Maybe she can change his ways. The woman agrees and the parrot goes back with the vicar. As soon as he is put in the female parrot's cage, his awful behaviour begins.

"C'mon girl, let's get to it, let's get a bit of screwing done."
Lo and behold, before the vicar or the lady can intervene, the female parrot replies, "At long bloody last, my prayers have been answered."

★ ★ ★

Two mates are out walking when one suddenly rushes behind a bush to have a pee. Unfortunately, there's a snake hiding in the undergrowth and when Jack gets out his penis the snake bites it. Hearing Jack's screams, Bob rushes over and, seeing what has happened, rushes off to the doctor's.
"You'll have to hurry, otherwise your friend will die," says the doctor.
"Cut a small incision in the wound and suck out all the poison, but be quick."
Bob goes back to his mate who's looking very pale and weak.
"What did the doctor say?" he whispers.
"I'm sorry, mate, you're going to die."

★ ★ ★

A man comes home from work one day to find a rat shagging the backside off a cat in the garden. The next evening he returns home to find the rat doing the same thing to a bull terrier. Unable to believe his eyes, he takes the rat into the house to show his wife but as soon as she sees it she screams, "Aahh, get that sex maniac out of here."

★ ★ ★

Three dogs meet up in the vet's. The Alsatian tells the other two he's being put down for biting his next door neighbour. "Same here", says the second dog – a Rotweiler. "I've scared too many children at the local school."
The third dog, a Great Dane, says, "I'm here because yesterday my gorgeous blonde owner got out of the bath, bent down to dry her feet and without a second thought I mounted her and did what comes naturally."

"So you're being put down as well," ask the other two dogs.
"Oh no, I'm here to have my nails cut."

★ ★ ★

A female elephant is having an awful time with flies who keep biting her on a part of her back too far away for her to shoo them off with her tail. When a little blackbird sees this he quickly lands on her back and within a minute has eaten up all the flies.
"Oh thank you so much!" cries the elephant. "If ever you need a favour doing, please don't hesitate to ask."
"Well, actually," stutters the bird, "I did often wonder what it would be like to shag an elephant. Would you mind?"
The elephant gives her permission and the blackbird gets on with the business. Suddenly a bunch of bananas fall off a tree and hits the elephant on the head. "Ouch!" she yells.
"Oh sorry," replies the bird. "I didn't mean to hurt you."

★ ★ ★

This is the story of the three bears. One of them married a giraffe. The other two put him up to it.

★ ★ ★

A man goes into a bar with a giraffe and they both get horribly drunk until the giraffe collapses in a dead faint on the floor and the man gets up to leave.
"Hey," says the bartender. "You can't leave that lyin' there."
"It's not a lion, it's a giraffe," he replies.

★ ★ ★

Three friends are sitting round the fire talking about their dogs. The first one tells them his dog is called Woodman.
"Let me show you why. Woodman, go boy."
At that, the dog takes a log from the side of the fire and carves a

beautiful statue of a bird. Then the second explains why his dog is called Stoneman.

"Go, boy, go." Immediately the dog jumps up, takes part of the stonework away from the front of the fire and trims it into a stone carving of an Indian.

Finally, the third friend says, "My dog's called Ironman. Watch this." The man heats the fire tongs until they are blisteringly hot and then tells his mates, "I'll just touch him on the balls with this and you watch him make a bolt for the door."

★ ★ ★

"Hey, does your dog bite?" asks the man sitting down next to a guy with a dog at his feet. "No," he replies. But a moment later, the dog takes one almighty bite out of the man's ankle. "Heh, I thought you said your dog didn't bite," he says angrily.

"That's right, but this here's not my dog."

★ ★ ★

Two men are sitting on a park bench watching a dog licking its balls. One says, "Boy, I wish I could do that."

The other replies, "I think you'd better start by petting him first."

★ ★ ★

The elephant keeper at the zoo was grooming his animal when a man stopped to ask him the time. The keeper got down on his knees, swung the elephant's balls to and fro and replied, "Half past four."

Amazed, the man caught up with his friends and urged them to return with him to see this extraordinary occurrence. They agreed and all went back to the keeper. "Excuse me, do you know the time, please?" said one of the friends. Again the man got on his knees, gently handled the elephant's balls and replied, "Four forty five."

After the party moved on, the first man's curiosity got the better of him and he returned to the keeper.

"I'll give you £50 if you show me how you can tell the time."

"If that's what you want" said the keeper. He beckoned the man to get down on his knees also, then moved the elephant's balls to one side and said, "You see that clock tower over there?"

★ ★ ★

On safari in darkest Africa, a hunter got separated from his party and came face to face with a huge lion. Knowing his gun was empty, the hunter got down on his knees to say a last prayer and was amazed to find the lion praying. "Thanks be to God!" exclaimed the man joyously. "Quiet!" roared the lion, "I'm saying grace."

★ ★ ★

A goose goes into the local job centre and joins the back of the waiting queue. When his turn comes he goes up to the interviewer and asks what's on offer.
"My goodness!" gasps the interviewer. "You can talk."
"Well, of course," retorts the goose. "I'm not bloody stupid."
"OK, let me see, come back on Thursday and I'll have something for you."
After the goose has gone, the man rings the circus and persuades the owner to take on the goose, with 5% of the profits coming to him.
Thursday arrives and in waddles the goose.
"So what have you got for me?" he asks.
"Well, I've got you a great job in the circus," he enthuses. "Good money and full board."
"No, that's no good to me," says the goose. "I'm an electrician."

★ ★ ★

"What are those marks on your knees?" one girlfriend asks another.
"Oh, that's from making love doggie style," she replies.
"It looks painful to me, don't you know any other way?"
"Oh yes, I do but my dog doesn't."

★ ★ ★

This dog auditioned for a part in the new summer show. He told half a dozen jokes, using different accents, tap-danced and closed with a song.

"What d'you think?" the owner asked the agent.

"Well, I don't know," replied the agent, shaking his head. "The delivery's good, but the material's very weak."

★ ★ ★

As the stranger walked into the store, he saw a sign reading, "Beware of the Dog".

Next, he saw a shaggy old sheep dog sprawled out on the floor, fast asleep.

"Is that the dog referred to on that sign?" he asked the storekeeper.

"Yes, it sure is," came the reply.

"Well, it's hard to believe the dog is so dangerous. Why did you put the sign up?"

"Because since I've put the sign up, people have stopped tripping over him."

★ ★ ★

The woman went along to the dog behavioural centre to tell them about her problem pet.

"He keeps chasing cars," she explained.

"Well, not to worry. It's quite normal and in time the dog will grow out of it."

"But you don't understand," she wailed. "He keeps burying them in the back garden."

★ ★ ★

The man was very proud of his guard dog, which he would leave outside his house to warn off any would-be burglars. Then one day, there came a frantic knocking at the door and on opening it, the man saw a distressed woman.

"Is that your dog outside?" she cried.

"Yes," he replied.

"Well, I think my dog's just killed it."

"What!?" roared the man. "What sort of a dog have you got?"

"A peke."

"A peke!" he exclaimed. "How could your dog kill my big guard dog?"

"I think it got stuck in his throat," she replied sadly.

★ ★ ★

"Hey, come over here," hissed a voice. The man could see no one but an old mangy greyhound.

"Yes, over here," said the greyhound. "Look at the state of me. I'm stuck here in this shed when I should be out winning more races. I was a triple champion in my time, you know."

The man was dumbfounded. A talking dog! He could become famous. Everyone would want to see this. Millions could be made. He went to look for the dog's owner.

"I'd like to buy your dog," he said, "is it for sale?"

The owner shook his head and said,

"No, mate, you don't want that old thing."

"Oh but I do," persisted the man. "I'll give you £100 for it."

"Well, all right, but I think you're making a mistake."

"Why's that?"

"That dog's a bloody liar. He's never won a race in his life."

★ ★ ★

A variety show producer is on the look-out for a new act, and one day he happens to be walking round a country fair when he notices a group of people huddled around one particular stall. As he approaches, he sees a chicken dancing up and down on an old ceramic pot. The audience are obviously enjoying the act, so the producer asks the man if the chicken is for sale. After a lot of hard bargaining, they eventually decide on a sum of £1,500 and the producer goes off happily, with the chicken and the pot safely under his arm. However, two days later he storms back, very angry.

"You double-crossing bastard!" yells the producer. "You tricked me, that chicken hasn't danced a step since I bought him."

"Mmm," mused the man, thoughtfully. "Did you light the candle under the pot?"

★ ★ ★

A man walked into a country pub with a flea-bitten old dog on a lead. The bar was full of wise old country folk; most of them had big dogs lying at their feet. He addressed the crowd.

"See here," he said, pointing to his dog. "This dog understands everything I say. Not just command words like 'sit', 'lie', 'beg' and all that crap, but proper sentences. I'll wager anyone £2 that he'll do exactly as I say."

The customers looked down at the mangy old dog and one by one they look up the bet until there was nearly £100 in the kitty.

"Okay," said the man, putting up his £100. "Watch this." He picked up his dog and threw him on the open fire. "Patch, get off that fire!" he yelled.

★ ★ ★

Before the race meeting had begun, some of the horses were boasting about their achievements.

"Well, I've won over half the races I've been in, and I've been placed in the rest," said the bay horse.

"I've won 18 races out of 24," said the black.

"I've only lost one race in the whole of my career," said the white.

"Excuse me," interrupted a greyhound who'd been listening to them, "I've won 20 races out of 20."

The horses looked down at him in astonishment.

"Bloody hell," said one, "a talking dog!"

★ ★ ★

A woman was walking through the park when she spotted a man and a dog playing chess.

She watched the game for a few minutes and then remarked, "I can hardly believe what I'm seeing. A dog playing chess. What a clever animal!"

"He's not that clever, madam," replied the man. "I've beaten him four games out of six."

★ ★ ★

"My dog is a nuisance. He chases everyone on a bicycle. What can I do?"
"Take his bike away."

★ ★ ★

A blind rabbit and a blind snake meet each other for the very first time. Neither one can remember what kind of animal they are, so they decide to feel each other.
The rabbit says, "You feel me first." The snake says okay, and he starts feeling the rabbit. He says, "Well, you have fur all over, and a little cotton tail, and two long ears, and big back feet..."
The rabbit says, "I know! I'm a rabbit! Yippee!"
Then the rabbit feels the snake. He says, "Okay, you're long and thin, and slimy all over, and there's a little forked tongue..." The snake says, "Oh no, I'm a lawyer."

★ ★ ★

A police officer sees a man driving around with a pick-up truck full of penguins. He pulls the guy over and says, "You can't drive around with penguins in this town! Take them to the zoo immediately."
The guy says OK, and drives away.
The next day, the officer sees the guy still driving around with his truck full of penguins, and this time they're all wearing sunglasses.
He pulls him over and speaks his mind: "I thought I told you to take these penguins to the zoo yesterday?"
The guy replies, "I did... today I'm taking them to the beach!"

★ ★ ★

A lonely frog, desparate for any form of company, telephoned the Psychic Hotline to find out what the future held in store. His Personal Psychic Advisor advised him, "You are going to meet a beautiful young girl who will want to know everything about you." The frog was thrilled and said, "This is great! Where will I meet her, at work, at a party?" "No," says the psychic, "in a Biology class."

★ ★ ★

A pair of chickens walk into a public library, go over to the librarian and cluck, "Buk Buk BUKOOK." The librarian realizes that the chickens want three books, and promptly hands them over. Without further ado, the chickens walk out.

Around midday, the two chickens are back looking quite annoyed. One leans over to the librarian and says, "Buk Buk BuKKOOK!" The librarian decides that the chickens are asking for another three books and promptly gives them some more. The chickens leave as before. About an hour later the two birds march back in, approach the librarian, looking very angry now and nearly shouting, "Buk Buk Buk Buk BuKKOOOOK!"

The librarian is now starting to get worried about where all her stock is ending up. She decides to give them more books, but also to track the birds to find out what's happening. She follows them out of the library, out of town and into a park. At this point, she hides behind a tree, not wanting to be seen. She sees the two chickens throwing the books over to a frog in a pond, but the frog just keeps repeating, "Rrredit Rrredit Rrredit..."

★ ★ ★

A young woman is travelling with her young son on a train when a man walking down the aisle abruptly halts in front of her, does a double take and exclaims, "That's the ugliest baby I've ever seen."

The woman bursts into tears, and the conductor who has heard her crying tries to console her. "Don't worry about what those inconsiderate people have to say; they're just uncouth. I'll get you a nice cup of tea, my dear, and here's a banana for your monkey."

★ ★ ★

"I think animal testing is a terrible idea; they get all nervous and give the wrong answers."

★ ★ ★

A little old lady was in the kitchen one day, washing the dishes when suddenly a genie appeared. "You've led a long and good life" it said, "I have come to reward you by granting you three wishes.

The old lady was surprised and at first sceptical, but she decided to play along for a minute. "OK," she said, "turn all those dirty dishes into money."

With that there was a flash and the dishes had turned into a big pile of cash.

"My my," said the old lady, staggered that it had actually worked. "Perhaps you could make me look young and beautiful again."

There was another flash and the woman now looked lots younger. Excitedly she carried on, "Can you turn my dear old cat into a handsome young man?"

Instantly, the cat was replaced by a handsome young man. Smiling devilishly, she turned to the young man and said, "At last! Now I want to make love with you for the rest of the day and all night too!"

The young man just looked at her for moment then replied in a high-pitched voice, "Well, you should have thought about that before you took me to the vet's, shouldn't you?!"

★ ★ ★

Three men, one of whom is a bit simple, are captured by savages in the deepest part of the jungle and are told they have one last wish before being killed. The first man asks for a crate of bourbon which he drinks until he collapses unconscious on the ground. The savages then kill him and eat him, but keep his skin to make a canoe.

The second man asks for as much food as he can eat, and proceeds to stuff himself in turn until he collapses exhausted on the ground. The savages then do the same to this man.

Finally, it's the turn of the 'simple' man to pick a wish and he asks for a fork, which he then starts stabbing himself with all over his body. Puzzled, the savages ask him what he is doing and he replies, "You're not making a bloody canoe out of me!"

★ ★ ★

A young couple went on safari to Africa, accompanied by the woman's mother. On the second day, they got separated from their party and found themselves in a remote part of the jungle. Suddenly, a lion jumped out of the undergrowth and stood growling ferociously in front of the mother-in-law.

"Quick, George!" screamed his wife, "do something!"

"Not bloody likely," he replied. "That lion got himself into this mess, he can get himself out."

★ ★ ★

Two hunters are walking through the jungle, one is carrying a concrete post and the other is carrying a wooden shed.

"Why have you got that shed with you?" asks the first hunter.

The second replies, "Well, you see, if we get attacked by a wild animal, I can take refuge inside the shed."

They walk on a bit and the second hunter inquires, "So why are you carrying a concrete post?"

"Well, if we get attacked by a wild animal, I can drop the post and run a bloody sight faster."

★ ★ ★

"Jack, what happened?" gasped his friend on seeing him in the intensive care unit of the local hospital. "I thought you were touring in South America."

"I was," replied Jack weakly, "but it all went horribly wrong. Three weeks into the tour, our band played in this remote village and we went down such a storm that the Chief ordered all our instruments to be filled with fabulous jewels. Unfortunately, I was playing the flute at the time, so I didn't do quite so well out of it."

Jack stopped while the nurse mopped his fevered brow and then continued. "Anyway, later we found ourselves in another out-of-the-way village and this time the Chief hated our music so much, he ordered all the instruments to be shoved up our backsides."

"Wow!" exclaimed his friend, "it's a good thing you were playing the flute."

"Well, that's the trouble," said Jack sadly. "After I missed out on the jewels, I'd switched to the tuba."

★ ★ ★

This man walks into a bar in Alabama and orders a mudslide. The bartender looks him over and says, "You're not from around here, are ya?" "No," he responds. "I'm from Pennsylvania." The bartender asks, "Well, what do you do in Pennsylvania?" "I'm a taxidermist," replies the man. Looking very bewildered, the bartender asks, "What in the world does a tax-ee-derm-ist do?" "I mount dead animals," replies the man. The bartender stands back and hollers to the whole bar (which is staring at them now), "It's okay, boys! He's one of us!"

★ ★ ★

A burglar broke was looking round a home he had broken into. He heard a soft voice say, "Jesus is watching you." Thinking it was just his imagination, he continued his search. Again the voice said, "Jesus is watching you." By the light of his flashlight, he saw a parrot in a cage. He asked the parrot if he was the one talking and the parrot said, "Yes." He asked the parrot what his name was and the parrot said, "Moses." The burglar asked, "What kind of people would name a parrot Moses?" The parrot said, "The same kind of people who would name their pit bull Jesus."

★ ★ ★

Why didn't the baby goose believe anything his father said? He thought it was just *papagander*.

★ ★ ★

Nothing succeeds like a budgie with no teeth.

★ ★ ★

A dedicated professor of music decided to go deep into the African jungle to test his theory that wild animals could be tamed by playing them beautiful music. Sure enough, his theory proved to be true. As he began playing a beautiful piece of classical music on his violin, he soon had an appreciative audience – two giraffes, three snakes, four zebras and a host of monkeys. All of a sudden, a lion roared into the middle of them and bit off the professor's head.

"Why did you do that?" complained the other animals. "That was beautiful music and you've gone and spoilt it."

The lion put a paw to his ear and said, "What?"

★ ★ ★

An old snake goes to see his doctor.

"Doc, I need something for my eyes... can't see too well these days."

The doctor fixes him up with a pair of glasses and tells him to return in two weeks' time. The snake comes back two weeks later and tells the doctor he's very depressed. The doctor says, "What's the problem... didn't the glasses help you?"

"The glasses are fine thanks, doctor. I've just discovered I've been living with a hosepipe for the past two years!"

★ ★ ★

A panda bear walks into a bar, and tells the bartender that he wants to have lunch. The bartender gets him a menu and he orders.

The panda bear eats his lunch and, when he finishes, he gets up to leave. Suddenly, the panda bear pulls an AK-47 out of his fur, and shoots the bar to pieces. He then heads for the door.

The shocked bartender jumps out from behind the ruins of his bar and yells, "Hey, what do you think you're doing? You ate lunch, shot up my bar and now you're just going to leave?"

The panda bear answers calmly, "I'm a panda bear."

The bartender says, "Yeah, so what?"

The panda bear replies, "Look it up," and walks out of the door.

The bartender retreats behind his ruined bar and grabs his encyclopedia. He looks up "panda bear," and sure enough, there's a big picture of a panda bear.

He reads the caption, which says, "Panda Bear – a cuddly, black and white creature. Eats shoots and leaves."

★ ★ ★

Bill Clinton got off the helicopter in front of the White House with a baby hog under each arm. The Marine guard snapped to attention, saluted and said, "Nice pigs, sir."

The president replied, "These are not pigs, these are authentic Arkansas Razorback hogs.

"I got one for Hillary and one for Chelsea."

The Marine again snapped to attention, saluted, and replied, "Nice trade, sir."

★ ★ ★

A man wakes up early one morning and decides to go bear hunting.

He tells his wife, "You've got three choices: you can go bear hunting with me, or I'll do you anally, or you can give me a blowjob. Can't say fairer than that.

"I'm gonna load up the truck and get the dog out. Make up your mind before I get back."

The man returns twenty minutes later and says, "Well, what's it gonna be? Have you come to a decision yet?"

His wife replies, "There's no way I'm going bear hunting and you're not doing my ass, so I guess it's going to have to be a blowjob."

A couple of minutes later, she starts choking and spitting and says, "Jesus, you taste like shit."

"Oh yeah," he replies. "The dog didn't want to go bear hunting either."

★ ★ ★

BAD BEHAVIOUR

A man fishing off the end of the pier is amazed to see an old wizened woman in a wheelchair hurtling past him. To his dismay, he realizes she is determined to go over the edge, so just in time he stops her and asks what's wrong.

The old woman, who's wrinkled, half bald and toothless, starts to cry and tells him she's nearly 90 and has never been kissed. The man looks at her, hides his repulsion and gives her a kiss, although it's almost too much to stomach when she sticks her tongue down his throat. However, she goes away happy. But a couple of hours later he sees her again, hurtling down the pier.

"What's wrong now?" he asks.

Tears streaming down her face, she tells him she has never been hugged. So he closes his eyes, takes a deep breath and just manages to give her a big hug. The man returns to his fishing and after another hour he manages to catch a very big fish which he has trouble reeling in. At the crucial moment, the old woman returns, hurtling down the pier and, losing concentration for a moment, he loses his prize catch.

He turns to the tearful old hag who, this time, tells him she's never been fucked. So the man gently lifts her out of the wheelchair, and smiling toothlessly she asks him to lie her down on the sand under the pier where they won't be disturbed. The man agrees, pulls up two loose planks from the walkway of the pier and drops her through to the sand below. The woman laughs excitedly, repeating the words, "I've never been fucked before."

"Well, you will be now," replies the man. "The tide comes in in 15 minutes" and, with that, he walks away.

★ ★ ★

Three men are discussing how best to drive women wild. The first says he nibbles their ears and their toes and it really turns them on. The second says he kisses them all over and it drives them mad. The third says that after he's made love to them he wipes himself clean on their curtains – now that really does drive them wild!

★ ★ ★

How many men does it take to tile a bathroom?
Two. If you slice them very thinly.

★ ★ ★

A boy rushed into his friend's bedroom unannounced to find him lying face down on a life-size Arena poster of a vivacious starlet. "Ben, what the hell are you doing?"
His friend looks up breathless and flushes.
"It's all right, Martin, I've got the charwoman underneath."

★ ★ ★

"It's about time you got married, son."
"But why, dad?" the son replied. "Why should I buy a book when there's such a good lending library in town?"

★ ★ ★

Nursing one almighty hangover, Lady Ponsonby decided to get a breath of fresh air and take a walk around the grounds.
After a few minutes she met her husband's manservant and casually mentioned to him that she was feeling under the weather after the previous night's riotous hen party and couldn't remember a thing about getting to bed.
"I helped you, madam," replied the manservant. "I took off your dress and hung it up so it wouldn't get creased."
"But I woke up totally naked," she replied.
"That's right, madam, I removed your underclothes because I thought they might be a little uncomfortable."
"Gosh, I can't remember anything," she said. "I must have been tight."
"Not after the first time, Your Ladyship."

★ ★ ★

A young floozy was washing her hair when the phone rang and it was answered by her flatmate.
"It's an obscene phone call for you," she called out.

"Take down the number, tell him I'll call him back soon," came the reply.

★ ★ ★

"If you want an extra bit of sport in bed," one male said to the other, "mount her from behind and whisper in her ear, 'This is how I do it with your best friend.' Then try and stay on for 10 seconds."

★ ★ ★

Two men fell overboard when they were on a boat out at sea and only Jim could swim. "Jump on my back, John, and we'll swim for shore," he said.

For the next two hours, Jim swam towards land. Twice he was ready to give up, but urged on by John they eventually made it. "Bloody hell, I'm fucked," panted Jim as he crawled up the beach. "Yes, sorry about that," said John. "It was the only way I could hang on."

★ ★ ★

I says to my mate, "I like your hair, how do you get it like that?"

He replied, "My girlfriend strips and I rub my head between her tits and my hair goes like this. Try it." "I will."

Next day, we meet up and he says, "Did you try it?"

"Yeah," I says. "And you've got a lovely house as well."

★ ★ ★

Left stranded after falling off her horse some miles from home, a young cattleman's daughter was rescued by an Indian who brought her back to the ranch on his mount. When the father heard the sound of hooves, he went out to meet them and helped his daughter down from the back of the horse.

"How did you manage to stay on?" he asked her.

"Well, it was difficult at first, but then he told me to hold on to the saddle horn."

"Oh, my darling daughter, don't you realize, Indians always ride bareback."

★ ★ ★

A boy and girl stop for a kiss while walking through the park.
"Mmm, you smell nice," says the girl. "What have you got on?"
He replies, "I've got a hard on, but I didn't realize you could smell it."

★ ★ ★

Three men are discussing what to buy their wives for their birthdays.
"I'm going to get my wife some sexy underwear and a pair of Italian shoes, then if she doesn't like one, hopefully she'll like the other."
"That's a good idea," says the second man.
"I'll get my wife two presents as well and maybe one of them will be all right. Let's see – I think I'll get a gold necklace and an evening dress."
"What about you, Jack?" they say, turning to the third man who has remained morosely quiet.
"Oh, I know what I'm getting Doreen, a mink coat and a dildo. If she doesn't like the coat, she can go fuck herself."

★ ★ ★

Into a bar comes a man grinning all over his face. He says to the bartender, "I'll have three rums, one bourbon and two gin and blackcurrant, please."
The drinks are lined up before him and he downs them all straight away.
"Hey, what's the big occasion?" asks the bartender.
"I've just had my first blowjob," replies the man.
"Oh right, was it OK?"
"Not too bad, but even now I can still taste it."

★ ★ ★

For quite some time this man has been living next door to a very beautiful young girl and they have never done more than just say hello in passing.

One day, however, the girl comes out wearing a flimsy dressing gown and invites him over to her door. It's obvious she's flirting with him and he becomes very hot under the collar. All of a sudden she urgently whispers to him, "Let's go inside, I hear someone coming..."

He blindly follows her indoors and, once inside, she drops her dressing gown to the floor and stands there stark naked.

"So, honey," she coos, "what do you think my best attribute is?"

The man stutters, "It's, er.... It's got to be your ears."

"My ears!" she gasps. "Why? Have you ever seen such flawless skin, have you ever seen such beautiful breasts, have you ever seen such a firm backside? Yet you say my ears!"

"Well, it's like this" he explains. "When we were outside and you said you heard someone coming.... Well, that was me."

★ ★ ★

A confidence trickster bought a pet shop and put an advertisement in the window saying he had a very special dog, ideal for spinsters.

Sure enough, the ad attracted a lot of attention and one woman came into the shop asking for more details.

"It's a big alsatian, miss," he said, "and it keeps women warm on cold nights – if you know what I mean (wink wink)."

The woman bought the dog, but a few days later rang the pet shop complaining that the dog had done "nothing special!"

The man went round to the woman's flat and found her in bed while the dog was asleep on the floor.

"Come on, Rover," he said, taking his clothes off. "How many more times do I have to show you!"

★ ★ ★

Ever since the new cook had arrived at camp, he had been treated miserably. They'd thrown away his clothes, turned his bed upside down and hidden his post. Eventually, however, they grew bored and told him there would be no more tricks.

"You really mean that?" he said. "Yes" they assured him.

"OK, good, then I'll stop pissing in the soup."

★ ★ ★

Did you hear about the girl who swallowed a razor blade?

The doctor decided to let it come out naturally, but during the time it took for that to happen, it gave her an appendectomy, badly lacerated her husband, cut out the tongue of her next-door neighbour and damaged the hand of the milkman.

★ ★ ★

"I'm really fed up with my wife's slovenly ways," complained Bob. "This morning, I went to piss in the sink and it was full of dishes!"

★ ★ ★

"Two men talking over a pint. "I'm glad to see you and your wife are on better terms. Solved the eternal triangle problem, did you?"

"Oh yes," replied the other. "We ate the sheep."

★ ★ ★

When he showed her his big one, she exclaimed, "But if we have oral sex, won't you lose respect for me?"

"Not at all," he replied, "as long as you're good at it."

★ ★ ★

Did you hear about the man who entered his dog in the local pet show?

He got three months.

★ ★ ★

The beautiful blonde bimbo whispered to the handsome doctor.

"Oh, kiss me again, please kiss me again."

"It's ethically wrong you know," he said. "I shouldn't really be fucking you in the first place."

★ ★ ★

A very famous Member of Parliament was walking through the park when he suddenly got a huge erection and had to dash behind a tree to relieve himself.

Unfortunately, a passer-by caught him in the act and took a photo of him. Extremely alarmed at the bad publicity this would bring, he offered to buy the camera and film from the stranger. It took a great deal of haggling, but they finally agreed on £500. Walking back to work a little later with the camera slung over his shoulder, the MP met one of his colleagues.

"Is that a new camera?" he asked. "How much did you pay for it?"

"£500."

"My goodness, he must have seen you coming."

★ ★ ★

A miserly old woman was always trying to find ways of saving money and came upon the idea of feeding her husband cheap dog food.

It took a few days for him to get used to it but when she insisted it was the best minced steak he had no reason to be suspicious.

Three months had gone by when, one afternoon, she received a phone call from the local hospital to say her husband had been brought in following a mysterious accident. She arrived at Casualty 20 minutes later and asked the doctor on duty how her husband was and what had happened.

"Just a few broken bones, nothing too serious. An odd accident, though. It seems he was hit by a car when he suddenly sat down in the middle of the road and tried to lick his backside."

★ ★ ★

The rush hour train was packed to capacity and standing pressed up against a pretty young girl was a creepy-looking man.

"Will you stop pushing that thing at me," she whispered angrily.

"It's only my wallet," he replied.

"Well, you must have a bloody good job, you've had three rises since we left Waterloo."

★ ★ ★

A man out walking with his dog is amazed to see his doctor down on all fours with his fingers halfway down a rabbit hole. As he continues to watch, the doctor withdraws his hand and a moment later a rabbit pops his head out. The doctor knocks it out and puts it in his bag. After watching him catch ten rabbits this way, the man goes over and asks what the secret is.

"It's very simple," replies the doctor. "Before you come out, put your hand between a woman's legs; then when the rabbits smell your fingers they keep coming up for more. That's when you get them."

"I can hardly believe it," says the man. "Are you sure?"

"Of course, you can trust me: I'm a doctor."

The man ponders the doctor's words on the way home and when he sees his wife bending over the oven he quickly puts his hand between her legs. Without looking round, his wife says, "Hello, doctor, off rabbit hunting again?"

★ ★ ★

Three hikers stop for a rest in the Yorkshire Dales and looking over into an adjoining field they see some sheep.

"Hey, I think that sheep's smiling at you," jokes one of them. "I wish it was Cindy Crawford."

The second says, "I wish it was Sharon Stone."

The third says, "I wish it was dark."

★ ★ ★

A DJ on a local radio station decides to launch a new competition.
He asks people to ring in with a word used in everyday speech but not found in the dictionary. It's not long before a man rings up with the word 'goan'.
"Well, thanks for that word. I'll just check it's not in the dictionary – no, it's not. So how would you use this word?"
"Goan fuck yourself," came the reply.
Lost for words, the DJ quickly puts on some music.
An hour later, he gets another call and this time the word is 'smee'.
He looks it up and once more it's not there.
"So how would you use this word?" he asks the caller.
"It's smee again; go fuck yourself."

★ ★ ★

Three blokes were talking in a pub in Wales about the best way to shag a sheep. The first two agreed it was the back legs down the wellies and the front legs over the wall. But the third said, "No, it's the back legs down the wellies and the front legs over the shoulders."
"Doesn't that make it difficult?" said the other two. "Why don't you do as we suggested?"
"What! And miss out on all the kissing?"

★ ★ ★

"You look happy this morning, Jack" said his mate.
"Yeah, I came into some money last night – a girl with gold caps on her teeth."

★ ★ ★

"You will still love me now we're married, won't you?" asked the newly wed girl.
"Oh, even more," he replied. "I've got a thing about married women."

★ ★ ★

A poor simple young girl went to the doctors and was told she was pregnant. "But how can that be?" she said. "I haven't been with a man." Patiently, the doctor explains the birds and bees to the young girl. "Oh no," she gasped. "The first aid teacher told me it was artificial respiration."

★ ★ ★

Jack and Flo had a distant cousin staying with them and one night when she was taking a bath, Flo went in to give her some more towels and noticed she didn't have any pubic hair. "Really," said Jack, when Flo told him about it later. "That's very odd, you must be mistaken."

"No, I'm not," said Flo angrily. "You can see for yourself."

Flo told him that the cousin usually had a bath on his darts night. As they had a bungalow, he could nip back, look through the window and see for himself. The darts night came around and sure enough the cousin went for her bath. A little later, Flo walked in and this time felt compelled to say something.

"Why haven't you got any hair on your fanny?" she asked.

"I didn't know I was supposed to," said the naive girl.

"Oh yes, look I'll show you," And with that Flo lifted her skirt, pulled down her knickers and showed the girl her thatch.

Jack came home 30 minutes later in a very angry mood. "What the hell were you doing exposing yourself like that," he shouted.

"Oh don't be silly, Jack, you've seen me hundreds of times."

"Maybe, but the bloody darts team haven't."

★ ★ ★

Lucy's mother looked so young that many people mistook them for sisters. Now it just so happened that Lucy was courting a local dairyman but, unknown to her, the dairyman was also seeing her mother.

One day, Lucy came home in tears.

"What's wrong?" asked her mother.

"William and I stopped seeing each other a month ago because I'm sure he was being unfaithful. But I've just seen him in the High Street and I still love him!" she cried.

"Never mind, you'll find someone else. You'll just have to forget about him. Did you return all the presents he gave you?"

"Yes, I did and what's more I put tiny pinpricks in all his condoms – that'll teach him… Oh, Mother, you've gone pale, are you all right?"

★ ★ ★

What two other purposes have hill farmers found for sheep?
Wool and meat.

★ ★ ★

How can you tell if a woman is wearing pantyhose?
When she farts her ankles swell up.

★ ★ ★

"And another thing, Terry," said the macho man, "masturbation is a waste of fucking time."

★ ★ ★

A young man was meeting his future in-laws for the first time at their large mansion in the country. They sat down to lunch and the first course went by without incident, but just as the young man was about to tuck into the roast, he was unable to stop a small fart escaping.

"Jasper!" exclaimed the hostess to the dog.

Unfortunately, less than five minutes later, another, larger fart began to build up until he was unable to contain it any longer.

Again, the hostess shouted, "Jasper!"

Feeling pleased that the dog was getting blamed, the young man relaxed but in doing so he let out a rip roarer that fairly rattled the crockery. "Jasper, get the hell over here quickly before that bugger dumps on you."

★ ★ ★

A bloke was walking home late one night when he was set upon by two muggers who beat him up and stole his wallet. They also managed to break his dentures. Lying on the ground battered and bruised, he was found by a kindly gentleman and helped to his feet.

"You look as if you could do with a stiff drink," said the gentleman. "My house is just round the corner; you're welcome to come and sit for a while until you're feeling better."

Two large whiskies later, the man started to recover and in doing so remembered his dentures were broken. "Wait a minute," said the gentleman, "I think I can help you out."

He disappeared for a few minutes and came back with a selection of different dentures. "See if any of these fit."

After trying on several different pairs, he found some that were perfect. "I can't thank you enough" he said. "You rescue me from the pavement, help me to recover my wits and on top of all that you're a dentist as well."

"Oh no," said the gentleman, "I'm not a dentist, I'm an undertaker."

★ ★ ★

"Hey, Bob," they said laughing. "What's the difference between your sister and a Porsche?

"Most of us haven't been in a Porsche."

★ ★ ★

A man got on a crowded train and the only seat available was occupied by a dog. "Excuse me, madam, can you move the dog?"

"Bugger off!" she said. "Go and find somewhere else to sit."

But there was nowhere else and as the train slowed down at the crossing he picked the dog up and threw it out of the door.

The woman jumped up, shouting, "Did you see that… did you see him molest poor Fou Fou? What a terrible thing to do."

"You're right there, madam," said a voice from the back. "It really was a terrible thing to do – he threw out the wrong bitch.

★ ★ ★

Did you hear about the girl who said she'd do anything for a mink coat?
Now she can't do it up!

★ ★ ★

"Your kisses really burn."
"Sorry, perhaps I ought to put my cigarette out!"

★ ★ ★

Why do Australian men come so quickly?
Because they can't wait to get down to the pub to tell their mates.

★ ★ ★

What does a prat call his best friend's wife?
A really good fuck.

★ ★ ★

The Head of State would just like to say in defence of the sexual harassment charge against him, that the woman must have been slightly deaf. What he did say was, "Hold my calls and sack my cook."

★ ★ ★

The man was so drunk, he slipped and fell as he came out of the pub, causing one car to swerve out of his way and plough into the back of a bus which caused a two-mile tailback. As the drunk was helped to his feet, one of the crowd asked him what had happened.
"I don't know," he slurred. "I've only just got here myself."

★ ★ ★

Well, I've stuffed the goose. All we need to do now is kill it and buy some apple sauce, and we'll have a great Christmas dinner.

★ ★ ★

The man staggered into the bar and shouted, "A double whisky, bartender, and a drink for all your customers... and have one yourself."

"Well, thank you, sir."

Moments later, the man shouted again, "Let's have another drink all round and one for yourself, bartender."

"Excuse me, sir, but I think you ought to pay for the other round first."

"But I haven't got any money."

The bartender was beside himself with rage.

"Then fuck off out of here and don't ever come back!" he roared.

However, ten minutes later, the man reappeared, and once more staggered to the bar.

"Double whisky," he slurred, "and a drink for all my friends."

"I suppose you'll be offering me a drink as well," growled the bartender sarcastically.

"Oh no," replied the man, "you get nasty when you drink."

★ ★ ★

A man stormed into a bar and yelled, "Okay, you bastards, which prat just painted the back of my car pink?"

From the corner, a huge Hells Angel stood up and growled, "I did. You got a problem with that?"

"No, no," stuttered the man. "I just thought you'd like to know, the first coat is dry."

★ ★ ★

An Englishman, an Irishman and a Scotsman walked into a bar and each ordered a pint of beer. However, when the drinks arrived, all three pints had a fly swimming around in the froth. The Englishman looked at his pint in disgust and pushed it away. The Irishman picked his fly out with his fingers, threw it on the floor and drank the beer. The Scotsman also picked his fly out of the froth, then began shaking it over his pint, saying, "Spit that beer out now, y'thieving little bastard!"

★ ★ ★

A drunk staggers into a bar and spots a man drinking in the corner. He goes up to him and says at the top of his voice, "I've just been out with your mum, it was great."

There's a hushed silence as everyone waits to see a reaction, but the man ignores the comment and the drunk wanders away. But 10 minutes later he shouts at him again from the other end of the bar, "And I'll tell you now, your mum's the best lay for miles."

Again, everyone waits with baited breath but nothing happens. They all return to their drinks but by now the drunk can't leave it alone. He staggers over to the man once more and yells, "And another thing, she says she wants it from me every night!"

Sighing audibly, the man puts down his beer and places his hand on the drunk's shoulder.

"Just go home, dad, you've had enough."

★ ★ ★

Two old men had drunk a pint together, every day for over 20 years. Sadly, one day Tom died, and Albert was left on his own. The last words that Tom had ever uttered were: "Albert, me old buddy, in memory of me, have an extra pint each day."

Albert kept his promise and each day he ordered an extra drink. Then one day, to the amazement of the bar staff, he only had one drink.

"What's up, Albert, no drink for your friend?"

"Oh yes, I've just had the pint for Tom, but I can't have one myself. The doctor's told me my liver's packing up."

★ ★ ★

Two drunks missed the last bus home so ended up trying to walk. But as they reached open countryside, one of them sank to his knees in the middle of the road and refused to go any further. He laid down, closed his eyes and was soon fast asleep. The other drunk eyed his mate in astonishment.

"You silly bugger, you'll end up like a squashed hedgehog," he remarked as he settled himself on the grass verge and fell asleep as well. Just after midnight, a car came down the road, swerved to avoid the man asleep in the road, and ploughed straight across the grass verge.

★ ★ ★

A drunk sets out to go fishing. He gets his tackle box, rods and net, and staggers off to look for a likely spot. It's a cold day and he searches far and wide.

Eventually, he comes across a huge area of ice and starts to saw a hole.

All of a sudden a booming voice speaks from nowhere, "There are no fish under that ice."

The drunk looks round but can't see anyone so he continues to saw. Again the voice booms, "I've told you once, there are no fish under that ice. You're wasting your time."

The drunk looks up, there's still no sign of anyone so he continues sawing unconcerned.

"That's enough!" shouts the voice. "Pick up your gear and get out of here, or there'll be trouble"

"Where are you?" yells the drunk. "If you're a ghost trying to scare me, then bugger off."

"No," replies the voice. "I'm the manager of this bloody ice rink."

★ ★ ★

A man walks into a pub and is greeted by a crocodile.

"What'll it be?" asks the crocodile.

The man just stares at him open-mouthed.

"Come on," he says, "haven't you seen a crocodile before?"

"Oh sorry," he stutters, "it's just that I never thought the horse would sell this place."

★ ★ ★

What a landlord!

I asked him for something tall, cold and full of gin and he introduced me to his wife.

★ ★ ★

I saw this white horse standing behind a bar.
I said, "Do you know there's a whisky named after you?"
He said, "What, Adrian?"

★ ★ ★

A man walked into a pub carrying a red, long-nosed, short-legged dog.
"Ugh, that's an ugly dog," commented a man standing at the bar with his prize bull terrier at his feet.
"Maybe," replied the first man, "but she's a mean bitch."
"Oh yeah? Listen, I'll bet you £50 my dog will have chased her off in less than a minute."
"OK, it's a deal," and with that they lined the two dogs up. On the word 'Attack' the two dogs flew at each other and, in no time at all, the bull terrier has been bitten in half.
"Christ Almighty!" sobbed the owner, aghast. "What the hell kind of dog is that?"
The man replied, "Well, before I docked her tail and painted her red, she was a crocodile."

★ ★ ★

A giant of a man, very drunk and very mean, throws open the doors of the pub and shouts loudly, "All you on the right side are cock-suckers and all you on the left are mother-fuckers!"
Suddenly a man runs from the left side to the right.
"Where are you going, wimp?" roars the drunk.
"Sorry, sir, I was on the wrong side," he replies.

★ ★ ★

A man walked into the pub with a dog.
"I'm sorry, sir, no dogs allowed in here."
"Yes, but he's a really intelligent dog; ask him to do anything and he will."
"OK," said the barman. "Tell him to go and get me a newspaper."
The man hands the dog £5 and off he goes. Two hours go by and

there's still no sign of the dog, so the anxious owner goes looking for him.

After roaming the streets, shouting his name, he eventually finds him in a back alley with a bitch, doing the business.

"What's all this about?" asked the owner. "You've never done this before, have you?"

"No, but I've never had so much money before," replied the dog.

★ ★ ★

A bloke goes into a pub and orders a triple whisky and a pint of beer. As soon as the barman puts them in front of him he drinks them all down in one gulp.

"I shouldn't be drinking all this," he says.

"Why's that?"

"Because I've only got 20p on me."

★ ★ ★

A man goes into a bar and asks the barman if it would be all right to tell an Irish joke.

"I think you ought to know," said the barman, "that my name's O'Riley and many of my fellow countrymen use this pub. That group over there is the local darts team – they're Irish. Those two men over there are Irish. They work round the corner on the building site, and (lowering his voice) that big Irish bastard in the corner is the local hard man."

The newcomer thought for a moment and then said, "Okay. It would take too bloody long to explain the joke to you lot anyway."

★ ★ ★

An anti-drink campaigner walks into a local bar and calls for the customers' attention.

"I would like to show you all something about drinking," he announces and at that point he puts two jars on the table. One he fills with whisky, the other with water.

Then he produces two earthworms and drops one into each jar. The one in the whisky jar breathes his last and sinks to the bottom, while the other swims happily around in the water.

"So what does this show you about drinking?" asks the campaigner, and a voice at the back replies, "Drinking stops you getting worms!"

★ ★ ★

A man walks into a bar with a toy poodle on a lead.

"No dogs allowed in here," says the barman. "Only guide dogs for the blind."

"But I am blind," insists the man.

"Well, that's not a guide dog."

"Why, what is it?"

"It's a poodle."

"Bugger, I've been conned."

★ ★ ★

A fire engine came racing around the corner and disappeared up the road, bells clanging wildly. As it passed 'The Flying Horse', a drunk staggered out and started chasing it, but after a minute or so he collapsed on the ground breathing heavily.

"Sod it!" he gasped. "Keep your bloody ice creams."

★ ★ ★

A man walked up to the bar and asked for a pint of less.

"Less?" questioned the barmaid. "I've never heard of it, is it a new beer?"

"I don't know," replied the man. "When I went to the doctor's this morning, he told me I should drink less."

★ ★ ★

"Whisky on the rocks, bartender, please," says the man, and as he gulps it down in one go he takes out a picture from his back pocket.

"Another whisky please," and again he gulps it down and looks at the picture in his back pocket.

For the next two hours he goes through the same routine, time and time again. By the end of the night he turns to stagger out when the bartender taps him on the shoulder.

"Sorry, mate, but I have to ask," said the bartender. "You've ordered whiskies all night and each time you've drunk one, you've taken out a picture in your back pocket and looked at it. Can I ask why?"

"Sure," replied the man sounding very pissed. "It's a picture of my wife and when I think she's looking good, then it's time for me to go home."

★ ★ ★

A man walks into a bar with a Cornish pasty on his head and asks the barman for a pint of beer.

Unable to conceal his curiosity the barman hands the man the beer and says, "Excuse me, sir, I couldn't help but notice that you have a Cornish pasty on your head."

"That's right," replies the man. "I always have a Cornish pasty on my head on a Thursday."

"But, sir, it's Friday today."

"Oh no," says the man. "I must look a right prat."

★ ★ ★

Saturday morning at the library, Martin spots his mate Kevin over in the non-fiction section.

"Hello, Kevin, been away? Haven't seen you for a while."

"Oh hello, Martin. As a matter of fact I have. I went on a weekend course to that big hotel just off the A1. It was all about reincarnation. Very good. Mind, it cost £400."

"Phew! That's a bit steep."

"Yes, I suppose it was. Still, you only live once."

★ ★ ★

A man walks up to the bar and asks for an entendre.
"Would you like a single or a double?" asks the barmaid.
"A double please," he replies.
"OK, sir, so yours is a large one."

★ ★ ★

A bloke walked into the pub and was astounded at the sight of the barman. He was built like the side of a brick shithouse with muscles bulging out all over the place, tattoos everywhere; he was also unshaven and sweaty.

After a moment or two the barman became aware of the looks he was getting and said, "What the bloody hell are you looking at?"

"Sorry, mate, it's just that you look just like someone I know. You're almost identical... if it wasn't for the moustache..."

"But I haven't got a moustache," said the barman.

"No, but my wife has."

★ ★ ★

DRINKING: A TROUBLESHOOTING GUIDE

SYMPTOM: Feet cold and wet.
FAULT: Glass being held at incorrect angle.
ACTION: Rotate glass so that open end points toward ceiling.

SYMPTOM: Feet warm and wet.
FAULT: Improper bladder control.
ACTION: Stand next to nearest dog, complain about house training.

SYMPTOM: Beer unusually pale and tasteless.
FAULT: Glass empty.
ACTION: Get someone to buy you another beer.

SYMPTOM: Opposite wall covered with fluorescent lights.
FAULT: You have fallen over backward.
ACTION: Have yourself chained to bar.

SYMPTOM: Mouth contains cigarette butts.
FAULT: You have fallen forward.
ACTION: See above.

SYMPTOM: Beer tasteless, front of your shirt is wet.
FAULT: Mouth not open, or glass applied to wrong part of face.
ACTION: Retire to toilets, practise in mirror.

SYMPTOM: Person you are speaking to no longer appears to have
the film star good looks of ten minutes ago.
FAULT: You are becoming sober.
ACTION: Add vodka to beer.

SYMPTOM: Floor blurred.
FAULT: You are looking through bottom of empty glass.
ACTION: Get someone to buy you another beer.

SYMPTOM: Floor moving.
FAULT: You are being carried out.
ACTION: Find out if you are being taken to another bar.

SYMPTOM: Everyone looks up to you and laughs.
FAULT: You are dancing on the table.
ACTION: Fall on somebody cushy looking.

SYMPTOM: Beer is crystal clear.
FAULT: It's water. Someone is trying to sober you up.
ACTION: Punch him.

SYMPTOM: Hands hurt, nose hurts, mind unusually clear.
FAULT: You have been in a fight.
ACTION: Apologize to everyone you see, just in case it was them.

SYMPTOM: Don't recognize anyone, don't recognize the room you're in.
FAULT: You've wandered into the wrong party.
ACTION: See if they have free beer.

SYMPTOM: Your singing sounds distorted.
FAULT: The beer is too weak.
ACTION: Have more beer until your voice improves.

SYMPTOM: Don't remember the words to the song.
FAULT: Beer is just right.
ACTION: Play air guitar.

SYMPTOM: Room seems unusually dark.
FAULT: Bar has closed.
ACTION: Confirm home address with bartender, take taxi home.

SYMPTOM: Truck suddenly takes on colourful aspect and textures.
FAULT: Beer consumption has exceeded personal limitations.
ACTION: Cover mouth.

SYMPTOM: Cold and unable to unlock door to hotel room.
FAULT: Woke up in hotel room, got up to go to bathroom and chose wrong door.
ACTION: Knock loudly on door to wake sleeping wife. If this fails, find a hotel worker to unlock door for you.

★ ★ ★

Bruce and Tom were a couple of drinking buddies, who worked as aeroplane mechanics in Melbourne. One day the airport was fogged in and they were stuck in the hangar with nothing to do. Bruce said, "Man I wish we had something to drink." Tom said, "Me too. You know I have heard you can drink jet fuel and get a buzz. You want to try it?" So they poured themselves a couple of glasses of high-octane hooch and got completely smashed. The next morning Bruce wakes up and is surprised at how good he feels. In fact he feels great. No hangovers! No bad side-effects. Nothing! Then the phone rings... it's Tom. Tom says, "Hey, how do you feel this morning?" Bruce says, "I feel great, how about you?" Tom says, "I feel great, too. You don't have a hangover?" Bruce says, "No, that jet fuel is great stuff – no hangovers, nothing. We ought to do this more often." "Yeah, well there's just one thing…" "What's that?" "Have you farted yet?" "No." "Well don't, 'cos I'm in Adelaide."

★ ★ ★

Two old drunks were drinking in the pub together, when the first one says: "You know, Mick, when I was 30 and got a hard-on, I couldn't bend it with both hands. When I was 40, I could bend it about 10 degrees if I tried really hard.

"By the time I was 50, I could bend it about 20 degrees, no problem at all. I'm going to be 60 next week and now I can almost bend it in half with just one hand."

"So," says the second drunk. "What's your point?"

"The point is quite straightforward: I'm just wondering how much stronger I'm going to get."

★ ★ ★

Ole was sitting at the bar, getting sloshed, and mentioned something about Lena being out in the car. After quite a while, the bartender became concerned about Lena, as it was cold that night, and went outside to check on her. When he looked in the car, he saw Ole's buddy, Sven, going at it with Lena. The bartender shook his head and returned to the bar. He told Ole he thought it might be a good idea to go out and check on Lena. Ole staggered off his bar stool, went outside to the car and, sure enough, he saw Sven and Lena still going at it. Ole walked back into the bar, laughing and laughing. The bartender asked him what was so funny. Ole said, "That damned Sven! He's so drunk, he thinks he's me!"

★ ★ ★

Someone who teaches at a Middle School in Safety Harbor, Florida forwarded the following letter. The letter was sent to the principal's office after the school had sponsored a lunch for the elderly.
This story is a credit to all human kind. Read it and forward it to all those who could use a lift. It's a heartwarming story:

Dear Safety Harbor Middle School

God blesses you for the beautiful radio I won at your recent senior citizens' luncheon. I am 84 years old and live at the Safety Harbor Assisted Home for the Aged. All of my family has passed away. It's nice to know that someone really thinks of me. God blesses you for your kindness to an old, forgotten lady.

My roommate is 95 and always had her own radio, but would never let me listen to it, even when she was napping. The other day her radio fell off the night stand and broke into a lot of pieces. It was awful and she was in tears.

She asked if she could listen to mine, and I said, "Fuck you."

★ ★ ★

A man and woman are riding up in an elevator.
The man looks at the woman and says, "Can I smell your pussy?"
She replies, "Hell, no!"
The man says, "Well, it must be your feet then."

★ ★ ★

A man is sitting in a bar when a beautiful woman walks up and whispers in his ear, "I'll do anything you want for 50 bucks." He puts his drink down and starts going through his pockets. He pulls out a ten, two fives, a twenty and ten ones. He thrusts the wadded-up money into the woman's hand and says, "Here... paint my house."

★ ★ ★

A man walks into a bar and orders a 12-year-old scotch. The bartender, believing that the customer will not be able to tell the difference, pours him a shot of the cheap three-year-old house scotch that has been poured into an empty bottle of the good stuff.

The man takes a sip and spits the scotch out on the bar. "This is the cheapest three-year-old scotch you can buy. I'm not paying for it. Now, give me a good 12-year-old scotch."

The bartender, feeling a bit of a challenge, pours him a scotch of much better quality, six-year-old scotch. The man takes a sip and spits it out. "This is only six-year-old scotch. I won't pay for this, and I insist on a good, 12-year-old scotch."

The bartender finally relents and serves the man his best-quality, 12-year-old scotch.

An old drunk from the end of the bar, who has witnessed the entire episode, walks down to the finicky scotch drinker and sets a glass down in front of him and asks, "What do you think of this?"

The scotch expert takes a sip, and in disgust violently spits out the liquid, yelling, "Why, this tastes like piss."

The old drunk replies, "That's right, now tell me how old I am."

★ ★ ★

A woman is shopping in the supermarket. She selects some milk, some eggs, a carton of juice, and a packet of bacon.

As she unloads her items at the cash register, a drunk standing behind her in the queue watches her place the four items on the belt and states with assurance, "You must be single."

The woman looks at the four items on the belt, and seeing nothing unusual about her selection says, "That's right. How on earth did you know?"

He replies, "Because you're ugly."

★ ★ ★

Larry finally found the nerve to tell his fiancee that he had to break off their engagement so he could marry another woman.

"Can she cook like I can?" the distraught woman asked between sobs.

"Not on her best day," he replied.

"Can she buy you expensive gifts like I do?"

"No, she's broke."

"Well then, is it sex?"

"Nobody does it like you, babe."

"Then what can she do that I can't?"

"... Sue me for child support."

★ ★ ★

A knight and his men returned to their castle after a hard day of fighting. "How are we faring?" asked the king. "Sire!" replied the knight. "I have been robbing and pillaging on your behalf all day, burning the towns of your enemies to the west."

"What?" shrieked the king, "I don't have any enemies to the west!"

"Oh!" said the knight. "Well, you do now."

★ ★ ★

A Minister decided to do something a little different one Sunday morning.

He said, "Today, church, I am going to say a single word and you are going to help me preach. Whatever single word I say, I want you to sing whatever hymn comes to your mind."

The pastor shouted out "Cross".

Immediately the congregation started singing in unison 'The Old Rugged Cross'.

The Pastor hollered out "Grace".

The congregation rapidly began to sing 'Amazing Grace, how sweet the sound'.

The Pastor said "Power".

The congregation sang 'There is Power in the Blood'.

The Pastor said "Sex".

The congregation fell into total silence. Everyone was in shock. They all nervously began to look around at each other, afraid to say anything.

Suddenly, from the back of the church, a frail little 87-year-old grandmother stood up and, in a tiny quavering voice, began to sing, 'Precious Memories'.

★ ★ ★

A guy walks into a post office one day to see a middle-aged, balding man standing at the counter methodically placing 'Love' stamps on bright pink envelopes with hearts all over them. He then takes out a perfume bottle and starts spraying scent all over them.

His curiosity getting the better of him, this guy goes up to the balding man and asks him what he is doing. The man says, "I'm sending out 1,000 Valentine cards signed 'Guess who?'"

"But why?" asks the man.

"I'm a divorce lawyer," the man replies.

★ ★ ★

THE 13 BIGGEST LIES

13. Your cheque is in the post.
12. You get this one, I'll pay next time.
11. You look great.
10. Of course I love you.
9. It's not the money, it's the principle of the thing…
8. … but we can still be good friends.
7. She means nothing to me.
6. Don't worry, I can go another 20 miles when the gauge is on "empty".
5. Don't worry, he's never bitten anyone.
4. I'll call you later.
3. I've never done anything like this before.
2. I'm from your government, and I am here to help you.
1. I DO.

★ ★ ★

BED CHAMBER

"Why are you taking so long?" complained his wife.
"I'm trying really hard," he replied,"but I can't think of anyone."

★ ★ ★

Did you wake up grumpy this morning?
No, I let him sleep.

★ ★ ★

The best way to drive your husband mad is to smile in your sleep.

★ ★ ★

The small guest house was full, but taking pity on the stranded traveller the owner agreed to the man sharing a bed with his daughter. However, when the man tried some hanky panky she replied, "Stop that at once or I'll call my father."
Some time went by and he tried again but got the same reply: "Stop that or I'll call my father."
Then to his amazement, third time lucky, she agreed and they spent a passionate 20 minutes bonking.
Five minutes later she tapped him on the shoulder and asked for more. He obligingly agreed and away they went. Exhausted afterwards, he was just about to go to sleep when she tapped his shoulder again. This was repeated half the night until he was so knackered he turned to her and said, "Stop that or I'll call your father."

★ ★ ★

How does a French girl hold her liquor?
By the ears.

★ ★ ★

What's the macho man's idea of foreplay?
A tap on the shoulder and the words "Are you awake?"

★ ★ ★

A wife with a large sexual appetite calls to her husband. "Guess what I have hidden in my hands and I'll reward you with a full night of passion."

The poor harassed husband replies, "An elephant".

"Not quite," she says, "but it's close enough."

★ ★ ★

A young girl tells her devoted father she wants to get married. He's a bit shocked at this and decides to sit her down and talk to her about the birds and the bees. He also tells her that if her husband asks her to roll over she doesn't have to.

"Oh father," she says, "I know all there is to know, you don't have to worry."

A year goes by and one night in bed her husband asks her to roll over.

"Oh no," says the girl. "I don't have to if I don't want to."

"But, darling, what's wrong, don't you ever want to get pregnant!"

★ ★ ★

In a recent survey it was discovered that 15% of men liked women with thin legs, 10% liked women with fat legs and the rest liked something in between.

★ ★ ★

One night as they were going to bed Mabel asked her old husband how they would manage when he could no longer work.

"Just look out of the window," said Bill. "I own those two shops and three houses."

Mabel wanted to know how exactly he'd managed to do that on such a low wage.

"From the moment we were married I put 50p under the mattress every time you let me have my way and if you hadn't been such a frigid old cow, we'd have had two supermarkets and three pubs by now."

★ ★ ★

If you suffer from insomnia, have sex. It won't help you sleep but you'll have more fun while you're awake!

⋆ ⋆ ⋆

There's a shop next door that sells strobe lighting for the bedroom. It makes it look as if your wife is moving during sex.

⋆ ⋆ ⋆

Looking through an open bedroom window one night, a Peeping Tom came upon a young couple playing a rather kinky game. Stark naked, they were sitting in opposite corners of the room, a bag of marbles besides the man, and a pile of hoops besides the woman. As he watched the woman threw a hoop across the room and it landed on the man's erect penis.

"Hooray!" she said. "One to me".

Then the man rolled a marble straight between her legs and cheered. "Now, it's one all."

The next day the Peeping Tom's wife was going shopping and asked him if there was anything he needed.

"Yes," he replied with a secret grin on his face. "A bag of sprouts and a packet of polo mints."

⋆ ⋆ ⋆

Now I know why my wife closes her eyes when we're making love. She hates to see me having a good time.

⋆ ⋆ ⋆

Have you heard about the ideal couple? He's got a premature ejaculation problem and she's got a short attention span.

⋆ ⋆ ⋆

One night, unsure whether his wife would respond to his amorous advances, Ken suddenly had a really great idea. As he clambered into

bed he handed his wife two paracetamol pills and a glass of water.
"What's that for?" she asked.
"For your headache."
"But I haven't got a headache."
"Good, then let's fuck."

★ ★ ★

After many years of making love in the dark, the wife turns the light on one night to find her husband using a dildo on her.
"What's going on?" she cries horrified. "What's the meaning of this?"
"I can explain," he says, "but first you tell me how we got the kids."

★ ★ ★

Old proverb: You can't take sex with you, so you might as well get plenty down here.

★ ★ ★

"My darling, will you love me always?"
"Of course, sweetheart, which way do you want to try first?"

★ ★ ★

Have you heard of the new style in women's nightdresses?
They have fur hems to keep a man's neck warm.

★ ★ ★

"Darling, do you think we might try making love doggie style?" said husband to wife.
"OK, we can think about it but not on a street in this particular neighbourhood where someone might come along who knows us," she replied.

★ ★ ★

"I love you very much," said the ardent young lover. "I may not have much money, like my mate Martin. I may not have a sports car or a cottage in the country like him. But I love you with all my heart and everything I have is yours."

"Very nice," she replied, preoccupied, "but just tell me a little more about this Martin guy."

★ ★ ★

"Sweetheart," said the young man, "since I met you, I can't eat, I can't drink, in fact I can't do anything."

Thinking he was lovesick, she replied confidently, "Why's that?"

"Because I'm flat broke," came the reply.

★ ★ ★

"Sir," said the young man to the girl's father, "your daughter has told me she loves me so much she can't live without me, and she wants us to get married."

"I see. So you want my permission."

"No. I want you to tell her to leave me alone."

★ ★ ★

John sat down and put pen to paper.

My dear Lucy
Can you ever forgive me?

I'd had a lot of pressure at work and I wasn't thinking straight when I broke off our engagement. Of course I love you more than anything in the world. Let's not let my moment of madness spoil our future happiness.
Hugs & kisses
John
P.S. Congratulations on winning top prize on the lottery.

★ ★ ★

Karl met a woman in a pub and asked her if she would like a drink.

"No thanks," she replied. "I don't drink alcohol."

"How about a cigarette?"

She shook her head. "I don't smoke," she replied.

"Packet of crisps?"

Again she shook her head. Secretly congratulating himself on spending so little, he asked her if he could see her home and when she said 'yes', he was delighted.

They arrived at her front door, and in the hall was a dead horse. Seeing the look on his face, she said, "Well, I didn't say I was tidy."

★ ★ ★

Attending a wedding for the first time, a little girl turned to her mother and asked, "Mummy, why is the bride wearing white?"

Not wanting to get bogged down in complicated explanation, her mother replied, "Because white means happiness, and today is the happiest day of the bride's life."

"So why is the groom wearing black?" asked the little girl.

★ ★ ★

As the wife watched her husband's coffin disappear into the ground, she turned to her friend and said, "You know, Ethel, I blame myself for his death."

"Oh why?"

"Because I shot him," she replied.

★ ★ ★

"I'm getting a divorce," said Jack to his mate, Bill. "The wife hasn't spoken to me for six months."

Bill thought about this for a moment and then replied, "Just make sure you know what you're doing, Jack. Wives like that are hard to find."

★ ★ ★

Two men talking over a pint of beer. "Me and the wife had a terrible argument last night," said Alf. "She's a bloody stubborn woman. But I got the last word in."
"Good for you, Alf!" said his mate. "What did you say?"
"Okay, buy the damned thing!" he replied.

★ ★ ★

Laying on his deathbed, the old man's eyes rested on the face of his sorrowful wife.
"Dear Agnes," he rasped, "we've been through a lot together. When I was just 20 my parents were killed in a car accident, and you were there for me. Then we had the terrible floods of '64 when we lost all our possessions and you helped me through it. Now I've caught this fatal disease and here you are by my side. Do you know," he continued with a spark of anger, "I'm beginning to think you're a bit of a jinx!"

★ ★ ★

Angry wife to husband: "You were twice as long on the golf course today. Why's that?" "A slight problem," replied the husband. "Old Jack died on the ninth hole and from then on in it was play the hole, drag Jack, play the hole, drag Jack, play the hole..."

★ ★ ★

A man sat staring sadly into his pint of beer.
"Hello, George, what's wrong?" asked his mate, sitting down next to him.
"It's the wife," he replied. "We had a terrible fight last night and she came crawling over to me on her hands and knees..."
"Oh Lord! That's awful," interrupted his friend.
"... and she said, 'Come out from under that bed or I'll put you in hospital.'"

★ ★ ★

"It's no good!" cried the downtrodden husband. "I can't go on. I'm off to join the Foreign Legion."

"Very well," retorted the wife, "but don't let me find you trailing sand all over my nice new carpet when you get back."

★ ★ ★

Walter was hammering away in the garden when George popped his head up over the wall. "Fancy a pint, Walt?" he asked.

"No, I can't," replied Walter sadly. "The wife's ill in bed, so I've got to look after her."

As if on cue, they heard terrible noises coming from the house.

"Is that her coughin'?" asked George.

"Don't be daft," replied Walter. "She couldn't get inside this. It's far too small. It's going to be a new kennel for the dog."

★ ★ ★

A man took his dog to the vet's and asked for its tail to be completely removed.

"But why?" asked the vet. "That's a bit drastic."

The man replied, "My mother-in-law's coming to stay next week and I want to be sure there are no signs of welcome."

★ ★ ★

Old Jake only had moments to live. At his bedside were his family – his wife and four sons, three of which had blond hair, the other ginger.

"Mavis, I've always wondered why one of our sons had red hair. Tell me truthfully, is he really my son?"

Mavis put her hand on her heart and swore fervently that, yes, he was his son.

"Oh thank goodness," croaked the old man and he died with a smile on his face.

As the family left, the room, the wife sighed deeply, "Thank God, he didn't ask about the other three."

★ ★ ★

The couple had been married a year when the husband was called away on business on the other side of the country. It meant he would be away for a month so the wife's friend moved in to keep her company. As it happened, the job finished earlier than expected, so he jumped on a plane and on landing rang his wife from the airport. Her friend answered the phone to say that Tracy was in the bath.

"OK, can you tell her I'll be there about midnight, so if she can wear something sheer and sexy we'll make it a night to remember."

"OK," said the friend, "and who shall I say called?"

★ ★ ★

A man rang his wife to tell her he had the afternoon off and would be coming home. The phone was answered by a small boy.

"Hello, son, can I speak to mum?"

"No," said the boy. "Mum's in bed with the milkman and they've told me to stay downstairs."

The man was stunned by the news but after a moment or two he said to the boy, "Son, go and get my shotgun from the garage, load it with two cartridges and go and blast them."

After an agonizing 10 minutes the little boy came back on to the phone. "I've done it, dad," he said.

"Well done, son. I'll finish off when I get back. Go and have a swim in the pool to clean yourself up and I'll see you later."

"But, dad, we don't have a pool," said the boy.

"What! Hold on, is that 0397 46461?"

★ ★ ★

A woman was in bed with her lover when she heard her husband open the front door. "Quick!" she whispered urgently. "It's my husband, hide in the wardrobe."

"Ooh, it's dark in here," said a little voice.

"Who's that?" gasped the man.

"That's my mum you've been with and I'm going to call my dad."

"Now, now, son, not so hasty, I'm sure we can work this out."

"OK," said the small boy. "But it'll cost you."

"How about £5?"

"I'm going to call Dad."

"Well, £10 then."

"I'm going to call dad."

"OK, let's say £20."

"No, £30."

"Well, that's all I've got. Here you are." The man handed over the money and made his escape. A few days later mum took the little boy to church and as she prayed he wandered off into the confessional.

"Ooh, it's dark in here," he said.

"Oh no, don't start that again!" replied the priest.

★ ★ ★

The simple man was beside himself with anger when he discovered his wife in bed with another man.

"How could you!" he yelled, and taking a gun out of the bottom drawer of the bedside table he placed it to his head and cocked the trigger.

"Don't, Jim, please don't," sobbed the woman. "Put the gun down."

"Say your prayers, you're next," snapped the man.

★ ★ ★

A man turns to his friend and asks him why he's looking so puzzled. He replies, "I've received this letter today and it's from a man who says he'll beat me senseless if I don't stay away from his wife."

"So what's puzzling you?"

"Well, he hasn't signed it."

★ ★ ★

When a man arrives home from work one evening, he's greeted by his wife, who's got a bottle of hair conditioner in her hand.

"What's that for?" he asks. "My hair's OK."

"Yours maybe, but this is for your girlfriend whose hair keeps coming out all over your clothes!"

My best friend ran away with my wife, and do you know – I miss him.

* * *

Jack lived his life to a very strict routine and would go out for a pint every Monday, Wednesday and Friday. However, one Friday night he didn't feel very well, so he decided to stay in and watch television with his wife. Halfway through the evening the phone rang and his wife heard him say, "Why the hell are you ringing me? Get on to the Met Office!" and he slammed down the phone.

"Who was that?" she asked.

"Some silly bugger asking me if the coast was clear."

* * *

Husband comes home from the office and sees his wife in the garden.

"Sarah, I have some good news and some bad news to tell you. I'm leaving you for Molly."

"I see," says the wife, "and what's the bad news?"

* * *

A man was going away on business for a month. Highly suspicious that his wife would get up to no good while he was gone, he hired a private investigator to follow her wherever she went.

On his return, the PI confronted him with his wife's infidelity. All the evidence was on video. The man was shown film of his wife at glamorous parties, dancing the night away at exclusive nightclubs, intimate dinners with one of his work colleagues, overnight stays at luxury hotels...

"Well," gasped the man, "I can hardly believe it."

"Is it because she's involved with one of your colleagues?" asked the PI in concerned tones.

"No, no," replied the man. "I just didn't believe my wife could be that much fun."

* * *

WARNING: consumption of alcohol may cause you to thay shings like thish; it may cause you to tell the boss what you REALLY think while photocopying your butt at the office Christmas party; it may create the illusion that you are tougher, handsomer and smarter than that vicious guy over there in the corner named 'Psycho'; worse still, it may also lead you to think people are laughing WITH you.

★ ★ ★

The man turned to his wife and said angrily, "You silly cow, locking the dog in the boot of the car has got to be the most stupid thing ever."
"Oh yeah?" she retorted, "wait till I tell you about the car keys."

★ ★ ★

A married couple are driving down the interstate doing 55 mph. The wife is behind the wheel.
Her husband looks over at her and says, "Honey, I know we've been married for 15 years, but, I've decided I want a divorce."
The wife doesn't say a single thing, but slowly increases her speed to 60 mph.
He then says, "I don't want you to try to talk me out of it, because I've been having an affair with your best friend, and she's a far better lover than you."
Again the wife stays quiet and just speeds up as her anger increases.
"I want the house," he says.
Again the wife speeds up, and is now doing 70mph.
"I want the kids too," he says.
The wife just keeps driving faster and faster – now she's up to 80mph.
"I want the car, the checking account, and all the credit cards too," he continues.
The wife slowly starts to veer toward a bridge overpass piling, as he says, "Is there anything you want?"
"No, I've got everything I need," says the wife.
"What's that?" he asks.

The wife lets him know, just before they hit the wall at 90mph, "I've got the airbag!"

★ ★ ★

The woman picked the phone up and a voice said, "Hello, Sandy, fancy a drink tonight?"
"No, I'm working late," she replied.
"Well, how about tomorrow?"
"No, I'm meeting friends for dinner."
"Okay, let's make it this weekend?"
"Sorry, I'm off to my mother's."
"Oh for goodness sake. Sometimes I wonder why we ever got married!"

★ ★ ★

"Now listen, son, you'll look back on this time as the happiest in your life," confided the boy's father.
"But, dad, I'm not getting married for another week."
"That's what I mean, son," he nodded sadly.

★ ★ ★

Did you hear about the girl who advertised for a husband in the personal column of the local paper?
She had over 200 replies saying, "You can have mine."

★ ★ ★

A reporter from the local newspaper was interviewing a couple who were celebrating their 25th anniversary.
"And after all this time, can you still say you're in love?" he asked.
"Oh yes," said the husband, "I'm in love with her sister and she's in love with the man next door."

★ ★ ★

"I'm worried about my wife. It's her appearance, she's let me down."
"Oh, how come?" replied the other.
"Well, I haven't seen her for three days."

★ ★ ★

A man said, "Was that your wife who answered the door?"
"Of course it was," replied the husband. "You don't think I've got an au pair that ugly?"

★ ★ ★

My wife gets so easily upset that she cries when the traffic lights are against her.

★ ★ ★

Moaning man: "Is there anything worse than a wife who never stops talking about her last husband?"
"Yes – a wife who never stops talking about her next husband," his friend replied.

★ ★ ★

"Oh my darling, drink makes you look so sexy."
"But I haven't been drinking."
"No, but I have."

★ ★ ★

A woman comes home to find her husband crying his eyes out.
"What's wrong?" she asks.
He looks up at her and says, "Do you remember 15 years ago when I got you pregnant? Your father was so angry he said I had to marry you or go to jail?" "Yes, I remember," she replies, "but why are you thinking of that now?"
"Well, today is the day I would have been released!"

★ ★ ★

An efficiency expert concluded his lecture with a note of caution.
"You need to be careful about trying these techniques at home."
"Why?" asked somebody from the audience.
"I watched my wife's routine at dinner for years," the expert explained. "She made lots of trips between the refrigerator, stove, table and cabinets, often carrying a single item at a time. One day I told her, 'Honey, why don't you try carrying several things at once?'"
"Did it save time?" the guy in the audience asked.
"Actually, yes," replied the expert. "It used to take her 30 minutes to make dinner. Now I do it in ten..."

★ ★ ★

A man and his young wife were in divorce court, but the custody of their children posed a problem.
The mother leaped to her feet and protested to the judge that since she brought the children into this world, she should retain custody of them.
The man also wanted custody of his children, so the judge asked for his justification.
After a long silence, the man slowly rose from his chair and replied,
"Your Honour, when I put a pound in a vending machine and a Coke comes out, does the Coke belong to me or the machine?"

★ ★ ★

Scott finally got his girlfriend into bed, and things were becoming very hot and heavy.
"Slow down, baby," she said. "Foreplay is an art."
"You'd better get your canvas ready soon," he panted, "because I'm about to spill my paint!"

★ ★ ★

Two deaf people get married. During the first week of marriage, they find that they are unable to communicate in the bedroom when they turn off the lights because they can't see each other using sign language. After several nights of fumbling around and misunderstandings, the wife decides to find a solution. "Honey," she signs, "why don't we agree on some simple signals? For instance, at night, if you want to have sex with me, reach over and squeeze my left breast one time. If you don't want to have sex, reach over and squeeze my right breast one time."

The husband thinks this is a great idea and signs back to his wife, "Great idea, Now if you want to have sex with ME, reach over and pull on my penis one time. If you don't want to have sex, reach over and pull on my penis... fifty times."

★ ★ ★

A man meets a gorgeous woman in a bar.

They talk, they connect, they end up leaving together.

They get back to her place, and as she shows him around her apartment, he notices that her bedroom is completely packed with teddy bears.

There are hundreds of small bears on a shelf all the way along the floor, medium-sized ones on a shelf a little higher, and huge bears on the top shelf along the wall.

The man is kind of surprised that this woman would have a collection of teddy bears, especially one that's so extensive, but he decides not to mention this to her.

He turns to her, they kiss... and then they rip each other's clothes off and make love.

After an intense night of passion, as they are lying there together in the warm afterglow of love, the man rolls over and asks, smiling, "Well, how was it?"

The woman says, "You can have any prize from the bottom shelf."

★ ★ ★

A husband and wife are in bed busy watching *Who Wants to be a Millionaire* on TV.

The husband asks for sex.

The wife says, "No".

Her husband asks, "Is that your final answer?"
She responds, "Yes."
He says, "Then, I'd like to phone a friend."

★ ★ ★

A man and a woman were deeply in love. She, being of a religious nature, had held back from the worldly pleasure that he wanted so badly. In fact, he had never even seen her naked.
One day, as they drove down the freeway, she remarked about his slow driving habits.
"I can't stand it anymore," she told him. "Let's play a game. For every 5 miles per hour over the speed limit you drive, I'll remove one piece of clothing."
He enthusiastically agreed and sped up the car. He reached the 55 mph mark, so she took off her blouse. At 60, off came the pants. At 65 it was her bra and at 70 her panties.
Now, seeing her naked for the very first time, and travelling faster than he ever had before, he became far too excited and lost control of the vehicle.
He veered off the road, over an embankment and wrapped the car around a tree.
His girlfriend was thrown clear, but he was trapped. She tried to pull him free, but alas he was stuck.
"Go up to the road and get help," he said.
"But I haven't anything to cover myself with!" she replied.
The man felt around, but could only reach one of his shoes. "You'll have to put this between your legs to cover it up," he told her.
So she did as he said and went up to the road for help. Along came a truck driver. Seeing a naked, crying woman along the road, he pulled over to hear her story. "My boyfriend, my boyfriend!" she sobs. "He's stuck and I can't pull him out!"
The truck driver, looking down at the shoe between her legs, replies, "Ma'am, if he's in that far, I'm afraid there's no hope for him."

★ ★ ★

131

A boy just takes his girlfriend back to her home after being out together, and when they reach the front door he leans with one hand on the wall and says to her, "Sweetie, why don't you give me a blowjob?"

"What? You're crazy!"

"Don't worry, it will be quick, no problem..."

"No! Someone may see – a relative, a neighbour..."

"At this time of the night no one will show up."

"I've already said NO, and NO."

"Honey, it's just a small blowie... I know you like it too."

"NO!!! I've said NO!!!"

"My love... don't be like that."

At this moment the younger sister shows up at the door in a nightgown with her hair totally in disorder, rubbing her eyes and says, "Dad told you to blow, or that I must blow, or he will come down and blow himself, but for Christ's sake to tell your boyfriend to take his hand off the intercom."

★ ★ ★

BITTERNESS

A bitter woman who buried her husband on the Monday returned with his headstone on the Thursday. On it she had inscribed, "Here lies my husband, stiff at last."

★ ★ ★

A bitter old lady turned to her neighbour and said, "I see Edith's buried her tenth husband. Now at last they're together again."
"What d'you mean, her husbands?"
"No, silly, I'm talking about her legs."

★ ★ ★

What's the difference between a whore and a bitch?
A whore sleeps with everyone; a bitch sleeps with everyone except you.

★ ★ ★

A bitter old woman turned to her friend and said, "If it wasn't for orgasms, that old tart over there wouldn't know when to stop screwing."

★ ★ ★

A man who had done so much for his village was complaining about the lack of respect he had received from the rest of the inhabitants.
"For instance," he said, "see all those beautifully mown lawns, the abundance of flowers, the avenue of trees? I did all that, but do they call me John the Horticulturist? No, they bloody well don't. And look at the stunning new village hall and the ornate wall around the church. I did all that, but do they call me John the Builder? Not bloody likely! But just one, just one bloody sheep..."

★ ★ ★

When the bitter woman was asked what the meaning of life was she replied, "It's like a bed of roses – full of pricks."

★ ★ ★

Did you hear about the bitter old nurse?
On the night her husband got married again she put anaesthetic in the lubricating jelly.

* * *

Two women, who were at school together, bump into each other 10 years later. The first one is a bit of a show-off.
"Yes, I can't complain. I went for a job on an estate just outside Henley and ended up marrying the Lord of the Manor. Ha Ha."
"Oh, how nice," said the second.
"And Jack darling encouraged me to start a stud farm and we've now got one of the best in southern England."
"Oh, how nice."
"We've got two lovely boys... at Eton, of course."
"Oh, how nice."
"Anyway, listen to me blathering on! What happened to you?"
"Me? Oh, I went to finishing school after we left, and learnt how to say, 'Oh how nice' instead of 'Fuck you'."

* * *

Overheard on the top deck of a bus:
"I'm knackered, Bill, it's been a hell of a day at work. You know, compared to us, women have it so easy. Why, they even sit down to take a piss."

* * *

Walking round the art gallery, Bob is stopped by one of the local artists.
"I'm sorry to bother you, but I must say your wife is quite stunning and I would deem it an honour to paint her portrait."
"Oh yes?" said Bob, watching his wife flirting with yet another local dignitary. "Yes, you're right, she reminds me of the Venus de Milo."
"How extraordinary," said the artist, looking closer at Bob. "In what way?"

"She's beautiful all right, but not all there!"

★ ★ ★

Joan, the town gossip and supervisor of the town's morals, publicly accused her neighbour George of being an alcoholic because she saw his pick-up truck parked outside the town's only bar.

George stared at her for a moment and said nothing. Later that evening, he parked his pick-up in front of her house and left it there all night.

★ ★ ★

Dennis Rodman finds a bottle on the beach and picks it up... suddenly a female genie appears from the bottle. "Master, I may grant you one wish," says the genie with a smile.

"Hey, Bitch... don't you know who I am? I don't need no woman to give me nuttin!" barks Rodman.

The genie pleads, "But Master I must grant you a wish or I will be returned to this bottle forever."

Dennis thinks for a moment, then grumbling about the inconvenience of it all, he says, "OK, OK, I wanna wake up with three women in my bed in the morning. So just do it!" He gives the genie an evil glare. "Now leave me alone!" he screams.

So the very annoyed genie says, "So be it!" and disappears back into the bottle.

Next morning, he wakes up with Lorena Bobbitt, Tonya Harding and Hillary Clinton. His penis is gone, his leg is broken, and he has no health insurance.

★ ★ ★

The first wonderful quote of the century, and one that may well prove extremely hard to top...

Monica Lewinsky (on CNN's *Larry King Live* discussing her miraculous Jenny Craig weight-loss): "I've learned not to put things in

my mouth that are bad for me..."
Now I ask you, are these words to live by, or what...

★ ★ ★

CHEEKINESS

It was too late for Bob to drive home, so he was invited to stay the night at his mate's house.

"We've only the one bed," said Bob's mate, "so you'll have to share with me and the wife."

They all went to bed and soon the husband was snoring. Then Bob got a nudge from the wife inviting him over for a bit of shagging.

"I can't do that, your husband will wake up at the noise," he whispered.

"Don't worry, there's no chance of that. But if you're worried, pull out one of his pubic hairs and see if he wakes up."

Bob did just that, but the husband never moved a muscle and went on snoring. So Bob and the wife got down to it and enjoyed a very pleasant 30 minutes. It wasn't long before she was nudging him again and this went on half the night, each time Bob plucking the husband's pubic hair out before he started.

However on the twelfth time, the husband turned to Bob and said, "Listen, mate, I don't mind you shagging my wife, but bloody hell I do mind you keeping score on my arse."

★ ★ ★

A man travelling home late from work falls asleep on the train and ends up at the terminus. There's a taxi outside but the driver refuses to take him because he hasn't enough money for the fare and the driver won't let him pay the balance on getting home. The poor man ends up sleeping rough. A few days later, having plotted his revenge, he stays on to the terminus and sees four taxis waiting, the last one in the line being the driver who refused him last time. He goes up to the other three taxis in turn, asks how much the fare is, says he can't pay but offers to give them a blow job. Each driver in turn tells him to bugger off. He then goes up to the fourth taxi, asks how much the fare is and gets in. As they pass the three waiting taxis, he looks out of the back window, smiles and gives them the thumbs-up.

★ ★ ★

Do you know what the heaviest thing in the world is?

The body of a woman you no longer love.

★ ★ ★

My wife's got long black hair running down her back. Wish it was on her head.

★ ★ ★

FEMALE put-down:
I bet when you climax you call out your own name.

★ ★ ★

How do you know when your girlfriend is putting on weight?
When she sits on your face and you can't hear the radio.

★ ★ ★

Porter to man, "Can I carry your bag, sir?"
"No, let her walk."

★ ★ ★

Do you know what a constipated greeting is?
It's when you ask someone, "How are you?" but don't give a shit.

★ ★ ★

"My darling," whispered the naive young man, "will I be the first man to sleep with you?"
"You will be if you doze off," she replied.

★ ★ ★

"You are the world's worst lover!" yelled his wife.
"Get away," he replied. "That really would be too much of a coincidence."

★ ★ ★

The butler was summoned to the master bedroom to find her ladyship lying naked across the bed.

"There you are, Edward" she said. "Are you a good sport?"

"I believe so, ma'am," replied the startled butler.

"And are you a good fuck?" she continued.

"Yes, I believe I am."

"Well, in that case, fuck off – it's April Fools' Day."

★ ★ ★

There were mixed reactions when Lady Godiva rode side-saddle through the town. Those on the right cheered, shouted and whistled, those on the left were strangely quiet.

★ ★ ★

My wife saw the dustbin lorry leaving our house. "Am I too late for the rubbish?" she asked. "No," they answered. "Jump in."

★ ★ ★

A young man takes refuge in an old couple's house when his car breaks down on the moor. "We've only got two bedrooms, young man, one for us and the other for our spinster daughter, Aida, but you're quite welcome to sleep on the sofa."

In the middle of the night it turns bitterly cold, so the old woman pops downstairs to see how the man is doing. "I hope you're not too cold, would you like our eiderdown?" "Good gracious, no thanks," he replied. "She's been down three times already."

★ ★ ★

"Well, I never!" cried the outraged mother when she walked into the front room to find her daughter and boyfriend having it away on the sofa. "Oh, mother," replied the daughter. "Of course, you did."

★ ★ ★

As Jack drew up at the lights, a car screamed to a stop behind him and out jumped the driver and rushed over.

"I've been trying to get your attention for the last three miles," he said. "Didn't you realize your wife had fallen off when you took that sharp bend?"

"Oh, I am relieved" said Jack. "I thought I'd gone deaf."

★ ★ ★

What makes taxi drivers the world's worst lovers? They never check to see if you're coming before they pull out.

★ ★ ★

Did you hear about the dwarf who was expelled from the nudist colony?

He was always poking his nose into other people's business.

★ ★ ★

"But, darling, you're only saying I've got a beautiful body to get me into bed," she said.

"No, no, that's not true," he replied. "It's not just me that thinks that. I took some secret shots of you in the shower, showed them to my mates and they all agree. You really do have a beautiful body."

★ ★ ★

"Listen, mate," said one man to another in the local bar. "Do the same as me. After sex when you're knackered and she's not, record your voice and keep the machine under your pillow, so you can switch it on and make her think you're still talking to her."

★ ★ ★

How can you tell a short-sighted man in a nudist colony?
It isn't hard.

★ ★ ★

Did you hear about the blind man who went to a nudist colony?
It was a touching sight.
Who's the most popular man in a nudist colony?
The one who can carry two teas and ten doughnuts all at the same time.

★ ★ ★

Doctor, do you agree with eating everything raw?
No, always keep your clothes on.

★ ★ ★

A nudist never has to hold his hand out to see if it is raining.

★ ★ ★

A young man, finding himself stranded in the middle of nowhere, comes upon a little cottage. On knocking, the door is opened by a Chinaman who allows him to stay the night as long as he goes nowhere near his daughter. If he disobeys, the three most horrible tortures will be inflicted upon him.

However, the young man is rather stupid and when he sees the Chinaman's beautiful daughter he forgets all about his promise. That night when everything is quiet, he steals into the daughter's room and they enjoy a night of non-stop rollicking.

He wakes to find a boulder on his chest and pinned to it is a little note which says, "Beware, large boulder on chest – Torture 1."

The young man is arrogant enough to throw the boulder out of the window immediately. As he does so he notices another note which says, "Beware boulder tied to left testicle – Torture 2."

Quickly thinking that the lesser of two evils was to break a few bones jumping out of the window, he did just that before the rope tightened. However, as he fell to the ground, another sign was waiting for him. It read, "Beware, right testicle tied to bedroom door – Torture 3."

★ ★ ★

A man walks into the local hotel and sees a pretty girl drinking by herself at the bar.

"Do you mind if I join you?" he asks.

At that she screams at the top of her voice, "No, I will not go up to your room!"

Everyone stops talking, looks at him as he turns a bright red and slowly shuffles away.

A few minutes later she walks over to him, apologises and explains that she is studying human behaviour and people's reactions to embarrassing situations.

The man listens quietly to her explanation and then shouts at the top of his voice, "£150, you've got to be joking."

★ ★ ★

What is the difference between erotic sex and kinky sex?

For erotic sex you use a feather, during kinky sex it's the whole chicken.

★ ★ ★

"What's wrong, mate? You look tired."

"I am," said Bob. "I think I pulled a muscle this morning."

"It's odd that it should make you so tired."

"Not really, if you pull it 450 times."

★ ★ ★

A rather haughty woman walked into the menswear section of a major department store and asked the wizened old assistant whether he fitted trusses.

"Indeed we do," came the puzzled reply.

"Well, in that case, wash your hands thoroughly before you serve me with some of those gentlemen's cigars," she demanded.

★ ★ ★

A divorced couple still remained good friends and would often meet in the local pub to catch up on all the gossip.

So it wasn't all that surprising that when he broke a leg skiing she would frequently go round to his place to help him out.

One day, she was lifting him out of the bath when she noticed he had an erection.

"Oh look, Bob," she remarked. "He still remembers me."

★ ★ ★

Driving down a very busy high street, the man's car suddenly stalled and nothing he did would get it moving again.

Feeling more and more flustered, his temper eventually boiled over when a man behind him repeatedly beeped his horn. Out got the man and strode up to the car behind, opened the door and pushed his fingers hard down on the horn.

"Here, we'll do a swap. I'll blast your horn for you, while you go and start that bugger up."

★ ★ ★

A 'dirty old man' picked up a beautiful young girl in the local pub and invited her out for dinner.

To his surprise she accepted and they went off to the most expensive restaurant in town where she ordered all the most expensive food and drink on the menu. Astonished, the man asked her if she always had such a big appetite.

"Only when someone wants to get into my knickers," she replied.

★ ★ ★

Have you heard about the miserly man? He always stays in with his dates and plays snap. It's cheap on wining and dining; the only expense is the elastic.

★ ★ ★

"According to the latest MORI poll 50% of male adults sing in the bath – the rest are wankers. And do you know what they sing?"

"No."

"I didn't think so."

★ ★ ★

Walking along the seashore, a man finds a bottle washed up on the sand and when he opens it, a genie pops out. As thanks for setting him free, the genie grants the man one wish.

"Er... I wish I was always hard and had lots of arse," he says.

So the genie turns him into a toilet seat.

★ ★ ★

Do you know the difference between a woman trying to slim and a virgin? One's trying to diet and the other's dying to try it.

★ ★ ★

"I'll tell you what eternity feels like," said the unscrupulous woman. "It's the time it takes between you coming and him leaving."

★ ★ ★

"Sweetheart," said the young man to his girlfriend. "What I'd really like is a little pussy."

"Me too," she replied. "Mine's as big as an elephant's."

★ ★ ★

A sales rep was staying overnight at an hotel and took a great fancy to the waitress but when he tried to entice her up to his room she flatly refused. "I'm not that sort of girl," she said. "Besides, I don't like sex very much."

"Oh come now! Do you realize I'm a shoe salesman? You might like to inspect some of the latest and most fashionable ladies shoes upstairs in my room."

In the end the girl relented and it wasn't long before he was on top of her in bed. Much to his surprise she reacted very enthusiastically, wrapping her legs around him and twisting and turning quite vigorously. "There, I knew you'd find me good," said the arrogant man. "Oh no," she replied. "I'm just trying on the shoes."

★ ★ ★

A very large lady visits the doctor complaining of a sore throat. The doctor shines a light down her throat and after a few moments says to her, "Would you like to take all your clothes off and then get down on all fours?"

This the fat lady does.

"Very good," says the doctor. "Now would you please crawl over to the wall behind the door."

So the fat lady does as she's told.

"Mm Mm, yes, I see. Right now, will you please crawl to the wall between the lampstand and the glass-fronted cabinet. Good... excellent. OK, you may get dressed now."

When the fat lady is dressed and sits back down she asked him what is wrong.

"Oh, you have a sore throat, I'll give you a prescription for it."

"But why on earth did you have me crawling around the room on all fours with no clothes on?" she asks impatiently.

"Ah well you see, tomorrow I'm having a pink sofa delivered and I was just trying to find the best place to put it."

★ ★ ★

What's the difference between an ugly girl and rubbish?
Rubbish gets taken out once a week.

★ ★ ★

He bought an apple for the teacher and she kissed him. So the next day he took a cantaloupe melon.

★ ★ ★

Her husband was so ugly, every time he went to the zoo he had to buy two tickets – one for going in and one for getting out.

★ ★ ★

"I can't go out with you tonight, I'm getting married."
"OK. How about tomorrow night then?"

★ ★ ★

"Father, I have something to confess. My girlfriend is pregnant and I need £150."
The man hands over the money. Then a few days later the other son arrives home with similar news.
"How much do you need?"
"£170."
Time passes and one day the daughter comes to see her father.
"I'm sorry, but I am pregnant," she says.
"Never mind," he says smiling. "It's about time we were on the receiving end."

★ ★ ★

A young punk rocker gets on the tube and sits opposite an old man who stares at him constantly. The punk has spiky red, blue and orange hair, rings in his nose, his eyebrows, lips and ears, and long dangling feather earrings. After 10 minutes, the punk can't take any more of the staring and shouts at the old man, "What are you looking at, you old fart, didn't you do anything crazy when you were young?"
"Yes," replies the old man. "When I was young and in the navy, I shagged a parrot when I was on shore leave. I thought maybe you were my son."

★ ★ ★

"How dare you tell that dirty, filthy joke before my wife!"
"I do apologise, I didn't know she wanted to tell it herself."

★ ★ ★

A very attractive woman walks up to the bar in a local pub and, smiling seductively, signals for the barman to come close to her. When he does, she starts to run her fingers through his hair and whispers, "Are you the landlord?"

"No, I'm sorry. He's not here at the moment"

And he gasps with delight as she brings her fingers down through his hair and begins to gently stroke his beard.

"Is there anything I can do?" he whispers.

"Yes, will you please give him a message?" By this time, she's put her fingers in his mouth and he's sucking on them sexily.

"Will you please tell the landlord that there's no toilet paper in the Ladies?"

★ ★ ★

Two burglars broke into a house in the village, tied up the old spinster who lived there and ransacked the rooms. The boss turned to his mate and said, "Before we go, I think I'll give her one to remember me by."

"I don't think we've got time, Boss. Let's get out of here before someone sees something and calls the police."

"Now hold on a minute," said the spinster. "Just who's in charge of this robbery?"

★ ★ ★

A market gardener and his daughter went into town to sell their produce and pick up some supplies for the following month. They made a healthy profit on the vegetables and spent some of it on buying onion sets, seed potatoes and the like, for the coming Spring. However, on the way back, they were attacked by a gang of thieves who took everything they had.

"Oh dear, our Josie!" said the distraught man. "How are we going to manage to live without any money?"

"Don't worry, father, I've saved the money."

"But how, they searched you thoroughly."

"I hid it in that place that women have."

151

"Oh my goodness, if your mother had been here, we could have saved half the supplies as well."

★ ★ ★

Have you heard about the miserly man who keeps a crate in the boot of his car?

He's filling it up with all the small furry animals he runs over on the road, so when he's got enough he'll get it made up into a fur coat for the wife.

★ ★ ★

Due to engine trouble, a scheduled flight from New York to London had to be cancelled and the airline staff were left to try and re-book all the passengers on to other flights. The queues were enormous, but one angry, pompous man strode to the front and interrupted the booking staff mid-conversation.

"Now look here, I have to be on the next flight, and I have to travel first class," he said forcefully.

"We will do all we can to help you, sir," replied one of the staff. "If you will just get back in line while I finish attending to this gentleman here."

Annoyed at being fobbed off, the man replied loudly so that everyone could hear, "Young lady, do you have any idea who I am?"

She smiled and picked up the microphone for the public address system.

"All passengers in the airport terminal, may I have your attention please. I have a passenger here at Gate 5 who does not know who he is. If anyone can help in this matter, please come to the gate as soon as possible. Thank you."

★ ★ ★

After doing his rounds in a remote part of the Lake District, the doctor stops off at Bill Higgins' house to see how he is since his wife died.

"Thanks for asking," he says. "I do feel a bit lonely now she's gone, but she's never far from my thoughts. I buried her in the garden, face down with her bum in the air."

"My goodness, why?"

"Well, you've got to have somewhere to park the bike."

★ ★ ★

A passing motorist sees a man fishing in a flower bed next to the mental institution.

He thinks he'll have a laugh, so he sticks his head out of the window and shouts, "Have you caught many?"

"Just three, apart from you," the man replies.

★ ★ ★

A high school English teacher reminds her class of tomorrow's final exam. She also tells them that there will be no excuse for failing to show up, except for serious injury, illness or a death in the student's immediate family.

A smart-ass jock in the back of the room pipes up and asks the teacher out loud, "What about extreme sexual exhaustion?"

The entire class does all it can to keep from breaking up, being barely able to stifle its laughter and snickering.

When silence is restored, the teacher smiles sympathetically at the student, shakes her head and sweetly says, "You can write with your other hand then."

★ ★ ★

A man moves into a nudist colony. He receives a letter from his mother asking him to send her a current picture. But being too embarrassed to let her know that he lives in a nudist colony, he cuts a photo in half and sends her the top part.

Later, he receives another letter asking him to send a picture to his grandmother. The man cuts another picture in half, but accidentally sends her the bottom half. He is really worried when he realizes that he sent the wrong part, but then remembers how bad his grandmother's eyesight is and hopes she won't notice.

A few weeks later, he receives a letter from his grandmother. It says, "Thank you for the picture. One piece of advice: change your hair style... it makes your nose look long!"

★ ★ ★

CHURCHYARD

The Reverend James was taking his usual morning walk through the woods when he met a frog that was looking very unhappy.

"I wish you could talk and tell me what is wrong," said the Reverend.

"I can," said the frog. "I used to be a choirboy, but an evil old crone turned me into a frog and the spell can only be reversed if someone takes me home, looks after me and lets me sleep in their bed."

Being such a caring soul, the Reverend did as the frog requested and the next morning the frog turned back into a choirboy.

"And that, your honour, is the case for the defence."

★ ★ ★

The local vicar is on his parish rounds when he comes to a house playing very loud music. When he knocks at the door, it is opened by a young lad smoking a cigarette, holding a bottle of scotch and accompanied by two young girls.

"Excuse me, son," says the vicar, "are your mum or dad in?"

"Does it fucking well look like it?" replies the boy.

★ ★ ★

The vicar was doing his parish rounds when he came upon a house that had eight children, from ages two to 12, playing in the garden. He knocked at the door but couldn't get any reply, so he peeped through the window. To his horror he saw a couple going at it hammer and tongs on the dining room carpet, so he beat a hasty retreat and went to the house opposite.

"Your neighbours across the road love having children, don't they?" he commented to the man.

"They sure do, vicar. His wife is in hospital at the moment having another baby, so my wife's popped over to see if there's anything she can do."

★ ★ ★

A young woman and a clergyman found themselves to be the only ones in the tea-room. So to be polite, the clergyman said, "That's a lovely baby you have there." The woman explained that it had taken six years of marriage before she conceived. Indeed it had taken so long that she had almost given up hope.

"Yes, indeed," replied the clergyman. "Persistence is the answer. Look at me: I breed pigeons, but for years never won a race. Now I'm winning gold cups all the time."

"Indeed," replied the woman, "and why's that?"

"Oh, I changed the cock," he said.

"Yes, that's what I did, too."

★ ★ ★

A very pretty young girl was just about to walk into the church in a topless dress when the vicar turned towards her.

"I'm afraid you can't come into church dressed like that," he said.

"But I have a divine right," she replied.

"My dear, I agree," nodded the vicar. "You have a divine left as well, but I still can't let you into my church."

★ ★ ★

The vicar returned to the rectory complaining bitterly that someone had stolen his bicycle while he'd been out on his parish calls.

"I've got an idea," replied the verger. "This Sunday in church make the Ten Commandments the theme of the sermon and when you get to 'Thou shalt not steal', watch their faces carefully for any tell-tale signs."

So that Sunday the vicar began his sermon, but halfway through he suddenly dried up and finished early.

"What happened?" asked the verger later.

"Well, I was going to do as you suggested, but when I got to 'Thou shalt not commit adultery', I suddenly remembered where I'd left my bicycle."

★ ★ ★

A young man and a bishop were sharing a railway carriage. The bishop spent the journey doing *The Times* crossword, but after some time began shaking his head and muttering.

"Can I help you, sir?" asked the young man.

"Well, I'm having trouble with one word – the clue is 'Essentially feminine' – four letters, the last three U-N-T."

"Why, sir, that'll be 'aunt'."

"Of course," said the bishop. "Do you have a rubber by any chance?"

★ ★ ★

A churchman, staying overnight at an hotel, struck up an acquaintance with the receptionist and at the end of the evening invited her up to his room for a bedtime drink.

One thing led to another and it wasn't long before they were having it away in bed.

"I'm not sure I should be here," said the receptionist. "After all, you are a man of the cloth."

"It's all right," he replied. "I read about it in the Gideon Bible here on my bedside table."

"Oh, where?" she asked.

"Here, on the front cover," he replied. "Look it says, 'You're on to a winner with the receptionist downstairs.'"

★ ★ ★

A man was taken seriously ill and the vicar was summoned to come as soon as possible. Now this puzzled the vicar because he knew the man was not of his parish and indeed went to a different church. However, he rushed around to the house and, on knocking, the door was opened by a small child.

"Hello," he said. "Isn't it nice that your father thought of me at this time?"

The child replied, "Well, we thought it might be catching, so we didn't want to take any risks."

★ ★ ★

The Mother Superior was late getting up and had to rush her morning prayers before visiting the young nuns at their work.

"Good morning, Sister Veronica, how are you? Those tomatoes are coming along very well."

"Thank you, Reverend Mother. Yes, I'm fine, though I'm sorry you got out of bed on the wrong side this morning."

Puzzled, the Reverend Mother moved on.

"Good morning, Sister Mary, what a lovely day."

"It is indeed, Reverend Mother; it's a shame you got out of bed on the wrong side this morning."

Even more puzzled, the Mother Superior approached Sister Elizabeth and asked cautiously, "Sister, do you get the impression I got out of bed on the wrong side this morning."

Sister Elizabeth blushed, "Yes, Reverend Mother."

"Why?"

"Because you're wearing Father O'Neal's slippers."

★ ★ ★

Three nuns went to confession. The first said, "Forgive me, Father, for I have sinned. I looked at a man's private parts."

"Then go and wash your eyes with holy water," replied the priest.

The second nun went to confession. "Forgive me, Father, for I have sinned. I touched a man's private parts."

"Then go and wash your hands with holy water."

The third nun went in and after a short while came out saying, "Won't be long, sisters, I've just got to go and gargle."

★ ★ ★

A nun and a priest are travelling through the desert when suddenly the camel collapses on the sand. It is the hottest time of the day and the nun realizes they must have shelter or they will collapse as well. So she takes off her clothes to make a shelter, and on seeing a nude woman for the first time in decades the priest gets a huge erection.

"What's that?" asks the nun.

"It's the giver of life," he replies.

"In that case, stick it up the camel's arse and see if we can get to the next town."

★ ★ ★

Every week before Bob and his two mates went out on the town, Bob would pop into the local church for confession.

"Father, forgive me for I have sinned with a woman."

The priest replied, "Was it Rosy from the Frog and Toad?"

"No, Father."

"Was it Cute Kate from the Cosie Cafe?"

"No, Father."

"Then it must have been whoring Helen from the Greasy Spoon. However, I'll give you your penance. But think carefully about what you have done."

"Thank you, Father, I will."

Then Bob would rush back outside and say to his two mates, "I've got the names of three little ravers for tonight, lads."

★ ★ ★

Two monks who belonged to a silent order spent the day fishing together. Nothing was caught until the very end of the day, when one of the monks caught a mermaid. He looked at the beautiful naked creature, fondled her enthusiastically and then threw her back in. Unable to keep silent, the other monk shouted, "Why?"

"How?" he replied.

★ ★ ★

It was a young priest's first time at hearing confession and the old priest said he'd sit at the back to see he did it right.

When it was all over, the young priest looked quite pleased with himself.

"That didn't seem to go too badly," he said.

"No, not too bad, but maybe when it comes to next time a little less of the "Wow! Really!" and a bit more tut tutting would be appropriate."

★ ★ ★

"Is there a Roman Catholic priest on the train?" called a man, walking along the aisle from carriage to carriage. A little while later, he was back, shouting, "Is there an English Catholic priest on the train?" but still no response.
Then a man got up and tapped him on the shoulder.
"Excuse me, sir, can I be of any help? I'm a Methodist minister."
"No, thanks," replied the man. "I'm just looking to borrow a corkscrew."

★ ★ ★

Late for church, a woman says to the man at the door, "Is mass out?"
"No," he replies, "but your hat's on crooked."

★ ★ ★

First night in the Garden of Eden and Adam warns Eve, "You'd better stand back a bit, I don't know how big this thing gets."

★ ★ ★

Who was the world's first bookkeeper?
Adam – he turned over a leaf and made an entry.

★ ★ ★

Moses came down from Mount Sinai and addressed the waiting Israelites. "I've got good news and bad news. The good news is I've got them down to ten, but the bad news is that Adultery is out."

★ ★ ★

Why don't men believe in the return of the Messiah?
A second coming is beyond their understanding.

★ ★ ★

"Father, I had it off with two voluptuous blondes last night," confessed the young man.

"Tut, tut, that's not the way a good Catholic man should behave," replied the priest.

"But, I'm not a Catholic," he said.

"Then why are you telling me?"

"I'm telling everyone," came the reply.

★ ★ ★

A young and very shy vicar was out on his parish rounds for the very first time. His first call was at the house of an old lady living on her own. She invited him in and made a pot of tea while he sat there frantically trying to think of something to say.

"Um... winter draws on then, Mrs Hubbard," he finally stammered.

"In fact, I did put them on this morning," she retorted. "But it's got nothing to do with you."

★ ★ ★

"Okay, darling," said Mummy to her five-year-old daughter. "Why don't you say grace for us today."

"Yes, Mummy," replied the dutiful daughter. She closed her eyes, put her hands together and said innocently, "Give us some food, for Christ's sake. Amen."

★ ★ ★

The number of children attending Sunday School had dropped dramatically and it was thought that perhaps the lessons had become too serious. As it happened, a visiting Minister had come to stay and the vicar asked him if he would mind speaking to the children a bit more informally.

"Of course," replied the Minister and he sat with the children saying, "All right, children, can you tell me what eats grass, goes moo and gives us milk?"

For a moment, there was complete silence and then a small boy slowly put his hand up. "Please, sir, I suppose the answer is Jesus, but it sounds just like a cow to me."

★ ★ ★

A new vicar had taken over at the small village church of St Gregory and he was eager to make a good impression. After the service, the congregation emerged from the church and each shook hands with the vicar.

"Lovely sermon," said one.

"It really made me stop and think," said another.

All of a sudden, a rather scruffy man appeared and as he shuffled past he mumbled, "Load of old cobblers!"

Determined not to be affected by this, the vicar carried on greeting his parishioners.

"Splendid sermon," they said, "thank you very much, most inspiring."

The vicar beamed gratefully.

"Load of old cobblers! Call himself a vicar," came the mumbling of the scruffy man as he passed the vicar again. This time, the vicar was more upset and the situation worsened as the man kept appearing and making comments.

"Bored to tears! Waste of time! What a prat!"

The vicar could take it no longer. He turned to one of the congregation and pointed out the scruffy man.

"Oh, you mustn't worry about Old Ned, vicar," said a kindly old woman. "He's not right in the head, he just goes round repeating what everyone else says."

★ ★ ★

A Catholic priest, an Anglican vicar and a rabbi are talking one morning, and the subject of collection arises: more specfically, how do they decide how much of the collection they give to the Church, and how much they keep for themselves? The Catholic priest says, "Well, it's very simple really. I draw a chalk circle on the ground, and throw all the money into the air. Whatever falls outside the circle, I give to the Church; whatever falls inside the circle, I keep to provide for

myself. It's a simple method, and I have never gone hungry yet."
The Anglican replies, "That's very similar to the method I use myself, except that when I throw the money in the air, God keeps whatever falls inside the circle, and I keep for myself whatever falls outside."
"You both have very good methods there," says the rabbi, "and I have a similar one myself, except that I don't use a chalk circle."
"Oh?" asks the vicar. "How does that work?"
"Well," says the rabbi, "it works like this: I throw the money into the air. Whatever God catches, he keeps; whatever falls to the ground I keep."

★ ★ ★

One Sunday a cowboy went to church. When he entered, he saw that he and the preacher were the only ones present. The preacher asked the cowboy if he wanted him to go ahead and preach. The cowboy said, "I'm not too smart, but if I went to feed my cattle and only one showed up, I'd feed him." So the minister began his sermon.
One hour passed, then two hours, then two-and-a-half hours. The preacher finally finished and came down to ask the cowboy how he had liked the sermon. The cowboy answered slowly, "Well, I'm not very smart, but if I went to feed my cattle and only one showed up, I wouldn't feed him all the hay."

★ ★ ★

The night porter in a Welsh hotel saw one of the guests coming down the stairs in his pyjamas at four o'clock in the morning. Tapping him on the shoulder, he asked, "What are you doing here at this time?" The man replied, "I'm sorry, I'm a somnambulist." "I don't care what chapel you belong to," said the porter, "you can't go wandering round the hotel like this."

★ ★ ★

An old vicar was retiring and selling his horse so he put an ad in the local newspaper. It wasn't long before it was bought by Bob who decided to ride it home. But when he mounted up, the horse wouldn't move.

"I trained this horse from a little foal," said the vicar. "He only moves when you say 'Jesus Christ' and stops when you say 'Amen'."

Bob thanked the vicar and, sure enough, when he said 'Jesus Christ', the horse set off.

However, on the way home they got caught up in a ferocious thunderstorm and the horse bolted at a particularly loud crack of thunder. Soon they were galloping madly through the countryside. It took Bob a moment or two to remember to say 'Amen'.

Immediately, the horse came to a standstill teetering right on the edge of a deep canyon.

"Jesus Christ!" he said.

★ ★ ★

A group of young boys were always getting into trouble on the estate so the local vicar decided to intervene and speak to each of them about their behaviour. When it was Johnny's turn to go in, he sat down nervously wondering what was going to happen. As with the other boys, the vicar decided to find out how much the boy knew about God and whether he understood the difference between right and wrong. The vicar began with the question, "Where is God?"

Johnny stared at him in amazement but did not answer. Again the question was asked, this time more forcibly.

"I said, where is God?" he bellowed.

Frightened out of his skin, Johnny raced from the room, ran all the way home and hid in the wardrobe. His older brother followed him upstairs and shouted through the door, "What's happened?"

"Oh, Tom, we really are in trouble this time. God has gone missing and they think we did it."

★ ★ ★

A wife is so distressed at her husband's excessive drinking that she decides to try and scare him into stopping. After pub closing time one night, she waits for him in the church graveyard, crouched down behind one of the tombstones. Sure enough, he takes the short cut home and, as he staggers past her, she jumps up in full devil's costume and shouts, "Beware, beware, Arthur Chivers, carry on drinking as you are, and you'll soon be joining me down below!"

"What!" he exclaims, somewhat befuddled, "who the hell are you?"

"I am the devil himself!" she booms.

The drunk begins to smile and holds out his hand to greet him.

"Well, I never," he says, "you'll know me then. I'm married to your sister."

★ ★ ★

The bishop was not looking forward to his meeting with the new vicar. The latter had only been in his parish for a few weeks, but already there were many complaints.

"So why did you decide to enter the ministry?" asked the bishop.

"I was called," replied the vicar. "The Lord appeared to me in a vison and told me to become ordained."

"Mmm," mused the bishop. "Are you sure that's what he said?"

★ ★ ★

"The Canon's here to see you, bishop."

"Tell him he's fired."

★ ★ ★

The priest and the C of E vicar bumped into each other by chance in the public library.

"What a coincidence," said the vicar. "I had a dream last night about a Catholic heaven. It was full of people, drinking, singing and dancing."

"Really?" replied the priest. "I had a dream about a protestant heaven. It was very peaceful, beautiful countryside, gorgeous gardens and gently flowing streams."

The vicar smiled contentedly. "And what were the people doing?"

"What people?" replied the priest.

★ ★ ★

A vain, middle-aged woman went to confession.

"Forgive me, Father, for I have sinned. I spent an hour this morning in front of the mirror admiring my beautiful body. Will I have to do a penance?"

"No, no," said the priest. "You only do a penance when you have done something wrong, not for making a mistake."

★ ★ ★

A gloomy, lugubrious-looking minister was travelling on a slow train across Wales with only one other passenger in the compartment. Suddenly he turned to his fellow traveller and demanded, "Have you ever reflected that at any moment we may be launched into eternity?"

"Yes," said the stranger, "many times."

"And do you ever meditate on the great uncertainty of life?"

"Yes, indeed, I think of this many times a day," replied the other.

"Indeed," said the preacher with sudden interest, "can it be that I am talking to a fellow minister?"

"No," said the stranger, firmly, "you are not. I am a travelling agent for the London and Cardiff Life Assurance association."

★ ★ ★

A hippie gets on a bus and spies a pretty young nun.

He sits down next to her, and asks her, "Can we have sex?"

"No," she replies. "I'm married to God."

She stands up, and gets off at the next stop.

The bus driver, who overheard, turns to the hippie and says, "I can tell you how to get to have sex with her!"

"Yeah?" says the hippie.

"Yeah," says the bus driver. "She goes to the cemetery every Tuesday night at midnight to pray. So all you have to do is dress up in a robe with a hood, put some of that luminous powder stuff in your beard, and pop up in the cemetery claiming to be God."

The hippie decides to give it a try and arrives in the cemetery dressed as suggested on the next Tuesday night.

"I am God," he declares to the nun in the darkness, keeping the hood low about his face. "Have sex with me."

The nun agrees without question, but begs him to restrict himself to anal sex, as she is desperate not to lose her virginity.

'God' agrees and promptly has his wicked way with her.

As he finishes, he jumps up and throws back his hood with a flourish.

"Ha-ha," he cries. "I am the hippie!"

"Ha-ha," cries the nun. "And I am the bus driver."

★ ★ ★

The new priest was so nervous at his first mass, he could hardly speak. Before his second appearance in the pulpit he asked the monsignor how he could relax.

The Monsignor replied, "Next Sunday, it may help if you put some vodka in the water pitcher. After a few sips, everything should go smoothly."

The next Sunday the new priest put the suggestion into practice and was able to talk up a storm. He felt great. However, upon returning to the rectory, he found a note from the Monsignor. It read:

1. Next time, sip rather than gulp.
2. There are 10 commandments, not 12.
3. There are 12 disciples, not 10.
4. We do not refer to the cross as "the big T".
5. The recommended grace before meals is not "rub-a-dub-dub, thanks for the grub, yeah God".
6. Do not refer to our saviour, Jesus Christ, and his apostles as "JC and The Boys".
7. David slew Goliath. He did not "kick the shit out of him".
8. The Father, Son and Holy Spirit are never referred to as "Big Daddy, Junior and The Spook".
9. It is always the Virgin Mary, never "Mary with the Cherry".
10. Last, but not least, next Wednesday there will be a taffy pulling contest as St Peter's. There will not be a Peter pulling contest at St Taffy's.

11. Jesus was Consecrated, NOT constipated.
12. Jesus said,"Take this and eat it, for it is my body" – he did not say, "Eat me."
13. Jacob wagered his donkey, he didn't "beat his ass".
14. David was hit by a rock and knocked off his donkey, he wasn't "stoned off his ass".

★ ★ ★

Twelve monks were about to be ordained. The final test was for them to line up naked in a garden, while a nude model danced before them. Each monk had a small bell attached to his privates, and they were told that anyone whose bell rang would not be ordained because he had not reached a state of purity. The model danced before the first monk candidate with no reaction. She proceeded down the line with the same response until she got to the final monk.

As she danced by him, his bell rang so loudly it fell off and clattered to the ground. Embarrassed, he bent down to pick it up and all the other bells went off in unison.

★ ★ ★

The new priest is nervous about hearing confessions, so he asks an older priest to sit in on his sessions. The new priest hears a couple confessions, then the old priest asks him to step out of the confessional for a few suggestions.

The old priest suggests, "Cross you arms over your chest, and rub your chin with one hand."

The new priest tries this.

The old priest suggests, "Try saying things like, 'I see', 'Yes, go on' and 'I understand'. Or 'How did you feel about that?'"

The new priest practises saying these phrases.

The old priest says, "Now, don't you think that's a little better than slapping your knee and saying, 'No shit?!? What happened next?'"

★ ★ ★

Two men considering a religious vocation were having a deep and meaningful conversation.

"What is similar about the Jesuit and Dominican Orders?" the one asked.

The second replied, "Well, they were both founded by Spaniards – St Dominic for the Dominicans, and St Ignatius of Loyola for the Jesuits. They were also both founded to combat heresy – the Dominicans to fight the Albigensians, and the Jesuits to fight the Protestants."

"What is different about the Jesuit and Dominican Orders?"

"Met any Albigensians lately?"

★ ★ ★

Top Reasons For Joining The Church Choir

- You're running out of clean clothes and the robe saves on laundry.
- The church is usually crowded and you want to make sure you always have a seat.
- You've just been selected for jury duty and you want to get used to sitting with a large group of people.
- The collection plate is never passed to the choir.
- There's a clock in the back of the church and you want to know when one hour has passed.
- For years you have wanted to know who sits in the back of the church, but were afraid to turn around and look.
- You've been known to nod off during the service and don't want the minister/priest to catch you.
- The chairs for the choir are padded and are the most comfortable seats in the church.

★ ★ ★

Christian Pick-up Lines

1. Nice Bible.
2. I would like to pray with you.
3. You know Jesus? Me too.

4. God told me to come and talk to you.

5. I know a church where we could go and talk.

6. How about a hug, sister?

7. Do you need help carrying your Bible? It looks heavy.

8. Christians don't shake hands, Christians gotta hug.

9. Oh, you are cold, Ecclesiastes 4:11.

10. Did it hurt when you fell from Heaven?

11. What are your plans for tonight? Feel like a Bible study?

12. I am here for you.

13. The word says, "Give drink to those who are thirsty, and feed the hungry" – how about dinner?

14. You don't have an accountability partner? Me neither.

15. Do you want to come over and watch *The Ten Commandments* tonight?

16. Is it a sin that you stole my heart?

17. Would you happen to know a Christian woman (man) that I could love with all my heart and wait on hand and foot?

18. Nice bracelet. What would Jesus date? I mean "do".

19. Do you believe in Divine appointment?

20. Have you ever tried praying at a drive-in movie before?

21. Excuse me, I believe one of your ribs belongs to me.

22. My friend told me to come and meet you. He said that you are a really nice person. I think you know him. Jesus, yeah, that's the name.

23. You know they say that you have never really dated, until you have dated a Christian.

24. Yeah, I predicted David over Goliath.

★ ★ ★

DAYS ON THE GAME

After a long spell at sea, the old captain comes ashore and goes straight down the whorehouse. He's taken upstairs by one of the girls, they agree a price and he gets to work.

Pleased with his performance, he says to the girl, "How's it going? I'm not too fast am I? How fast am I going?"

The girl yawns and says, "You're doing about three knots. You're not in, you're not stiff and you're not getting your money back!"

★ ★ ★

A husband and wife went to London, he to a meeting and she to the shops. The meeting finished earlier than planned, so he went into Mayfair to look for a "quickie".

He met a high-class girl, but she gave him the push when he said he only had £20, and her rate was £200. So the man left, met up with his wife and they went off to a restaurant. At the next table sat the "high-class lady" he'd approached earlier. When she saw him she leant over and said, "Serves you right, that's what you get for twenty quid."

★ ★ ★

A hooker goes to the hospital to visit a work colleague who is about to have a heart transplant. She's concerned about her friend, so she says to the doctor, "I'm worried about Lulubelle, doc. What if her body rejects the organ?"

The doctor replies, "Well, she's 36 years old and healthy. How long has she been in the business?"

The prostitute says, "She's been working since she was 19 years old, but what does that have to do with anything?"

"Well, she's been working 17 years and hasn't rejected an organ yet!"

★ ★ ★

Did you hear about the man who was so tight with his money he rang up a hooker and asked her what night she was free?

★ ★ ★

A businessman goes to a brothel, pays £150 and proceeds to make mad, passionate love to one of the girls. In fact he is so good, she offers a screw on the house. Again it is so fantastic the girl says she'll pay him £150 if he will do it a third time.

However, although the mind is willing the body is weak and as she looks down at his shrivelled penis he says to it, disgustedly, "You're good at spending money, but when it comes to earning some…!!"

★ ★ ★

A brothel is like a circus, except that a circus is a cunning array of stunts.

★ ★ ★

The Soho police have just raided the local whorehouse and lined the girls up along the street ready to take down the nick. At that moment an old woman comes along and, when she sees the queue, asks the girl at the end why they are all there.

"We're queueing up to get a nice juicy ice lolly," replies one of the girls sarcastically. The old woman takes it literally and joins the end of the queue. Time passes as the coppers question each of the girls in turn and when one sees the old woman he says, "You're a bit old for this sort of thing, aren't you?"

"Indeed not," replies the old woman angrily. "I may not have any teeth, but I can still suck."

★ ★ ★

A man with both his arms and legs in plaster knocks at the door of the local brothel.

"I'm looking for a woman," he says when the madam opens the door.

"And what can you do in that state?" she asks.

"I knocked on the door, didn't I?"

★ ★ ★

An old man goes to the local brothel and asks the price. Madam tells him prices start at £50.
"You're putting me on!" he exclaims.
"OK," she replies, "that'll be an extra £10."

★ ★ ★

"When I grow up I want to be a prostitute," said a young lush girl to the Reverend Mother. The Reverend Mother threw up her hands in horror "What did you say?" "I said I want to be a prostitute."
"Oh praise the Lord!" replied the Reverend Mother. "I thought you said Protestant."

★ ★ ★

Negotiations are still continuing over a new pay deal for the Soho girls. They are demanding more money on the table, even more money on the floor and danger money on top of the piano.

★ ★ ★

A man went up to town and engaged the services of a young lady. After doing the business, she asked for £75. "Good gracious, you're expensive." "Well, haven't you heard of me? I'm Polly, the best in town." "Did you say your name was Polo?" "No, Polly. Why?"
He replied, "Because you've definitely got a hole with a mint in it."

★ ★ ★

"Hey dad," teenage son says to his father. "I've got this homework problem. I've got to show the difference between possible and real."
"Well, son, here's what you do. Go and ask your mum if she would sleep with Mel Gibson for a thousand pounds. Then go and ask your sister if she would sleep with Leonardo di Caprio for a thousand pounds. Come back and tell me the answer."
Son goes off to his mother, who replies she would (but keep it to himself) and to his sister, who's wild about the idea. He then returns

to his Dad and says, "I see what you mean. We are sitting on a possible £2,000, but in real terms we are living with a couple of whores."

* * *

"Son, if you ever go to a whorehouse you will die. They are places of sin. Be warned." But the son's curiosity got the better of him. He ended up at the local brothel and was taken upstairs to Fifi's room. She was lying naked on the bed and suddenly his father's warning came back to him. "Bloody hell, dad was right, I can feel myself going stiff already."

* * *

An old man of 95 went to a brothel and told the woman on the door he wanted a big, buxom girl. The old man was very shaky on his legs and looked as if he would collapse any minute. Seeing this, the woman replied, "Listen, grandpa, you've had it."
"Oh bugger," he said, looking confused. "How much do I owe you?"

* * *

A man invited a prostitute back to his hotel bedroom and, with only a few words spoken, got her down on the bed and started giving her a good seeing to. After an hour of energetic sex, he suddenly got up and said, "Just one moment, please," and walked into the bathroom. He returned a moment later, jumped into bed and began once more. After another hour, he suddenly got up again and disappeared into the bathroom, to return a moment later and begin again. Hour after hour went by until the prostitute jumped up, saying, 'Won't be a moment,' and going into the bathroom she found the man's three brothers.

* * *

What did the nymphomaniac say after having sex?
"So which football team do you guys play for?"

* * *

A man landed up in a very seedy part of town where the whorehouses were the lowest of the low. Knocking at one of the doors, he shouted, "Come on, let me in." And a voice replied, "Put £50 through the letter box first."

He did this, but nothing happened.

"Hey," he bellowed. "I want to be screwed."

"What! Again!" he heard her reply.

★ ★ ★

A man was very surprised that on visiting a foreign whorehouse he was given £500 on leaving. Unable to believe his luck, he returned the following day and again on leaving was given £500. However, on the third day he left without anything and, disappointed, asked why.

"We're not filming today, sir," came the reply.

★ ★ ★

A good time girl went into the DIY store to buy some hinges. When she was paying, the storekeeper asked, "Need a screw for those hinges?"

"No, but how about a blow job for the shelves over there?"

★ ★ ★

This guy has a spare £10 that he decides to spend on his first hooker ever. He goes out, he gets one, then he brings her home.

The next morning, he wakes up and discovers that he has crabs, so he goes, finds the hooker again and says, "Hey, lady, you gave me crabs!" She replies, "Well, for the measly sum of £10 what did you expect, lobsters?"

★ ★ ★

If a fire fighter's business can go up in smoke, and a plumber's business can go down the drain, does a hooker get laid off?

★ ★ ★

A panda visits a brothel and heads for the exit after half an hour. "Hold on a minute, haven't you forgotten something? I'm a prostitute and that means you have to pay me for the last thirty minutes, including all those bamboo shoots." "So what?" replies the Panda. "You should know by now that the definition of a panda is an animal that eats shoots and leaves. Goodbye."

★ ★ ★

"How much will it cost?" the man asked the streetwalker.
"£15 up the alley, £120 if we spend the night in a comfortable hotel."
"OK, here's £120."
"Good, it's cold out here tonight. I could do with a nice hotel room."
"Not bloody likely!" replied the man. "I want it eight times up the alley."

★ ★ ★

Thor, the mighty God of War, decides to come down to earth and sample some of the local talent. He stops off at a brothel and demands the services of their best girl. For two days he shags her unmercifully and is just about to leave when he realizes he never told her his name. "I'm Thor."
"You're sore! Bloody hell, I can't even walk!" she complains.

★ ★ ★

An old couple find themselves down to their last few pennies and unable to pay their bills. In one last desperate attempt to keep the bailiffs from the door, the old girl decides to go on the game. She takes her curlers out, puts her teeth in and struggles into a mini skirt before disappearing into the night. Just before dawn, she staggers home to her husband who asks her how much she's made. "£120.50," she replies. "Bloody hell, who was the prick who only gave you 50p?"
"They all did," she cries.

★ ★ ★

A man goes into a brothel and tells the madam that he's only got £5, what can she offer him? The madam gives him a duck and off he goes to one of the rooms where he shags it for 25 minutes. The following week, he goes back but this time he's got £10 – he can afford something better.

The madam shows him into a room where there is a line-up of blokes looking through peepholes. He takes his turn and through the peephole he sees three women and one man up to all sorts of things on a trapeze.

"It's good this, isn't it?" he says, turning to the bloke next to him.

"Yes," replies his neighbour, "but you should have been here last week, there was a man shagging a duck."

★ ★ ★

A huge, 6ft 6in, 18-stone man was having great trouble finding anyone who would have sex with him because one look at his gigantic penis frightened the girls away. The poor man roamed London seeking satisfaction but with no luck. He ended up sitting in a boozer looking sadly into his beer.

"What's up, mate?" said a man sitting down opposite. "You look as if you've got the problems of the world on your shoulders."

The big man told him of his fruitless search.

"I know just the answer," replied the newcomer. "If you come with me I'll take you to Madam Cyn. She's got girls who've seen and done everything."

They arrived at the whorehouse door and the big man explained his problem. "Just how big is it?" Madam Cyn asked.

"Five inches," he replied.

She laughed, "Five inches long! Goodness, that's a lot of fuss about nothing."

"No, madam, five inches thick."

★ ★ ★

Three men are walking around Soho looking for a screw when they see a prostitute hanging round the street corner. The first man goes over and asks her what she can do for a tenner. She beckons him into an alley where they stay for ten minutes before he rejoins his mates.

"What did she do, what did she do?" they urged.

"It was wonderful," said the man with a big grin on his face. "She put this doughnut on the end of my knob and then slowly ate it off."

This really got the other two men going. So the second went over to her and asked what she could do with £20. Again, she took him into the alley and he reappeared 20 minutes later full of smiles.

"Wow, she really knows how to turn you on!" he said. "She put two doughnuts on the end of my knob, sprinkled them with sugar and then slowly licked them off."

By this time, the third man couldn't wait to have a go, but he didn't tell the others he had £50 on him. However, after only a few minutes he was back looking very pissed off.

"What's wrong, mate? That was quick," they said.

"Well, she had these four doughnuts which she put over my knob, covered them with raspberry jam, sugar, chocolate, whipped cream and amaretto."

"Go on, what happened?"

"Well, it looked so good, I ate it myself."

★ ★ ★

"I've met some disgusting people in my time, but you are the worst ever. You're a dirty, dreadful old man," said the prostitute to her client. "Listen, I've paid you, haven't I? So I'll ask you to keep a civil tongue in my arse."

★ ★ ★

A Colonel-in-Chief arrives back home after spending six months on a distant outpost and heads straight for the local brothel. Once inside, he goes upstairs with one of the girls and into a bedroom where she starts to fiddle with his flies.

"Now, now," he says as he pushes her hand away. "Any more of that familiarity and the fuck's off."

★ ★ ★

"My dear, what would your mother say if she saw you?" said the kindly social worker to the street corner prostitute.

"She wouldn't say anything. She'd kill me. I'm on her patch."

★ ★ ★

A soldier, on weekend leave, goes into the nearest town looking for a bit of sex. He ends up staying the night at one of the seedy brothels and next morning, when he wakes up, he groans and says to the girl, "Bloody hell, I feel terrible; you haven't got AIDS, have you?"

"No," she replies.

"Thank goodness, I wouldn't want that again."

★ ★ ★

A man visited a brothel in the middle of an African jungle and a sign inside the door advertised a special 'Jungle Roulette'.

"What's that?" he inquired.

"Well, it's a special service where six girls offer to give you a blow job and you can choose up to three of them."

"Wow, that sounds good. What's the catch?"

"One of the girls is a cannibal."

★ ★ ★

The President's housekeeper was horrified to see the family parrot escape from his cage and fly out of the window. Feeling partly to blame, she rushed down to the local pet shop to buy another that looked exactly the same.

"I've only one like that," said the man, "but it's a bit risky because this parrot has come from a whorehouse and has picked up some foul language."

"Never mind, I'll just have to take a chance."

Later on in the day, the President and his family arrive home and as they enter, the parrot speaks.

"Too young," he says as the daughter comes in.

"Too old," he says of the wife.

Then, as the President enters, he squawks excitedly, "Hello, big boy, long time no see."

★ ★ ★

Why don't prostitutes vote?
Because they don't care who gets in.

★ ★ ★

A guy is hanging out in his favourite bar when he spots a fabulous babe walking in on the arm of some ugly man.

He asks the bartender about her and is surprised to discover that she's a prostitute.

He watches her the rest of the night, amazed that someone so attractive could be available to him.

The next night he goes back to the bar, and sure enough she shows up again, only this time alone.

The guy gets up his nerve and approaches her. "Is it true you're a prostitute?"

"Why, sure, big boy. What can I do for you?"

"Well, I dunno. What do you charge?"

"I get $100 just for a handjob. We can negotiate from there."

"$100!! For a handjob? Are you nuts?"

"You see that Ferrari out there?" The guy looks out the front door, and sure enough there's a shiny new Ferrari parked outside.

"I paid cash for that Ferrari with the money I made on handjobs. Trust me, it's worth it."

The guy mulls it over for a while, and decides what the hell.

He leaves with her, and gets the most unbelievable experience he's ever had.

This handjob was better than any complete sexual experience in his miserable life.

The next night he's back at the bar, waiting eagerly for her to show up. When she does, he immediately approaches her. "Last night was incredible!"

"Of course it was. Just wait till you try one of my blowjobs."

"How much is that?"

"$500."

"$500!?! C'mon, that's ridiculous!"

"You see that apartment building across the street?"

The guy looks out front at a 12-story apartment building.

"I paid cash for that building with the money I made on blowjobs. Trust me, it's worth it."

Based on the night before, the guy decides to go for it.

He leaves with her, and once again is not disappointed.

He nearly faints – twice. The next night he can hardly contain himself until she shows up.

"I'm hooked, you're the best! Tell me, what'll it cost me for some pussy?"

She motions for him to follow her outside.

She points down the street, where between the buildings he can see Manhattan.

"You see that island?"

"Aw, c'mon! You can't mean that!"

She nods her head. "You bet. If I had a pussy, I'd own Manhattan!"

★ ★ ★

One very hot dry day, a local cowboy visited the reservation.

He went there from time to time to mingle with the Indians.

There was this one Indian that the cowboy has become friends with.

This Indian was pretty much a loner.

He was all alone, his parents got killed in battle, and he had no squaw that he claimed as his own.

This cowboy felt sorry for the lonely Indian.

He told him that he could help him overcome being so lonely.

But, he would have to go into the nearby town.

He told him to go into the town saloon and walk up to the bar.

There would be a lady standing behind the bar.

"Tell her that you want a woman, she will take care of you.

I will tell her to be expecting you."

185

Next day the Indian went into town and walked up to the bar in the saloon.

The Indian began this conversation with the lady.

Indian: "Me want a woman."

Lady: "How much money do you have?"

Indian: "What is money?"

Lady: "It is something that you must have to spend time with one of my girls."

She explained to the Indian what money was. So the Indian left and told her that he would return. A couple of days passed and the Indian returned. He approached the bar.

Indian: "Me want a woman."

Lady: "Did you get you any money?"

Indian: "Yeah, me got plenty of money."

Lady: "Do you have any experience with women?"

Indian: "What you mean by experience?"

Lady: "You have to be experienced to spend time with my girls."

The Lady explained to the Indian how he could get his experience.

Lady: "You go to the mountains and find a big tree. Make sure it is one that has a knot hole in it. You will be able to get all the experience you wish. Then when you feel that you have all the experience that you can get, you can come back here and I will have one of my girls take care of your needs."

The Indian left the town and went up into the mountains.

One week passed by before the Indian returned. He was very angry and very aggressive with the lady behind the counter.

Indian: "Me want a woman, and me want woman right now!"

Lady: 'Have you gotten any experience since you were here last?"

Indian: "Me got all kinds of experience, and a bag full of money. Me want woman now."

Lady: "All right! Follow me to the top of the stairs."

The Indian followed her to the top of the steps to a door.

He opened the door and there stood the most lovely woman he had ever seen.

He closed the door behind him and walked up to the woman.

She asked, "What would you like for me to do?" The woman began removing all of her clothes and so did the Indian.

The Indian asked, "Turn around and bend-em over and touch your toes."

She liked that idea, so she turned around and bent over like the Indian asked.

The Indian stepped up behind the woman and pulled back his leg and kicked her in the ass.

The woman jumped up in surprise. She ask the Indian, "What in the hell did you have to do that for?"

The Indian looked at the woman and replied, "Me checking for bees in that knot hole."

★　★　★

Harry approached a prostitute and asked, "How much for a blow job?"

"Hundred Bucks."

"OK," he said and began to jerk off.

"What the hell are you doing that for?"

"For a hundred bucks you don't think I'm going to give you the easy one, do you?"

★　★　★

As a hooker was dressing, she turned to her customer and asked, "Have you just gotten out of prison?"

"Yeah," the guy replied. "How did you guess? Is it because I wanted to have sex from the rear?"

"Partly," she said. "But more because when we finished, you ran around in front of me, bent over and shouted, 'YOUR TURN'."

★　★　★

Two midgets go into a bar where they pick up two prostitutes and take them to their separate hotel rooms. The first midget, however, is unable to get an erection. His depression is enhanced by the fact that, from the next room, he hears cries of "ONE, TWO, THREE... UUH!" all night long. In the morning, the second midget asks the first, "How did it go?" The first whispered back, "It was so embarrassing. I simply couldn't get a hard-on."

The second midget shook his head. "You think that's embarrassing?" he asked. "I couldn't even get on the fucking bed."

★ ★ ★

DESERT ISLAND

A man is abandoned on a desert island. After six years, a beautiful, shapely blonde in a wet suit gets washed ashore, and they get into conversation.

"How long have you been here?" she asks.

"Six years," he says.

"That's a long time. Would you like a drink?"

"I'd love one."

With that she unzips a pocket in her wet suit and gets out a bottle of Scotch. The blonde then asks if he would like a cigarette.

"Yes, please," he replies and she unzips another pocket to produce a packet of cigarettes and a lighter.

"How long did you say you'd been here?" she asks again.

"Six years."

"Ah... then would you like to play around?"

He was astonished. "Don't tell me you've got a set of golf clubs in there as well."

★ ★ ★

Only two people survived the sinking of the luxury liner and separately they managed to make it to a desert island. The man who had been travelling economy class couldn't believe that his companion was none other than one of Hollywood's most famous starlets.

At first they remained on platonic terms, but as the weeks passed natural desires took over until one night they tore each other's clothes off and went at it like the clappers.

The next day he turned to her and asked whether she would mind doing him a favour. Would she dress up in some of his clothes? He had a pair of trousers and a shirt.

Puzzled, she agreed and when they met up later he patted her on the back and boasted, "Hello, mate, you'll never guess who I fucked last night."

★ ★ ★

A man was stranded on a desert island with a sheep and a dog. After some months, he became romantically attached to the sheep but every time he tried to get near to her the dog would start barking. Then one day his prayers were answered when a beautiful girl was washed ashore. He looked after her until she'd recovered her strength and in gratitude she asked him if there was anything she'd like him to do.

"In fact, there is," he said. "Would you mind taking the dog for a walk while I shag this sheep?"

★ ★ ★

A bloke found himself stranded on a desert island with six women. To keep it fair, it was decided he would service a different woman every night and have Mondays free. After a few months the man was exhausted, realizing how tiring it was to perform constantly every night except one. Then one day to his joy, he found a man washed up on the beach who would be able to take some of the workload from him. However, his hopes were shattered the first words the man said were, "Hello, pretty boy, you've got a big one."

Oh fuck, thinks the man, there go my Mondays.

★ ★ ★

A man was stranded on a desert island and one day found a bottle washed up on the beach.

Inside the bottle was a genie, who was so grateful for being let out that he said he would grant the man one wish.

After some thought the man said he had always wanted to visit the Far East, so could the genie build a road from the island to the Great Wall of China?

"My goodness," replied the genie. "I'm not sure I can do that. Imagine all the work involved in building across oceans, and mountainous landscapes, all the materials… no, I don't think that's such a good idea."

"OK," said the man. He thought for a moment and said, "Another thing I've always wanted is to understand women. I want to know what makes them laugh, why they get so angry, why they cry…"

At this the genie replied, "Now about this road, do you want a dual carriageway or a motorway?"

★ ★ ★

After two months of being shipwrecked on a desert island, this man sees a barrel floating towards the shore and holding on to the barrel is a stunningly beautiful naked woman. As he rushes down to meet her she says, "I think I have something you want."
The man's eyes light up. "I don't believe it," he gasps. "You've got beer in that barrel."

★ ★ ★

This man had been stranded on a desert island for two years. One afternoon, looking out to sea, he shouted excitedly to himself, "Oh boy, oh boy, a boat's coming and there's a beautiful, young, voluptuous blonde on board, and she's stark naked… and she's waving to me, blowing me kisses and rolling her hips."
By this time, he had a mighty erection which he suddenly grabbed with both hands."Fooled you, fooled you," he laughed. "There ain't no fucking boat."

★ ★ ★

Three men had been marooned on a desert island for three months when one day a man-made raft was washed ashore, carrying a beautiful young girl.
"She's mine," said the Frenchman. "Look, she's got a red, white and blue blanket covering her." He pulled the blanket away, only to reveal a pair of tartan knickers.
"There," said the Scotsman triumphantly. "She was made for me." And he pulled them off.
"Aaah!" said the Indian, falling to his knees. "Behold, the sacred beard of our holy prophet…"

★ ★ ★

A young wife, her boorish husband and a young good-looking sailor were shipwrecked on an island. One morning, the sailor climbed a tall coconut tree and yelled, "Stop making love down there!"

"What's the matter with you?" the husband said when the sailor climbed down. "We weren't making love."

"Sorry," said the sailor. "From up there it looked like you were."

Every morning thereafter, the sailor scaled the same tree and yelled the same thing. Finally the husband decided to climb the tree and see for himself.

With great difficulty, he made his way to the top. The husband said to himself, "By golly he's right! It DOES look like they're making love down there!"

★ ★ ★

Two lawyers had been stranded on a desert island for several months. The only other thing on the island was a tall coconut tree, which provided them with food. Each day one of the lawyers would climb to the top of the tree to see if he could see a rescue boat coming.

One day, the lawyer yelled down from the tree, "WOW, I can't believe my eyes. There is a girl out there floating in our direction."

The lawyer on the ground was sceptical and said, "I think you're hallucinating and you've finally lost your mind."

But within a few minutes, a naked blond woman floated up to the beach, face up and totally unconscious.

The two lawyers went over to her, dragged her up on the sand and discovered, yes, she was alive.

One said the other, "You know, we've been on this island for months now without a woman. It's been such a long time. Do you think we should, you know, screw her?"

The second lawyer, asked, "Out of what?"

★ ★ ★

A man had been stranded on yet another desert island for two years when the ground began to shake and he noticed a great tidal wave bearing down upon him.

"Oh Lord, please help me," he prayed. Suddenly, a boat appeared and a man aboard shouted to him, "Quick, get on board, before the tidal wave comes!"

"No, no, I have faith in Jesus," said the castaway. A few moments passed and another boat appeared.

"Quick man, don't be silly, get on board, there's not much time left." But again he replied, "No, thank you, I have faith in Jesus."

With only seconds to go, another boat appeared and a voice called out in panic, "If you don't get over here right this minute, it'll be too late!"

"No, thank you. I have faith in Jesus."

The next moment, the tidal wave hit the island, smashing everything to pieces. The poor castaway drowned.

Later in heaven the man met Jesus and said reproachfully, "I had faith in you. I can't believe this has happened."

"What do you mean, you can't believe it!" cried Jesus "I sent three bloody boats, didn't I?!"

★ ★ ★

A man (okay, this is a different man) and his dog got stranded on a desert island, and as time passed, they ran out of food and things looked pretty grim.

"I'm sorry, Rex," said the man, "one of us has got to eat," and with that he killed the dog and put him in the cooking pot.

For three days, he dined well until there was nothing left of Rex but a pile of bones. The man looked at them sadly and said to himself, "It's a pity old Rex isn't here. He'd have loved those bones."

★ ★ ★

On a group of beautiful deserted islands in the middle of nowhere, the following people are suddenly stranded, as you might expect, following a shipwreck:

- 2 Italian men and 1 Italian woman

- 2 French men and 1 French woman

- 2 German men and 1 German woman

- 2 Greek men and 1 Greek woman

- 2 Englishmen and 1 Englishwoman

- 2 Bulgarian men and 1 Bulgarian woman

- 2 Japanese men and 1 Japanese woman

- 2 Chinese men and 1 Chinese woman

- 2 American men and 1 American woman

- 2 Irishmen and 1 Irishwoman

One month later on these same absolutely stunning deserted islands situated bang in the middle of nowhere, the following things have occurred:

- One Italian man has killed the other Italian man because he wants the Italian woman.

- The two French men and the French woman are living happily together in a menage-a-trois.

- The two German men have a strict weekly schedule of alternating visits with the German woman.

- The two Greek men are sleeping with each other and the Greek woman is cleaning and cooking for them.

- The two Englishmen are waiting for someone to introduce them to the Englishwoman.

- The two Bulgarian men took one long look at the endless ocean, then one long look at the Bulgarian woman, and started swimming.

- The two Japanese men have faxed Tokyo and are awaiting instructions.

- The two Chinese men have set up a pharmacy, a liquor store, a restaurant and a laundry, and have got the woman pregnant in order to supply employees for their stores.

- The two American men are contemplating the virtues of suicide because the American woman keeps endlessly complaining about her body; the true nature of feminism; how she can do everything they can do; the necessity for fulfilment; the equal division of household chores; how sand and palm trees make her look fat; how her last boyfriend respected her opinion and treated her better than they do; how her relationship with her mother is improving and how at least the taxes are low and it isn't raining.

- The two Irishmen have divided the island into North and South and set up a distillery. They do not remember if sex is in the picture because it gets sort of foggy after the first few litres of coconut whisky. But they're quite happy, because at least the English aren't having any fun.

★ ★ ★

A man has been shipwrecked on a desert island for ten years. Then one day he is down at the shoreline when he spots a ship on the horizon. He frantically waves his arms and jumps up and down shouting, until he spies a rowboat being let down into the water from the ship. About ten minutes later the rowboat reaches the shore carrying a man in a captain's uniform.

'Thank Christ for that!" says our shipwrecked hero, "I thought I was never going to be rescued."

"How long have you been here?" asks the Captain.

"Ten years, ten long years," replies the man.

"Ten years?" says the Captain. "How have you coped all that time on your own?"

"Well, I'm quite a resourceful fellow. I've built my own house; there it is, over there, Number 1!"

"But ten years!" says the Captain, "ten years without sex!"

"Ah well, that's not quite true," says the man shyly.

"What do you mean?" inquires the Captain.

"Well, about six months ago I was down here on the shore washing my feet, when I noticed an ostrich up the beach with its head buried in the sand and its ass facing me. Well, I thought it's been nine and a half years, so I crept up behind it and WALLOP!"

"Ugh God, that must have been disgusting!" cries the genuinely shocked Captain.

"Well, it was all right for the first five miles, but then we got out of step."

★ ★ ★

DOTAGE

Three old men were discussing who had the worst health problem.
The 80-year-old said, "Every morning I get up to take a pee, but I have to stand there for half an hour because it trickles out so slowly."
The 85-year-old said, "That's nothing, every morning I go for a shit and have to sit there for two hours because of my constipation… it's terrible."
The 90-year-old said, "I wish I had your problems. Me, every morning at 7.30 I piss like an elephant and shit like a pig. Trouble is… I don't wake up until nine."

★ ★ ★

An old widower of 80 married a young girl of 26 and, not long after, astounded the vicar by telling him he would soon be needed for a christening. Recovering from the news, the vicar congratulated the old man and asked him if this was going to be the first of many.
"Oh no, vicar, you see my eldest son is going abroad."
Of course the vicar thought the worse but said, "I don't understand. What's your son got to do with it?"
"Well, you see, he used to lift me on and off."

★ ★ ★

A feisty spinster reached 100 years old and attracted the attention of the press.
"How's your health?" asked one.
"Let me tell you, I've never been to a doctor in my life," she replied.
"That's incredible – do you mean to say you've never been bedridden in your life?"
"Of course I have, young fella, in fact table-ended as well, but there's no need to put that in the paper."

★ ★ ★

One resident at the Green Fields retirement home is sitting outside enjoying the early afternoon sun. Every now and again he leans over to the left and immediately a care helper rushes over and straightens him up. Later that day his son comes to visit and the son asks his father if the home is treating him well.

"Yes and no," comes the reply. "The beds are comfortable, the food's tasty, but they won't let me fart."

★ ★ ★

The old man has such a bad memory, the only thing to stay in his head for longer than 12 hours is a cold.

★ ★ ★

You know you're getting old when you bend down to tie up your shoes and look around to see if there's anything else needs to be done while you're down there.

★ ★ ★

An old man stopped to comfort a little boy who was crying on a park bench.

"What's wrong, son?" he said.

"I'm crying because I can't do what the big boys do."

So the old man sat down and cried too.

★ ★ ★

Two old ladies in the Pastures Green retirement home.

"Did you hear old Ben had a massive stroke?"

"He always did," came the reply. "That's why he was always so popular with the ladies."

★ ★ ★

Getting old is when you don't comb your hair, you just start re-arranging it.

★ ★ ★

Grandma was 102. She didn't have wrinkles; she had pleats.

★ ★ ★

He's so old that, when he asks for a three-minute egg, they ask for the money up front.

★ ★ ★

"I don't understand," said the young widow's friend.
"You say your husband was killed by the bells. What does that mean?"
"Well, my husband was 75 and he would save up all his strength for us to make love on a Sunday to the rhythm of the church bells. He would still be here with us today if it hadn't been for that blasted ice cream van driving past."

★ ★ ★

An old man of 85 was sitting hunched up over his pint, crying his eyes out.
"What's wrong?" asked a fellow drinker.
"I got married two weeks ago to a beautiful curvaceous young redhead who's a gourmet cook, a wonderful conversationalist and fantastic in bed," replied the old man.
"That's wonderful; you're a very lucky man. I don't understand why you're so upset."
"I can't remember where I live!" he cried.

★ ★ ★

It's good to exercise. My grandpa started walking five miles a day when he was 60. Today he's 95 and we don't know where the hell he is.

★ ★ ★

First prize at a fancy dress party for nudists went to a woman who wore black gloves and black shoes and went as the five of spades.
The second prize went to a 98-year-old man for the best dried fruit arrangement.

★ ★ ★

You know old age has overtaken you when the phone rings and a sexy voice at the other end says, "Do you know who this is, lover?" And you say, "No," and put the phone down.

★ ★ ★

You know it's old age when you try to straighten out the wrinkles in your socks and realize you're not wearing any.

★ ★ ★

You know you're getting old when the phone rings on a Saturday night and you hope it isn't for you.

★ ★ ★

They say life begins at 40. But so does lumbago, rheumatism, deafness and repeating oneself more than three times to the same person in the same day.

★ ★ ★

Two old men sitting on a park bench. One turns to the other and says, "Do you remember when we used to chase the girls down the street?" The other replied, "Yes, I remember chasing them but I can't remember for the life of me why."

★ ★ ★

An old spinster sees a sign offering three cucumbers for 50p.
"Well, I can always eat the other two," she says.

★ ★ ★

An old lady went to the doctor complaining of constipation among other ailments.
"I sit there for hours," she said.
"Ah yes, but do you take anything?" asked the doctor.

"Oh yes, I take my knitting."

* * *

Two old men meet on a park bench and one says to the other, "Hello, Bob, I haven't seen you around for a few weeks. Where have you been?"
"In jail," came the reply. "Never! What happened?"
"Well, I was walking down the street when this beautiful curvaceous blonde rushes up to me with a policeman in tow and accuses me of sexually assaulting her. I was so flattered I didn't deny it."

* * *

Four very old ladies were walking through the park when a man approached and flashed at them. Two of the ladies had strokes, but the other two weren't quick enough.

* * *

"Are you sure it's a good idea to marry such a young, energetic girl?" said the doctor to his elderly patient. "You know, such energetic sex could prove fatal."
"Oh well," said the old man, "if she dies, at least she dies happy."

* * *

A very old man went to the doctor's to find out if he was fit enough to have sex. "Let me see your sex organs, please," replied the doctor, so the man stuck out his tongue and held up his index finger.

* * *

Old man looked at his withered penis and said, "We were born together, we've lived through childhood together, had adventures together, known marriage together, even played together. So now, why now, did you have to die first?" he sighed.

* * *

A man getting on in years visited his doctor complaining about his poor love life. The doctor's advice was to give up smoking, stick to one pint of beer a day and take up jogging. He was to build up to running about an hour a day. Four weeks later, the man rang his doctor to let him know how it was going.

"Thank you, doctor, I feel so much better. I've done all you've said and there's been a great improvement in my health."

"Well, that's good to hear," replied the doctor with interest, "and how's your love life?"

"I've no idea," he answered. "I'm 200 miles from home now."

★ ★ ★

What is the similarity between men and old age? They both come too soon.

★ ★ ★

A rich old man of 88 married a beautiful young girl of 23 and it wasn't long before she was expecting a baby. Overjoyed at the news, the old man was taken aside by his kindly doctor, who had known his patient for a long time and was concerned for his wellbeing.

"Listen, Jack, it's about the baby. Let's see if I can explain what I mean. There was a big game hunter who'd spent all his life in Africa but was now really too old to last the distance. He decided to go out one last time but being so absentminded, instead of his gun, he took his walking stick with him. Some time went by when suddenly a man-eating lion confronted the man. He lifted his stick and shot the animal dead."

"But, that can't be!" cried his patient. "Someone else must have shot it."

"Absolutely," replied the doctor. "That's what I'm trying to tell you."

★ ★ ★

An old woman is walking along the road when she comes upon a frog. "Excuse me, Miss," says the frog. "If you pick me up and kiss me I'll turn into a Robert Redford lookalike and I'll stay with you forever."

The old woman picks up the frog and puts it in her handbag and continues on her way.

Puzzled, the frog calls from her bag, "Excuse me, aren't you going to kiss me then?"

"Oh no," replies the old woman. "At my age, it's far more exciting to have a talking frog."

★ ★ ★

The interfering old busybody from next door was complaining that her neighbour's old husband was chasing all the young girls.

"I think it's disgusting," she said.

"Oh, there's nothing to it," replied the wife calmly. "After all, you've seen dogs chasing cars many times, but have you ever seen them catch one, and even if they did, I doubt whether they could drive."

★ ★ ★

Rosie was bored. In her younger days she'd been known as 'Good time Rose', but since moving to the retirement home there was nothing to do. Then she had a great idea and on the door of her room she pinned a notice saying, "The Good Times are back. £30 in bed, £10 on the table."

Nothing happened for a couple of days and then one night there was a knock at the door and old Alfred was standing there.

"I've got £30 here," he said.

"OK, hop into bed."

"Not bloody likely, I want three on the table."

★ ★ ★

The Duty Officer answered the phone at the police station.

"Hurry please, I want to report a burglar trapped in the bedroom of an old spinster."

"We'll be right round," said the policeman. "Who am I talking to?"

"The burglar," he answered frantically.

★ ★ ★

An old retired colonel was invited to a reunion dinner and halfway through the proceedings he rang his wife.

"Agnes, this reunion is turning out to be more than I bargained for. They've got naked girls dancing on the table and then giving their favours to anyone who's interested. What do you think I should do?"

She replied, "If you think you can do anything you'd better get home straightaway."

★ ★ ★

It's the old man's 100th birthday and as a special treat, all his mates pay for a naked lady to come over and do the business. The doorbell goes and when he opens the door she's standing there in her coat which she lets fall open to reveal that she's totally bare underneath.

"Hello, darling," she says seductively. "I'm here for 'Supersex'."

"I'll just have the soup, thanks," says the old man.

★ ★ ★

Jack and Flo went to stay for a weekend with his parents. There wasn't much room in the tiny flat so Jack ended up sleeping with his dad. In the middle of the night he got an elbow in the ribs.

"Jack, Jack," whispered his dad, "I'm going next door to give your mum a good rogering!"

"What! Dad, it's the middle of the night and you're 75 years old."

"Yes, but I've got such a mighty fine erection – the first for 15 years – and I don't want to waste it, son."

"Well, in that case, I'll have to come with you," said Jack. "You're holding my cock."

★ ★ ★

A woman knows when she's getting old.

It's when her girdle pinches, but her husband doesn't.

★ ★ ★

"Now, remember, Bert, let that bald man go ahead of you in the toilet. I've heard that hair loss and incontinence usually start at the same time in men over 50."

★ ★ ★

A man of 75 retires to a golfing community and spends every day out on the course. But as time passes, he realises he can't see where the ball is going after a particularly long tee shot, so he goes to visit the eye doctor.

The doctor examines him and says, "There's nothing wrong with your eyes except the fact that you're getting on in years. It might be a good idea if you hired a caddy to spot the ball for you."

The old man follows the doctor's advice and places an ad in the local newspaper. Early the next day the doorbell rings and standing there is a man of 85.

"I've come about your ad in the local paper," he says.

"Gosh!" says the golfer. "Are you sure you'll be able to see the ball at such long distances?"

"No problem at all, I've got the eyes of a hawk," he replies.

So the next day they go out on to the course and the golfer tees off, sending the ball flying down the fairway.

"Did you see where that went?" asks the golfer.

"Sure did," replies the old man.

"Good," says the golfer. "Where?"

"I forget," he replies.

★ ★ ★

An 85-year-old man married a young girl of 25 and the event made headline news on the local radio. The old man was interviewed and asked about his sex life.

"Oh, it's nearly every night," he replied. "Nearly on Monday, nearly on Tuesday…"

★ ★ ★

Two old seadogs were mulling over old times in the Black Dog public house. One had a wooden leg and the other had an eye patch and a hook on the end of his arm.

"So how did you lose your leg?" asked one-eyed Jack.

"It were back in '49. Our ship went down in rough seas off the coast of China and some bloody big shark came along and bit it off before I'd had time to think. The bastard! So what about you and your hook. How did that happen?"

"That was down to Hardacre's lads. They chased us halfway across the channel before boarding us. But we put up a great fight. Shook the beggars off in the end. Just a shame it wasn't before one of them cut my arm off."

"And what about the eye patch?"

"Seagull crap."

"What! I don't believe it."

"As true as I'm sitting here," said Jack. "I happened to look up at the sun and this seagull crapped in my eye."

"And that's what made you blind?"

"No, but it was the first day with my new hook."

★ ★ ★

What's the difference between a stick-up and a hold- up?

Age.

★ ★ ★

The social worker was doing the rounds at the local residential home and she stopped to talk to Bob who was 92. After she'd helped him to cut up his food, she noticed a bowl of nuts on a small table next to him. "I was given them as a present," he said, "but I don't like them much. You're very welcome to have them."

Now the social worker was very fond of nuts so she nibbled away on them as she continued to chat to old Bob. As she was about to go she commented, "Thanks for the nuts, it's an odd present to give to someone with no teeth."

"Oh no," he replied. "When I was given them, they had chocolate on."

★ ★ ★

An old man decides he would like to join a nudist colony so he goes along to spend a day there, before joining up. He strips off, spends half an hour walking around and then, feeling tired, sits down to rest on a park bench. Moments later a beautiful young woman comes along and he finds himself with a raging erection. On seeing this, she gets down on her knees and gives him a blow job. "This is wonderful," he thinks and immediately goes along to the office to sign up. The rest of the day passes pleasantly and just before he goes home, he drops his cigarette. Bending down to pick it up, a young man comes up and takes him roughly from behind. Immediately the poor old man returns to the office to cancel his subscription.

"I'm so sorry you've changed your mind," said the owner. "You seemed to like it so much."

"That's true," said the old man, "problem is, at my age I only get excited once a month, but I'm always dropping cigarettes."

★ ★ ★

Two old ladies were on holiday in Greece and had landed up at one of the local museums.

As they wandered around they came across a magnificent 12-foot statue of a greek god, naked apart from a fig leaf. One of the old ladies stood transfixed.

"Come on, Mabel," said the other. "What are you waiting for – Christmas?"

"No, just autumn," she replied.

★ ★ ★

An old married couple stopped at a roadside cafe to have a cup of tea before resuming their journey. Thirty minutes later, the man realized he'd left his glasses on the cafe table, so they had to turn round and drive back, the woman complaining all the way about his forgetfulness. They arrived back at the cafe and as he got out of the car she said, "While you're in there, you might as well get my umbrella too."

★ ★ ★

"Let me tell you," said old William, slurring into his pint of beer. "Alchohol's a dreadful thing, dreadful. It killed my wife, you know." "I'm so sorry," replied his listener. "Alcoholic was she?" "No, no, I came home drunk and shot her."

★ ★ ★

A short-sighted spinster was ill in bed and got a visit from what she thought was the vicar. After he had been with her for some time, he left as her friend arrived.
"That was nice of the vicar to call, wasn't it?" said the spinster.
"No, dear, that was the doctor."
"Oh," replied the spinster. "I thought the dear vicar was very familiar."

★ ★ ★

An old couple are sitting in deck chairs enjoying a few rays of sun when all of a sudden, a seagull flies overhead and drops his load on top of the man's head.
"Just a moment, dear," says the wife. "I think I've got some tissue paper in my bag."
"Don't be daft, Dora, it'll be miles from here by now," he replies.

★ ★ ★

Two women were in the kitchen engaged in listening to their husbands' conversation.
"It's incredible," said the first lady, "that all they can talk about is golf and sex."
"Oh I don't know," replied her friend. "You must remember at their ages that's all they can do – talk about it."

★ ★ ★

Three little old ladies are sitting in a restaurant one day, talking about this and that. The first lady said, "You know, I'm really getting forgetful. This morning I was standing at the bottom of the stairs and I couldn't remember if I was just about to go up or if I had just come down."

"Oh, that's nothing," the second lady said. "The other day I was sitting on the edge of my bed, wondering if I was going to bed or if I had just gotten up."

The third lady smiled pleasantly at the other two. "Well, my memory is just as good as ever, knock on wood."

She rapped on the table with her knuckles, then gave a start and said, "Who's there?"

★ ★ ★

Two old men reminiscing about the old times. "Do you know, Sid, when I was just a lad I never slept with my wife before we got married. Did you?" "I don't know," said Alf. "What was her maiden name?"

★ ★ ★

He was so old that when he asked the doctor how long he might live, the doctor replied, "Put it this way, don't go buying any green bananas."

★ ★ ★

Two old men go to an escort service house. The madam asks them what they want. They say women. She asks, "How old are you?" They say 90.

So she tells one of the girls to take them upstairs and put each of them in a room with a blow up doll. So they go upstairs and do their thing. When they come back downstairs the first old man asks the other 'How was it?" The other one says, "I think she was dead, she just lay there, how was yours?"

213

"I think mine was a witch."

"A witch?"

"Yeah, I bit her on the tit, she farted and flew out the window."

★ ★ ★

YOU KNOW YOU'RE BECOMING "MARVELLOUSLY MATURE" WHEN...

1. You and your teeth don't sleep together.
2. Your try to straighten out the wrinkles in your socks and discover you aren't wearing any.
3. At the breakfast table you hear snap, crackle, pop and you're not eating cereal.
4. Your back goes out but you stay home.
5. When you wake up looking like your driving licence picture.
6. It takes two tries to get up from the couch.
7. When your idea of a night out is sitting on the patio.
8. When happy hour is a nap.
9. When you're on vacation and your energy runs out before your money does.
10. When you say something to your kids that your mother said to you and you always hated it.
11. When all you want for your birthday is to not be reminded of your age.
12. When you step off a kerb and look down one more time to make sure the street is still there.
13. Your idea of weight lifting is standing up.
14. It takes longer to rest than it did to get tired.
15. Your memory is shorter and your complaining lasts longer.
16. Your address book has mostly names that start with Dr.
17. You sit in a rocking chair and can't get it going.
18. The pharmacist has become your new best friend.
19. Getting "lucky" means you found your car in the parking lot.
20. The twinkle in your eye is merely a reflection from the sun on your bifocals.

21. It takes twice as long – to look half as good.

22. Everything hurts, and what doesn't hurt – doesn't work.

23. You look for your glasses for half an hour and they were on your head the whole time.

24. You sink your teeth into a steak – and they stay there.

25. You give up all your bad habits and still don't feel good.

26. You have more patience, but it is actually that you just don't care anymore.

27. You finally get your head together and your body starts falling apart.

28. You wonder how you could be over the hill when you don't even remember being on top of it.

★ ★ ★

A little old lady goes to the doctor and says, "Doctor, I have this problem with gas, but it really doesn't bother me too much. They never smell and are always silent. As a matter of fact, I've farted at least 20 times since I've been here in your office. You didn't know I was farting because they don't smell and are silent."

The doctor says, "I see. Take these pills and come back to see me next week." The next week the lady goes back. "Doctor," she says. "I don't know what the hell you gave me, but now my farts, although still silent, stink terribly." The doctor says, "Good!!! Now that we've cleared up your sinuses, let's work on your hearing."

★ ★ ★

On their way home after celebrating their 25th anniversary, she thanks him for a wonderful evening.

Oh. it's not over yet, says he. Once in the house, he gives her a little black velvet box. She opens it in anticipation, But what are these two little pills? Aspirin, says he.

But I don't have a headache, says she.

GOTCHA!!!

★ ★ ★

Two elderly ladies, Ethel and Martha, had been the best of friends for over 50 years. Over the decades they had spent together, they had worked together, lived next door to each other, and even vacationed together with their husbands. In their golden years, they would meet every afternoon to play cards and chat enthusiastically. One day, as they were wrapping up a game of pinochle, Ethel looks at Martha sheepishly and says, "Now please don't get angry with me. I know we've been friends for a long time, but I just can't seem to remember your name! I've been wracking my brain for the past hour, but it still escapes me. Please remind a forgetful old lady!" Martha glares angrily at her. For five minutes, she doesn't speak, only giving her friend stares of disappointment. Finally, Martha asks, "How soon do you need to know?"

★ ★ ★

Two elderly women, Mildred and Hazel, were out driving in a large car, barely able to see over the dashboard.
As they're driving along to the grocery store, they approach an intersection. The light is red, but Mildred just drives on through, not hesitating for a second.
Bewildered, Hazel thinks to herself, "I must be losing it. I could've sworn we just drove through a red light."
A few minutes later, they come up to another red light. Again, Mildred drives right on through. Hazel is alarmed, but is still not sure if she's imagining things.
At the next intersection, however, Mildred drives through another red light, prompting Hazel to turn to her friend. "Mildred, are you aware that we just ran through three red lights in a row?"
Mildred replies, "You know, I noticed that too!"
Hazel, flabbergasted, stammers, "You could have gotten us both killed!"
Mildred turns to her slowly, and says, "Me?! I thought you were driving!"

★ ★ ★

An eighty-year-old man was sitting on the couch with his wife when she said to him, "Why don't you come sit close to me like you used to." So he did.

After a moment she said, "Why don't you put your arm around me like you used to."

He put his arm around her and held her tight.

Then she said, "Why don't you nibble on my ear like you used to."

The man got up and left the room. "Where are you going?" she called out. "To get my teeth," he replied.

★ ★ ★

An elderly gentleman had serious hearing problems for a number of years. He went to the doctor and the doctor was able to have him fitted for a set of hearing aids that allowed the gentleman to hear 100%.

The elderly gentleman went back in a month to the doctor and the doctor said, "Your hearing is perfect. Your family must be really pleased that you can hear again."

The gentleman replied, "Oh, I haven't told my family yet. I just sit around and listen to the conversations. I've changed my will three times!"

★ ★ ★

This couple in their nineties are both having problems remembering things. During a check-up, the doctor tells them that they're physically okay, but they might want to start writing things down to help them remember. Later that night, while watching TV, the old man gets up from his chair.

"Want anything while I'm in the kitchen?" he asks.

"Will you get me a bowl of ice cream?"

"Sure."

"Don't you think you should write it down so you can remember it?" she asks.

"No, I can remember it."

"Well, I'd like some strawberries on top, too."

"Maybe you should write it down, so's not to forget it?"

He says, "I can remember that. You want a bowl of ice cream with strawberries."

"I'd also like whipped cream. Do you want to write it down?" she asks. Irritated, he says, "I don't need to write it down! Ice cream with strawberries and whipped cream – I got it, for goodness sake!"

Then he toddles into the kitchen. After about 20 minutes, the old man returns from the kitchen and hands his wife a plate of bacon and eggs. She stares at the plate for a moment. "Where's my toast?"

★ ★ ★

A 90-year-old man goes to the doctor's and says, "I want my sex drive lowered." The doctor says, "You are 90 years old man, it's all in the mind." The bloke says, "I know it is, that's why I want it lowered."

★ ★ ★

Do you know the website for the incontinence society is www.slash slash slash?

★ ★ ★

With a few hours to kill before the pubs open a man limps into a faith healing meeting and finds a seat on the front row. After the 30-minute service, the faith healer comes down from the platform and starts to touch some of the people. To the first one he puts his hands over the woman's eyes and she jumps up shouting, "I can see, I can see!"

He then lays his hands on a man who cannot walk and to everyone's delight he gets up out of his wheelchair and begins to dance. And so it goes on, people are being healed left, right and centre. Suddenly, the healer is standing in front of the newcomer and is just about to put out his hands when he shouts, "No, no, don't touch me! I've waited weeks for the orange disability stickers for my car, and they only came this morning."

★ ★ ★

Three old women were having tea on the lawns of the retirement home and the subject turned to memory.

"I may be 75," said the first old lady, "but I can still remember lying in my cot, just days after being born."

"Oh, that's nothing," said the second woman scornfully. "I can remember being born. Horrible it was. Going from a nice warm dark place into blinding light and getting my bum smacked. Aagh!"

Not to be outdone by the other two storytellers, the third woman piped up, "I'm 86 and I can remember going to Blackpool with my father and coming back with my mother!"

★ ★ ★

Two old spinsters were catching up on the local gossip.

"I see old Violet Henshaw has just cremated her third husband," said one.

"So I see," replied the other. "Some of us can't get a husband at all, and Violet's got husbands to burn!"

★ ★ ★

The old couple went to Eastbourne for their two-week summer holiday but alas, the day before they were due to return, Maurice collapsed and died. As friends and relatives filed past his coffin at the funeral, Rose turned to the widow and remarked, "Gosh, Ethel, he looks wonderful."

"Oh yes," agreed Ethel, "those two weeks in Eastbourne did him a power of good."

★ ★ ★

An old man had just lost his wife. All he had left was his cat and because he was lonely and had no one to talk to, he thought he would try to teach the cat to talk. He decided to feed his cat the very finest food and then speak to him every day for an hour.

Wonderful salmon, the very best rabbit, an endless variety of birds, this, and much more, was fed to the cat every day. The animal obviously enjoyed the gourmet menu but never said a word. Then one day, the man had just served up a plate of specially prepared mice when the cat suddenly shouted, "Look out!"

The old man was so dumbfounded, he just sat there with his mouth open and the next moment the ceiling collapsed on top of him, killing him stone dead.

"Silly bugger," said the cat. "Spends two years trying to get me to talk and then when I do, he takes no bloody notice!"

★ ★ ★

The old man was addressing the class of 14-year-olds as part of 'people in the community' week.

"I'm fighting fit," he said. "I've never smoked, I've never had a drink, I don't eat between meals and I've been faithful to my wife for fifty years. Tomorrow I'll be celebrating my 80th birthday."

A voice from the back called out, "How?"

★ ★ ★

"It's funny how old age affects you," said one old man to the other. "Do you know, it's made my wife's arms shorter." "Really?" "Yeah, when we were first married, she could put her arms right round me."

★ ★ ★

An elderly couple had dinner at another couple's house, and after eating, the wives went into the kitchen. The two gentlemen were talking, and one said, "Last night we went out to a new restaurant and I would recommend it very highly." The other man said, "What is the name of the restaurant?" The first man thought and finally said, "What is the name of that flower you give to someone you love? The one that's red and has thorns." "Do you mean a rose?" "Yes, that's the one," replied the man. He then turned towards the kitchen and yelled, "Rose, what's the name of that restaurant we went to last night?"

★ ★ ★

220

Two old men were sitting on the beach watching the bikini-clad girls walking by, running into the water and playing beach volleyball.

"Do you think all this exercise keeps you fit?" asked one.

"I should say so," replied the other. "I walk two miles every day just to watch this."

★ ★ ★

Two old men were sitting in the park talking over past times. They'd got on to the subject of pubs.

"They're more like restaurants these days," said one.

"And the beer's not so good," replied the other.

"But it's the spittoons that I miss," continued the first.

"You always did," came the reply.

★ ★ ★

Three aged women were sitting in the park when they heard the sound of the ice cream van and decided to have a cornet each. They played eeny, meeny, miney, mo to see who should go and the task fell to Beryl.

She took their money, struggled to her feet and set off. It was more than an hour later when Cath turned to the other woman and commented, "I don't know where our Beryl's got to, I think the old bugger's run off with the money."

"Don't you bloody start," came Beryl's voice from a few yards behind the bench, "or I won't go at all."

★ ★ ★

Two old blokes were talking.

"Come on, Bert, cheer up," said Alfred. "Let's go and have a pint of the dark brew. I hear it puts lead in your pencil."

"No thanks, if it's all the same to you," replied Bert. "I haven't really got anyone to write to."

★ ★ ★

Two old men were sitting in the park watching the girls walking by in their skimpy outfits. God!" said one, " it makes you want to sit them down on your knee and kiss and cuddle them!" "Oh yes," replied the other, "but wasn't there something else we used to do as well?"

★ ★ ★

Morris, an 82 year-old man, went to the doctor to get a physical.
A few days later, the doctor saw Morris walking down the street with a gorgeous young woman on his arm.
A couple of days later, the doctor spoke to Morris and said, "You're really doing great, aren't you?"
Morris replied, "Just doing what you said, Doc. 'Get a hot mamma and be cheerful.'"
The doctor said, "I didn't say that. I said, 'You've got a heart murmur; be careful."

★ ★ ★

Two old women limp towards each other along the pavement. As they pass, one points at her foot and says conspiratorially, "Bad arthritis, had it ten years."
The other replied, pointing at her foot, "Dog mess, got it round the corner a minute ago."

★ ★ ★

A little old man shuffled slowly into an ice cream parlor and pulle himself slowly, painfully, up on to a stool. After catching his breath, he ordered a banana split. The waitress asked kindly, "Crushed nuts?" "No," he replied, "Arthritis."

★ ★ ★

An 85-year-old man went to his doctor's office to get a sperm count. The doctor gave the man a jar and said, "Take this jar home and bring back a semen sample tomorrow." The next day the 85-year-old man reappeared at the doctor's office and gave him the jar, which was as clean and empty as on the previous day. The doctor asked what happened and the man explained, "Well, doc, it's like this – first I tried with my right hand, but nothing. Then I tried with my left hand, but still nothing. Then I asked my wife for help. She tried with her right hand, then her left, still nothing. She tried with her mouth, first with the teeth in, then with her teeth out, and still nothing."

"We even called up Eileen, the lady next door, and she tried too, first with both hands, then an armpit and she even tried squeezin' it between her knees, but still nothing." The doctor was shocked and said, "You asked your neighbour?!" The old man replied, "Yep. And no matter what we tried we still couldn't get the jar open!"

★ ★ ★

An old man and his wife lived really deep in the hills and seldom saw any other people.

One day a peddler came by to sell his goods and asked the man if he or his wife wanted to buy something. "Well, my wife ain't home, she's gone down to the creek to wash clothes, but lemma see what you got," said the man. The peddler showed him pots and pans, tools and gadgets, but the old man wasn't interested.

Then the man spotted a mirror and said, "What's that?" Before the peddler could tell him it was a mirror, the old man picked it up and said, "My God how'd you get a picture of my Pappy?" The old man was so happy, he traded his wife's best pitcher for it. The peddler left before the wife came back and spoiled his sale.

The old man was worried that the wife would be mad at him for trading her best pitcher, so he hid it in the barn behind some boxes of junk. He would go out to the barn two or three times a day to look at the "picture" and eventually the wife got suspicious. One day she got fed up and after he retired for the night, she went out to the barn. She saw the mirror behind the boxes, picked it up and said, "So this is the hussy he's been foolin' around with!"

★ ★ ★

Two old men were sitting on a bench outside a nursing home having a chat. "How are you, Richard?" asked George. "I'm not feeling too good today, I'm utterly exhausted," replied Richard. "I've pulled a muscle, and it's killing me." "I'm surprised that a pulled muscle makes you feel so tired," said George. Richard yawned and said, "Well, it does if you pull it a hundred times in one night."

★ ★ ★

An old man in a nursing home awoke one day and trundled down the hallway to the community breakfast room looking rather forlorn. Ms Smith, a nurse, met him in the hallway. She greeted him smilingly and asked how he was.

Mr Jones admitted that all was not well; in fact, his penis had died during the night. Ms Smith knew that Mr Jones was occasionally a little off mentally, so she merely replied that she was sorry to hear the bad news and went on her way.

The next morning Mr Jones was on his way to breakfast again, but today he was dressed in a coat and tie, and his penis was hanging out of his pants. Sure enough, he met Ms Smith, whereupon – although somewhat startled – she calmly reminded him that the day before he had told her his penis had died and asked why it was hanging out of his pants.

Mr Jones replied simply, "Today is the viewing."

★ ★ ★

Two elderly gentlemen, Sam and Harry, were having breakfast. Sam said to Harry, "Harry, why do you have a suppository in your ear?" Harry took the suppository out, looked it over and said, "Sam, I'm really glad you saw this thing, now I think I know where my hearing aid is."

★ ★ ★

EMPLOYMENT

Three girls arrive at the hotel to be interviewed for the job of chambermaid. The manager asks each of them in turn what they would do if they found a £10 note.

The first said, "Finders keepers."

The second said she would hand it in and after three months, if it had not been claimed, would take it herself.

The third answered the same as the second except that, with the money, she would buy everyone who worked in the hotel a drink and then give the rest to the local hospice.

Now… which girl got the job?

The one with big tits, of course.

★ ★ ★

Two businessmen were travelling home on the train. One turns to the other and asks how his business is doing.

"Very well, very well indeed, ever since I've taken on this new salesman. Sadly, there's just one problem. He's seduced both my wife and my daughter and made two of the office girls pregnant."

"Good gracious, what are you going to do?"

"Don't worry, I'm watching him very closely and if he tries to fiddle the books, I'll sack him on the spot."

★ ★ ★

It is the conference season and three dentists and three bankers find themselves together at the railway ticket office. The dentists each buy a ticket, but the bankers buy one between them.

"How are you all going to travel on one ticket?" ask the dentists. "You'll see," they reply.

On boarding the train the dentists take their seats, but the bankers all cram into the one toilet. The conductor comes round shouting, "Tickets please!," knocks on the toilet door and a ticket is passed to him. The dentists are impressed and decide to do the same on the return journey. They only buy one ticket, but to their amazement the bankers don't buy a ticket at all.

"How come?" ask the dentists.

"You'll see," the bankers reply.

They all got on to the train, the three dentists cram into one toilet, the three bankers get into another.

A few minutes later one of the bankers leaves his toilet, knocks on the other toilet door and shouts, "Tickets please!"

★ ★ ★

A man goes for an audition as a pianist in a local night-club. He starts by playing a stunning blues number which has everyone stopping work to listen to it. When he's finished the club owner is delighted and asks him about the music.

"I wrote it myself," said the man. "It's called 'I want to shag you long and hard'."

After a stunned silence, the owner asks him to play something else and this time it's a funky jazz number. Absolutely superb: there are cheers all round the bar. The man tells them he also wrote it and called it, "Give me a blow job and I'll show you what for."

After some embarrassment the owner comes to a decision.

"You've got the job, on one condition; you never ever tell the audience the titles of the music you play."

Although not too happy about it, the man agrees. After all, the pay is good.

Some weeks go by and the club's popularity goes from strength to strength. People come from miles around to hear the pianist and his reputation spreads like wildfire. The night after a particularly successful session, the pianist staggers off to the toilet. He's been given free drinks all night by the admiring public and is feeling a bit the worse for wear. In fact he's so far gone he forgets to do his flies back up. On the way back to the stage a lady taps him on the shoulder. "Excuse me, do you know your fly is open and your dick is hanging out?"

He replies, "Bloody hell, I do, I wrote it."

★ ★ ★

A silly young man lived for his work, nothing else mattered. Every night and all weekend he would bring papers home to work on. Then one day he left some important papers at home and in a panic rushed home to get them. As he was leaving his spare room he saw his wife and boss in bed together.

Later that day he mentioned what he had seen to a colleague.

"Why, that's appalling, are you going back tomorrow to try and catch them at it?"

"Good gracious no, it was lucky he didn't see me this time."

★ ★ ★

A man went for a job in an undertaker's and was found to be ideal for the job apart from the fact that he kept winking.

"Mr Smith, I'd very much like to give you the job but in these terribly sad situations, it would be very callous to keep winking at the bereaved customers."

"Oh, that's no problem", replied the man. "I just need to take a paracetamol and the winking will immediately stop."

The man looked for the pills in his briefcase which, to the undertaker's astonishment, was full of an amazing variety of condoms.

"Good gracious," gasped the undertaker. "I'm surprised you've got any time left to work. Your leisure time must be very tiring…"

"Oh no," smiled the man. "I've got a lovely wife at home. But have you ever tried to buy a bottle of paracetamol from a chemist, winking all the time?"

★ ★ ★

It was the day of the inspector's visit to the local bakery and as he was doing his rounds he came upon a man pressing down the outsides of the fruit pies with his thumb.

"Hey, haven't you a tool for that?" asked the inspector.

"Yes," said the man, "but I use that for putting holes in the doughnuts."

★ ★ ★

Unable to get any answer when he knocked on the door, the postman went round to the back of the house, only to find a beautiful young woman sunbathing stark naked in the garden.

Now the young lady was very strong-willed and determined to outstare the man. Their eyes locked for a good long minute in the hope that she could shame him into looking away.

It worked.

All of a sudden the postman yelled, "What the bloody hell are you looking at. Haven't you seen a postman before!"

★ ★ ★

The two handsome delivery boys carried the woman's box of groceries into her kitchen.

"That will be £15, please," said the first one.

At this, the woman let her dressing gown fall open to reveal she was stark naked underneath.

"Perhaps, there's some other way we could settle the bill," she said smiling.

"Just a moment, then," said the second. "I'll have to see if it's all right with our driver. This morning we've already screwed away two orders, one on Beech Street and the other on the High Street."

★ ★ ★

The taxi was hurtling down the road at such a tremendous speed that the man tapped the driver on the shoulder, saying, "Why are you going so fast?"

"Well, I heard someone say 'faster, faster'!" said the cabbie.

"Yes, but she wasn't talking to you, so slow down, please."

★ ★ ★

The phone rang and a voice at the other end said, "Mr Smallman? We have one of your employees staying at our hotel. He has run up quite a large bill and I'm checking to see that it will be paid."

"How much is it?" asked Mr Smallman.

"£550," came the reply.

"What?" he spluttered. "For three days! That's impossible."

"I've got the chits here," said the hotel man.

"You've got the chits! What do you think I've got after hearing that?"

★ ★ ★

A successful company is taken over by three business whizz kids and its time for them to decide on the management structure. The first one says, "I've got 42% of the shares, so I'll be Chairman."

"I've got 37% of the shares, so I'll be Managing Director" says the second.

"What about me?" says the third man. "You needed me to buy the other 21%, but you've carved the power up between yourselves."

After a moment's consultation the other two turn to him and say, "You can deal with sexual matters."

"What the hell does that mean?"

"When we want your fucking advice, we'll ask for it."

★ ★ ★

'Simple Sam' is the local odd-job man in the village, not too bright but always willing to have a go. One day, he hears there are vacancies in the local sawmill, so he goes along in the hope of getting a job. Reluctantly, the boss takes him on, emphasizing how dangerous the job is and how he must always think "Safety". However, only two hours into the job and Sam stumbles over a plank of wood, puts his hands out to save himself and gets all his fingers and thumbs sawn off by a giant blade. There's no one else about, so he runs off in shock to the local hospital, where he faints on the doorstep. Later, as he regains consciousness, he hears the doctor's voice.

"Sam, Sam, if only you'd brought your fingers in with you we might have been able to sew them on before it was too late."

"I would have" cried Sam, "but I couldn't pick them up."

★ ★ ★

A woman went into a butcher's shop and asked for a Norfolk Turkey. "Just a moment," said the assistant, and disappeared into the backroom. He came back with the bird, which he showed to the woman.

Immediately, she put her fingers right up its backside and after a minute exclaimed, "This isn't a Norfolk Turkey, this is a Shropshire. How dare you try to trick me?"

Astonished at her outburst, he apologised profusely and returned to the backroom where he picked up another turkey. On returning, the woman shoved her hands up its arse, smiled and said, "That's better. Wrap it up, please."

After she had left the shop, the butcher came out of his office and asked what all the commotion was about. When the assistant recounted the incident the butcher said, "It's no good trying to fool that old biddy, she knows her turkeys. You should know them too by now. Where have you been?"

Fed up with the butcher's jibes, the assistant turns round and sticks his bum in the air.

"You're the expert, you tell me!"

★ ★ ★

"Jenkins, what on earth do you think you are doing?" said the boss to his employee when he found him in the toilets masturbating. Jenkins thought quickly and said, "Oh that! It's not what it seems."

"Really, then what does it mean?"

"Well, sir, I've got ESP and I'm just bonking my girlfriend in Bristol."

★ ★ ★

A big strapping boy went up to the big house for a job as a handyman but returned home very disappointed.

"Oh, dad, I'm so ashamed, I really made a cock-up."

"How come, son?"

"The lady was very nice, she asked me lots of questions, seemed pleased with what I had to say, I told her I was a hard worker but then right at the end she asked to see my testimonials... that's when I lost it completely!"

★ ★ ★

The business is doing badly and one of two people from middle management will have to go. It's not an easy decision, as both Doreen and Jack have been there a long time and they're both very good. The first one to leave work tomorrow will get their cards, decides the Personnel Manager; that's the only way he can think of doing it. The following evening, 30 minutes before she usually leaves, Doreen tells Jack she has a bad headache. It could be a migraine coming on, so she's going to go home early. As she gets her coat, the Personnel Manager spots her and decides to take action. He goes over to her and says, "There's something I have to say to you, Doreen. I'm going to have to lay you or Jack off."

"Jack off!" she retorted angrily. "I've got a bad headache."

★ ★ ★

What's the definition of a faithful servant?
One who carries out his master's wishes when he's told, "Drive over that cliff, Jenkins, I've reached the end of my tether."

★ ★ ★

A man walking along a country road comes across a shepherd with a huge flock of sheep. He says to the shepherd, "I will bet you £150 against one of your sheep that I can tell you the exact number in this flock." There's a pause for a moment while the shepherd thinks it over but he feels quite confident because the flock is so big.

"OK," he says. "You're on." "964," says the man.

"Good gracious!" splutters the farmer. "You're absolutely right. You'd better take one of the sheep."

The man picks one up and begins to walk away, when the shepherd cries, "Hold on a minute, will you give me a chance to get even? Double or nothing, that I can guess your occupation."

"OK," replies the man.

"You are a government economist," says the shepherd.

"I'm amazed," responds the man. "That's absolutely right, but tell me, how did you deduce that?"

"Well," says the shepherd. "Put down my dog and I will tell you."

★ ★ ★

As the man parks his Rolls-Royce in the car park, a local businessman approaches.

"That's a lovely car you have there; how much did it cost?"

"About £200,000."

"Blimey, how much petrol does it take?"

"29 gallons."

"And how many miles does it do to the gallon?"

"About two miles. I work for Cunard you know."

"Well, I work fucking hard as well, but I still can't afford a Rolls-Royce," he retorts.

★ ★ ★

The new assistant is being shown round the lighthouse and given a grand tour of all the facilities.

"It's not a bad life," says the keeper. "There's not much time to get bored, we've got something on most nights. On Monday, we have the local chef in from one of the top hotels round here and he puts on a sumptuous banquet. Then on Tuesday, we have the casino, and Wednesday, a visit from some of the call girls. That's a real passionate night, eh?"

He looks at the man who seems to be shaking his head.

"Oh dear, you're not a poofter, are you? Cos you'll hate Thursdays."

★ ★ ★

A crow was sitting on a tree, doing nothing all day. A small rabbit saw the crow, and asked him, "Can I also sit like you and do nothing all day long?"

The crow answered: "Sure, why not."

So, the rabbit sat on the ground below the crow, and rested which was extremely relaxing for a while. All of a sudden, a fox appeared, jumped on the rabbit and ate it.

Moral of the story is:

To be sitting and doing nothing, you must be sitting very, very high up.

★ ★ ★

The woman rushed into the chemist's, crying.

"Do you realize what you've done?" she wailed. "You gave my husband rat poison instead of stomach salts."

"Oh dear," replied the chemist. "That is truly awful; you owe me another £2.

★ ★ ★

"Great news, boss," said the salesman.

"You remember that checked suit in green and yellow... The one you thought you'd be stuck with forever? Well, I've sold it, and at the asking price."

"Well, that's fantastic," replied the boss, very impressed. "Well done, I think you deserve a bonus for that. By the way, why have you got a bandage on your hand?"

"Oh, that's where his guide dog bit me."

★ ★ ★

The man knocked on his manager's door.

"Excuse me, Sir, may I have tomorrow off, the wife wants to go shopping."

"Certainly not," replied the manager.

"Oh thank you, sir, you've saved my life!"

★ ★ ★

WORK VS. PRISON

In prison you spend the majority of your time in an 8x10 cell.
At work you spend most of your time in a 6x8 cubicle.

In prison you get three meals a day.
At work you get a break for one meal and you have to pay for it.

In prison you get time off for good behaviour.
At work you get rewarded for good behaviour with more work.

In prison you can watch TV and play games.
At work you get fired for watching TV and playing games.

In prison a guard locks, unlocks, opens and closes all doors for you.
At work you must carry around a security card and unlock and open all doors yourself.

In prison you get your own toilet.
At work you have to share.

In prison they allow you to visit your family and friends.
At work you can't even speak to family and friends.

In prison all expenses are paid by taxpayers, with no work required.
At work, you get to pay all the expenses to go to work, and then they deduct taxes from your salary to pay for the prisoners.

In prison you spend most of your life looking through bars from the inside wanting to get out.
At work you spend most of your time wanting to get out and inside bars.

In prison you can join many programmes that you can leave at any time.
At work there are some programmes you can never get out of.

In prison there are wardens who are often sadistic and psychotic.
At work we call them managers!

★ ★ ★

A man was strolling around an old antique market when he spotted a long forgotten brass rat pushed into a far corner of one of the shops. As he was a collector of brass objects, the purchase was soon made and the man departed. However, he hadn't gone too far when he noticed a rat running up behind him and within minutes, the whole area was swimming in the vermin. Frightened for his life the man raced down the road to the river and threw the brass rat into the water. Lo and behold all the rats ran into the water and drowned. Some time later, he returned to the antique market and sought out the man who had sold him the rat. When the shopkeeper recognized him, he said, "Back again already, sir? Is there something wrong with your figurine?"

"Oh no, not at all," replied the man, "I was just wondering if you had any brass figures of lawyers."

★ ★ ★

There was only one supermarket basket left at the door of the shop as a woman and a man approached from separate directions.

"Excuse me," said the woman, "do you want that basket?"

"No, thanks," he replied, "I'm only after one thing."

"Typical male," she said to herself as he walked away.

★ ★ ★

A woman walks into a pet shop and asks the owner for some wasps.

"I'm sorry, Madam, we don't sell wasps in here."

"But you do," she insists.

"No, I think you're mistaken," replies the owner.

"Well, in that case, why have you got two in the window?"

★ ★ ★

Secretary to her boss, "Excuse me, sir, the invisible man's here."

"Tell him I can't see him."

★ ★ ★

His secretary was absolutely naff.

"Why don't you answer the bloody phone?" he said in exasperation.

"Because I'm fed up," she replied. "Nine times out of ten it's for you."

★ ★ ★

As the new office manager walked into the building, he noticed a youth sitting down on a stool, reading a magazine.

"Hey, you," he called, throwing him £200. "That's a week's wages, pack up and get out immediately... and don't come back."

As the astonished boy left the site, the boss turned to the under manager and said, "That's the way to treat idle buggers like that, just get rid of them on the spot. So how long had he been working here?"

"He hadn't," replied his assistant. "He just popped in to deliver lunch from the deli, and he was waiting for his change."

★ ★ ★

A large, well-established, Canadian lumber camp advertised the fact that they were looking for a good lumberjack.

The very next day, a skinny little guy showed up at the camp with his axe, and knocked on the head lumberjacks' door. The head lumberjack took one look at the little man and told him to scram.

"Just give me a chance to show you what I can do," said the skinny man.

"Okay, see that giant redwood over there?" said the lumberjack. "Take your axe and go cut it down!" The skinny man headed for the tree, and in five minutes he was back knocking on the lumberjack's door. "I cut the tree down," said the little man.

The lumberjack couldn't believe his eyes and said, "Where did you get the skill to chop down trees like that?"

"In the Sahara Forest," replied the puny man.

"You mean the Sahara Desert," said the lumberjack.

The little man laughed and answered back...

"Oh sure, that's what they call it now!

★ ★ ★

The multinational company was looking for a new Director General and three men were up for the job. To test their undying loyalty to the company, they were all asked to do the same thing.

"Go into the other room and shoot your wife," they ordered the first man, handing him a gun.

"Oh no," gasped the man. "My wife means more to me than anything, I can't do it."

So he was dismissed.

The second man was given similar instructions. Handing him a gun they ordered him to go next door and shoot his wife dead.

"I can't do it," replied the ashen-faced man. "Tomorrow is our 25th anniversary and we've lived a very happy life."

So the second man was dismissed.

The third man came in, a gun was passed to him and he was told to go into the next room and kill his wife. The man did as he'd been instructed and went next door. At first there was complete silence, but all of a sudden they heard an awful scream, furniture falling over and then all went quiet. A moment later the third man returned.

"What happened in there?" they asked.

"Some prat put blank cartridges in the gun, so I had to strangle her," he replied.

★ ★ ★

Jack went down to the Job Centre and as he was scanning situations vacant, he spotted a card asking for a film scene assistant. The successful candidate would need to have a steady hand to be a bikini line shaver on the latest series of an English version of *Baywatch*. Drooling at the very thought, he took the card over to the desk and told the employment officer he was interested in the job.

"Very well," she replied, not batting an eyelid. "You'll need to go to the service station, two miles out of town."

"Really? Is that where they're interviewing?"

"No, that's the end of the queue," she replied.

★ ★ ★

A couple moved into a new house, close to a busy main road. Unfortunately, every time a bus trundled by, the wardrobe door would fly open so the woman rang up a local carpenter who came round that afternoon. He inspected it closely but could find nothing wrong. "I'll just have a look inside," he said, but as he disappeared through the doors, her husband walked into the bedroom.

"What's going on here?" he demanded, opening the wardrobe door.

"You'll never believe this," said the carpenter sheepishly. "I'm waiting for a bus."

★ ★ ★

Jack was a plumber. He worked for himself and had just finished a job for Mr Crabtree on Gowan Avenue. As he left, he handed him a bill.

"Prompt payment would be appreciated," he said.

However, a couple of weeks went by without payment, so Jack sent a reminder. Another month went by and still no sign of a cheque, so he sent a second reminder. After another four weeks, he wrote a letter and enclosed a picture of his wife and two children, writing on the back, "This is the reason I need money – to feed my family."

Lo and behold, two days later a letter arrived in the post. It was from Mr Crabtree. But alas there was no cheque. The envelope contained just one photo. A picture of a voluptuous blonde, wearing a bikini and standing next to a zippy little sports car. On the back of the photo was written, "And this is the reason I can't pay."

★ ★ ★

"Waiter, I see on the menu that you have a chicken tarka. Shouldn't that be chicken tikka?"

"No, sir, it's like chicken tikka only a little 'otter."

★ ★ ★

A good artist can draw a crowd.

A roofer on the job is above it all.

Usually violinists just string along.

Lazy bakers loaf on the job.

★ ★ ★

A man in a hot air balloon realized he was lost. He reduced altitude and spotted a woman below. He descended a bit more and shouted, "Excuse me, can you help me? I promised a friend I would meet him an hour ago, but I don't know where I am." The woman below replied, "You're in a hot air balloon hovering approximately 30 feet above the ground. You're between 40 and 41 degrees north latitude and between 59 and 60 degrees west longitude." "You must be an engineer," said the balloonist. "I am," replied the woman, "How did you know?" "Well," answered the balloonist, "everything you told me is technically correct, but I've no idea what to make of your information, and the fact is I'm still lost. Frankly, you've not been much help at all. If anything, you've delayed my trip."

The woman below responded, "You must be in Management." "I am," replied the balloonist, "but how did you know?" "Well," said the woman, "you don't know where you are or where you're going. You have risen to where you are due to a large quantity of hot air. You made a promise which you've no idea how to keep, and you expect people beneath you to solve your problems. The fact is you are in exactly the same position you were in before we met, but now, somehow, it's my fault."

★ ★ ★

"Ladies and gentlemen," announced the airline pilot, "due to a loss of power in one of our four engines, we will now land in San Francisco an hour late. Our apologies for any inconvenience caused."

Five minutes later, he made another announcement.

"A second engine has failed but please be assured that the plane can fly on the two remaining engines. It will just mean a further delay of another thirty minutes."

Then, later still, he made a third announcement.

"Due to the failure of a third engine, we will now be landing at San Francisco three hours later than scheduled."

At this point, one of the passengers exclaimed loudly, "Let's hope we don't lose the fourth engine, otherwise we'll be up here all bloody night."

★ ★ ★

The plane is about to taxi down the runway when passengers see the pilot and co-pilot walking up towards the cockpit. Both look as if they are virtually blind, carrying white sticks and bumping into everyone. At first, the full plane of passengers cannot believe what they have just seen, but as the plane taxis to the end of the runway and turns to pick up speed, a slight panic begins. By the time it's hurtling down the runway, there is ever-increasing panic and as the plane lifts into the air an earth-shattering scream goes up from the cabins. This sudden change in pitch is followed by the plane rising into the sky.

"Aaah, thank goodness," says the pilot to his colleague. "Safe again. You know, one day the passengers aren't going to scream and then we're really done for."

★ ★ ★

A man is walking around the streets of New York one day when he spies an old friend of his from college. "Boris!" he yells. "I haven't seen you in ages! How have you been?"

"Well," Boris replies. "I am the piccolo player for the International Orchestra."

"Spectacular!" the man replies.

"It is not what you might think, my friend. We play for the King of England, and he loves the music. He says, 'Fill the instruments with gold!' and they fill the tuba with gold and they fill the trombone with gold, and me with the goddamn piccolo."

"We play for the Queen of France, and she loves the music. She says, 'Fill the instruments with silver!' and they fill the tuba with silver and they fill the trombone with silver, and me with the goddamn piccolo."

"Then we play for the Czar of Russia, and he hates the music. He says 'Shove the instruments up their asses!' and the tuba doesn't fit and the trombone doesn't fit. AND ME WITH THE GODDAMN PICCOLO!"

★ ★ ★

10 REASONS WHY YOU SHOULD ASK YOUR BOSS FOR A RAISE

10. You take your pay cheque to the bank and the clerk bursts out in hysterical laughter.

9. The Red Cross calls and offers you emergency assistance.

8. Your only charge card is for the Salvation Army.

7. You work full time and you still qualify for food stamps.

6. You empty out your piggy bank and then cook the bank and serve it for your Easter ham.

5. All you can think about morning, noon and night is clipping grocery coupons.

4. You file your income taxes and the Inland Revenue returns them stamped, "Charity Case – Return To Sender."

3. You set the world record for mailing £1.00 rebate requests to Young America, Minnesota.

2. You pay all your bills, put your remaining fiver into your wallet and it goes into shock.

and the Number 1 reason you need to ask for a raise...

1. You get arrested for taking the coins out of the fountain in the shopping centre.

★ ★ ★

Why did the Lone Ranger kill Tonto?
He found out what 'Kemo Sabe' meant.

★ ★ ★

The Lone Ranger and Tonto are riding along a narrow canyon, when suddenly an arrow comes flying through the air and thuds into the ground in front of them. They look up quickly, to see both sides of the canyon lined with hostile Indians, and even as they watch, more appear in front of them at the end of the canyon.

They turn their horses around to get the hell out of it, but there are hundreds of Indians coming up behind them, and it is obvious they have ridden into a trap.

"Well, old friend," says the Lone Ranger, turning to Tonto, "looks like we're really in trouble this time."

"Oh yeah?" replies Tonto. "What d'you mean 'we', white man?"

★ ★ ★

Sherlock Holmes and Doctor Watson went on a camping trip to Dartmoor and as they lay down for the night Sherlock Holmes said,
"Doctor Watson, my old friend, when you look up into the darkness, please tell me what you see."

"Well, I can see a very clear sky, there are no clouds and the stars are out in their millions. I can see the Milky Way and I believe that extra-bright star over there is the planet Venus which you can see at this time of the year. I also deduce that being such a clear night will mean that it will get quite chilly."

Watson laughed and said, "But knowing you, Sherlock, I'm sure there are many things I have missed. What have you deduced?"

There was a moment's silence and then Holmes replied, "Somebody's nicked our tent."

★ ★ ★

The Lone Ranger and Tonto have just spent a month riding through the desert before landing up at Prickly Gulch Creek where they go into the saloon for a much-needed drink. They've only been in there a few minutes when a man runs in asking customers if anyone owns a big white horse.

"That's mine," replies the Lone Ranger. "Is there anything wrong?"

"Sure is, the animal's collapsed," said the man.

The Lone Ranger and Tonto go outside to see poor Silver lying prostrate on the ground, but after giving him some water he seems to revive a bit.

The Lone Ranger turns to Tonto and says, "Will you just run around it for a few minutes so it can feel a breeze and that'll soon put him right."

Tonto starts to run around Silver while the Lone Ranger goes back inside to finish his drink. A moment later another man rushes in asking who owns the white horse outside.

"Bloody hell!" says the Lone Ranger. "That's mine, now what the hell's wrong?"

"Oh, your horse is all right," says the man, "but you've left your injun running."

★ ★ ★

Her husband was so ugly, every time he went to the zoo he had to buy two tickets – one for going in and one for getting out.

★ ★ ★

Drawbacks to working in a cubicle
1. Being told to "Think Outside the Box" when I'm in the darn box all day long!
2. Not being able to check E-mail attachments without first seeing who is behind me.
3 Fabric cubicle walls do not offer much protection from any kind of gun fire.
4. That nagging feeling that if I just press the right button, I will get a piece of cheese.
5. Lack of roof rafters for the noose.
6. My walls are too close together for my hammock to work right.
7. Twenty-three power cords, one outlet.

8. Prison cells are not only bigger, they have beds.
9. When tours come through, I get lots of peanuts thrown at me.
10. Can't slam the door when you quit and walk out.
11. If you talk to yourself it causes all the surrounding cubicle inhabitants to pop their heads over the wall and say, "What? I didn't hear you."
12. If your boss calls you and askes you to come into his office for a minute, the walk there is like a funeral march... people hand you tissues as you pass and refuse to make eye contact.
13. You always have the feeling that someone is watching you, but by the time you turn to look they're gone.

★ ★ ★

"So tell me, Mrs Smith," began the interviewer, "have you any other skills you think might be worth mentioning?"
"Actually, yes," said the applicant modestly. "Last year I had two short stories published in national magazines, and I finished my novel."
"Very impressive," he commented, "but I was thinking of skills you could apply during office hours."
Mrs Smith explained brightly, "Oh, that was during office hours."

★ ★ ★

An office manager arrives at his department and sees an employee sitting behind his desk, totally stressed out. He gives him the following advice: "I went home every afternoon for two weeks and had myself pampered by my wife. It was fantastic, and it really helped; you should try it too!"
Two weeks later, when the manager arrives at his department, he sees the man happy and full of energy at his desk. The faxes are piling up, and the computer is running at full speed. "I see you followed my advice." "I did," answers the employee. "It was great! By the way I didn't know you had such a nice house!"

★ ★ ★

FARMYARD

It was market day in the small town and towards the end of the day a vet approached one of the old farmers.

"Have you ever considered artificial insemination for your herd of cows, Mr Woodall?"

"No, thanks. I'll stick w'old-fashioned way if it's all the same to you."

"OK, but if you change your mind, give us a ring and we'll take it from there."

On the way home, the farmer pondered the man's words, but couldn't imagine how a cow could be served without a bull. His curiosity eventually got the better of him and he rang the man asking for his cow to be serviced as soon as possible.

"OK," replied the vet. "If you can get a few things ready. Wash down the cow's backside, put down some clean straw and have a bucket of hot water and a stool ready."

When all was ready, the vet arrived.

"Have you done everything I asked?"

"That I have," replied the farmer. "I've even hammered a nail in the door for you to hang your trousers on."

★ ★ ★

A farmer was getting fewer and fewer eggs from his hens and decided he would have to replace the old rooster who wasn't carrying out his job properly. So he bought a new rooster. Later in the henhouse the old rooster turned to the new rooster and said, "Look, let's make a deal. Let me just have three of the hens and I'll leave the rest to you."

"No way," came the reply. "This is all mine now."

"OK," said the crestfallen rooster, "but let me have some pride. If we have a race across the farmyard and back, the winner takes all."

"All right," said the new rooster, thinking there was no way he was going to lose to this tired old bird.

They set off, but just as the new cock was about to overtake, the farmer burst out of his house and shot him dead.

"Bloody hell, that's the third queer rooster I've bought this month."

★ ★ ★

Over a pint in the local pub a farmer was telling his neighbour about the trouble he was having with his chickens. They weren't laying, they weren't breeding. At this, his neighbour told him not to worry because he had a cockerel that was forever on the job, in fact he'd worn his chickens out, so he was quite happy to sell him. The transaction took place and the rooster went home to the new farm. In no time at all he was servicing all the chickens with amazing results, and not only that the ducks were looking a lot livelier, as were the geese. The farmer was overjoyed.

However, two days later the farmer couldn't find his prize rooster anywhere and it took a lot of searching before he was eventually discovered behind the barn, lying stiff with his legs in the air.

"Oh no," said the farmer, "my poor bird, all that work has killed him."

"Don't be daft, you fool," whispered the rooster "I'm just trying to entice that hovering vulture down."

★ ★ ★

A shapely young farmer's daughter took a cow over to the neighbouring farm to be serviced by their bull. The farmhand opened the gate and it wasn't long before both animals were well away.

"Oh my!" said the farmhand, breaking out in sweat. "I wish I was doing that."

"OK, do," she said, "I'm not stopping you."

"Thanks," he said, "but maybe the cow wouldn't like it."

★ ★ ★

A man taking his driving test is asked to make a U turn.

"Fetch me my wellies, I'll make her eyes water."

★ ★ ★

A man's car broke down in the middle of nowhere and he ended up seeking refuge at a farmer's cottage.

"Well, we've only got two bedrooms," he said, "but you can share a bed with my daughter as long as you don't bother her."

The man agreed and not wanting to disturb her, slipped into bed without turning the light on. In the morning he thanked the farmer for his hospitality and commented on how cold his daughter was.

"Oh yes," replied the farmer sadly. "We're burying her this morning."

★ ★ ★

A ventriloquist was being shown around a farm by a local yokel.

As a joke the ventriloquist made the bull look as if he was saying, "Hello there." The yokel did not react. So he then made the hen say, "This man has been stealing all my eggs." At which point the yokel got very flustered and said, "When we get to the sow, don't believe a word she says."

★ ★ ★

A farmer stopped work to have a mid-morning snack and as he sat there he watched the cock chasing the chicken around the farmyard. Having finished, the farmer threw his scraps on the ground and immediately the cock ran over to gobble them up.

"Bloody hell!" he said, "I hope I never get that hungry."

★ ★ ★

At the summer fayre, Farmer Brown has brought along his favourite horse and is making a lot of money by taking bets on anyone who could make him laugh. One cunning local comes up and takes up the bet. He whispers something in the horse's ear and the animal starts to laugh uncontrollably. Not to be outsmarted the farmer offers him double or nothing if he can make the horse cry.

The local goes round to the other side of the horse, out of sight of onlookers, and after a moment the horse starts to cry uncontrollably. As the farmer pays up, he asks the man how he managed to make the horse laugh and then cry.

"Well, first I told him my knob was bigger than his, and the second time I showed him."

★ ★ ★

Finding himself lost, a motorist stops to ask a farmer for directions and as they are talking he notices a pig with a wooden leg.

"Why's that pig got a wooden leg?" he asks.

"Oh, that pig is a real hero. Do you know he's been a life-saver. About four months ago our barn caught alight and if it hadn't been for that pig alerting us by his noise, we'd have lost all our horses."

"Very good," replies the motorist, "but why has he got a wooden leg?"

The farmer continues, "And do you know, not long after that I fell into a fast-flowing river and he saved my life by running for help."

"Yes, I see, but that doesn't explain why he's got a wooden leg."

"Oh, come on, sir, after all that pig's done for us, we couldn't bear to eat him in one go."

★ ★ ★

Backing out of the farmyard on his milk float, the man drove over and killed the prize rooster. Feeling very bad about it, he sought out the farmer's wife to let her know the bad news.

"Excuse me, madam, I'm so sorry but I've run over your prize rooster and I would like to replace it."

"Well, that's fine with me," she said. "You'll find the chickens behind the barn."

★ ★ ★

How can you stop a rooster from crowing on Monday morning?
Eat him for Sunday lunch.

★ ★ ★

A local crop dealer is on his way to visit a farm out in the middle of nowhere. It's a long distance to travel, so he puts his foot down and is going at 60mph when he's passed by a three-legged chicken that soon disappears into the distance.

He gets to the farm, carries out his business when he suddenly remembers the chicken and asks the farmer about it.

"Oh yes, one of our three-legged chickens. We raised them ourselves.

You see, there's me, my wife and our John and we all like the legs, but it was a waste when we had to kill two chickens for our Sunday lunch."
"And are they tasty?" asked the crop dealer.
"I don't know, we still haven't caught one of the buggers yet!"

★ ★ ★

A little girl was walking along the street pulling a cow by a rope. She passed the old village busybody, Mrs Seebad, who said, "My dear child, where on earth are you going with that animal?"
"I'm taking it to the bull," she said.
"Oh, fancy asking you to do a thing like that. Can't your dad do it?"
"Oh no, it has to be the bull," she said, smiling sweetly.

★ ★ ★

"Don't worry about the cow," said the vet to the farmer. "It just needs a pessary up its backside. Take this tube, simply insert it in the cow's bum and blow." When the farmer returned to his farm, he explained the method to his cowman and left him to it. Half an hour later, the cowman came looking for him. "I'm sorry, Mr Brooks, I can't seem to blow the damn thing up." Farmer Brooks went back to the cow shed, took the tube out, turned it round and re-inserted it. He then blew the pessary up first time. "Mr Brooks, why did you turn the tube round?" asked the cowman. "I didn't want to suck the end that had been in your dirty mouth!" he replied.

★ ★ ★

The vicar's out for his morning constitutional when he sees the local farmer in the field, shagging a pig. He walks further on and sees the farmer's son, shagging a sheep. Then just behind the barn he spots the grandfather tossing off. Unable to contain his anger, he goes up to the farmhouse and knocks loudly on the door. When the wife opens it, he yells, "It's absolutely disgusting: your husband's shagging pigs, your son's shagging sheep and then what do I see behind the barn but your father tossing himself off!"

"I know," she says sadly, "but, you see, dad's too old to go chasing the animals anymore."

★ ★ ★

An Australian tourist travelling through Wales sees a farmer with the back legs of a sheep stuck down his wellingtons.
"Are you shearing that sheep?" he asks.
"No bloody way, catch one of your own," comes the reply.

★ ★ ★

The old farmer wasn't a very friendly man; in fact, most of the time he was downright rude. One day a travelling salesman stopped by and, as they were talking, a fly landed on the man's chin.
"Is there something on my chin?" he asked.
"Ay," said the farmer. "It's a fanny fly – you usually find them on cows."
"Are you trying to imply that my chin looks like a fanny?" he demanded.
"I ain't saying that at all," said the farmer and then added, "but you can't fool the fly."

★ ★ ★

A man knocked on the door of a farmer's cottage and said, "I happened to notice you had some canary grass down in that bottom meadow, would you mind if I picked myself a few canaries?"
"Go right ahead, but you won't get any canaries" replied the farmer.
A little while later, the farmer spotted the man heading for home and was flabbergasted to see he had a cage full of canaries.
Some weeks later, the man returned.
"Would you mind if I took a walk down towards the stream. I've seen some toad flax and would like to collect a few toads."
"That's OK," said the farmer, "but you won't get any toads from toad flax."
An hour later the farmer couldn't believe his eyes when he saw the man had a bag full of toads.

The following week the man knocked at the door again. "Good morning, I've just noticed you have some pussy willow in those woods…"

"Just a moment, sir, I'll get my boots, I'm coming with you."

★ ★ ★

Three bulls had serviced the farmer's herd of cows for more than five years. During that time they had split the herd between them, each having an amount appropriate to their size, the biggest bull getting the most, and the smallest the fewest. This was an arrangement that suited them all. Then one day, the bulls discovered a fourth bull was going to join them.

"Stuff that," said the biggest bull, "he's not having any of my cows," and the others agreed they were not sharing either.

The following morning a huge lorry arrived at the gate of the field and out stormed the largest bull they had ever seen.

He stood in the field with his legs braced, and looked around extremely arrogantly.

"Oh well," said the biggest bull nervously. "I guess he can have a few of my cows. It'll be nice not to have to work so hard."

"Yeah, I agree," said the middle-sized bull, "there's no reason why we can't share a bit. He can have some of mine."

Suddenly the smallest bull started snorting and stamping his feet on the earth, sending up clouds of dust.

"Hey, listen," hissed the other two, "you don't want to go starting anything with him, he'll kill you. All you have to do is let him have some of your cows."

"He can have all my bloody cows," replied the small bull. "I just want him to know I'm a bull. Can't have him mistaking me for a cow!"

★ ★ ★

Two chickens were standing at the side of the road. One said to the other, "For God's sake don't cross, we'll never hear the end of it."

★ ★ ★

Why Did The Chicken Cross The Road?

JERRY FALWELL:
"Because the chicken was gay! Isn't it obvious? Can't you people see
the plain truth in front of your face? The chicken was going to the
'other side'. That's what 'they' call it: the 'other side'. Yes, my friends,
that chicken is gay. And, if you eat that chicken, you will become gay,
too. I say we boycott all chickens until we sort out this abomination
that the liberal media whitewashes with seemingly harmless phrases
like 'the other side'. That chicken should not be free to cross the road.
It's as plain and simple as that."

PAT BUCHANAN:
"To steal a job from a decent, hardworking American."

DR. SEUSS:
"Did the chicken cross the road?
Did he cross it with a toad?
Yes!
The chicken crossed the road,
But why it crossed,
I've not been told!"

ERNEST HEMINGWAY:
"To die. In the rain."

MARTIN LUTHER KING, JR:
"I envision a world where all chickens will be free to cross roads
without having their motives called into question."

GRANDPA:
"In my day, we didn't ask why the chicken crossed the road.
Someone told us that the chicken crossed the road, and that was good
enough for us."

ARISTOTLE:
"It is in the nature of chickens to cross the road."

KARL MARX:
"It was a historical inevitability."

SADDAM HUSSEIN:
"This was an unprovoked act of rebellion and we were quite justified in dropping 50 tons of nerve gas on it."

RONALD REAGAN:
"What chicken?"

CAPTAIN JAMES T KIRK:
"To boldly go where no chicken has gone before."

FREUD:
"The fact that you are at all concerned that the chicken crossed the road reveals your underlying sexual insecurity."

BILL GATES:
"I have just released eChicken 09, which will not only cross roads, but will lay eggs, file your important documents, and balance your checkbook and Internet Explorer is an inextricable part of eChicken."

EINSTEIN:
"Did the chicken really cross the road or did the road move beneath the chicken?"

BILL CLINTON:
"I did not cross the road with THAT chicken. What do you mean by chicken? Could you define chicken, please?"

LOUIS FARRAKHAN:
"The road, you will see, represents the black man. The chicken crossed the 'black man' in order to trample him and keep him down."

THE BIBLE:
"And God came down from the heavens, and He said unto the chicken, 'Thou shalt cross the road'. And the chicken crossed the road, and there was much rejoicing.

COLONEL SANDERS:
"I missed one?"

★ ★ ★

A horse walks into a bar, he sits down and the bartender asks him, "Why the long face?" A second horse walks in with jump leads attached to its head, he sits down and the bartender says, "I don't mind the long face, but don't you try starting anything!"

★ ★ ★

The farm inspector was on his annual tour of the county and had arrived at Farmer Giles' place. "So how many sheep do you have?" he asked. "I don't know," replied the farmer, "every time I try to count them, I fall asleep."

★ ★ ★

A kindly man came across a young boy whose cart had shed its load of manure. "Come back with me," he said, "we'll soon get you cleaned up, have a spot of lunch then I'll bring back my two sons to help you clear the road."
The boy hesitated. "I'm not really sure," he faltered, "my dad might not like that."
"I think your dad will be pleased you're doing something about it," said the man and eventually the boy was persuaded.
A couple of hours later, they returned with his two sons to begin clearing the load. "By the way, where is your dad?" asked the man.
"Under the manure," came the reply.

★ ★ ★

Deep within a forest a little turtle began to climb a tree. After hours of effort he reached the top, jumped into the air waving his front legs and crashed to the ground. After recovering, he slowly climbed the tree again, jumped and fell to the ground. The turtle tried again and again while a couple of birds sitting on a branch watched his sad efforts. Finally, the female bird turned to her mate. "Dear," she chirped, "I think it's time to tell him he's adopted."

★ ★ ★

Psychiatrist: What's your problem?
Patient: I think I'm a chicken.
Psychiatrist: How long has this been going on?
Patient: Ever since I was an egg!

★ ★ ★

Bill Clinton and his driver were cruising along a country road one night when all of a sudden they hit a pig, killing it instantly.
Bill told his driver to go up to the farmhouse and explain to the owners what had happened.
About one hour later Bill sees his driver staggering back to the car with a bottle of wine in one hand, a cigar in the other and his clothes all ripped and torn.
"What happened to you?" asked Bill.
"Well, the Farmer gave me the wine, his wife gave me the cigar and his 19-year-old daughter made mad passionate love to me."
"My God, what did you tell them?" asks Clinton.
The driver replies, "I'm Bill Clinton's driver, and I just killed the pig."

★ ★ ★

A big-city lawyer was representing the railroad in a lawsuit filed by an old rancher. The rancher's prize bull was missing from the section through which the railroad passed. The rancher claimed that the bull must have been hit by the train, and wanted to be paid the fair value of the bull.

The case was scheduled to be tried before the justice of the peace in the back room of the general store.

As soon as the rancher showed up, the attorney for the railroad pulled him aside and tried to get him to settle out of court. The lawyer did his best selling job, and finally the rancher agreed to take half of what he was asking. After the rancher had signed the release and took the check, the young lawyer couldn't resist gloating a little over his success, telling the rancher, "You know, I hate to tell you this, old man, but I put one over on you in there. I couldn't have won the case. The engineer was asleep and the fireman was in the caboose when the train went through your ranch that morning. I didn't have one witness to put on the stand. I bluffed you!"

The old rancher replied, "Well, I'll tell you, young feller, I was a little worried about winning that case myself, because that darned bull came home this morning."

★ ★ ★

While waiting for a bus, the blind man's dog decided to piss all over the blind man's legs. A passer-by commented to the blind man, "What! That dog just pissed all over your legs, and you are petting him?! Are you crazy?"

To which the blind man replied, "Madam, I am not petting him, I am feeling for his bottom, so I can kick him."

★ ★ ★

FILMS

A sleazy young man went to the cinema and sat next to a pretty girl. As the film started, he put his hand on her leg but she slapped him away. A little later, he tried again and put his hand on her knee, only to be pushed off again. Then when he put his hand on her thigh, she turned to him angrily and said, "You've got no chance. You're just wasting your time. I'm Picasso's daughter and what you're looking for is on the back of my neck!"

★ ★ ★

Did you hear about the film at the Soho sex club?
It must have been very emotional, there wasn't a dry fly in the place.

★ ★ ★

At long last the Cisco Kid is captured by the Sioux Indians, who bury him up to his neck in the sand to face a long and painful death. Out of respect for the 'Kid', the Indians grant him one last wish and he asks them to free his old trusty horse.
So the horse is freed and the Cisko Kid, whistles him over and whispers in his ear. The horse then runs away but appears an hour later with a beautiful girl on its back. The girl gets off, comes over to the Cisco Kid and lifts her skirt to show she has no knickers on. She then sits on his face and wiggles around.
As the Cisco Kid comes up for air, he shouts to his horse, "You silly bugger, I said go and get me a posse."

★ ★ ★

It was a glamorous Hollywood party and a beautiful, curvaceous blonde came up to one of the show business agents and said, "Wow, you really turn me on. Let's go somewhere quiet and I'll make mad, passionate love to you all night."
The agent replied, "I don't know, what's in it for me?"

★ ★ ★

Little Red Riding Hood is walking through the woods when she spots the big bad wolf hiding behind a tree.

"Come out, come out. I can see you, Mr Wolf," she shouts.

"How can you see me?" he asks.

"I saw your big bushy tail sticking out."

Mr Wolf turns and disappears deeper into the woods, but a few minutes later, Little Red Riding Hood shouts, "Come out, come out, Mr Wolf. I can see you behind the rocks."

Out comes the wolf and asks, "How can you see me?"

"I saw your big ears sticking out," she says.

Once again the wolf runs off further into the woods, but again he hears her shouting.

"Come out, come out, Mr Wolf. I can see you behind that bush."

"How did you see me this time?"

"I saw your long nose sticking out."

"Just who are you anyway?" asks the wolf angrily.

"I'm Little Red Riding Hood."

"And what are you doing in here?"

"I'm going to see my grandma."

"Well, fuck off and go and see her because I'm dying for a shit!" he yells.

★ ★ ★

Two girls are watching a film in the local cinema when one turns to the other in panic.

"Tracy, the man next to me is masturbating."

"Well, just ignore him."

"I can't, he's using my hand."

★ ★ ★

Did you hear why Snow White was asked to leave Fairyland?

She was found sitting on Pinocchio's face saying, "Tell a lie, tell the truth, tell a lie, tell the truth...."

★ ★ ★

An usherette in the local cinema was known to be an 'easygoing girl' and one night she bestowed her favours on the cinema manager. After an hour of humping, he was about to leave when he gave her two passes to the film premier of a much-advertised new drama. But instead of being grateful, she complained, "This isn't going to put food in my childrens' mouths."

"If it's food you wanted, you should have fucked a grocer," he retorted.

★ ★ ★

The film had only been on 20 minutes when a woman came rushing out into the foyer of the cinema looking very upset.

"I've been interfered with," she complained to the manager. He eventually managed to calm her down and took her to another section of the cinema. However, a short time later another woman ran out complaining of the same thing.

This was too much for the manager, so he took his torch and went to investigate. Lo and behold the torch picked up a bald-headed man crawling along on all fours.

"What's going on?" he demanded.

"I've lost my hairpiece" said the man. "I put my hand on it twice but it got away."

★ ★ ★

A reporter from the Hollywood gutter press was interviewing one of the industry's hottest starlets.

"Will you be telling all in your memoirs?" he asked.

"Oh yes, but the book won't be published until after my death."

"Oh great, I hope it's soon."

★ ★ ★

At the local cinema a man noticed a young woman sitting all by herself.

He was excited to see she had both hands under her skirt and was fingering herself furiously.

He moved to the next seat to her and offered his help.

She agreed, and the man started fingering her like crazy.

When he tired and withdrew his hand, he was surprised to see her go back to work on herself with both hands.

"Wasn't I good enough?" he asked sheepishly.

"You were great," she said, "but these crabs are still itching!"

★ ★ ★

HARD TIMES

A tramp was roaming the streets when he suddenly came across a £10 note lying on the pavement. Picking it up, he looked down at his old worn-out shoes and said, "Feet, I'm going to get you some new shoes." A little later he looked at his tattered clothes and said, "Legs, I'm going to get you some new trousers." A little later he noticed his willy had grown into a right big stonker. "Oh, oh," he said. "Who told you we'd come into money."

★ ★ ★

A frustrated young lady heard that men with big feet also had big members, so when a tramp came to the door with the biggest feet she'd ever seen he was invited inside. After wining and dining him, she then took him to bed. The next day, as he was leaving, she called out crossly, "By the way, in future try and wear shoes that fit you."

★ ★ ★

A couple of old tramps who haven't eaten for many days suddenly come upon a dead dog. The first tramp cries out, "At last, food", and he starts to eat the dog. "Don't you want any?" he asks his mate, who replies, "No thanks, mate, not at the moment."
When the first tramp has finished, they go on their way but after a few minutes the tramp that ate the dog groans in pain and vomits it up.
"Oh great!" exclaims the second tramp. "At last, just what I've been waiting for – a hot meal!"

★ ★ ★

Walking down the street, a man is approached by a tramp who begs him for some money. "Let me give you a drink," said the man.
"I don't drink," replied the tramp.
"Then let me give you a cigarette." "No, thanks. I don't smoke."
"How about this betting slip for the 2.30 at Cheltenham tomorrow."
Again the tramp refused, saying, "I don't gamble either."
Suddenly the man had an idea. "Why don't you come back with me and I'll cook you a three-course meal with all the trimmings?"

"Look," said the tramp. "Wouldn't it be just easier to give me the money?"

"Maybe, but I want my wife to see what happens to someone who doesn't drink, smoke or gamble."

★ ★ ★

Two down-and-out alcoholics had run out of money and were unable to buy any more grog. It was sending one of them completely round the twist, so his mate came up with a great idea. They just had a few pence left, enough to buy a sausage, which Bert shoved in Dick's flies. "OK, Dick, now watch this."

The two men went into a bar, ordered drinks which they soon polished off, and when the barman asked for the money Bert got down on to the floor and started sucking the sausage.

"Why, you disgusting buggers!" shouted the barman, "Get out of here or I'll have the law on you."

All day they repeated the trick and drank freely until they were completely sozzled.

"You know, Dick, my knees are bloody sore from kneeling on the floor so often."

"That's nothing," replied Bert "I lost the sausage after the second pub."

★ ★ ★

Did you hear about the two old tramps at Christmas?

Unable to afford turkey and stuffing, they bought two budgies and a pair of chest expanders.

★ ★ ★

A tramp, wearing only one boot, was shuffling down the street when he was stopped by a busybody woman.

"Do you realize you've lost a boot?" she said.

"Oh no," he replied. "I've just found a boot."

★ ★ ★

Two tramps are so hungry, they haven't eaten for days and are beginning to get quite desperate.

"John," said one, "I've got to have a crap; I'll just go behind that bush." So off he goes. Meanwhile, John remains where he is and he suddenly hears a very strange noise. "Bob, what's that funny noise I can hear? It sort of goes oh... oh... oh... oh..."

"How should I know, I can't hear anything." And he squats down again.

"Bob, Bob, it's that noise again. Look, I'll have to come round and see what it is." So John goes behind the bush trying to locate the noise – "oh... oh... oh... oh..."

"Oh, I see," he says triumphantly, "it's just your arse eating the grass."

★ ★ ★

An old tramp walks into Social Services with a pig on a lead.

"Can you find somewhere for me and my pig to live?" he asks. "Just a bed if that's all you've got. My pig can sleep underneath it."

"But what about the smell?" asks the official.

"Oh, the pig don't mind."

★ ★ ★

The East End gang boss had always been very careful whom he employed, for fear of being grassed up. He thought he'd been really clever with his crooked accountant who was deaf and dumb. There wasn't much of a risk that he would overhear too much. However, it eventually dawned on the boss that someone was stealing money from him. A lot of money! And it didn't take long for him to discover it was his crooked accountant.

"Benny," he ordered, "get that bastard down here pronto and get Marty to come with him. He can read the hand signs."

Later in his office, the boss started interrogating him.

"Marty, ask him what he's done with the money."

At first the terrified accountant signalled his ignorance of the theft but when a gun was put to his head, he spilled the beans.

With rapid hand movements, he explained that he'd hidden all the money in a trunk in an old derelict factory, two miles from the office.

"So what did he say?" demanded the boss impatiently.

Marty thought quickly and replied, "It's no good boss. He says you haven't got the bottle to shoot him, you can get stuffed."

★ ★ ★

A millionaire had been going out with a croupier from the local casino for two months. They'd had a great time, often staying out until the early hours of the morning, but both of them knew nothing serious would come of it.

Then one evening the croupier turned to the man and said, "Why don't we get married?"

The man looked shocked.

"Oh come on, Rose, you know that's not possible. When I marry it has to be to a titled family."

"I know," she sighed.

"Then why did you ask?"

"I just wanted to know how it felt to lose a fortune."

★ ★ ★

A rich couple decided to hire a full-time handyman to look after the house, all the outbuildings and also the garden. They offered very low wages so it took a while to select a candidate, but out of despair they eventually chose a man from the neighbouring village.

The following weekend they left him in charge while they visited friends in the next county. Alas, when they returned, they discovered the man sitting in their lounge with water pouring through the ceiling.

"What the hell's going on?" they demanded. "We hired you to make any necessary repairs. Why haven't you mended the roof?"

"Can't," he replied. "It's raining. It's too wet."

"Well, why didn't you do it while it was dry?" they said in exasperation.

"Couldn't, it wasn't leaking then."

★ ★ ★

A woman rings her husband up at work to tell him she's won the jackpot on the lottery and that he'd better start packing.

"Darling, that's wonderful!" he shouts with glee. "Where are we going?" "I'm not bothered," she replied. "Just make sure you're gone by the time I get home."

★ ★ ★

A man who thought he could charm the birds out of the trees met his match one night. The man had just learned that his father only had days to live and then he would inherit over half a million pounds. Overjoyed at the promised wealth, he celebrated at the local wine bar, where he saw a ravishing long-legged blonde. He couldn't wait to brag to her and indeed she was so interested in him, they went back to his house together. The next day she became his stepmother.

★ ★ ★

"It's no good, sir," said the DSS man to his interviewee. "It's no good saying you feel like 65 – you have to be 65."

★ ★ ★

Two men sitting on a park bench reading newspapers. Suddenly one of them puts down his paper and bursts uncontrollably into tears.

"Excuse me," says the other. "I can't help but notice you're very upset about something. Can I help?"

"I've just read that the richest man in the whole world has died."

"I'm sorry to hear that. You look very upset, were you related to him?"

"No," sobbed the man, "that's why I'm crying."

★ ★ ★

What's green and takes an hour to drink?
The family allowance cheque.

★ ★ ★

Flo's husband dies and because he was such a popular fella, she decides to put an announcement in the paper. But not having a lot of money, she tells the local newspaper she wants to keep it as short as possible. "Just put 'Ben Potts dead'."

"Actually, Madam, you can have up to six words for the same price. Would you like to add anything?"

Flo thinks for a while and then says, "Yes, OK, can you add 'Ferret for sale'?"

★ ★ ★

A man was always thinking up ways of making easy money and one day he thought he was on to a certainty. He taught his parrot to say the 23rd psalm and then took it down the local pub.

"I bet anyone £5 my parrot can recite the 23rd psalm, from beginning to end," he said.

Quite a lot of interest was shown and the money laid out on the bar.

"Go on then, parrot, recite the psalm."

But the parrot remained completely dumb and eventually the man took it home, having lost quite a lot of money.

"Why the bloody hell didn't you do what we'd practised for so long, you feathery little git?"

"Now hold on," said the parrot. "Think what the odds will be tomorrow when we go back."

★ ★ ★

At a party to celebrate her 21st birthday, the daughter put all her presents on display including a cheque from her father to buy a new car. During the evening the guests would wander over to take a look at the presents and on one occasion a man was standing at the table looking at the cheque, doubled up with laughter.

"Mum," whispered the girl, "who is that man?"

"Him? Oh, he's your dad's bank manager."

★ ★ ★

The rich and elegant old woman stopped to reverse her Rolls into the only free parking space.

But as she was slowly backing in, a young girl in a nifty little sports car, came up behind her and nipped into the space.

"You've got to be young and daring to do that," laughed the girl.

The old woman ignored her and continued to reverse into the parking spot, pushing the sports car out of the parking space and down a slope, where it smashed into a wall and burst into flames.

The old woman finished parking, then turned to the dumbfounded girl and said, "And you've got to be old and rich to do that."

★ ★ ★

A woman has her portrait painted by a local artist and asks him if he would paint her dripping with fabulous jewels.

She explains, "If I die before my husband and he gets married again, I want his second wife to go crazy looking for the stones."

★ ★ ★

The retired colonel is striding out through the village when he is accosted by one of his manservants who's a little the worse for wear.

"Hello, your colonelship sir," grins the man. "How the devil are we?" he mimics.

Not only drunk but insulting! The colonel is outraged and remarks forcefully, "Drunk as a skunk!"

The man whispers conspirationally, "Don't worry, sir, your secret's safe with me, I've had a bit to drink myself."

★ ★ ★

The poor man was in great difficulties. His business was failing and it looked as if he was facing bankruptcy.

As a last resort he popped into the local church and kneeling down he prayed fervently.

"Oh God, please don't let this happen to me, please let me win the lottery."

But on Saturday night, he had no luck. The following week, the situation got worse.

The man lost his house and all his possessions, so once again he went into Church and prayed desperately, "Oh please, I beg you, please let me win the lottery."

But on Saturday, he had no luck.

On the following Monday, his wife and children left him and he was now completely on his own.

He ran into church, got down on his knees and pleaded, "Oh God, all has gone, I have nothing left. Have pity on me, I beg you. Please help me win the lottery."

At that moment, there was a tremendous thunderclap, a bright flashing light and God boomed out, "Help me out on this one, Amos; buy a bloody ticket!"

★ ★ ★

The down-and-out man had spent his morning begging from street to street. He hadn't done very well and was just about to give up when he noticed a very posh woman walking up the private road to her mansion.

"Excuse me, madam," he said as politely as possible. "Can you spare a bob or two?"

"I'll do better than that," she said. "How are you with a paint brush?"

"Erm, okay, I suppose," he replied, puzzled.

"Good, there's a can of orange paint here. If you paint the porch round the back, then I'll pay you a decent day's wages."

The tramp disappeared and nothing was seen of him for the next three hours at which point he reappeared with an empty can.

"All finished?" she asked.

"It is," he replied. "But just one thing," he added helpfully, "it's a Ferrari round the back, not a Porsche".

★ ★ ★

Two tramps were walking along the railroad tracks one day and one tramp said to the other, "I'm the luckiest guy in the world."

"Why is that?" said the other tramp.

"Well, I was walking down these tracks last week and I found a £20 note. I went into town and bought a case of wine and was drunk for three days.'

The other tramp said, "That must have been pretty good, but I think I'm the luckiest guy in the world. I was walking down these very tracks about two weeks ago, and just up ahead was a gorgeous naked woman tied to the tracks. I untied her and took her up there in the trees and I had sex with her for two days."

"Jesus," said the first tramp. "You are the luckiest guy; did you get a blow job, too?"

"Well, no," the other tramp said, "I never found her head."

★ ★ ★

A blonde named Barbara appeared on *Who Wants To Be A Millionaire*...

Host: "Barbara, you've done very well so far – £500,000 and one lifeline left. The next question will give you the million pounds if you get it right... but if you get it wrong you will drop back to £32,000 – are you ready?"

Barbara: "Sure I'll give it a go."

Host: "Which of the following birds does not build its own nest? Is it...

A Robin
B Sparrow
C Cuckoo
D Thrush

"Remember, Barbara, the question is worth one million pounds."

Barbara: "It's a cuckoo."

Host: "You're sure now? You can walk away with the £500,000 or play on for the million."

Barbara: "I want to play, I'll go with C – Cuckoo."

Host: "Is that your final answer?"

Barbara: "It is."

Host: "Are you confident?"

Barbara: "Absolutely!"

Host: "Barbara, you had £500,000 and you said C – Cuckoo. Well... you're right! You have just won ONE MILLION POUNDS. Here is your cheque. You have been a great contestant and a real gambler. Audience, please put your hands together for Barbara."

That night Barbara calls her friend Carol and they go to a local bar for a celebration drink.

As they are sipping their champagne. Carol turns to Barbara and says, "Tell me, how did you know that it was the cuckoo that does not build its own nest?"

"It was so simple," Barbara replied. "Everybody knows that cuckoos live in clocks."

★ ★ ★

A young man was having money problems, and needed £200 to get his car fixed and roadworthy. The problem was, he had run out of people to borrow from. So, he calls his parents via the operator, and reverses the charge and says to his dad, "I need to borrow two hundred quid." At the other end, his father says, "Sorry, I can't hear you, son, I think there may be a bad line."

The boy shouts, "Two hundred. I need two hundred pounds!"

"Sorry, I still can't hear you clearly," repeats his father.

The operator cuts in, "Sorry to butt in, but I can hear him perfectly."

The father says, "Oh, good. YOU lend him the money!"

★ ★ ★

HONEYMOON DAYS

The honeymoon couple couldn't wait to get to their bridal suite. As soon as the door closed they tore their clothes off and dived under the sheets. But suddenly the bride began to shake.

"I caaaan't heeeelp it."

She explained she had a curious ailment which only happened once a year, but it meant she had uncontrollable shakes.

Quickly, the bridegroom had an idea. He rang for room service and asked them to send up four waiters.

When they arrived he got them each to take either an arm or a leg and hold her down on the bed. Then he inserted his todger and shouted, "OK, lads, let her go!"

★ ★ ★

It was decided that the newly weds would spend their honeymoon night with her parents. But the walls were very thin and mum and dad were disturbed by all the humping noises.

"I know," said the father, "every time they do it, we will do it."

After an hour, the honeymooners went quiet and everyone fell asleep. But two hours later they started again and after 45 minutes, peace was restored and the parents fell into an exhausted sleep. However, around dawn activity began again and the father was forced to shout out, "Stop it, you're killing your mother."

★ ★ ★

A young hillbilly returns alone from his honeymoon and when asked where his new wife is, replies, "I found out she was a virgin, so I shot her."

"Quite right," comes the reply. "If she wasn't good enough for her family then she sure ain't good enough for ours."

★ ★ ★

"Oh sure," said the frustrated wife. "My husband's a winner all right! When it comes to lovemaking, he always finishes first."

★ ★ ★

After a wonderful first night of their honeymoon, the man came down to breakfast in the hotel dining room. Looking through the window at the magnificent scenery one of his fellow guests greeted him warmly. "Good morning, a delightful spot, sir."

"Oh yes," replied the man, "and so well concealed."

★ ★ ★

A young couple got married but on the first night of their honeymoon quarrelled about politics – she's Liberal, he's Conservative. Sometime later, having turned their backs on each other, she said, "Sweetheart, there's a split in the Liberal Party and I think it's a good time for the Conservative Party to get in."

"Well, it's too damned late. The Conservative stood as an Independent and now he's lost his deposit."

★ ★ ★

On the morning after their honeymoon night, the husband came down to breakfast to see a lettuce, and only a lettuce, on his plate. "What's this?" he asked puzzled, "I just wanted to see if you ate like a rabbit too," she replied.

★ ★ ★

A middle-aged couple went to Las Vegas for their second honeymoon, but lost all their money gambling and didn't have enough left to pay the hotel bill. Feeling quite desperate, they happened to pass a poster advertising a rodeo. Enormous prizes could be won for staying on the bucking bronco. The husband decided to have a go even though many had tried before him and all had fallen off. To the amazement of the onlookers he managed to stay on and won $30,000. The wife was dumbfounded. "How did you manage that? You've never been on a horse in your life." "I know, but don't you remember when we went on our honeymoon and you had that dreadful cough?"

★ ★ ★

Two friends get married at the same time and go on honeymoon together. They decide to have a bet on who will perform the most times on the first night. They will put the score up outside the bedroom door.

John performed three times and notched up 111 outside the door.

Next morning, when Bill staggered down after seeing John's score, he said, "Well done, mate, a hundred and eleven, you beat me by two!"

★ ★ ★

A young newly wed couple were staying with his folks but when they went to bed that night they were unable to allow their passions to erupt for fear of making too much noise and waking them up.

"Let's go to a hotel," he suggested.

So they packed the suitcase but had trouble closing the lid.

Next door, the father heard her say, "Let me sit on it," and a moment later he heard his son say, "Let's both sit on it."

Amazed, the father jumped out of bed and rushed to the door saying, "I've just got to see this!"

★ ★ ★

The night before they are due to get married, the intended groom suffers a very bad accident and the part of his body most affected is his willy.

When the doctor realizes the man's getting married the next day, he bandages up the injured member as carefully as possible and surrounds it with little splints.

The following night in the bridal suite his wife starts to strip for him. She takes off her top, exposes her boobs and says, "These have never been touched by any other man."

Then she takes her knickers off and says, "And no man has ever seen this."

At that point the man opens his dressing gown and says, "Well, look at this. It's still in the original packaging."

★ ★ ★

"Darling, what's wrong?" asked the newly wedded husband of his tearful wife.

"Didn't you like last night?"

"Oh yes," she sobbed, "but look at it now, we've used it all up."

★ ★ ★

A 90-year-old man and his 19-year-old wife came back from their honeymoon and the man was asked if he'd had a good time.

"Not bad, I suppose," he said. "Trouble is, have you ever tried putting a marshmallow into a child's piggy bank?"

★ ★ ★

A girl married a quiet, humble man and after one week, he came home flustered. "When I got to work this morning, I found a pencil tied to my willy." "That's right," she said. "I thought if you couldn't come, at least you could write."

★ ★ ★

A couple on their honeymoon ask for a suite in the local hotel.

The clerk asks them if they want the bridal. "No, that's all right," replies the groom. "I'll hold on to her ears until she gets the hang of it."

★ ★ ★

A 75-year-old man and 19-year-old girl get married. On their wedding night he gets into bed and holds up four fingers.

Surprised, the girl says, "You want to do it four times tonight?"

"No, no," replies the old man. "I meant pick a finger."

★ ★ ★

It is a special honeymoon hotel and on the big night three men find themselves stranded on their balconies. "Bloody hell," complains the first man. "She's pushed me out here and locked the door just because I slapped her on her backside and said she had a beautiful big arse."

"Same here," groans the second man. "I just said my wife had great big tits."

They look over at the third man and one of them says, "I guess you've put your foot in it as well?"

"No," retorts the man, "but I sure as hell could have."

On their honeymoon night, he stripped off and his wife exclaimed, "Oh, what a cute dinky winky!"

"Doreen," he said sternly, "that's no dinky, winky, that's my cock."

"Oh no," she replied, "a cock is big and fat and long."

★ ★ ★

Have you heard about the miserly man who got married and went to Cornwall for his honeymoon, on his own? His wife had been there before.

★ ★ ★

It was their honeymoon night. The Reverend Johns and his new wife retired to the honeymoon suite and he disappeared into the bathroom to get ready. When he came out, his wife was already in bed.

"Oh, Mabel, I thought you'd be on your knees," he said.

"Oh, we can do it that way later. For the moment, I just want to see your face," she replied.

★ ★ ★

A five-times divorced woman is convinced that the only way she will be happy is if she marries a man who has had no sexual experience with women.

For three years she searches the country and eventually finds a strapping young man in Wales.

After a short courtship, they get married and retire to the honeymoon suite. She disappears into the bathroom to make herself as sexy as possible and when she returns, she's astonished to find all the furniture has been moved over to one wall.

"What's going on?" she asks astonished.

"I don't know what it's like to shag a woman, but if it's anything like a sheep, I want as much room as possible," he replies.

★ ★ ★

Man and woman had been dating for about a year and their relationship was taking a turn towards getting serious.

Man proposed and she accepted, however she told him that she wanted him to know that her chest was just like a baby's.

He said that he loved her and that her measurements didn't matter to him.

He told her that his penis was also like a baby.

She said that she loved him and size didn't matter.

Come the day of the wedding and all went well.

That night the happy couple checked into the honeymoon suite at the resort hotel.

The blushing bride was in the bathroom putting on a sexy nightie.

Her husband was in the bed waiting.

As she entered the bedroom, she reminded him of her confession about her chest being like a baby's.

"Don't worry, honey," he said.

She took her night gown off and her breasts were the smallest he had ever seen.

He said that he was going to get undressed and reminded her of his confession about his penis being like a baby.

As he took his pants off, the new bride said, "Good God All Mighty. I thought you said your penis was like a baby."

"It is," he said, "9 pounds and 19 inches long!"

★ ★ ★

JUDGEMENT

A man is up before the courts for walking down the High Street completely naked.

"Is it true that you didn't have a stitch on?" asks the Judge.

"That's right, Your Honour."

"Well, have you no shame? Are you married?"

"Yes, Your Honour."

"And how many children do you have?"

"Sixteen, Your Honour."

"Release this man, he was only in his work clothes."

★ ★ ★

"You have been brought before this court to answer the allegation that you stole a young woman's bicycle. How do you plead?"

"Not guilty, M'lord," said the young man. "I was walking down the lane when this lady cycled by, stopped when she saw me and asked me to kiss her. Then she took all her clothes off and said I could have anything I wanted. Well, Your Honour, I don't wear ladies clothes, so I took the bicycle."

★ ★ ★

"Mrs Mopps, you are up before the court for beating your husband black and blue. Do you have anything to say for yourself, before I pass sentence?"

"Yes, M'lud. Our Jack came home so drunk I locked him out of the house because of his disgusting behaviour. But he was hammering on the door, and said he was sure I'd open up if I knew what he was knocking with. So I opened the door, M'lud, and he gave me a box of chocolates. That's when I hit him."

★ ★ ★

Judge to husband, "I'm awarding your wife £300 a month."

"Well, that's very generous, M'lud, I'll try and chip in a couple of pounds myself."

★ ★ ★

"Madam, you are up before this court for driving on the wrong side of the road. Do you have anything to say in your defence?"

"Yes, M'lud, the other side was full."

★ ★ ★

When a witness was asked if a certain event had surprised him, he replied, "Why, you could have buggered me through my oilskins."

The Judge leaned over to the Counsel and said, "I think he means he was taken aback."

★ ★ ★

A young girl was in the witness box giving evidence against her boss for his sexual advancements towards her.

"And what did he say?" asked the barrister.

At this point, the girl was too embarrassed to repeat it, so it was suggested that she write it down for the jury and the judge to read.

First it was passed to the Foreman, who read, "Get your knickers off and meet me in the basement."

The Foreman then handed it to Miss Wantin, an elderly spinster who had fallen asleep and had to be woken up. She read the note, gave Fred a wink and a toothless smile, and put the note in her pocket.

★ ★ ★

A policeman, his dog and a policewoman were on night duty. It was very cold and the policewoman shivered.

"Are you all right?" asked the policeman.

"Yes," she replied. "I just forgot to put on my black woollen knickers before coming out."

"Don't worry," said the policeman. "My dog's well trained. Let him sniff between your legs and we'll send him back to the station to get them."

Some time passed before the dog reappeared with part of the sergeant's hand between his teeth.

★ ★ ★

Police have announced that they would like to interview a man wearing high heels and black lace knickers, but the Chief Constable has stated they must wear their uniforms instead.

★ ★ ★

Last week, a policeman stopped me driving the wrong way up a one-way street.
He said, "Didn't you see the arrow?"
"No," I replied. "Honestly, officer, I didn't even see the Indians."

★ ★ ★

"Good morning, I'm a criminal lawyer," said the man to his new client. "Oh well, at least you're not ashamed about describing yourself," came the reply.

★ ★ ★

A policeman on night duty thought he heard a noise up an alley and when he shone his torch he saw a woman with her blouse undone and her knickers round her ankles eating a packet of mints.
"What's going on?" he asked.
"Blimey, has he gone?" she replied.

★ ★ ★

A crafty barrister was defending a beautiful, shapely blonde accused of fraud and in his final address he turned to the all-male jury and said, "Gentlemen, are we going to see this poor, very friendly woman spend the next few years in jail, or should she return to her private and secluded flat at 48 Green Walk, telephone number 491 7360?"

★ ★ ★

"Before I pass sentence have you anything to say?" demanded the judge.
"Fuck all," came the reply.

The judge turned to one of the court officials and said, "I didn't hear that; what did he say?"

"He said fuck all, M'lud," whispered the official.

"Oh, that's odd. I was sure I'd seen his lips move."

★ ★ ★

Driving home from the pub one night a couple were stopped for speeding.

"You were doing 40mph in a 30mph zone," said the officer.

"Oh no, you're wrong," said the driver.

"I assure you, sir, that my instruments are very accurate and that you were driving much too fast."

At that point his wife leant across and said to the officer. "It's no good arguing with him now, not when he's had a drink."

★ ★ ★

A man was up before the court on a charge of vagrancy. He had lost his job, house and family and fallen on hard times.

The judge found him guilty as charged and looking down at him said, "Young man, it is drink and drink alone that have brought you before this court today."

On hearing this, the young man cheered up considerably. "Oh thank you, M'lud, everyone else says it's my fault."

★ ★ ★

A man was up in court on a charge of soliciting. He had approached one of the principal bass singers in the local opera company, the judge was told. "If that's so, then case dismissed," replied the judge. "I've heard the singers and in my opinion they all need fucking."

★ ★ ★

A young boy of 12 was in court charged with being the father of a new-born baby.

In his defence, counsel asked the boy to show the court his penis. "There," he said triumphantly. "Such a small, limp exhibit." And taking it in his hand he tossed it from side to side, saying, "Consider, members of the jury, whether this immature penis could possibly ever have fathered a child." At this point, the young boy tapped his defence counsel on the shoulder and whispered, "If you don't let go, we're going to lose this case."

★ ★ ★

When the man was found humping his girlfriend in the railway carriage he was charged with having a first-class ride in a second-class carriage.

★ ★ ★

"John Smith and Mary Owen, you are up before the court today for causing a serious breach of the peace and very nearly forcing the number 49 bus off the road. Have you anything to say in your defence?"
"Yes, Your Honour. We're very sorry for our behaviour but we were the victims of circumstance. Mary collapsed in the middle of the road and I knelt down to give her mouth-to-mouth resuscitation, but before we knew what was happening, passion took over and away we went. All of a sudden, I was coming, she was coming, and the bus was the only one that had brakes."

★ ★ ★

A woman got a divorce on the grounds that her husband's penis was too big. Two years later she was up before the same judge, this time requesting a divorce because her husband's penis was too small. Her divorce went through but as she was leaving court the judge warned, "Madam, this court will not look too favourably upon you if you appear before us again with a third husband. We have more important things to do than sort out the right fitting for you."

★ ★ ★

The judge addressed the defendant, a sickly 65-year-old man.

"You have been charged with kerb crawling on September 4 of this year; how do you plead?"

"Guilty, Your Honour," said the man, going into a coughing spasm.

"You are also charged that on September 21, you were found in an illegal club watching pornographic films; how do you plead?"

"Guilty, Your Honour," replied the man suffering another bout of bad coughing.

"And finally, last week you were found with a well-known prostitute in a compromising position in a dark alley; how do you plead?"

During a bout of coughing that shook the man's whole body, he replied, "Guilty, Your Honour."

In a sudden moment of compassion, the judge said. "Look, before I pass sentence, would you like to suck a Fisherman's Friend?"

"No, thanks. Don't you think I'm in enough trouble already?"

★ ★ ★

"Young man, you are up before the court for bad behaviour towards Penny Ball, our celebrated referee's one and only daughter. You are fined £100 for handling, bad tackling and pulling off the jumper."

★ ★ ★

A shoplifter was caught red-handed trying to steal a watch from an exclusive jewelry store.

"Listen," said the shoplifter, "I know you don't want any trouble either. What do you say I just buy the watch and we forget about this?"

The manager agreed and wrote up the sales slip.

The crook looked at the slip and said, "This is a little more than I intended to spend. Can you show me something less expensive?"

★ ★ ★

Farmer Joe decided his injuries from the accident were serious enough to take the trucking company (responsible for the accident) to court. In court, the trucking company's fancy lawyer was questioning farmer Joe. "Didn't you say, at the scene of the accident, 'I'm fine'?" said the lawyer.

Farmer Joe responded, "Well, I'll tell you what happened. I had just loaded my favorite mule Bessie into the..."

"I didn't ask for any details," the lawyer interrupted. "Just answer the question. Did you not say, at the scene of the accident, 'I'm fine!'"

Farmer Joe said, "Well, I had just got Bessie into the trailer and I was driving down the road..."

The lawyer interrupted again and said, "Judge, I am trying to establish the fact that, at the scene of the accident, this man told the Highway Patrolman on the scene that he was just fine. Now several weeks after the accident he is trying to sue my client. I believe he is a fraud. Please tell him to simply answer the question."

By this time the Judge was fairly interested in Farmer Joe's answer and said to the lawyer, "I'd like to hear what he has to say about his favourite mule Bessie."

Joe thanked the Judge and proceeded, "Well, as I was saying, I had just loaded Bessie, my favourite mule, into the trailer and was driving her down the highway when this huge semi-truck and trailer ran the stop sign and smacked my truck right in the side. I was thrown into one ditch and Bessie was thrown into the other. I was hurting real bad and didn't want to move. However, I could hear ole Bessie moaning and groaning. I knew she was in terrible shape just by her groans. Shortly after the accident a Highway Patrolman came on the scene. He could hear Bessie moaning and groaning so he went over to her. After he looked at her he took out his gun and shot her between the eyes. Then the Patrolman came across the road with his gun in his hand and looked at me. He said, "Your mule was in such bad shape I had to shoot her – how are you feeling?"

★ ★ ★

A good lawyer knows the law. A great lawyer knows the judge.

★ ★ ★

The cross-eyed judge looked at the three defendants in the dock and said to the first one, "So how do you plead?"

"Not guilty," said the second defendant.

"I wasn't talking to you," the judge replied.

"I never said a word," the third defendant replied.

★ ★ ★

"And where do you think you're going at this time of night?" the police officer asked the staggering drunk.

"To a lecture," he replied.

"Come off it. It's one o'clock in the morning. Who'd be giving a lecture at this time of night?"

"My wife."

★ ★ ★

Our town was so lawless, if you went to buy a pair of tights, they'd ask you for your head size.

★ ★ ★

"Luigi, Luigi," shouted the children as they lined up outside the ice cream van.

But Luigi was nowhere to be seen. The motor was running, the music was playing loudly, but no-one was serving.

"Stand back, kids," said a policeman attracted by all the noise. "What have we here?"

The policeman peered inside the van and caught sight of Luigi lying on the floor. He was covered in chocolate sauce, mixed nuts and lots of fresh cream.

"Sarge," he said, speaking into his radio. "This is PC Mann, I need some back-up at Luigi's ice-cream van on Prospect Street. It's bad news I'm afraid, Luigi's topped himself."

★ ★ ★

This particular evening, the traffic cop was determined to crack down on drunk and disorderly drivers. He parked near one of the toughest, noisiest and rowdiest bars in town, sat back and waited.

A little later, a man staggered out of the bar, tripped over and then attempted to open three cars before he eventually found his own. The man got in and immediately fell asleep. Feeling very pleased with himself, the officer waited all evening until everyone left the bar, got into their cars and drove away. Finally, the sleeper woke up, started the engine and began to pull away.

"Got you," said the police officer to himself and he pulled the driver over and administered a breathalyzer test. He was astonished to find the man passed with a zero blood-alcohol reading.

"But how can that be?" he said.

"Well, you see, officer," said the man, "it's like this: tonight I'm the designated decoy."

★ ★ ★

A man went to his lawyer and said, "I would like to make a will, but I don't know exactly how to go about it."

The lawyer said, "No problem, leave it all to me."

The man looked upset and said, "Well, I knew you were going to take the biggest slice, but I would like to leave a little to my children too!"

★ ★ ★

What do you call a lawyer with an IQ of 10? A lawyer.
What do you call a lawyer with an IQ of 15? Your honour.

★ ★ ★

A music hall entertainer is stopped by the police for having a faulty break light and on the back seat of the car, the policeman spots a whole set of knives. He asks the man why he has them – doesn't he know it's against the law to carry knives?

The man explains that the knives are used in his act – he juggles them. The policeman insists the man gets out to show him so he gets out and stands at the roadside performing his act. Just then, another car drives by and the driver turns to his wife saying, "Thank God, I gave up the drinking, those tests just get tougher every day!"

★ ★ ★

The traffic police spotted a man staggering towards his car and opening the driver's door. They stopped and confronted him.
"Excuse me, sir, but I hope you are not intending to drive the car?"
"Of course I am, officer," he slurred. "I'm in no state to walk."

★ ★ ★

A naive young man found himself in the wrong part of town late at night, and got attacked by a gang of muggers. He put up a terrific fight, but was eventually overcome and lay bleeding on the ground. When the muggers went through his pockets, all they found was a handful of loose change. "You went through all that just to protect a few coins?" they asked amazed. "Oh, I see," said the man. "For a while I thought you were after the £500 hidden in my shoe."

★ ★ ★

A lawyer passed on and found himself in Heaven, but was not at all happy with his accommodation. He complained to St Peter, who told him that his only recourse was to appeal. The lawyer gave notice that he intended to appeal, but was then told that he would have to wait at least three years before his appeal could be heard. The lawyer was then approached by the devil, who told him that he would be able to arrange an appeal to be heard in a few days, if the lawyer was willing to change his abode to Hell. The lawyer asked, "Why can appeals be heard so much sooner in Hell?" The devil answered, "All the judges end up down here with us."

★ ★ ★

"If you don't keep the noise down, I'm going to have to arrest you," advised the policeman to the drunk who was staggering down the road singing at the top of his voice.

"Oh, have a heart, officer," slurred the man, "it's the works' outing."

The policeman looked round him, "So where are the others then?"

"There aren't any others," he replied. "I'm self-employed."

★ ★ ★

The defendant stood up in the dock and said to the judge, "I don't recognize this court!" "Why?" asked the Judge.

"Because you've had it decorated since the last time I was here."

★ ★ ★

"You didn't stop at the last junction," said the policeman to the motorist. "I'll have to breathalyze you." The officer held up the bag.

"What's that?" asked the driver.

"This tells you if you've had too much to drink," he replied.

"Well, I never!" he exclaimed. "I'm married to one of those."

★ ★ ★

The trial was going badly for the defendant. He was charged with murder and although the body had never been found, there was enough evidence to convict him. As a last desperate effort, the defending lawyer decided to play a trick. He stood up, looked at the jury and said, "Ladies and gentlemen, I have an announcement to make. In exactly 30 seconds, the person presumed murdered will walk into this courtroom." There was stunned silence as all the jury looked towards the door, but nothing happened.

The defending lawyer continued, "So members of the jury, although I made that last statement up, because you all looked at the door proves there is an element of doubt. Therefore, I put it to you that you have no other course than to find the defendant not guilty."

A short while later the jury retired to consider their verdict and it was only 20 minutes before they returned.

"We find the defendant guilty," they proclaimed.

"But how can that be?" protested the lawyer. "You all looked towards the door, you must have had some doubt."

The foreman of the jury replied, "That's true, we did all look towards the door. But your client didn't."

★ ★ ★

The shopaholic, 'money-mad' woman told the judge she couldn't serve on the jury because she didn't believe in capital punishment. "But, madam," replied the judge patiently. "This is not a murder trial; it's a simple case of a husband reneging on his promise to buy his wife a new sports car." "Okay, okay," she conceded. "Maybe there is a case for capital punishment after all."

★ ★ ★

The judge said to the drunk, "Please stand, Mr Havermore. Before passing sentence, I need to know if you are sober enough to understand you have been brought here for drinking."

"Oh, that's very kind, Your Honour, but I won't if you don't mind. I'm trying to give to give it up, you see."

★ ★ ★

There had been so much trouble in the border settlement, that a curfew had been enforced from 10pm. Two men set out to patrol the eastern part of town and were walking down the main street. Suddenly a shot rang out and the first patrolman ran over to find his partner holding out his smoking gun and a man lying dead at his feet.

"Why did you have to shoot him?" he asked. "There's still 20 minutes to go before curfew."

"Maybe," replied his partner, "but I know where this man lives and he wouldn't have got home in time."

★ ★ ★

A man was in court for killing his wife. When he saw the jury – only two men and the rest women, he felt his chances of getting off were slim. Now he was quite a handsome man, so in desperation he thought he would try to seduce one of the women jurors and persuade her to drop the murder verdict to one of manslaughter. He succeeded and when the trial came to an end, the jury left to consider their verdict. A few hours later they returned and found him guilty of manslaughter. He sighed with relief and later managed to speak to the woman to thank her for all she'd done. "Well, it wasn't that easy," she replied. "The others wanted to acquit you."

★ ★ ★

"Hey! That bottle of magic potion you sold me was supposed to make me more intelligent... I'm beginning to think it's a big con."
"There, you see! You're more intelligent already."

★ ★ ★

The local game warden in a small town in Oregon arrested a man for killing and eating an egret. The judge asked him why he did it. "I was just trying to feed my hungry family and I've never done anything like it before." The judge agreed to let the man go free, since it was his one and only offence. "Before you go, though, I want to ask you a question," the judge quipped, "What does egret taste like?" "Well, Your Honour," the man told him. "It's not as tender as Spotted Owl, but it's better than Bald Eagle!"

★ ★ ★

A man walks into a bar. He sees a beautiful, well-dressed woman sitting on a bar stool alone. He walks up to her and says, "Hi there, how's it going tonight?"
She turns to him, looks him straight in the eyes and says, "I'll screw anybody at any time, anywhere, your place or my place, it doesn't matter to me."

The guy raises his eyebrows and says, "Really? What law firm do you work for?"

★ ★ ★

YOU NEED A NEW LAWYER WHEN...

1. During your initial consultation he tries to sell you Amway.

2. He tells you that his last good case was a "Budweiser".

3. When the prosecutors see who your lawyer is, they high-five each other.

4. He picks the jury by playing "duck-duck-goose".

5. During the trial you catch him playing his Gameboy.

6. He asks a hostile witness to "pull my finger".

7. A prison guard is shaving your head.

8. Every couple of minutes he yells, "I call Jack Daniels to the stand!" and proceeds to drink a shot.

9. He frequently gives juror No. 4 the finger.

10. He places a large "No Refunds" sign on the defence table.

11. He begins closing arguments with "As Ally McBeal once said..."

12. He keeps citing the legal case of Godzilla v. Mothra.

13. Just before trial starts he whispers, "The judge is the one with the little hammer, right?"

14. Just before he says "Your Honour", he makes those little quotation marks in the air with his fingers.

15. The sign in front of his law office reads, "Practising Law Since 2:25 PM."

16. Whenever his objection is overruled, he tells the judge, "Whatever".

17. He giggles every time he hears the word "briefs".

★ ★ ★

Did you hear that the Post Office just recalled their latest stamps? They had pictures of lawyers on them and people couldn't figure out which side to spit on.

★ ★ ★

How can a pregnant woman tell that she's carrying a future lawyer? She has an uncontrollable craving for baloney.

★ ★ ★

How does an attorney sleep? First he lies on one side, then he lies on the other.

★ ★ ★

How many lawyer jokes are there? Only three. The rest are true stories.

★ ★ ★

How many lawyers does it take to change a light bulb? How many can you afford?

★ ★ ★

How many lawyers does it take to screw in a light bulb? Three. One to climb the ladder. One to shake it. And one to sue the ladder company.

★ ★ ★

If a lawyer and the tax man were both drowning and you could only save one of them, would you go to lunch or read the paper?

★ ★ ★

What did the lawyer name his daughter?
Sue.

★ ★ ★

What do you call 25 skydiving lawyers?
Air pollution.

★ ★ ★

What do you call a lawyer gone bad?
An MP.

★ ★ ★

What do you call a lawyer with an IQ of 50?
The judge.

★ ★ ★

What do you get when you cross a bad politician with a power-mad lawyer?
Chelsea Clinton.

★ ★ ★

What do you throw to a drowning lawyer?
His partners.

★ ★ ★

What does a lawyer use for birth-control?
His personality.

★ ★ ★

What happens when you cross a pig with a lawyer?
You can't. There are some things a pig just won't do.

★ ★ ★

What's the difference between a lawyer and a vulture?
The lawyer gets frequent flyer miles.

★ ★ ★

What's another difference between a lawyer and a vulture?
Removable wingtips.

★ ★ ★

A man walks into a bar and loudly says to the bartender, "All lawyers are assholes." A man sitting at the other end of the bar says, "I resent that remark." The first man says, "Why, are you a lawyer?" He says, "No, I'm an asshole!"

★ ★ ★

A big-city California lawyer went duck hunting in rural Texas. He shot and dropped a bird, but it fell into a farmer's field on the other side of a fence.

As the lawyer climbed over the fence, an elderly farmer drove up on his tractor and asked him what he was doing.

The lawyer responded, "I shot a duck and it fell into this field, and now I'm going to retrieve it."

The old farmer replied, "This is my property, and you are not coming over here."

The indignant lawyer said, "I am one of the best trial attorneys in the US and, if you don't let me get that duck, I'll sue you and take everything you own."

The old farmer smiled and said, "Apparently, you don't know how we do things in Texas. We settle small disagreements like this with the Texas Three-Kick Rule."

The lawyer asked, "What is the Texas Three-Kick Rule?"

The Farmer replied, "Well, first I kick you three times and then you kick me three times, and so on, back and forth, until someone gives up."

The attorney quickly thought about the proposed contest and decided that he could easily take the old codger. He agreed to abide by the local custom.

The old farmer slowly climbed down from the tractor and walked up to the city fella. His first kick planted the toe of his heavy work boot into the lawyer's groin and dropped him to his knees.

His second kick nearly wiped the man's nose off his face.

The barrister was flat on his belly when the farmer's third kick to a kidney nearly caused him to give up.

The lawyer summoned every bit of his will and managed to get to his feet and said, "Okay, you old coot! Now, it's my turn!"

The old farmer immediately smiled and said, "No, I give up. You can have the duck!"

★ ★ ★

A carpet layer had just finished installing carpet for a lady. He stepped out for a smoke, only to realize that he had lost his cigarettes. In the middle of the room, under the carpet, was a bump.

"No sense pulling up the entire floor for one pack smokes," he said to himself. He proceeded to take his hammer and flatten the hump.

As he was cleaning up, the lady came in.

"Here," she said, handing him his pack of cigarettes. "I found them in the hallway."

"Now," she said, "if only I could find my sweet little hamster."

★ ★ ★

At a convention of biological scientists, one prominent researcher remarked to another, "Did you know that in our lab we have switched from mice to lawyers for our experiments?"

"Really?" the other researcher replied. "Why did you switch?"

"Well, for three reasons. First we found that lawyers are far more plentiful. Second, the lab assistants don't get so attached to them, and thirdly there are some things even a rat won't do."

★ ★ ★

A lawyer's wife dies. At the cemetery, people are appalled to see that the tombstone reads, "Here lies Phyllis, wife of Murray, L. L. D., Wills, Divorce, Malpractice."

Suddenly, Murray bursts into tears. His brother says, "You should cry, pulling a stunt like this!" Through his tears, Murray croaks, "You don't understand! They left out the phone number!"

★ ★ ★

TRUE COURTROOM HUMOUR

Q. Now, Mrs Johnson, how was your first marriage terminated?
A. By death.
Q. And by whose death was it terminated?

Q. Doctor, did you say he was shot in the woods?
A. No, I said he was shot in the lumbar region.

Q. What is your name?
A. Ernestine McDowell.

Q. And what is your marital status?
A. Fair.
Q. Are you married?
A. No, I'm divorced.

Q. And what did your husband do before you divorced him?
A. A lot of things I didn't know about.

Q. How did you happen to go to Dr Cherney?
A. Well, a gal down the road had had several of her children by Dr Cherney, and said he was really good.

Q. Do you know how far pregnant you are right now?
A. I will be three months on November 8th.

Q. Apparently then, the date of conception was August 8th?
A. Yes.
Q. What were you and your husband doing at that time?

Q. Mrs Smith, do you believe that you are emotionally unstable?
A. I should be.

Q. How many times have you committed suicide?
A. Four times.

Q. Doctor, how many autopsies have you performed on dead people?
A. All my autopsies have been performed on dead people.

Q. Were you acquainted with the deceased?
A. Yes, sir.
Q. Before or after he died?

Q. Officer, what led you to believe the defendant was under the influence?
A. Because he was argumentary and he couldn't pronunciate his words.

★ ★ ★

A Mafia Godfather, accompanied by his attorney, walks into a room to meet with his former accountant.

The Godfather asks the accountant, "Where is the three million bucks you embezzled from me?" The accountant does not answer.

The Godfather asks again, "Where is the three million bucks you embezzled from me?"

The attorney interrupts, "Sir, the man is a deaf mute and cannot understand you, but I can interpret for you."

The Godfather says, "Well ask him where my damn money is!"

The attorney, using sign language, asks the accountant where the three million dollars is.

The accountant signs back, "I don't know what you are talking about."

The attorney interprets to the Godfather, "He doesn't know what you are talking about."

The Godfather pulls out a 9 millimeter pistol, puts it to the temple of the accountant, cocks the trigger and says, "Ask him again where my damn money is!"

The attorney signs to the accountant, "He wants to know where it is!"

The accountant signs back, "OK! OK! OK! The money is hidden in a brown suitcase behind the shed in my backyard!"

The Godfather says, "Well... what did he say?"

The attorney interprets to the Godfather, "He says... go to hell... that you don't have the guts to pull the trigger."

★ ★ ★

The staff at a local United Way office realized that it had never received a donation from the town's most successful lawyer. The person in charge of contributions called him to persuade him to contribute and said, "Our research shows that out of a yearly income of at least $500,000, you give not a penny to charity. Wouldn't you like to give back to the community in some way?"

The lawyer mulled this over for a moment and replied, "First, did your research also show that my mother is dying after a long illness, and has medical bills that are several times her annual income?"

Embarrassed, the United Way representative mumbled, "Um... no."

"Or," the lawyer continued, "that my brother, a disabled veteran, is blind and confined to a wheelchair?"

The stricken United Way representative began to stammer out an apology, but was interrupted when the lawyer added, "Or that my sister's husband died in a traffic accident," the lawyer's voice rising in indignation, "leaving her penniless with three children?"

The humiliated United Way representative, completely beaten, said simply, "I had no idea..."

On a roll, the lawyer cut him off once again, "So if I don't give any money to them, why should I give any to you?"

★ ★ ★

"Your Honour," a defence attorney began, "I have a series of witnesses that can testify that Mr Johnson was nowhere near the scene of the crime when it occurred."

The judge looked at the defence table and said, "This is the third time you've been in this court room this week, and I'm getting sick of hearing your lies."

The defendant stood up with a confused expression and said, "Your Honour, you must be mistaken. I've never been here in my life."

Waving his finger, the judge replied, "I was referring to your lawyer."

★ ★ ★

Two attorneys boarded a flight out of Seattle.

One sat in the window seat, the other sat in the middle seat. Just before take-off, a physician got on and took the aisle seat next to the two attorneys.

The physician kicked off his shoes, wiggled his toes and was settling in when the attorney in the window seat said, "I think I'll get up and get a coke." "No problem," said the physician, "I'll get it for you."

While he was gone, one of the attorneys picked up the physician's shoe and spat in it.

When he returned with the coke, the other attorney said, "That looks good, I think I'll have one too."

Again, the physician obligingly went to fetch it and while he was gone, the other attorney picked up the other shoe and spat in it.

The Physician returned and they all sat back and enjoyed the flight. As the plane was landing, the physician slipped his feet into his shoes and knew immediately what had happened.

"How long must this go on?" he asked. "This fighting between our professions? This hatred? This animosity? This spitting in shoes and pissing in cokes?"

★ ★ ★

An elderly spinster called the lawyer's office and told the receptionist she wanted to see the lawyer about having a will prepared.

The receptionist suggested they set up an appointment at a

convenient time for the spinster to come into the office. The woman replied, "You must understand, I've lived alone all my life, I rarely see anyone, and I don't like to go out. Would it be possible for the lawyer to come to my house?"

The receptionist checked with the attorney who agreed and he went to the spinster's home for the meeting to discuss her estate and the will. The lawyer's first question was, "Would you please tell me what you have in assets and how you'd like them to be distributed under your will?"

She replied, "Besides the furniture and accessories you see here, I have $40,000 in my savings account at the bank."

"Tell me," the lawyer asked, "how would you like the $40,000 to be distributed?"

The spinster said, "Well, as I've told you, I've lived a reclusive life, people have hardly ever noticed me, so I'd like them to notice when I pass on. I'd like to provide $35,000 for my funeral."

The lawyer remarked, "Well, for $35,000 you will be able to have a funeral that will certainly be noticed and will leave a lasting impression on anyone who may not have taken much note of you! But tell me," he continued, "what would you like to do with the remaining $5,000?"

The spinster replied, "As you know, I've never married, I've lived alone almost my entire life, and in fact I've never slept with a man. Before I die, I'd like you to use the $5,000 to arrange for a man to sleep with me."

"This is a very unusual request," the lawyer said, adding, "but I'll see what I can do to arrange it and get back to you."

That evening, the lawyer was at home telling his wife about the eccentric spinster and her weird request. After thinking about how much she could do around the house with $5,000, and with a bit of coaxing, she got her husband to agree to provide the service himself. She said, "I'll drive you over tomorrow morning, and wait in the car until you're finished."

The next morning, she drove him to the spinster's house and waited while he went into the house. She waited for over an hour, but her husband didn't come out. So she blew the car horn.

Shortly, the upstairs bedroom window opened, the lawyer stuck his head out and yelled, "Pick me up tomorrow! She's going to let the County bury her!"

★ ★ ★

One afternoon, a wealthy lawyer was riding in the back of his limousine when he saw two men eating grass by the roadside. He ordered his driver to stop and he got out to investigate.

"Why are you eating grass?" he asked one man. "We don't have any money for food," the poor man replied.

"Oh, come along with me then."

"But sir, I have a wife with two children!" "Bring them along! And you, come with us too!" he said to the other man. "But, sir, I have a wife with six children!" the second man answered. "Bring them as well!"

They all climbed into the car. It was no easy task to fit them, even for a car as large as the limo. Once under way, one of the poor fellows says, "Sir, you are too kind. Thank you for taking all of us with you."

The lawyer replied, "No problem, the grass at my home is about two feet tall!"

★ ★ ★

A defendant in a lawsuit involving large sums of money was saying to his lawyer, "If I lose this case, I'll be ruined."

"It's in the judge's hands now," said the lawyer.

"Would it help if I sent the judge a box of cigars?" asked the defendant.

"Oh no!" said the lawyer. "This judge is a stickler for ethical behaviour. A stunt like that would drastically prejudice him against you. He might even find you in contempt of the court. In fact, you shouldn't even smile at the judge."

Over the course of time, the judge came up with a decision in favour of the defendant. As the defendant left the courthouse, he said to his lawyer, "Thanks for the tip about the cigars. It worked."

"I'm sure we would have lost the case if you'd sent them," said the lawyer smugly.

"But I did send them," said the defendant.

"What? You did?"

"Yes, That's how we won the case."

"I don't understand," said the lawyer.

"It's simple. I sent the cheapest cigars that I could find to the judge, but enclosed the plaintiff's business card..."

★ ★ ★

A lawyer named Strange died, and his friend asked the tombstone-maker to inscribe on his tombstone, "Here lies Strange, an honest man and a lawyer."

The inscriber insisted that such wording would be confusing, for passers-by would tend to think that three men were buried under the stone. However he suggested an alternative. He would inscribe, "Here lies a man who was both honest and a lawyer."

That way, whenever anyone walked by the tombstone and read it, they would be certain to remark, "That's Strange!"

★ ★ ★

Two guys were picked up by the cops for smoking dope and appeared in court before the judge.

The judge said, "You seem like nice young men, and I'd like to give you a second chance rather than jail time. I want you to go out this weekend and try to show others the evils of drug use and pursuade them to give up drugs forever. I'll see you back in court on Monday."

Come Monday, and the two guys were back in court.

The judge said to the first one, "How did you do over the weekend?"

"Well, Your Honour, I persuaded 17 people to give up drugs forever."

"17 people? That's wonderful. What did you tell them?"

"I used a diagram, Your Honour. I drew two circles like this: O o and told them this (the big circle) is your brain before drugs and this (small circle) is your brain after drugs."

"That's admirable," said the judge and, turning to the second guy, he added, "And you, how did you do?"

"Well, Your Honour, I persuaded 156 people to give up drugs forever."

"156 people! That's amazing! How did you manage to do that!"

"Well, I used the same two circles. I pointed to the small circle and told them, 'This is your asshole before prison...'"

★ ★ ★

After a lengthy two-week criminal trial in a high-profile bank robbery case, the jury finally ended its 14 hours of deliberations and entered the courtroom to deliver its verdict to the judge.

The judge turns to the jury foreman and asks, "Has the jury reached a verdict in this case?"

"Yes, Your Honour," the foreman responded.

"Would you please pass it to me," the judge declared, as he motioned for the bailiff to retrieve the verdict slip from the foreman and deliver it to him.

After the judge read the verdict himself, he delivered the verdict slip back to his bailiff to be returned to the foreman and instructed the foreman, "Please read your verdict to the court."

"We find the defendant NOT GUILTY of all four counts of bank robbery," stated the foreman.

The family and friends of the defendant jump for joy at the sound of the "not guilty" verdict and hug each other as they shout expressions of divine gratitude. The defendant's attorney turns to his client and asks, "So, what do you think about that?"

The defendant looks around the courtroom slowly with an extremely bewildered look on his face and then turns to his defence attorney and says, "I'm real confused here. Does this mean that I have to return the money?"

★ ★ ★

A salesman was testifying in his divorce proceedings against his wife. "Please describe," said his attorney, "the incident that first caused you to entertain suspicions about your wife's fidelity."

"Well, I'm pretty much on the road all week," the man testified. "So naturally when I am home, I'm attentive to the wife."

"One Sunday morning," he continued, "we were in the midst of some pretty heavy love-making when the old lady in the apartment next door pounded on the wall and yelled, 'Can't you at least stop all that racket on the weekends?'"

★ ★ ★

How can you tell that an attorney is about to lie? His lips move.

★ ★ ★

The devil visited a lawyer's office and made him an offer. "I can arrange some things for you," the devil said. "I'll increase your income five-fold. Your partners will love you; your clients will respect you; you'll have four months of vacation each year and live to be a hundred. All I require in return is that your wife's soul, your children's souls, and their children's souls rot in hell for eternity."
The lawyer thought for a moment. "What's the catch?" he asked.

★ ★ ★

Did you hear they just released a new Barbie doll called "Divorced Barbie"? Yeah, it comes with half of Ken's things and alimony.

★ ★ ★

A lawyer was driving his big BMW down the highway, singing to himself, "I love my BMW, I love my BMW." Focusing on his car, not his driving, he smashed into a tree. He miraculously survived, but his car was totalled. "My BMW! My BMW!" he sobbed.
A good Samaritan drove by and cried out, "Sir, sir, you're bleeding! And my god, your left arm is gone!"
The lawyer, horrified, screamed, "My Rolex! My Rolex!"

★ ★ ★

A man woke up in a hospital bed and called for his doctor. He asked "Give it to me straight. How long have I got?" The physician replied that he doubted that his patient would survive the night. The man then said, "Call for my lawyer." When the lawyer arrived, the man asked for his physician to stand on one side of the bed, while the lawyer stood on the other. The man then laid back and closed his eyes. When he had remained silent for several minutes, the physician asked what he had in mind. The man replied, "Jesus died with a thief on either side, and I thought I'd check out the same way."

★ ★ ★

What do you get if you send the Godfather to law school?
An offer you can't understand.

★ ★ ★

As Mr Smith was on his death bed, he attempted to formulate a plan that would allow him to take at least some of his considerable wealth with him. He called for the three men he trusted most: his lawyer, his doctor and his clergyman. He told them, "I'm going to give you each $30,000 in cash before I die. At my funeral, I want you to place the money in my coffin so that I can try to take it with me." All three agreed to do this and were given the money. At the funeral, each approached the coffin in turn and placed an envelope inside. While riding in the limousine to the cemetery, the clergyman said, "I have to confess something to you fellows. Brother Smith was a good churchman all his life, and I know he would have wanted me to do this. The church needed a new baptistry very badly, and I took $10,000 of the money he gave me and bought one. I only put $20,000 in the coffin." The physician then said, "Well, since we're confiding in one another, I might as well tell you that I didn't put the full $30,000 in the coffin either. Smith had a disease that could have been diagnosed sooner if I had this new machine, but the machine cost $20,000 and I couldn't afford it then. I used $20,000 of the money to buy the machine so that I might be able to save another patient. I know that Smith would have wanted me to do that." The lawyer then said, "I'm ashamed of both of you. When I put my envelope into that coffin, it held my personal cheque for the full $30,000."

★ ★ ★

LEARNING YEARS

"Mummy, the milkman's here. Are you going to pay him or shall I go out to play?"

★ ★ ★

Sweet little Sally-Anne goes into the garden to play, only to see her beloved cat lying stiff with his legs in the air. She runs in crying to daddy, who comes out and has to tell her that poor little Fluffy is dead.

"But why are his legs sticking up in the air," she asks.

For a moment, he is lost for words but quickly recovers and tells her it is so that Jesus can grab the legs more easily and take Fluffy to heaven. Sally-Anne seems to accept her pussy-cat's death, but a week later daddy comes home from work to find her crying her eyes out.

"Oh daddy, mummy nearly died today."

"How?" he stammered, very shocked. "What happened?"

"Mummy was lying on the kitchen floor with her legs in the air shouting, 'I'm coming, I'm coming!' and if it hadn't been for Mr Brown next door holding her down, Jesus would have taken her away."

★ ★ ★

A woman was walking along the street with her little daughter when they came upon two dogs humping. When the daughter asked her mother what they were doing, embarrassed mum did some quick thinking and replied, "The dog on top has hurt itself so the one underneath is carrying it."

"Well, isn't that just the truth?" said the little girl. "You try and do someone a good turn and all they do is turn round and fuck you."

★ ★ ★

"Mummy, mummy, I didn't know birds were made of metal."

"Why do you think that, son?"

"Because I've just heard dad telling his friend he would like to screw the arse off the bird next door."

★ ★ ★

A little girl in a convent school asks her teacher, an old nun, who came first, Adam or Eve.

"Adam," replied the nun, "but then men always do come first."

★ ★ ★

"My dad's got two of those," said little Tommy as he watched his grandfather urinating.

"No, you're mistaken there," replied grandfather.

"I'm not," replied the little boy, "he has one for weeing with and a great big purple one for cleaning the au pair's teeth."

★ ★ ★

When she was a little baby, she was so shy, she used to pin her own nappies.

★ ★ ★

A little boy went unannounced into his mother's bedroom when she was dressing.

"What big balloons you have," he said.

"Why Johnny, why do you call them that."

"Well, I saw father blowing up the maid's yesterday when you went out."

★ ★ ★

Little boy goes to his mum looking confused. He asks, "Mum, is it bad to have a willy?"

"No, dear," replies mum.

"Then why is daddy in the bedroom trying to pull it off?"

★ ★ ★

I always knew my parents really hated me.
My bath toys were a kettle and toaster.

★ ★ ★

"Mummy, mummy, the au pair is in bed with a strange man. Ha ha, got you! April fool. It's only daddy."

★ ★ ★

A father was very upset about his young son's betting habits, so he went up to school to talk to the boy's teacher, who promised to have a word with him.

"Maybe if he lost heavily on a bet, it would cure him," she suggested. That night after school she asked the boy to stay behind and confronted him about the bad ways he was getting into.

"It's not only me, miss," replied the boy. "You're a cheat; you pretend to be a natural blonde but you've got dark hair between your legs."

"I have not!" she blurted out without thinking.

"Oh yes you have, and I'll bet you next month's pocket money."

The teacher was in a bit of a quandary. She had promised to help and this could be an expensive bet for him to lose. So she lifted her skirt and dropped her knickers. Having won the bet she rang the boy's father to tell him the good news.

"Damn, damn, damn!" he said. "This morning he bet me he'd see your bush before the day was out."

★ ★ ★

The junior teacher decided to play a little guessing game with her class.

"Listen, everyone, I'm going to turn around and hold something in my hand and you have to guess what it is. Here's a clue, it's yellow and you can eat it."

One of the children guessed a melon but another guessed a banana.

"That's right," she said. "Now I'm holding something red in my hand, and this is also something you can eat." A little girl guessed apple.

"Well done, it shows all of you are really thinking." At this point a boy at the back asked if he could have a turn. With his back to the class he said, "I've got something in my hand that's long and has a little red tip."

"Now, John, enough of that," said the teacher.

"It's all right, miss, it shows you were thinking, but look what it is." He turned around to show a match.

★ ★ ★

Little Billy peeped into his big sister's bedroom one day to see her rubbing her hands between her legs, saying, "I need a man, please, I need a man."
The next night he peeped into her bedroom again and was amazed to find a man in bed with her. Later on that night if anyone had looked in Billy's room they would have seen him rubbing his hands between his legs, saying, "I need a PlayStation, please, I need a PlayStation."

★ ★ ★

A woman who lost the top half of her bikini in the sea was running back up the beach with her arms across her breasts when a little boy stopped her.
"Please, miss," he said. "If you're selling those puppies, can I have the one with the pink nose?"

★ ★ ★

A little girl said to her mummy, "Mummy, mummy, now I know how babies are made. I looked in your bedroom last night and saw daddy stick his willy in your mouth."
Mummy replied, "No, dear, that's not how babies are made, that's how mummy gets her new jewellery."

★ ★ ★

"Mummy, mummy, why do fairy stories always start, 'Once upon a time…'?"
"They don't always, sweetheart, sometimes they start, 'Had to work late again…' or even 'Damn traffic, it took ages…'"

★ ★ ★

"Mummy, mummy, Bobby's got something I haven't got," said the upset little girl, pointing between her legs.

"Oh, don't worry about that," said Mummy relieved. "As long as you've got one of these you'll always be able to get one of those."

★ ★ ★

Little girl goes into her parents' bedroom to find her mummy sitting astride her daddy. "What are you doing?" she asks.

"It's all right, my love. I'm just flattening daddy's tummy."

"Don't bother," replies the little girl, "because as soon as you go out the au pair blows it up again."

★ ★ ★

"Daddy, daddy, are you still growing?" "Why do you ask, son?"

"Because the top of your head is coming through your hair."

★ ★ ★

Once a week the boy would travel across town to pick up child support money from his father and take it back to his mum. This money had come regularly for 16 years but on the boy's 16th birthday his dad told him it was the last payment and to tell his mum he wasn't the father anymore. "OK, dad," replied the boy. "Mum says you never were."

★ ★ ★

The children go back to school after Christmas and are asked by the teacher what they received from Father Christmas.

"I got a brmm brmmm," says one little boy, but the teacher is quite angry and tells him he's not a baby and should use the right names.

"Sorry, Miss, I got a car."

"Well done, Bobby, and how about you, Tracy?"

"I got a woof woof," she said.

Again the teacher had to remind the class to use proper words.

"I got a puppy, Miss," she replied.

"Jason, what did you get?"

The little boy hesitated because he didn't want to get it wrong and make teacher cross with him.

"I, er…. got a book," he stuttered.

"Well done," smiled the teacher. "And what was it called?"

"Winnie The Shit, Miss."

★ ★ ★

"Now try and get to sleep, son. Dream about what you would like for Christmas."

"I want a watch, daddy," he replied.

"Well, you can't," retorted Dad. "Now get to sleep."

★ ★ ★

"Shall we make love tonight?" says husband to wife.

"Jack, please don't talk like that in front of the children; instead, when you're in the mood just say, 'Can I use your washing machine, please'?"

So a couple of nights go past before wife turns to husband and says, "Jack, do you want to use my washing machine tonight?"

"No thanks. love. I didn't want to bother you, so I did it by hand."

★ ★ ★

A woman was breastfeeding her baby in the park when a young boy sat down next to her.

"What does the baby have to drink?" asked the boy.

"Just milk and orange juice," she replied.

After a few moments' thought, the little boy asked, "Which one is the orange juice?"

★ ★ ★

"Mummy, mummy, stop worrying. It's all right you can go to bed

now because dad's already gone and locked up for the night."
"I don't think so, sweetheart, he isn't home yet."
"But it's true, mum, the police have just been on the phone to tell you."

★ ★ ★

"Please, miss, I've hurt my finger," said little Rosie to her teacher.
"Have you got any cider?"
Puzzled, the teacher asked her why she wanted cider.
"Because I heard my sister telling her friend that when she gets a
prick in her hand she always put it in cider."

★ ★ ★

The parents were so proud when their son John went away to
university, but all he did was constantly write home for money to
spend on books, trips, membership fees and so on. Then halfway
through the term he wrote to tell them he had a lead role in the
university play but needed money for the costume. All this talk of
money was beginning to really grate on the parents, but they did as he
asked and it was a month later when he wrote again to say thanks.
"Everyone thought I looked a real count in the costume," he wrote.
On seeing this, the father retorted, "Bloody hell, I gave him all that
money for his education and he still can't even spell!"

★ ★ ★

A little boy walks into an off-licence and asks the woman behind the
counter for a packet of fags and a bottle of cider.
"Now, now, sonny, do you want to get me into trouble," she says.
"Nah, I'm not interested in sex, just give me what I asked for, please."

★ ★ ★

Mum arrived back from staying overnight with her mother and asked
her daughter if everything went all right. "Oh yes," said little Anne.
"Dad took me to the fair and I had some candy floss and an ice cream.

It was great. But last night, I had a tummy ache, so I went to look for daddy and he was in the au pair's room and he was in her bed and…"

"Stop," said mum angrily. "I want your daddy to hear this."

When dad came in, Anne repeated her story while Mum looked on, beside herself with rage.

"Tell us what they were doing?" she demanded.

"The same thing that you and the man from next door were doing last week, mum," she replied.

★ ★ ★

Marooned in the middle of the Yorkshire Dales, a man finds overnight accommodation with a local farmer, who tells him he can share a bedroom with his young son. That night, just before retiring, the young boy kneels down at the bottom of the bed and the man is so impressed he kneels down as well.

"What are you doing?" asks the boy.

"The same thing as you."

"Gosh, my mum's going to give you hell. There isn't one where you are, you know."

★ ★ ★

"Grandpa," said the little boy. "What position do you play in football?"

"I don't play football, son, why do you ask?"

"I heard dad telling mum that, when you kicked off, we'd be able to afford a holiday."

★ ★ ★

A little girl was found wandering down the crowded High Street, crying her eyes out. When the policeman asked her what was wrong, she told him she'd lost her father.

"What's your dad like?" he asked.

"Football, beer and fishing," she replied.

★ ★ ★

"Mummy, do babies come out of the same place that boys put their willies into?"

"That's right."

"So if I have a baby, will it hurt my teeth?"

★ ★ ★

When their small son wanders into the bedroom to find mum astride dad, they decide to pretend it's a game so as not to upset him.

"Can I join in, dad?" he asks.

"Of course, son."

The boy climbs aboard, jumping up and down on his dad as if he was a horse. As the climax draws near, the movements get faster and faster, and the little boy shouts to his mother.

"Hang on, Mum, this is where me and the au pair usually fall off."

★ ★ ★

A little boy was out walking with his mother when they met the new vicar.

"Good morning," he said, and looking down at the young boy he continued, "And who do we have here?"

"I'm Mr Coles' son," said the little boy.

Later, his mother corrected him on his answer.

"You don't say that," she said. "You say, 'I'm Billy Cole.'"

A few days later, the little boy was stopped by the local headmaster.

"You're Mr Cole's son, aren't you?"

"I thought I was, but mum says I'm not," he replied.

★ ★ ★

It was halfway through the English lesson when Miss decided to test her class on spelling.

"I want everyone to tell me what their fathers do for a living and then spell it out to me."

"Johnny, what does your Dad do?"

"He's a farmer, Miss."

"OK, spell that, please."

"F-A-R-M-E-R."

"Well done, Johnny. Now, Bob, how about you?"

"He's a police constable, Miss."

"Very well, please spell that out."

"P-O-L-I-C-E C-U..."

"No, try again."

"CCC-U-N-"

"No, no, you'll have to think carefully about this, go and practise in your book."

"Who's next? Oh yes, Colin, what does your father do?"

"He's a bookmaker, Miss."

"Now can you spell that for me, please?"

"No, Miss, but I can give you 5–4 on that Bob writes 'cunt' in his book."

★   ★   ★

Neighbour to little girl: "What's the name of your new baby sister?"

"I don't know; I can't understand anything she says."

★   ★   ★

"Mummy, mummy, why has daddy put his willy in the biscuit barrel?"

"Take no notice, darling, he's fucking crackers."

★   ★   ★

"Please, Miss, I want a wee wee," said little Annie, holding herself. "Annie, we don't use words like that in the classroom. When you want to go to the toilet just put your hand up and say you want to do number one," said her teacher. Soon afterwards, Jason yelled out, "Miss, I got to go and do a poo poo." "Now, Jason, when you want to do that, you say you need to go and do number two." The rest of the lesson went without interruption until five minutes before the bell when Gregory put his hand up and said, "Please, Miss, I want to fart. Would that be number three?"

★   ★   ★

A concerned father knew his son's pet hamster was dying and felt he ought to try and soften the blow.

"Son, I know your little Brownie is like one of the family but eventually he will die and go up to heaven. We must try not to be too sad. He's had a good life with us, so we must celebrate the happy times and not get too upset when he goes."

"Dad, can we have a party?"

"Yes, that's a good idea. You can invite some friends round."

"Dad?"

"Yes, son."

"Can I kill it now?"

★ ★ ★

"Please, Miss, I think I know where God lives."

"Where's that, Maisie?"

"At the corner of our street at number 47."

"Why's that?"

"On my way to school this morning I heard a lady in the room upstairs calling, 'Oh God, oh God…'!"

★ ★ ★

At a family gathering, a young boy suddenly lets out a noisy fart.

"Bobby, manners please, you shouldn't do that in front of your grandma."

"Sorry, dad, I didn't know it was her turn."

★ ★ ★

The teacher turned to her class and said, "Today, children, we are going to find out how many of you know the meaning of certain words by putting them into sentences. The first word is 'definitely'. Who can do that one for me?"

"Please, Miss, the sea is definitely blue."

"That's a good try, Tracy, but sometimes the sea is grey, or even green depending on the weather, so we can't be that definite."

"I have one, Miss," said John. "Apples are definitely red."

"Well done for trying, but apples can also be green."
"Yes, Tom, do you want to say something?"
"Please, Miss, does a fart have lumps?"
"Good gracious me, Tom, no… no, of course not."
"Then, Miss, I've definitely crapped in my pants."

★ ★ ★

"Now, children, tomorrow I'd like you to bring in something connected with your father's work so that we can all learn a bit more about the different jobs people do," says the primary school teacher. The next day, little Jimmy brings in a bus ticket. "That's because my father is a bus conductor, Miss".
"Well done, Jimmy, and how about you Lucy?"
"I've brought in a betting slip because my dad's a bookie, Miss."
"Fine… and you, Billy?"
"I've brought in a light bulb and a toilet roll. My dad works at the big car factory and this is what he brings home every night."

★ ★ ★

Q: Why were the early days of history called the Dark Ages?
A: Because there were so many knights!
Q: How did the Vikings send secret messages?
A: By norse code!
Q: Who invented fractions?
A: Henry the ¼th!
Q: What kind of lighting did Noah use for the ark?
A: Floodlights!
Q: What's purple and 5,000 miles long?
A: The grape wall of China.
Q: Who made King Arthur's round table?
A: Sir-Cumference
Q: Who built the ark?
A: I have Noah idea!

★ ★ ★

The teacher was called away to speak to the headmaster, so she told the class to make up a poem about Timbuctoo and she would hear them all when she got back.

The first child recited hers.

"When I was lying in my bed
I dreamt of a ship with funnels red
A beautiful ship, its hull was blue
I think it was going to Timbuctoo."

"Well done, Lucy. Now let's hear the next."

During the morning all the poems were heard, the last one coming from young Billy, a rather disruptive boy.

"As we were walking down a road in Kent
We saw two ladies in a tent
I said to Tim, what shall we do?
Then I bucked one and Tim bucked two."

"Get to the headmaster!" roared the teacher.

★ ★ ★

FAMILY ENTERTAINMENT

"Dad, Dad," said his son excitedly. "I've done it. I've got a part in the new play."

"Well done, lad. What is it?"

"It's an old man who's been married for 35 years."

"That's a promising start. Next time you might get a speaking part."

★ ★ ★

Just as the young girl is coming out of the school gates, a car draws up and a man leans over to ask her if she'd like a lift home.

"No, thank you," she replies.

But he asks again. "Come on, it's raining. You'll be soaked by the time you get home."

"No! Go away and leave me alone."

The man follows her up the road. "Look, get in please. I'll get you some sweeties."

"No!" she yells and starts to run.

"I'll get you some sweeties and your favourite comic."

"No, no, no!" shouts the girl. "Just 'cos you bought a Lada doesn't mean I have to ride in it, Dad."

★ ★ ★

Mother receives a telephone call from school telling her they are sending home her son for weeing in the swimming pool.

"But everyone does that," she says.

"Not from the top diving board, they don't."

★ ★ ★

Daddy is mowing the lawn when his young son comes running out of the house calling to him.

"Daddy, Daddy, what's sex?" asked the boy.

For a moment Dad is dumbstruck but then decides that, if his son has asked the question, then he must do his best to answer it.

For the next few minutes Dad talks about the birds and the bees, then human relationships, love, the sex act, having babies – in fact he does a pretty good job of covering every aspect. Eventually he comes to a stop when he sees how his son is looking at him.

"Why did you want to know?" he asks.

"Well, Mum said to come out and tell you that dinner would be ready in two secs."

★ ★ ★

"Okay, kids," said Dad, returning home from work. "My boss gave me a box of chocolates today, so I think it ought to go to the person who always does what Mummy says and never answers her back."

"Oh, Dad," wailed the four children, "that's not fair, you know that's you!"

★ ★ ★

332

The angry father opened the door to find his daughter canoodling in the porch with her boyfriend.

"It's nearly half past one in the morning," he bellowed. "Do you think you can stay here all night?"

"Gosh, I don't know," replied the boyfriend. "I'll have to ring my parents for permission."

★ ★ ★

A discontented woman had taken her small son for a walk in the woods, but within moments of her looking away, the boy had wandered off. She searched for him for over an hour and it was beginning to grow dark.

As a last resort, she looked heavenwards and cried, "Oh God, please don't let anything happen to my son, please take me instead."

Moments later, she heard crying and there, caught in some undergrowth, was her little son.

"Oh, thank you, thank you," she said happily, running up to him.

Then suddenly she stopped and remarked, "But just before you go, God, he did have his teddy bear with him!"

★ ★ ★

A father is keen to take his son for a plane ride, but the only person he knows who will organize it is a rather shady stuntman. The stuntman is always looking for a way to make easy money so he suggests that they can have the ride free as long as they don't say anything or make a noise. If they do, then they will have to pay double.

The father agrees and tells his son there must be complete silence or the pilot will not fly.

The next day, the trip takes place and very soon the small plane is soaring high into the sky. The stuntman smiles to himself, certain that once he begins to perform some of his incredible manoeuvres, one of them is sure to make a noise. He loops the loop, flies upside-down, drops like a stone from a great height and many other tricks over the 30-minute period, but to no effect.

Eventually, admitting defeat, he returns to base.

"That was quite amazing," he says to the father, shaking his hand. "I was sure one of you would have broken the silence."

"It was very hard," admits the father, "particularly when my son fell out halfway through the trip."

★ ★ ★

Did you hear about the couple who adopted a baby from Spain?

They signed up for evening classes in Spanish, so that they would be able to understand the baby when it started talking.

★ ★ ★

"My mother-in-law and I don't get along. Take our anniversary, for instance. She sent us some monogrammed bath towels: 'Hers and Its'."

★ ★ ★

"I knew my future mother-in-law didn't like me from the start, when she bit the groom on the wedding cake in half."

★ ★ ★

Two women talking over the garden fence.

"My husband's an efficiency expert."

"What's that then?"

"Well, I'll put it another way. If it was a woman doing it, they'd call it nagging."

★ ★ ★

The woman went to the beauty parlour and, after her treatment, said to the beautician,

"Do you think my husband will think I'm beautiful?"

"I should think so. He still drinks a lot, doesn't he?"

★ ★ ★

The husband came down to breakfast, holding his head in his hands and moaning. "So, Gerald," said his wife, "have you ever been told you're the most handsome man in town?"

"No, dear."

"And have you ever been told you're the best dancer in town?"

"No, dear."

"Or that you're irresistible to women?"

"Certainly not, dear."

"Then pray, where did you get all those silly ideas at the party last night?"

★ ★ ★

"Is that the obituary section of the *Clarion*?" asked the woman.

"Yes, madam, can I help you?"

"I'd like to put a notice in, reporting the death of my husband from gunshot wounds."

"Good gracious, when did it happen?"

"Just as soon as I find the cheating bugger."

★ ★ ★

"You're a fool to yourself, Ethel," said her neighbour scornfully. "That husband of yours has you running around in circles." "Oh, don't say that," replied Ethel with spirit. "He helps with the housework, you know. He sits in front of the television and gathers dust."

★ ★ ★

The old woman turned to her husband and said, "You know, James, we're not getting any younger. We've got to accept that it won't be too long before one of us passes on."

"Oh, come on, Ruby," he replied, "don't let's talk about such things."

"Well, okay, but I just want you to know I think I'll go to Eastbourne when that happens."

★ ★ ★

"The spark's gone out of our marriage, Flo," said the old dear sadly to her friend. "These days, when I bring out the animal in Alfred, he runs to the door, scratching and whining to be let out."

★ ★ ★

"Doctor, doctor. It's the wife. She's having trouble with her eyesight," said the agitated husband.
"Really?" replied the doctor. "In what way?"
"She keeps having visions of a pearl necklace."

★ ★ ★

A man walked into his home and yelled at his wife.
"Mildred, I just discovered our marriage is illegal!"
"How come?" she replied.
"Your father didn't have a licence for that shotgun."

★ ★ ★

"My wife caught a Peeping Tom last night just as she was getting ready for bed. Phew! She was so angry, she beat him black and blue."
"I'm not surprised. It's dreadful feeling that someone was watching you as you got undressed."
"No, no, it wasn't that. It was when he tried to close the curtains."

★ ★ ★

"Look at this!" exclaimed the angry husband to his wife, "the bank has returned the cheque you wrote last week."
"Oh great," she replied. "What shall I spend it on next?"

★ ★ ★

Some people grow old gracefully, while others fight it the whole way. Andy's wife, refusing to give in to the looks of growing old, goes out and buys a new line of expensive cosmetics guaranteed to make her look years younger. After a lengthy sitting before the mirror applying the "miracle" products, she says to her husband, "Darling, honestly, if you didn't know me, what age would you say I am?"

Looking over her carefully, Andy replied, "Judging from your skin, twenty; your hair, eighteen; and your figure, twenty five."

"Oh, you flatterer!" she gushed.

Just as she was about to name Andy's reward, he stopped her by saying, "WHOA, hold on there, sweety! I haven't added them up yet!"

★ ★ ★

"Colin," she whispered, nudging him in the ribs.

"I can hear noises downstairs, I think we've got burglars. Go and see."

But Colin refused to move. "What's happened to you?" she hissed.

"You were brave when you married me."

"I know," he replied, "that's what everyone said."

★ ★ ★

DOMESTIC BLISS

Several years ago, I returned home from a trip just when a storm hit, with crashing thunder and severe lightning. As I came into my bedroom about 2 am, I found my two children in bed with my wife, Mary, apparently scared by the loud storm. I resigned myself to sleep in the guest bedroom that night. The next day, I talked to the children, and explained that it was okay to sleep with mom when the storm was bad, but when I was expected home, please don't sleep with Mum that night. They said, "Okay". After my next trip several weeks later, Mary and the children picked me up in the terminal at the appointed time. Since the plane was late, everyone had come into the terminal to wait for my plane's arrival, along with hundreds of other folks waiting for arriving passengers. As I entered the waiting area, my son saw me, and came running shouting, "Hi, Dad! I've got some good news!" As I waved back, I said loudly, "What's the good news?" "Nobody slept with

Mummy while you were away this time!" Alex shouted.

The airport became very quiet, as everyone in the waiting area looked at Alex, then turned to me and then searched the rest of the area to see if they could figure out exactly who his mum was!

★ ★ ★

A simple young man is encouraged to broaden his knowledge by learning how to parachute. After a few lessons it's time for his first jump, so that afternoon he and his instructor go up in a plane. The instructor tells the man not to worry because he'll jump straight after him. So the man jumps out, pulls his rip cord and heads gently for earth. A moment later the instructor jumps out but when he pulls his rip cord nothing happens and within seconds he passes his pupil and plummets to earth at an amazing speed. "Oh no you don't!" says the young man on seeing his instructor race pass. "You didn't tell me it was a race." He undoes his parachute and shouts gleefully, "Last one home is a sissy!"

★ ★ ★

There was a skinny young boy who was constantly being teased by the older lads in the village. One of their favourite games was to prove how stupid he was by giving him the choice between picking a 20p piece or a 10p piece. The boy always chose the 10p piece which would send the bullies into fits of laughter.

"See!" they would say. "He always picks the 10p because it's bigger. He's so thick." On a number of occasions this trick had been witnessed by the local storekeeper who eventually took the lad aside and tried to put him right.

"I'm sure you know 10p isn't worth as much as 20p is it really because it's bigger?"

"Of course not!" whispered the boy, "but if I stopped picking the 10p they'd stop playing the trick!"

★ ★ ★

Q: What do you call a man who doesn't sink?
A: Bob!
Q: What do you call a woman with a sinking ship on her head?
A: Mandy Lifeboats!
Q: What do you call a man with a big truck on his head?
A: Laurie!
Q: What do you call a woman with a pint of beer on her head
playing snooker?
A: Beatrix Potter!
Q: What do you call a lion with toothache?
A: Rory!
Q: What do you call a man with turf on his head?
A: Pete!
Q: What do you call the ghost who haunts TV shows?
A: Phantom of the Oprah!
Q: What kind of illness does Bruce Lee get?
A: Kung Flu!
Q: What do you call a Rodent that has a sword?
A: A Mouseketeer!
Q: What do you call the bad lion tamer?
A: Claude Bottom

★ ★ ★

After a Christmas break, a teacher asked her young pupils how they spent their holidays. One small boy wrote the following:
"We always used to spend Christmas with Grandpa and Grandma. They used to live here in a big brick home, but Grandpa got retarded and they moved to Florida. Now they live in a place with a lot of other retarded people. They all live in little tin boxes. They ride on big three-wheeled tricycles and they all wear nametags because they don't know who they are. They go to a big building called a wrecking hall; but if it was wrecked, they got it fixed because it's all right now. They play games and do exercises there, but they don't do them very good.
"There is a swimming pool there. They go into it and just stand there

with their hats on. I guess they don't know how to swim.

"As you go into their park, there is a dollhouse with a little man sitting in it. He watches all day so they can't get out without him seeing them. When they can sneak out they go to the beach and pick up shells that they think are dollars.

"My Grandma used to bake cookies and stuff, but I guess she forgot how. Nobody cooks, they just eat out. They eat the same thing every night, Early Birds. Some of the people are so retarded that they don't know how to cook at all, so my Grandma and Grandpa bring food into the wrecked hall and they call it 'pot luck'.

"My Grandma says Grandpa worked hard all his life and earned his retardment. I wish they would move back up here, but I guess the little man in the dollhouse won't let them out."

★ ★ ★

A boy was assigned a paper on childbirth and asked his parents, "How was I born?"

"Well, honey..." said the slightly prudish parent, "the stork brought you to us."

"Oh," said the boy. "Well, how did you and daddy get born?" he asked.

"Oh, the stork brought us too."

"Well, how were grandpa and grandma born?" he persisted.

"Well, darling, the stork brought them too!" said the parent, by now starting to squirm a little in the Lazy Boy recliner.

Several days later, the boy handed in his paper to the teacher who read the opening sentence with some confusion: "This report has been very difficult to write due to the fact that there hasn't been a natural childbirth in my family for three generations."

★ ★ ★

What do you get when you put three ducks in a box?
A box of quackers.
Why couldn't the sesame seed leave the casino?
Because he was on a roll.

Why did the student eat his homework?
The teacher told him it was a piece of cake.
What did the cannibal order as a takeaway?
Pizza with everyone on it.
How can you tell if an elephant has been in your refrigerator?
Footprints in the cheesecake.
What's in an astronaut's favorite sandwich?
Launcheon meat.
What did the mayonnaise say to the fridge?
Close the door, I'm dressing!
What did the duck say when he bought lipstick?
Put it on my bill.
Why did the chewing gum cross the road?
It was stuck to the leg of a chicken!!!
Why did the turtle cross the road?
To get to the Shell Station!
How do you know if there's an elephant under your bed?
You bump your nose on the ceiling.
Why do cows have bells?
Because their horns don't work.

★ ★ ★

The woman was walking down the street when she saw a young boy standing on the corner, drinking a can of beer and smoking a cigarette. "Why, this is disgraceful!" she exclaimed. "You should be in school." "Sod off," he replied. "I'm only four years old."

★ ★ ★

It was the end-of-year exams and an examiner from another school had come in to adjudicate.
"You will start when I ring this bell," he told the class, "and you will finish when I ring it a second time. Anyone found writing after that will be disqualified. At the end, please bring your papers up and then you are free to leave."

The class started on the bell and Jake began writing feverishly. His concluding sentence was all important but it meant he finished a couple of seconds after the bell. When he got up to hand his paper in, the strict adjudicator informed him he was disqualified.

"Do you know who I am?" demanded Jake.

"No," replied the adjudicator frostily.

"Are you sure?"

"Absolutely."

"Good," replied Jake as he shoved his paper into the middle of the stack and ran out of the room.

★ ★ ★

A 7-year-old and a 4-year-old are upstairs in their bedroom.

"You know what?" says the 7-year-old, "I think it's about time we started swearing."

The 4-year-old nods his head in approval. "When we go downstairs for breakfast I'm gonna say 'hell' and you say 'ass', OK?"

"OK," the 4-year-old agrees with enthusiasm.

The mother walks into the kitchen and asks the 7-year-old what he wants for breakfast. "Aw, hell, Mom, I guess I'll have some Cheerios." WHACK!!

He flies out of his chair, tumbles across the kitchen floor, gets up and runs upstairs, crying his eyes out.

She looks at the 4-year-old and asks with a stern voice, "And what do YOU want for breakfast, young man?" "I don't know," he blubbers, "but you can bet your ass it won't be Cheerios."

★ ★ ★

On the first day of college, the Dean addressed the students, pointing out some of the rules, saying, "The female dormitory will be out-of-bounds for all male students, and the male dormitory to the female students. Anyone caught breaking this rule once will be fined $50."

He continued, "Anyone caught breaking this rule a second time will be fined $150. Being caught a third time will incur a hefty fine of $400.

Are there any questions?"
At this point, a male student in the crowd inquired, "How much for a season pass?"

★ ★ ★

A family was having dinner on Mother's Day. For some reason the mother was unusually quiet. Finally the husband asked what was wrong.
"Nothing," said the woman.
Not buying it, he asked again. "Seriously, what's wrong?"
"Do you really want to know? Well, I'll tell you. I have cooked and cleaned and fed the kids for 15 years and, on Mother's Day, you don't so much as say 'Thank you'."
"Why should I?" he said. "Not once in 15 years have I gotten a Father's Day gift."
"Yes," she said, "but I'm their real mother."

★ ★ ★

A little boy returning home from his first day at school said to his mother, "Mom, what's sex?"
His mother, who believed in all the most modern educational theories, gave him a detailed explanation, covering all aspects of the tricky subject.
When she had finished, the little lad produced an enrollment form which he had brought home from school and said, "Yes, but how am I going to get all that into this one little square?"

★ ★ ★

The Smith's were proud of their family tradition. Their ancestors had come to America on the *Mayflower*. They had included Senators and Wall Street wizards.
They decided to compile a family history, a legacy for their children and grandchildren. They hired a fine author.
Only one problem arose – how to handle that great-uncle George, who

was executed in the electric chair. The author said he could handle the story tactfully.

The book appeared. It said, "Great-uncle George occupied a chair of applied electronics at an important government institution, was attached to his position by the strongest of ties and his death came as a great shock."

★ ★ ★

A lady stopped unexpectedly by her recently married son's house.

She rang the doorbell and stepped into the house to see her daughter-in-law standing naked by the door.

"What are you doing?" she asked.

"I am waiting for my husband to come home from work," the daughter-in-law replied.

"Why are you naked?" asked the mother-in-law.

"This is my love dress," the daughter-in-law replied.

"LOVE DRESS! You're naked," said the mother-in-law.

"But my husband loves it when I wear this dress. It makes him happy and he makes me happy," said the daughter-in-law. "He will be home any minute now, so perhaps you could stop by a little later?"

Soured by all of this romantic stuff, the mother-in-law left. On the way home she thought about the "LOVE DRESS" and got an idea.

She undressed, showered, applied her best perfume and waited by the door for her husband to come home.

Finally, his pick-up truck drove up the driveway.

Her husband opened the door, and immediately saw his naked wife.

"What are you doing?" he asked.

"This is my love dress," she said, excitedly.

"Needs ironing," he replied.

★ ★ ★

LEISURE TIME

On her way home from an all-night party, the girl was stopped by the traffic cops and breathalyzed.

Looking at the results one of the policemen said, "You've had a few stiff ones tonight, Miss."

"How amazing, that's really fantastic," she said. "I didn't know you could tell that as well."

★ ★ ★

A fellow went to a dance and as he was going round on the floor he said to the girl, "Your name's Hyacinth."

"How did you know?" she said.

"By your scent."

Later he danced with another girl and this time guessed her name was Rose. Towards the end of the dance his new partner was overheard to say, "But how did you know my name was Fanny?"

★ ★ ★

Just before Bobby Davro is due to appear on stage at a cabaret/dinner, a stranger comes up to him and says, "Hey, Bobby, you're the tops with me. I'm your biggest fan and tonight I've got a red hot date.

I'd really like to impress her and wondered if you would pretend to know me and come over and say hello. My name's Jack and I'll be sitting on the first table."

And indeed Bobby Davro remembers the stranger's request and halfway through his act comes over to Jack's table.

"Hello, Jack, good to see you. Hope all is well."

"Fuck off, Bob, can't you see I'm busy?" replied Jack.

★ ★ ★

After a really wild party, two girls wake up the next morning and one says to the other, "Ugh, my mouth tastes like the inside of a bird's cage."

"Well, I'm not surprised," said the other. "You did have a cock or two in there last night."

★ ★ ★

A woman in a very chic French restaurant suddenly sneezes and her boobs pop out of her evening gown.

Moments later, her waiter is berated by the manager. "Pierre, please remember this is a high-class establishment, next time use warm spoons."

★ ★ ★

Three sisters, named Flora, Fiona and Fanny, lived in the same village in Yorkshire and were renowned for their beauty, although all of them had extra-large feet. One evening, Flora and Fiona went to the local village bop and were soon chatting to some lads from the next village.

"By gum," said one of the lads. "Haven't you got big feet!"

"Oh that's nought," they replied. "You should see our Fanny's."

★ ★ ★

Have you heard about the girl who gave up 10-pin bowling for sex? She found out the balls were lighter and she didn't have to wear shoes.

★ ★ ★

A rather shy man was dancing with a very shapely redhead when suddenly one of her earrings came off and dropped down the back of her dress.

"Would you mind getting that for me?" she asked him.

"Of course," he said, but the earring had dropped down a long way.

"Er..." he said embarrassedly, "I feel a perfect arse."

"My tits are good too," she purred.

★ ★ ★

A woman was being taught how to swim by the local swimming instructor, Sleazy Sid, who was holding her up in the water.

With an astonished look on her face, she said, "Are you sure I'll drown if you take your finger out?"

★ ★ ★

348

Jack was fanatical about his special racing bike and he would clean it mornings and evenings, rubbing a special lubricant over it to stop any rust.

One day, he was invited to dinner at his girlfriend's house and went round on the bicycle but was told he couldn't bring it inside. It would have to remain round the back of the house.

After the meal, the mother said she wasn't washing up, she'd done the cooking.

"Well, I'm not," said the daughter.

"And I'm not," said the father.

"Neither am I," said Jack. "It looks like rain and I've got to see to my bike."

They seemed to have reached a stalemate so the father shouted, "Right, the next one who speaks will do the dishes!"

It was so quiet you could hear a pin drop, but Jack was getting very agitated as he looked through the windows at the storm clouds gathering. He needed to get the lubricant on the bike.

In sheer desperation to make someone speak he suddenly jumped on top of his girlfriend and rogered her there and then on the dining-room floor. The parents were utterly shocked but no word was said. So as he saw the first few spots of rain he jumped on the wife and gave her a good seeing to as well. But still no words were uttered.

As the rain started to fall Jack knew he had failed, jumped up and said, "It's no good, I've got to use the lubricant."

At which point the father shot out of the room saying, "OK, OK, I'll do the dishes."

★ ★ ★

A man went for an audition at the local club.

"You'd better not be a hypnotist, they're not welcome here."

"No, I'm a singer," he replied, "but what's wrong with hypnotists?"

"Well, we had one here a couple of days ago. He had 12 people on stage in a trance when he tripped over the microphone wire and shouted 'Shit'. We've been clearing up ever since."

★ ★ ★

Overheard at a fancy dress party:
"I'm a turkey," said the girl. "What are you?"
"Sage and onion," he replied.

★ ★ ★

I was dancing in a night-club with this girl. I said, "Can I smell your fanny?" "No, you can't," she said. "Oh well, it must be your feet then."

★ ★ ★

The lift was packed solid with people as the doors closed and the attendant called out, "Which floors please?"
A man standing at the back shouted out, "Ballroom!" and a lady in front of him cried, "Oh, I'm so sorry, I didn't know I was crushing you that much."

★ ★ ★

It was the church social and everyone was having a good time singing and dancing. Suddenly during a lull in the noise, Mrs Riddler shouted over to the vicar, "What is it a man stands up to do, a woman sits down to do and a dog lifts up his leg to do?"
Blushing profusely, the vicar replied that he didn't know and amidst peals of laughter she cried, "Why, to shake hands of course!"

★ ★ ★

A young lad goes on a picnic with his Grandpa. After they've eaten, the old man opens a can of lager.
"Grandpa, can I have some?"
"Son, is your todger long enough to touch your backside?"
"No".
"Then you can't have a lager."
A little later Grandpa lights a cigarette.
"Grandpa, can I have one of those?"
"Is your todger long enough to touch your backside?"

"No."

"Then you can't have one."

On the way back to the house, they pop into the newsagent's and pick up a couple of scratch-cards. The man wins nothing but the boy wins £10,000.

"Are you going to share that with me?" asks grandpa.

"Is your todger long enough to touch your backside?" asks the boy.

"Yes," said the man.

"Then go fuck yourself."

★ ★ ★

A rather toffee-nosed couple moved into the area and to show off their new house invited the neighbours in for a cocktail party. They sent their adolescent son to bed and told him not to bother them but he kept coming down on any excuse – stomach ache, thirsty, couldn't sleep. Eventually, one of the guests, a retired colonel, suggested he take the boy back up to bed and he would soon get him settled.

Ten minutes later, the Colonel reappeared and they had no more trouble for the rest of the evening. As the party was breaking up, the couple took the Colonel aside and asked him what the secret was.

"Oh, simple really. I taught him to masturbate."

★ ★ ★

"I'm sorry you can't come in here, you have to wear a tie," said the bouncer at the night-club.

The man goes back to his car, but can only find a set of jump leads. He slings them round his neck and walks back to the club.

"Will this do?" he asks.

"OK, but don't start anything."

★ ★ ★

It was the night of the grand fancy-dress party and on arriving, everyone was announced. Shortly after 8pm, Jack arrived at the door wearing only his underpants.

"What are you?" insisted the announcer.

"I'm premature ejaculation," replied Jack.

"What! I can't say that, there are ladies present."

"OK, well just say I've come in my underpants."

★ ★ ★

It was a busy night in the Club and the crap table was doing a really roaring trade.

On one crucial throw a lot of money had been bet and, as the dice landed, a beautiful brunette opened her coat to reveal she had nothing on underneath as she shouted, "I've won." She collected all the winnings and walked away.

"What did she throw?" asked the croupier afterwards.

"I don't know," everyone replied. "We weren't looking at the dice."

★ ★ ★

A couple popped into the local hotel bar for a drink but when the man went to the gents he found it infested with flies.

Returning to the bar, he complained to the barman, who said to him reassuringly, "Don't worry, sir, the bell for lunch will be rung in five minutes."

"How will that help?" asked the puzzled man.

"They'll all come up to the dining room," he replied.

★ ★ ★

The final of *Mastermind* is being held in Leeds next week. The three contestants will be:

1. Brian Rawlings on British Rail 1949–1969.

2. Cynthia Prescott, English Poetry 1828–1858.

3. Kevin Shuttelworth on Yorkshire suit lengths £10.99–£40.

★ ★ ★

A rather shy young man went along to the village dance and met up with a rather pretty girl.

His chat-up lines were sadly lacking, so in a blind panic he said the only thing he could think of.

"You're Scottish, aren't you?"

"Aye, I am, how did ye ken that?"

"It's the way you roll your Rs."

"Oh no," she said. "It's these high-heeled shoes that do that."

★ ★ ★

A pirate walks into a bar and orders a drink. The bartender looks down and says, "You know that you have a steering wheel in your pants." The pirate replies, "Aye, it's drivin' me nuts."

★ ★ ★

A young man began courting a girl from a high-class family and one evening they invited him to join them at the opera. Worried about making a good impression, he calmed his nerves by downing a few pints beforehand. When it was time for the performance, they were shown to their seats – the first row of the balcony – but halfway through the first act the man needed to pee. The longer he sat, the more agonising it became, yet he was too embarrassed to disturb the whole row by getting out to go to the toilet. Eventually he hit upon an idea. Covering his lap with the programme, he slid out his dick and peed over the edge of the balcony. Such relief! But a moment later, a voice was heard from below: "For goodness sake, wave it about a bit."

★ ★ ★

"Hey, Jack, would you like a ticket for the local policemen's ball?"

"No thanks, I can't dance."

"That doesn't matter. It's not a dance, it's a raffle."

★ ★ ★

There was once a great actor who could no longer remember his lines. After many years he finds a theatre where they are prepared to give him a chance to shine again.

The director says, "This is the most important part, and it has only one line. You walk on to the stage at the opening carrying a rose. You hold the rose to your nose with just one finger and thumb, sniff the rose deeply and then say the line, 'Ah, the sweet aroma of my mistress.'"

The actor is thrilled. All day long before the play he's practising his line over and over again.

Finally, the time came. The curtain went up, the actor walked on to the stage and with great passion delivered the line, "Ah, the sweet aroma of my mistress."

The theatre erupted, the audience was screaming with laughter and the director was steaming!

"You bloody fool!" he cried. "You have ruined me!"

The actor was bewildered, "What happened, did I forget my line?"

"No!" screamed the director. "You forgot the rose!"

★ ★ ★

A rather well-proportioned young lady spent almost all of her vacation sunbathing on the roof of the hotel.

She wore a bathing suit the first day but, on the second, being a naturist, she decided that no one could see her way up there and she slipped out of it in the search for an all-over tan.

She'd hardly begun when she heard someone running up the stairs. She was lying on her stomach, so she just pulled a towel over her rear.

"Excuse me, miss," said the flustered little assistant manager of the hotel, out of breath from running up the stairs.

"The hotel doesn't mind you sunbathing on the roof but we would very much appreciate you wearing a bathing suit as you did yesterday."

"What difference does it make?" Joan asked rather calmly.

"No one can see me up here, and besides I'm covered with a towel."

"Not exactly," said the embarrassed little man.

"You're lying on the dining room skylight."

★ ★ ★

Paul was ambling through a crowded street fair when he decided to stop and sit at a Palm Reader's table.

Said the mysterious old woman, "For fifteen dollars, I can read your love line and tell your romantic future."

Paul readily agreed and the reader took one look at his open palm and said, "I can see that you have no girlfriend."

"That's true," said Paul.

"Oh my goodness, you are extremely lonely, aren't you?"

"Yes," Paul shamefacedly admitted. "That's amazing. Can you tell all of this from my love line?"

"Love line? No, from the calluses and blisters."

★ ★ ★

A little old lady wanted to join the Hell's Angels.

She knocked on the door of a local biker club and a big, hairy, bearded biker with tattoos all over his arms answered the door.

She proclaimed, "I want to join your biker club."

The guy was amused and told her that she needed to meet certain biker requirements before she was allowed to join. So the biker asked her, "You have a bike?"

The little old lady said, "Yeah, that's my Harley over there," and pointed to a Harley parked in the driveway.

The biker asked her, "Do you smoke?"

The little old lady said, "Yeah, I smoke. I smoke four packs of cigarettes a day and a couple of cigars while I'm shooting pool."

The biker was impressed and asked, "Well, have you ever been picked up by the Fuzz?"

The little old lady said, "No, I've never been picked up by the fuzz, but I've been swung around by my nipples a few times."

★ ★ ★

Frank was excited about his new rifle and decided to try bear hunting. He travelled up to Alaska, spotted a small brown bear and shot it.

Soon after there was a tap on his shoulder, and he turned around to see a big black bear. The black bear said, "That was a very bad mistake. That was my cousin. I'm going to give you two choices. Either I maul you to death or we have sex."

After considering briefly, Frank decided to accept the latter alternative. So the black bear had his way with Frank. Even though he felt sore for two weeks, Frank soon recovered and vowed revenge. He headed out on another trip to Alaska where he found the black bear and shot it dead. Right after, there was another tap on his shoulder. This time a huge grizzly bear stood right next to him. The grizzly said, "That was a big mistake, Frank. That was my cousin and you've got two choices: Either I maul you to death or we have rough sex."

Again, Frank thought it was better to cooperate with the grizzly bear than be mauled to death. So the grizzly had his way with Frank. Although he survived, it took several months before Frank fully recovered. Now Frank was completely outraged, so he headed back to Alaska and managed to track down the grizzly bear and shot it. He felt sweet revenge, but then, moments later, there was a tap on his shoulder. He turned around to find a giant polar bear standing there. The polar bear looked at him and said, "Admit it, Frank, you don't come here for the hunting, do you?"

★ ★ ★

LOCAL

A man goes into a bar with a cat and a heron and orders two pints of beer for himself and the cat, and a glass of wine for the heron.

"That'll be £4.20," says the barmaid.

"You get these, heron," says the cat, so the bird pays.

A little later, they order another round and this time the cat says to the man, "Your round, mate," so the man pays up.

The three stay at the bar all night drinking heavily but never once does the cat pay for a round, always having some excuse. Eventually, the bemused landlord cannot contain his curiosity any longer and asks the man what he's doing with the cat and heron. Sadly, the man explains that one night in bed he was visited by a genie who granted him one wish and he asked for a bird with long legs and a tight pussy!

★ ★ ★

You know you must be drunk when somebody says, "Go fuck yourself," and you ask for their telephone number.

★ ★ ★

A bloke who's well known for challenging people to dares walks into a pub with an alligator. He picks up a bottle, smashes it over the head of the alligator, which stuns the beast into slowly opening its mouth. At this point the man drops his trousers and puts his knob in the alligator's mouth, leaving it there for 10 seconds and removing it just as the jaws of the alligator snap shut.

"Now," said the man addressing the stunned onlookers. "Is there anyone here who will take on this dare?"

The room remains silent for a few moments and then an old lady stands up, saying, "I'll have a go, but please don't hit me too hard with the bottle."

★ ★ ★

Every day a man in the local bar would be surrounded by beautiful women, who swarmed round him like bees round a honey pot.

"I don't understand it," said the barman. "It's not as if he has a lot of money or dresses expensively; all he does is just sit there licking his eyebrows."

★ ★ ★

A man walks into a pub, orders a pint and is charged £1.80. A little later he orders another and hands over £1.80. But the third time, the barman gives it to him for free.

"How come?" asks the man.

"Well, the owner of this pub doesn't know that I know he's upstairs with my wife. So I'm doing to him down here, what he's doing to me up there."

★ ★ ★

A man walked into a bar with a tiny pianist on his shoulder. The pianist could only have been a foot tall. During the evening the pianist entertained the customers with his wonderful playing and eventually the barman asked the man where he got this wonderful entertainer.

"Well, I was walking in a wood and came across an old bottle. In the bottle was a genie who offered me anything I wanted but was a little hard of hearing. She thought I said a twelve-inch pianist."

★ ★ ★

A drunk staggered into the police station to report his car had been stolen.

"Where did you leave it, sir?"

"On the end of this key and now the bloody thing's gone."

The policeman was not in the mood for such nonsense.

"Look at you. You're a disgrace, you're so drunk you don't know what's going on. Why, you've even left your flies open."

"Bugger me!" said the drunk. "They've stolen my girlfriend as well."

★ ★ ★

Yo Mama:
yo moma is so drank she got hit by a parkt car.

★ ★ ★

A man thought up a clever way to make some money. His friend had an unusual anatomical feature in that he had three balls.
"We can make a fortune," he told him. "Come on, I'll show you how."
They went into the local pub and the man got everyone's attention by standing on a chair and shouting, "I'll bet anyone in this bar that my friend and the barman there have five balls between them."
People rushed forward and soon a lot of money had changed hands.
At that point the man turned to the barman and said, "I hope you don't mind taking part in this bet."
"Not at all," replied the barman. "It's amazing to find a man with four balls, you see I've only got one."

★ ★ ★

A lady at the far end of the bar waves her arm in the air to get the attention of the waiter and in doing so shows a good hairy underarm.
Down the other end of the bar is a very drunk man.
"Hey, waiter, get that ballerina a drink!" he shouts.
"How do you know she's a ballerina?"
"Well, no one else could get their leg so high."

★ ★ ★

A ranch hand goes into the saloon and orders a shot of whisky. He drinks it down in one gulp, rushes outside, kisses his horse's arse and comes back in again.
Another whisky is ordered and drunk before he rushes outside and kisses his horse's backside again.
After he has done this half a dozen times, the bartender's curiosity gets the better of him and he asks the man why, after each drink, he rushes outside to kiss the horse's bum.
"Chapped lips," replies the man.

"Oh, does that cure them?" asks the surprised bartender.

"No, but it sure as hell stops me licking them."

★ ★ ★

A crafty man goes into the pub and up to the bar where the bartender greets him.

"Good evening, sir, what's your pleasure?"

"Well, I'll have a pint of bitter, please, and a packet of crisps."

He puts 30p down on the bar. On seeing this, the bartender asks him what he's up to.

He replies, "That's for the crisps. I didn't want a drink, but I thought it would be rude to turn down your generous offer."

"I was only being polite," explains the bartender but the man refuses to pay, so he's banned from the pub.

A few weeks later he comes into the pub again and is immediately recognized by the bartender.

"You're barred!" he shouts.

"But why? I've never been here before. I live overseas."

Puzzled, the bartender apologizes.

"I'm sorry sir, you must have a double."

"Why thank you, and a packet of crisps, please."

★ ★ ★

Why does a man's penis have a hole in it?

So he can get oxygen to his brain.

★ ★ ★

A man walks into a bar with a stoat on his shoulder.

"Hey, what's this all about?" asks the bartender.

"Let me tell you, mate, this stoat gives the best blow job ever."

"Give me a break, now get out and take it with you."

The man persists. "No, really. Why don't you take it out the back and see?"

A little while later, the bartender reappears.

"That was fantastic, I'll give you £100 for it."

"No way," replies the man. They haggle for a while, but the man eventually sells for £600. After closing time, the bartender takes the stoat home and finds his wife in the kitchen.

"Mabel, teach this stoat to cook and then get the fuck out of here."

★ ★ ★

"You're so ugly, your mom had to be drunk to breastfeed you!"

★ ★ ★

A man is trying to decide what to call his new bar when he spots Lisa coming up the street. Now this man is really keen on Lisa, who's not only gorgeous-looking but has legs that go on for ever. That's it, he thinks, I'll call my new bar 'Lisa's Legs'.

The next day three men are waiting outside the bar when a cop stops to ask them what they are doing.

"We're waiting for Lisa's Legs to open, so we can go in and satisfy our needs," they reply.

★ ★ ★

There was a guy in a bar one night that got really drunk, I mean really, really, really drunk. When the bar closed he got up to go home. As he stumbled out the door he saw a nun walking on the sidewalk. So he stumbled over to the nun and punched her in the face.

Well, the nun was really surprised but before she could do or say anything he punched her again. This time she fell down and he stumbled over to her and kicked her in the butt.

Then he picked her up and threw her into a wall. By this time the nun was pretty weak and couldn't move. So then he stumbled over to her, put his face right next to hers and said, "Not very tough tonight, are you, Batman?"

★ ★ ★

"Same as usual, Jack," asks the bartender as he sees one of his regulars walk up to the bar.

"No, thanks, just an orange juice, please," replies the man dejectedly. Taken aback, the bartender asks why.

"It's my wife. She says if I come home one more time legless and covered in puke, she'll pack her bags and leave."

The bartender tells him he has a way to get around the problem.

"Have a £10 note handy and when you arrive home in your usual state, insist it was someone else who threw up all over you. Show her the money and say he offered to pay for the dry cleaning."

Jack's well pleased with the idea and spends the evening drinking pint after pint until he's blind drunk. Sure enough, by the time he's got home, he's thrown up on himself but still remembers the little trick. As soon as his wife starts shouting at him he shows her the money and explains what happened.

"But that's a £20 note," she retorts.

"Er… yes, that's right, the same guy messed in my pants as well."

★ ★ ★

A man walks into his local and finds a seat at the bar next to a drunk. For some five minutes the drunk looks at something in his hand and eventually the man's curiosity gets the better of him and he asks what it is.

"It's odd," replied the drunk. "It looks like plastic but feels like rubber."

"Here, let me see," said the man.

He takes the object and begins to roll it between his fingers.

"You're right," he says. "It does feel like rubber but looks like plastic. Where did you get it from?"

"My nose," replies the drunk.

★ ★ ★

Joe agrees to take his wife to the pub. They sit down at a table and the husband gets up and goes to get drinks. While he is gone, a man walks up to Joe's wife and tells her he wants to turn her upside down, fill her with beer and drink her dry. Joe's wife exclaims, "You sick pervert, get out of my sight." Joe returns and his wife tells him what happened and to go kick that guy's ass. Joe says, "No way – you don't mess with a guy who can drink that much beer."

★ ★ ★

After gulping down a Scotch in the local bar, the man bets the bartender £50 he can piss in the empty glass. Eager to make some easy money, the bartender agrees, so the man drops his trousers and starts to piss everywhere – on the floor, the bar, the tables, even over the bartender himself. But nothing goes in the glass. The bartender chuckles to himself and demands the £50.

"Just a second," replies the man who goes up to two guys sitting in the corner and comes back moments later with £200 in his hand.

"Here's your £50," he says and hands over the money.

Puzzled, the bartender asks, "What was all that about?"

"Well, you see, I bet them £200 that I could piss all over this pub, and over you, and you'd still be smiling at the end of it."

★ ★ ★

Four men in the pub were discussing what part of a woman they found most attractive. The first said he went for the lips – full, pouty, curvy lips. The second said he went for the eyes – dark and mysterious. The third went for the hair – long, blonde, fragrant.

At that point, the fourth man interrupted.

"Listen, lads, I feel like the rest of you. We all know what part of the female we find most attractive. It's just that I don't lie through my bloody teeth about it."

★ ★ ★

It has just been announced that Bob Swillall has been elected Chairman of Alcoholics Unanimous. He will be notified of this as soon as he comes round.

★ ★ ★

A man goes into a bar and asks for a pint of bitter. The barman serves him and the customer drinks it very quickly and then says, "Do you have any brown ale?"

"Of course, sir." And he's served the drink.

A little later the man again asks, "Do you have any lager?"

"Of course, sir. That's what pubs are for."

And a little later still he asks, "Have you got any stout?"

"Naturally," replies the barman.

The barman is pestered all night by these ridiculous questions until finally his temper snaps.

"Sir, this is a pub. We have everything you could wish for – dark ales, light ales, ciders, four kinds of beers, bottled drinks, red wine, white wine… so please, enough of these stupid questions."

A moment goes by before the man asks, "Do you have shorts?"

"Look, my good fellow, I've just said we have everything, so YES, we have shorts."

"Thank goodness for that," replied the man. "I'll have a pair in a large size because I've just pissed myself."

★ ★ ★

Jack was sitting at the bar gazing dejectedly into his beer.

"What's up?" asked the barman.

"It was last night," he replied. "I got so drunk I don't remember what I did but when I saw a woman in bed with me I naturally gave her £50."

"Well, that's reasonable, even if you don't remember it," consoled the barman.

"It's not that," said Jack. "It's the fact that it was my wife and she automatically gave me £10 change."

★ ★ ★

Eight football hooligans walk into a bar and one of them orders nine pints of beer.

"There's only eight of you," says the barman politely, but for his trouble he gets thrown up against the wall and punched.

"Of course, sir!" he gasps and pulls nine pints. Each of the hooligans takes one and the ninth is taken to a man sitting quietly in the corner. "Here you are, mate, have this one on us. It gives me a good feeling to help someone who can't walk."

"Gosh! Thanks, but I can walk, you know."

"Not for long, if you don't get the next round in."

★　★　★

A pony walks into a bar and says, "Bartender, may I have a drink?"

Bartender says, "What? I can't hear you. Speak up!"

"May I please have a drink?"

"What? You have to speak up!"

"Could I please have a drink?"

"Now listen, if you don't speak up I will not serve you."

"I'm sorry, I'm just a little hoarse."

★　★　★

A guy walks into a bar and sees a dog lying in the corner licking his balls. He turns to the bartender and says, "Boy, I wish I could do that." The Bartender replies, "You'd better try petting him first."

★　★　★

A bloke goes into a pub and orders a triple whisky and a pint of beer. As soon as the barman puts them in front of him he drinks them all down in one gulp. "I shouldn't be drinking all this," he says. "Why's that?" "Because I've only got 20p on me."

★　★　★

A gambling man goes into a pub and bets the customers that he can smell any wood and tell them what it is, blindfolded. They take on his bet, blindfold him and get him to smell the table.

After a moment he suddenly says, "That's mahogany."

Next, they get him to smell the top of the bar.

"Yes, I know that, it's oak," he answers confidently.

"OK, it's double or nothing."

They put a snooker cue under his nose. A minute goes by and then he replies, "I would say that's Canadian maple."

Feeling very dispirited, the regulars have one more trick up their sleeve. They get hold of Old Meg – the village's oldest tart – lay her out on the table, pull down her knickers and get the man to smell between her legs. After a good sniff, he asks them to turn it over, which they do, and he has another good sniff.

"Can you just turn it back again?" he asks, and again he has a good smell.

This goes on for a couple of minutes with the regulars turning Meg over time and time again.

"OK, your time's up," they say at last.

"Right," says the man. "I would say it's a shit-house door made out of fish boxes."

★ ★ ★

A man walks into a Wild West bar, itching for a fight. He takes immediate dislike to the piano player, so takes out his shotgun and drills four holes in the man's ear. He then turns to the barman and asks for a shot of whisky. As he serves the man, the barman says, "Mind if I give some advice? If I were you I'd shave down the metal sight and grease the barrel well."

"Why? Will that make me shoot better?"

"No, but it'll be easier for you. The piano player's father is Big Jake, a man much feared round these parts, and when he hears what you've done, he'll shove that gun right up your arse."

★ ★ ★

A man walked into a pub boasting that he could identify any drink blindfolded. Would anyone care to take up the challenge?

Half a dozen of the regulars agreed to the bet. They each put down £10 that he could not identify all six drinks offered to him. Along came the first. The man tasted it and said, "Yes, that's from a famous brewery called Jenkins and it's their special bitter."

He was correct.

Another was put before him.

"This is a tequila and is Jose Revello."

Correct; and so it went on. Each time the man was able to name the drink and the manufacturer. By the time the sixth drink came along the punters were getting desperate. This time when they put the drink before him, he tasted it, spat it out and swore profusely.

"Bloody hell, this is urine; this is just plain piss."

"Yes," said a voice, "but whose is it?"

★ ★ ★

A hippopotamus walks into a bar and asks the bartender for a beer. "That will be $7.50 please," says the bartender.

So the hippo gives the bartender his money and starts to sip his beer. "You know we don't very many hippos in here," mutters the bartender. The hippo replies, "At these prices it's no wonder!"

★ ★ ★

A man walks into a bar and orders a pint of beer. He looks around, admiring the room and he soon notices that there are big lumps of meat hanging on the ceiling. He then says to the bartender, "Why have you got all this meat hanging around?"

The barman says, "It's a little bet that we are running. If you can jump up and grab a bit of meat in your mouth then you can have all of your drinks bought for you. If you fail then you have to buy everyone else in the bar their drinks. Are you going to have a try?" The man shakes his head and says to the bartender, "No, the stakes [steaks] are too high."

★ ★ ★

A man goes into a pub carrying an octopus.

"Sorry, mate, you can't bring that in here," says the barman.

"Hold on a minute," says the man, "this isn't just any old octopus, this one can play every single musical instrument you care to put before him. How about a small wager? If he can play all the instruments you can produce, I get free drinks for the night. If not, then I'll buy everyone in here a drink."

The barman agrees and the wager begins. First, the octopus plays the piano and it's beautiful, then it plays the trumpet – a superb piece of jazz – followed by the double bass, violin and the harp. In fact, the harp is so well played it brings tears to the eyes of the customers.

"I'm not beaten yet!" thinks the barman. He goes upstairs into the attic and finds his old bagpipes. They haven't been played for years, but he dusts them down and hands them to the octopus. The creature looks at them, feels them but doesn't start to play.

"Gotcha," smiles the barman triumphantly. "Time to pay up."

"Just a moment," replies the man confidently. "When he realizes he can't fuck it, then he'll play it."

★ ★ ★

A guy walks into a bar, sits down, and orders a drink. He starts eating the beer nuts at the bar and he hears a voice say, "Wow! You look GREAT tonight!"

The man looks over at the bartender who didn't say anything and just keeps drinking and eating beer nuts.

Then he hears something again! "That's an awesome shirt! You are truly amazing!"

He looks around and he's the only guy in the place, so he asks the bartender if he had heard anything and the bartender says, "Was the voice saying bad things or good things?"

And the man replies, "Good things, why?" At which the bartender says, "It must have been the complimentary nuts."

★ ★ ★

Once upon a time, a guy was sitting at a bar. He was throwing money around, giving the barman hundred dollar tips and buying drinks for everyone. He was surrounded by a crowd of adoring women.

The barman liked the tips, but he was kind of curious about a little man that would jump from the rich guy's pocket.

The little man would run up and down the bar, kicking over the bowls of peanuts and giving people the finger.

Then the little guy would jump back into the man's jacket for a while. The barman went over and asked the guy what was up.

So the rich guy says, "Well, let me tell you a little story. I was walking along a beach one day, and I come across this lamp.

"I rub it, and a genie popped out. I got three wishes, so my first wish was to be fabulously wealthy. Then I wished for a harem. You can see I got both."

The barman asks, "So what about that little guy in your jacket?"

"Oh, that," mumbles the rich guy. "That's the twelve-inch prick I wished for."

★ ★ ★

Two men are sitting drinking at a bar at the top of the Empire State Building when the first man turns to the other and says, "You know, last week I discovered that if you jump from the top of this building, by the time you fall to the 10th floor, the winds round the building are so intense that they carry you around the building and back into the window."

The bartender just shakes his head in disbelief and disapproval while wiping down the bar.

The second guy says, "What are you, a nut? There is no way that could happen." "No, it's true," said the first man, "let me prove it to you."

He gets up from the bar, jumps over the balcony and plummets towards the street below. When he passes the 10th floor, the high wind whips him around the building and back into the 10th-floor window and he takes the elevator back up to the bar. He meets the second man, who looks quite astonished. "You know, I saw that with my own eyes, but that must have been a one-off fluke."

"No, I'll prove it again," says the first man and jumps. Again just as he is hurtling towards the street, the 10th-floor wind gently carries him around the building and into the window.

Once upstairs he urges his fellow drinker to try it. "Well, what the heck," the second guy says, "it works. I'll try it!" He jumps over the balcony, plunges downwards, passes the 11th, 10th, 9th, 8th floors... and hits the sidewalk with a 'splat'. Back upstairs the bartender turns to the other drinker, saying, "You know, Superman, sometimes you can be a real jerk."

★ ★ ★

Two buddies were out for a Saturday stroll. One had a Doberman and the other had a Chihuahua.

As they sauntered down the street, the guy with Doberman said to his friend, "Let's go over to that bar and get something to drink."

The guy with the Chihuahua said, "We can't go in there. We've got dogs with us." The one with the Doberman said, "Just follow my lead." At this point, the guy with the Doberman put on a pair of dark glasses and started to walk in. The bouncer at the door said, "Sorry, Mac, no pets allowed."

The man with the Doberman said, "You don't understand. This is my Seeing-Eye dog."

The bouncer said, "A Doberman pinscher?"

The man said, "Yes, they're using them now. They're very good."

The bouncer said, "Come on in then."

The buddy with the Chihuahua figured what the heck, so he put on a pair of dark glasses and started to walk in. He knew his would be more unbelievable.

Once again the bouncer said, "Sorry, pal, no pets allowed."

The man with the Chihuahua said, "You don't understand. This is my Seeing-Eye dog."

The bouncer said, "A Chihuahua?"

The man with the Chihuahua said, "A Chihuahua? They gave me a fucking Chihuahua?"

★ ★ ★

A brain goes into a pub and says, "Pint of lager, please."
"Sorry, mate, you're already out of your head," the barman replies.

★ ★ ★

A mushroom walks into a bar, sits down and orders a drink. The bartender says, "I'm afraid we don't serve mushrooms here.'
"Why not? I'm a fun guy!"

★ ★ ★

A drunk gets up from the bar and heads for the bathroom. A few minutes later, a loud, blood curdling scream is heard from the bathroom.
A few minutes after that, another loud scream reverberates through the bar. The bartender goes into the bathroom to investigate why the drunk is screaming. "What's all the screaming about in there? You're scaring the customers!"
"I'm just sitting here on the toilet and every time I try to flush, something comes up and squeezes the hell out of my balls."
With that, the bartender opens the door, looks in and says, "You idiot! You're sitting on the mop bucket!"

★ ★ ★

A guy walks into a bar with his pet monkey. He orders a drink and while he's drinking the monkey jumps all around the place.
The monkey grabs some olives off the bar and eats them, then grabs some sliced limes and eats them, then jumps on to the pool table, grabs one of the billiard balls, sticks it in his mouth and, to everyone's amazement, somehow swallows it whole.
The bartender screams at the guy, "Did you see what your monkey just did?"
The guy says, "No, what?"
"He just ate the cue ball off my pool table – whole!"
"Yeah, that doesn't surprise me," replied the guy, "he eats everything in sight, the little bastard. Sorry. I'll pay for the cue ball and stuff."
He finishes his drink, pays his bill, pays for the stuff the monkey ate,

then leaves. Two weeks later he's in the bar again, and has his monkey with him. He orders a drink and the monkey starts running around the bar again.

While the man is finishing his drink, the monkey finds a maraschino cherry on the bar. He grabs it, sticks it up his butt, pulls it out and eats it. The bartender is disgusted.

"Did you see what your monkey did now?" he asks.

"No, what?" replies the guy.

"Well, he stuck a maraschino cherry up his butt, pulled it out and ate it!" said the bartender.

"Yeah, that doesn't surprise me," replied the guy. "He still eats everything in sight, but ever since he swallowed that cue ball, he measures everything first."

★ ★ ★

A man walked into a bar and ordered a beer. He drank half and then poured the rest on his hand.

A few minutes later, the man ordered another beer and the bartender became suspicious. Again, he drank half and then poured the rest on his hand.

A short while later, the man ordered yet another beer. The bartender finally asked, "Excuse me, sir, but what the heck are you doing?"

The irritated guy replied, "Can't you see that my date and I are trying to have a drink?"

★ ★ ★

MARRIAGE

A couple had just got married and as they went upstairs to bed, the groom turned to his new wife and told her to put his trousers on.
"But they don't fit," she said.
"Exactly. Remember that. I wear the trousers round here."
Inflamed, the new wife took her knickers off and threw them at him.
"OK," she said, "put these on."
He replied, "I can't get into these."
"You're damned right you can't and you never will if you don't change your outdated attitude."

★ ★ ★

My mother in law called today… I knew it was her: when she knocked at the front door all the mice threw themselves on the traps!

★ ★ ★

The groom was so ugly he had to wear the veil!

★ ★ ★

On the day of their marriage a man said to his new wife, "Everything I have is yours. You can do anything you like in the house, but you must never look in the top right-hand drawer of my desk."
Twenty-seven years passed when one day during spring cleaning she couldn't resist opening the drawer. In it she found three golf balls and £10,000. When her husband came home, she confessed she'd looked in the drawer and couldn't understand why he had never allowed her to look.
"I must be honest," he said. "I decided that if I was ever unfaithful I would put a golf ball in the drawer."
"Well, that's all right" replied the wife. "Only three times in 27 years."
"But I have to admit that every time I got to a dozen golf balls, I sold them," he said.

★ ★ ★

It was their wedding night and they were spending it in a four-star hotel. As she went upstairs to their room to prepare herself, he stayed downstairs for a final drink. However, as he thought of what awaited him upstairs he abandoned his drink and soon followed her up. But as he entered the room he found her stark naked on her back with the night porter fondling her breasts and the elevator boy down below.

"Darling, how could you!" he wailed.

"Oh, come on, Ron, I always told you I was a bit of a goer," she said.

★ ★ ★

A disappointed husband said to his wife on seeing he put her bra on, "I don't know why you bother, you've nothing to put in it."

She retorted, "Listen, you, I don't complain when you go out to buy underpants."

★ ★ ★

"Now listen, son, you'll look back on this time as the happiest in your life," confided the boy's father.

"But, dad, I'm not getting married for another week."

"That's what I mean, son," he nodded sadly.

★ ★ ★

Why did the one-legged man settle down and get married?

He couldn't catch sheep anymore.

★ ★ ★

Three couples get married on the same day and find themselves in the same hotel for their wedding night.

When the girls have gone up to bed the men have one more drink before following them and they agree to swap stories of their night of passion the next morning after breakfast.

The next day they meet up and the first man describes the wonderful night he and his wife had.

"We made love five times. I can't wait for tonight."

The second man agrees.
"Neither can I. Last night we made love seven times, every which way we could think of."
The third man was strangely quiet.
"How about you?" asked the other two.
"We made love once," he said.
"Once! What did your wife say?"
"It's nearly breakfast time, we'd better get some sleep."

★ ★ ★

A couple went down to the register office to arrange a date for their marriage.
"Names please," said the official.
"My name's Robert Smith and this is Jenny Smith."
"Any connection?" she asked.
"Only once," blushed the girl. "Behind his dad's barn last Sunday."

★ ★ ★

After only one month of marriage, the tearful young girl confided in her friend that she was leaving her husband because he drank too much.
"But why did you marry him in the first place if you knew about his drinking?" she asked.
"Ah, but I didn't, not until he came home three nights ago sober."

★ ★ ★

My wife is so houseproud that, in the middle of the night I got up to get a drink and when I returned, the bed was made.

★ ★ ★

She can remember when she got married, and where she got married, but she can't for the life of her remember why.

★ ★ ★

379

A man came home from work early to find his wife bending down clearing out the cupboards. Quick as a tick, he lifted her dress, pulled down her knickers and took her from behind. When it was over he gave her two sharp smacks on her bare backside.

"You bloody sod," she said. "You have your wicked way and all the thanks I get is a good slapping."

"That's for not looking round to see who it was," he retorted.

★ ★ ★

Do you know what it means to come home at night to someone who gives you love, affection and understanding?

It means you're in the wrong house.

★ ★ ★

A man said, "Was that your wife who answered the door?"

"Of course it was," replied the husband. "You don't think I've got an au pair that ugly."

★ ★ ★

My wife gets so easily upset that she cries when the traffic lights are against her.

★ ★ ★

Moaning man:

"Is there anything worse than a wife who never stops talking about her last husband?"

"Yes – a wife who never stops talking about her next husband," his friend replied.

★ ★ ★

Two mates talking about marriage.

One complained that his wife never felt like sex, but the other replied, "I know what the trouble is, you need good technique. Tonight after supper open a bottle of champagne, put on some sexy music, slowly

undress her, fondle her breasts, stroke her thighs… then, then…"
"Yes, then what?"
"Call for me."

★ ★ ★

Did you hear about the girl who advertised for a husband in the personal column of the local paper?
She had over 200 replies saying, "You can have mine."

★ ★ ★

The eldest son was still masturbating at the age of 35 so his dad strongly advised him that it was time he got married.
A year later, having found a girl, the son got married but it was only six weeks later that his father caught him once again masturbating in the garden shed.
"What's going on. I thought this would be a thing of the past once you'd got married," said his father.
"Have a heart, Dad, Doreen's only small and her arms get tired very quickly."

★ ★ ★

A couple have been apart for nearly six months and when they eventually embrace again at the railway station he says, "FF," but she says, "No, EF."
He replies, "FF," and at that point the ticket inspector taps him on the shoulder and says, "I couldn't help but overhear – what's going on?"
The man replies, "She wants to eat first."

★ ★ ★

A newly married man comes home from work to find his wife crying in the kitchen. "What's wrong?" he asks, looking alarmed. "I'm trying so hard to be a good wife," she sobs, "and I've spent all afternoon in the kitchen cooking your dinner, but it's turned out to be a disaster."

"Never mind," he says, "Let's just go to bed." The following day, he comes home from work to find her crying again because she's burnt the dinner and once more he comforts her and takes her to bed. This happens the next night as well. Then on the fourth night he arrives home to find her sliding stark naked down the bannisters. When he asks what she's doing, she replies, "I'm just keeping your dinner warm."

★ ★ ★

Did you hear about the man who grew a moustache?
He was fed up with his wife calling him a barefaced liar.

★ ★ ★

A disgruntled man broke the flies on his trousers when he was putting them on and turned to his wife, saying he'd still wear them just to show his mates what he had to put up with.
"Oh no," replied his wife. "I'll mend them, I don't want them to know what I have to put up with."

★ ★ ★

A woman woke her husband in the middle of the night and told him, "There's a burglar downstairs in the kitchen and he is eating the cake my mother made for us."
The husband said, "Who shall I call first, the police or an ambulance?"

★ ★ ★

After a month of being married, the young rather naive wife turned to her husband and said, fondling his private parts, "I thought you said you were the only man who had one of these, but you were telling lies. The man next door has one as well."
"Oh that," he replied. "That's just a spare one I had so I let him have it." "Oh, you goon," she laughed. "You've given him the best one."

★ ★ ★

A newly married couple had experienced their first real argument and she had spent two nights in the spare bedroom. On the third night her husband brought her some flowers home as a way of apologising and it seemed to work.

She smiled at him and disappeared into the bedroom, where he found her lying on the bed with her legs wide apart.

"This is for the flowers," she murmured.

"Oh dear, I didn't know we hadn't got a vase," he replied.

★ ★ ★

Only one month into their marriage, a young girl finds her 80-year-old husband cheating on her with a woman of 65.

"Why are you doing this? Can't I satisfy you – what has she got that I haven't?" she complains

"Patience," he replies.

★ ★ ★

"It's very simple," said the newly wed husband to his bride. "I don't want to be too demanding, so if you want it, tug on this twice, but if you don't want it, tug on it 400 times."

★ ★ ★

A husband and wife were always arguing. This time it was about sex.

"You're so frigid, I wouldn't be surprised if you put cold cream between your legs!" he yelled.

"Oh yeah!" she sneered. "And I wouldn't be surprised if you put vanishing cream between yours."

★ ★ ★

A married couple are in bed one night when he turns to her and says, "Darling, I've got a new position for us to try. We must lie back to back." "But I don't understand," she says, "what's this about?"

"It's OK. We've got another couple joining us."

★ ★ ★

The snow was thick on the ground when Jack went into the public toilets for a pee. As he was fumbling around in his flies, his mate Bob walked in.

"Hello, Jack, it's hard to find in this weather, isn't it!"

"It is indeed," replied Jack. "Even at home when the two of us are looking for it!"

★ ★ ★

A woman comes back from the doctor's smiling all over her face.

"You're in a good mood," remarks her husband. "What's happened?"

"The doctor has just told me I've got the boobs of a 21-year-old."

"Oh yeah, what did he say about your 50-year-old arse?"

"Nothing – we didn't mention you," she retorted.

★ ★ ★

Did you hear about the totally selfish husband? Every night in bed he would shout, "Coming, ready or not!"

★ ★ ★

Overheard in a bus:

"I'm worried about my wife. It's her appearance, she's let me down."

"Oh, how come?" replied the other.

"Well, I haven't seen her for three days."

★ ★ ★

I took my mother-in-law to Madame Tussaud's chamber of horrors and one of the attendants said, "Keep her moving, sir, we're stocktaking."

Did you hear about the man who threw his mother-in-law into the lion's den at London zoo?

He's being sued for cruelty to animals by the RSPCA.

★ ★ ★

"Do you know I found a great way of getting my husband to increase the housekeeping. Last week I went shopping with him wearing a low-cut blouse with no bra on. When I bent down to get something from the bottom shelf one of my boobs fell out. He was so angry until I told him it was because I didn't have enough money to buy a good bra, so he increased the housekeeping straight away."

"What a tremendous idea," said her friend, "I'll have to try something like that."

The two women met up the following week but her friend looked very downcast.

"What happened, didn't it work?"

"I remembered what you said and just before we went out on Saturday night I lifted up my dress and said, 'Look, Alf, I'm wearing no knickers because I can't afford to buy any,' and you'll never guess what the old bugger did. He gave me a couple of quid to buy myself a comb, telling me that at least I should tidy myself up."

★ ★ ★

Three women are talking about their husbands and the subject of nicknames comes up.

"My husband's called Big Mac because he's got the largest, juiciest donger you ever did see," said the first woman happily.

"I call my husband Surfing Willy because when he gets going I feel like I'm floating on water," said the second.

"Mine's called Cointreau," said the third.

Puzzled, one of the other women asked, "Isn't that a special kind of liquor?"

"That's exactly what I mean," she answered dreamily.

★ ★ ★

A man and a woman find themselves sharing the same carriage on an overnight sleeper to Glasgow. After half an hour the woman shouts down to the man, "It's quite cold in here, do you think you could pass me another blanket?"

"I've got a better idea," he says. "Why don't we pretend we're married?"

"Well, OK then."

"Good, then get your own bloody blanket."

★ ★ ★

The young couple have been married for six months and one day when they are in bed he asks her if she is happy.

"Oh yes," she replies. "Everything is wonderful."

"But is there nothing that bothers you?" he persists.

"Well... only a couple of things. You're always picking your nose and we always make love with you on top."

"I can explain that," he says. "When I was growing up my father gave me two pieces of advice which always I try to follow: 'Keep your nose clean and don't fuck up.'"

★ ★ ★

A man receives a telegram informing him that his mother-in-law had passed away; it also asked him whether she should be buried, or cremated.

The man telegraphs back, "Take no chances, burn the body and bury the ashes."

★ ★ ★

Did you know you can calculate the age of your mother-in-law by counting the rings in the bathtub!

★ ★ ★

I saw six men kicking and punching my mother-in-law. My wife said, "Aren't you going to help?" "No, six should be enough," I replied.

★ ★ ★

The woman sobbed quietly into her handkerchief as the engineer came to cut off the gas supply for non-payment of bills.

"We just couldn't afford to pay it," she cried. "We've got ten children and it takes all our money to feed them."

"Perhaps you shouldn't have had so many children," replied the engineer. "It's irresponsible if you can't meet your bills. One of you is surely to blame, though I would guess it's six of one and half a dozen of the other."

★ ★ ★

Two men talking in the bookies:

"What's wrong, Charlie? You don't look so good this morning."

"It's the bloody wife; she's keeping me awake at night dreaming of this driving test she's taking next week. Every so often she grabs hold of my willie and moves it around like a gear stick. It's no joke."

"I've got an idea, Charlie. Next time she starts, turn her over and stick it up her backside – maybe that will stop her."

The next night, Charlie does as his mate suggests, turns her over and gives her one up the backside.

"£5 of four-star, please," she says.

★ ★ ★

"Doctor, you've got to help me. My dick isn't big enough to satisfy my wife," said the distraught man.

"Do you drink special brew?" asked the doctor.

"Yes."

"Well, that's your problem. Special brew tends to keep it small; you'd better try some brown ale."

A few weeks later, the doctor bumped into the man in the off-licence.

"Was it a success? I can see you've got some brown ale there," said the doctor.

"Oh yes, the sex is great now. Thanks, doc. I don't drink the brown ale, though; I give it to my wife."

★ ★ ★

On their second honeymoon night a couple discovered there had been a mix-up with the booking and they would have to sleep in a twin-bedded room. They got into bed and the man said, "Sweetie pie, are you going to bring that beautiful big body of yours over here so that I can show you how much I love you?"

As she came across to him, she bumped into the bedside table and knocked the lamp on the floor. "Never mind, my darling, accidents will happen." Some time later, when the 'party' was over, the wife slipped out of bed to return to hers. But again she bumped into the bedside table. "For goodness sake, watch what you're doing, you stupid, fat bitch!" he said.

★ ★ ★

After watching a steamy video at work, a man goes home to his wife and asks her why she doesn't moan when they make love.

"If that's what you want, I'll do it tonight," she says.

That night, in bed, he gets on top of her and after a couple of minutes she says, "When are you going to paint the kitchen? Why can't I have a new dress? Next door have got a far better car than we have…"

★ ★ ★

After a heavy night drinking with his pals, Jack staggers home at one in the morning and falls into bed. Three hours later, he wakes up to find he's wet the bed so being a real prat, he climbs over his wife on to the dry side and rolls her into the wet.

It's not long before the wife wakes up and an almighty row erupts over who has actually wet the bed.

"I'll prove it," says the wife, and she takes out the pot from under the bed, squats down and enjoys a nice long pee. "Now it's your turn, you won't be able to, because you've just peed the bed."

Jack takes his turn on the pot and tries with all his might until he's finally rewarded with a long and satisfying pee. Alas! One minute later he wakes up to find he's wet the other side of the bed.

★ ★ ★

"Hello, Fred, what have you been up to?"

"I've just got married to an identical twin."

"How can you tell them apart?"

"The other one's got a beard and a very deep voice."

★ ★ ★

"Oh, John, do you remember, the last time we were up here was 25 years ago and we made love for the very first time near an old disused barn. I wonder if we could find it again."

"I shouldn't think it'd be there after all this time," he said, "but we'll go and have a look."

Surprisingly enough, the barn was still there.

"Look, Doreen, I sat you on that fence over there and we made love, let's do it again."

She agreed and he sat her on the fence and began the business.

Doreen went completely wild, thrashing her arms in the air and waving her feet around.

"Wow, Doreen, you didn't do that last time."

"I know," she stammered, "but it wasn't electrified then."

★ ★ ★

A street busker is trying very unsuccessfully to play his cello and the noise he's making is driving most people away.

"Cor, Flo," said May, as they passed him by, "he reminds me of our Bert's nasty habits. He sits and scratches his instrument too, instead of learning how to use it properly."

★ ★ ★

A man living way up in the Highlands of Scotland goes down into the village to post a letter. His wife has not long died after 45 years of marriage.

"How's it going then, Jock?" asks the sympathetic store owner.

"Well, the sex is just the same, but the ironing is piling up."

★ ★ ★

"Now you've just got married, let me tell you about sex," said the man's father. "You go through three different stages. First of all, when you're newlyweds, you have sex anytime, anywhere – the kitchen, the bedroom, the garage, whenever the urge takes you. But then, when you've been married for a while, you usually keep sex to the bedroom – that's stage 2. Stage 3 comes after many years of marriage, it's when you pass each other in the hall and say, 'Fuck you!'"

★ ★ ★

What did you have for breakfast this morning?
Oh, the usual argument.

★ ★ ★

"Doreen, ring for the vet, I feel terrible."
"But why the vet?" "Because I lead a bloody dog's life."

★ ★ ★

My wife's so ugly she's even got a French pleat under her arms.

★ ★ ★

A wife went to the doctor's complaining that her husband couldn't make love. The doctor gave her some pills to give to him and told her to let him know whether there was any improvement. The following week, he met her in the street.
"How did it go?"
"Oh wonderful, doctor, thank you. On the first day we did it in the morning, on the second day in the morning and in the evening, and only yesterday he did it five times before he died."

★ ★ ★

A husband and wife decided they needed to use "a code" to indicate that they wanted to have sex without letting their children in on it. They decided on the word "typewriter".

One day the husband told his five-year-old daughter, "Go tell your mommy that daddy needs to type a letter."

The child told her mum what her dad said and her mother responded, "Tell your daddy that he can't type a letter right now because there's a red ribbon in the typewriter."

The child went back to tell her father what mummy had said.

A few days later the mum told the daughter, "Tell daddy that he can type that letter now."

The child told her father, and then returned to her mother and announced, "Daddy said never mind about the typewriter, he already wrote the letter by hand."

★ ★ ★

A couple just got married, and when the husband went back to his house he found that his bride had disappeared. He got very worried and gathered up all his friends to search for his wife without success. Two days after his wife disappeared the man returned home to find her in the kitchen. He asked her what she has been up to and why she hadn't been home for so long.

She replied, "These four men kidnapped me and had wild sex with me for a week."

The husband answered, "But it's only been two days – what do you mean by a week?"

"I am only here to get something to eat."

★ ★ ★

My wife rushed into the supermarket to pick up a few items. She headed for the express line where the cashier was talking on the phone with his back turned to her.

"Excuse me," she said. "I'm in a hurry. Could you check me out, please?"

The cashier turned, stared at her for a second, looked her up and down, smiled and said, "Not bad."

★ ★ ★

"Ever since we got married, my wife has tried to change me. She got me to stop drinking, smoking and running around until all hours of the night. She taught me how to dress well, enjoy the fine arts, gourmet cooking, classical music, even how to invest in the stock market."

"Sounds like you may be bitter because she changed you so drastically," remarked his friend.

"I'm not bitter. Now that I'm so improved, she just isn't good enough for me."

★ ★ ★

Ted and his wife were working in their garden one day when Ted looked over at his wife and said, "You're butt is getting really big, I mean really big! I bet your butt is bigger than the barbecue."

With that he proceeded to get a measuring tape and measure the grill and then went over to where his wife was working and measured his wife's bottom. "Yes, I was right: your butt is two inches wider than the barbecue!!!"

The wife chose to ignore her husband. Later that night in bed, Ted is feeling a little frisky. He makes some advances towards his wife who completely brushes him off.

"What's wrong?" he asks.

She answers, "Do you really think I'm going to fire up this big-ass grill for one little weenie?"

★ ★ ★

The night before her wedding, the bride-to-be talked with her mother.

"Mom," she said, "I want you to teach me how to make my new husband happy."

The mother took a deep breath and began, "When two people love, honour and respect each other, love can be a very beautiful thing…"

"I know how to fuck, mother," the bride-to-be interrupted. "I want you to teach me how to make a great lasagna."

★ ★ ★

A couple were having trouble, so they did the right thing and went to a marriage counsellor. After a few visits, and a lot of questioning and listening, the counsellor said he had discovered the main problem.

He stood up, went over to the woman, asked her to stand and gave her a hug. He looked at the man and said, "This is what your wife needs, at least once a day!"

The man frowned, thought for a moment, then said, "OK, what time do you want me to bring her back tomorrow?"

★ ★ ★

A murderer, imprisoned for life, broke free after 15 years and was on the run. He broke into a house and tied up the young couple he found in the bedroom; the man to a chair on one side of the room and his wife to the bed. The helpless husband watched him get on the bed, straddle his wife and start to nuzzle her neck. His wife started to move her head violently, at which the man got up and left the room.

The husband squirmed his chair across the room to his young wife and hissed, "Darling, I saw him kissing you. He probably hasn't seen a woman in years. Please cooperate. If he wants to have sex, just go along with it and even pretend you like it. Whatever you do, don't fight him or make him mad. Our lives may depend on it!"

"Darling," the wife said, spitting out her gag. "I'm so relieved you feel that way. He wasn't kissing me, he was whispering to me. He told me he thinks you're really cute and asked if we kept the Vaseline in the bathroom."

★ ★ ★

This man went out with the boys, and told his wife that he be home by midnight.

At around 3 am, drunk as a skunk, he headed for home.

Just as he got in the door, the cuckoo clock in the hall started up and cuckooed three times.

Quickly, he realized she'd probably wake up so he cuckooed another nine times.

He was really proud of myself, having a quick, witty solution, even when smashed, to escape possible conflict.

Next morning, his wife asked him what time he got in, and he told her 12 o'clock. She didn't seem worried at all.

Then she told him that they needed a new cuckoo clock. When he asked her why, she said, "Well, it cuckooed three times, then said, 'Oh fuck,' cuckooed four more times, cleared its throat, cuckooed another three, giggled, cuckooed two more times and finally farted.

★ ★ ★

MEN TALK

Two girls talking, one says, "I got picked up by the fuzz last night."
"Did it hurt?" the other asks.

★ ★ ★

It was pouring down with rain and two girls were late for their date.
"Come on, Jane, put your foot down or we'll never get there."
"Oh no," said the driver. "The ground is too wet for us to buy off any
speed cops today."

★ ★ ★

A lady sitting alone in a bar gets pestered all night long by men trying
to proposition her, but she sends them all away with a flea in their ear.
Then, towards the end of the evening, an alien walks in, sits down,
orders a drink and completely ignores her. She is intrigued and asks
him why he is not interested in her.
"On our planet we have sex in a different way and it's much more
powerful. Would you like to try it?"
He then puts his middle finger on her forehead and she immediately
begins to feel quite stimulated. This feeling gets more and more
powerful until she reaches an orgasm never experienced before by
any human being. It was so wonderful, she begs for more, but he says,
"Give me half an hour," as he holds up his bent finger.

★ ★ ★

The Sheikh always knows which wife to choose for the night.
He goes to the harem, throws a bucket of water over them all and
takes the one that fizzes.

★ ★ ★

Have you heard the mating call of a blonde?
"Oh I'm soooo drunk..."

★ ★ ★

What did the Jewish lady say to the flasher? "You call that a lining?"

★ ★ ★

Two girls are walking along the prom when a holiday photographer steps forward. "Hold on, Jean, he's going to focus."
"What! Both at the same time?"

★ ★ ★

A woman said to her friend, "Do you smoke after sex?"
"Gosh, I've never looked," she replied.

★ ★ ★

Three girls were talking on a bus about safe sex.
The first said she always carried a packet of condoms in her bag; the second said she was on the pill; and the third said she used a tin with a few pebbles inside. The other two looked at her in amazement.
"How does that work?"
"Oh, it's quite simple. I make him stand on it and when it starts to rattle I kick it out from under him."

★ ★ ★

Three daughters all got married on the same day and they all spent the first night of their honeymoon in their parents' house.
As mum locked up, turned out all the lights and went up to bed she passed her daughters' rooms.
In the first room she heard her daughter laughing, in the second her daughter crying, but in the third room not a sound.
Next morning at breakfast she asked her daughters about the noises she had heard.
The first said, "Well, you always told me to laugh when something really tickled me."
"And you always told me to cry when something really hurt me," said the second.

"And you always told me not to speak when I had my mouth full," said the third.

★ ★ ★

What do "good time" girls have written on their underwear?
Next.

★ ★ ★

Three women at an antenatal clinic were asked what position they were in when they conceived.
The first said he was on top.
"In that case you'll have a boy," said the doctor.
The second said she was on top.
"In that case you'll have a girl," came the reply.
But before the third woman could reply she burst into tears.
"Oh no, please tell me I'm not going to have puppies."

★ ★ ★

Two women were chatting on a bus: "I've got a dreadful sore throat," said one. "Oh, you poor thing! When I've got a sore throat I suck on a Life Saver." "Ah, that's easy for you to do. You live near the seaside."

★ ★ ★

Two women are talking on a bus and one says to the other, "I was so embarrassed this morning. I met my son's new teacher. What a hulk, he made me go weak at the knees and instead of telling him I had come about our Billy, I said I'd come about his willy."
"Never mind," replies the other. "Sometimes we all say things we didn't mean to say. For instance, this morning I made my husband his breakfast and accidentally told him I hated his guts and that was why I was sleeping with his best friend."

★ ★ ★

Two ladies talking in the laundrette:
"Has your husband been circumcised?" said one.
"No," replied the other. "He's always been a complete dick."

★ ★ ★

Two women talking:
"How do you keep your youth?" said the first.
"I lock him in the cupboard," replied the second.

★ ★ ★

Mother was trying to console her daughter who was crying her eyes out because her boyfriend had dumped her. In case it was sex that had caused the split, mother told her about the birds and the bees but was suddenly interrupted by daughter. "Oh no mum, I can fuck and suck with the best of them, but he says I'm a useless cook."

★ ★ ★

Two girls talking on a bus: "Last night I had three orgasms in a row."
"That's nothing, I had over 50."
"Golly, he must be good."
"Oh, you mean with just one guy?"

★ ★ ★

Two women talking on a bus:
"No, Doreen, you've got it wrong. If you think the way to a man's heart is through his stomach, you're aiming too high."

★ ★ ★

Two girls talking:
"What do you think of the new salesman? He dresses fashionably."
"And quickly too," replied the other.

★ ★ ★

Overheard on the top deck of a bus: "My husband's away at sea so much, when he comes home he's like a stranger."
"Oh, you lucky thing, how exciting."

★ ★ ★

Overheard on the top deck of a bus: "I've been out with every player in the rugby team and I haven't bonked one of them," said the girl.
"Oh, I know who that'll be," replied her mate. "It's got to be that timid scrum half."

★ ★ ★

Why do married women have so many wrinkles?
From squinting down and saying, "Pull what?"

★ ★ ★

"But, Joan, if sex is a pain in the arse, you're doing it wrong."

★ ★ ★

What's the definition of a lazy man?
One who weds a pregnant woman.

★ ★ ★

Why did God create men?
Because a vibrator can't dig the garden.

★ ★ ★

What are the three most popular female lies?

1. Of course you're the best lover I've ever had.

2. Size doesn't mean everything.

3. Only interested in your money? How can you say that? Of course not.

★ ★ ★

First Lady Hillary Clinton and Attorney General Janet Reno were having one of those girl-to-girl talks. Hillary says to Janet, "You're lucky that you don't have to put up with men having sex with you. I have to put up with Bill, and there is no telling where he last had his pecker."

Janet responded. "Just because I am considered ugly, doesn't mean I don't have to fight off unwelcome sexual advances."

Hillary asks, "Well, how do you deal with the problem?"

Janet: "Whenever I feel that a guy is getting ready to make a pass at me, I muster all my might and squeeze out the loudest, nastiest, fart I can. And believe me, that takes the wind out of his sails, so to speak!"

Hillary was impressed and thank the General for her sage advice and hurried home.

Well, that night, Bill was already between the sheets with the lights out when Hillary headed for bed. She could hear him start to stir, and knew that he would be wanting some action. She had been saving her farts all day, and was ready for him. She tenses up her butt cheeks and forces out the most disgusting sounding fart you could imagine.

Bill rolls over and says, "Is that you, Janet?"

★ ★ ★

MOMENT OF DOUBT

"Oh, Fred, I'm pregnant," said Eileen to her boyfriend. "And if you don't do the decent thing, I'll put my head in the gas oven."
He replied, "Oh, Eileen, that's great. Not only are you a good fuck, but you're also a good sport."

★ ★ ★

"I don't know what's going on," said worried Bob to his mate. "Last month we moved parishes and I left our church which had a message pinned up outside saying, 'Sex is your worst enemy,' only to get to the new church and read, 'Make your worst enemy your best friend.'"

★ ★ ★

An angry husband was complaining to his friend about his slovenly wife. "She never does any housework; I never get a cooked meal; everything's dirty, including her. I'm so fed up I sleep on my own and I wish she was dead."
The friend suggested that he try killing her with sex. It wasn't an offence, after all. So the man returned home, dragged his wife upstairs and kept her there all weekend. By the time Monday morning came, he could hardly drag himself to work, but when he came home that night the house was spotless, a steak was cooking and she was standing there with a sexy see-through nightie on. "You see, darling," she said. "Treat me right and I'll treat you right."

★ ★ ★

What do you do if a pet bull terrier gets randy and tries to mount your leg? Fake an orgasm.

★ ★ ★

She was so naive the man tricked her into marrying him by telling her she was pregnant.

★ ★ ★

It was so cold in the park last month that the local flasher was reported to be describing himself to the women he met.

★ ★ ★

A famous footballer was asked if he would appear nude in a glossy magazine.
"We'd like you to pose holding a ball," explained the editor.
"OK, but what do I do with my other hand?"

★ ★ ★

For 20 years, a man has been writing to a woman in Norway but they have never met. At long last, the man decides they ought to do something about it and he suggests that she should fly over and he'll meet her at the airport.
"I think that's a wonderful idea," she replies, "but I think I ought to tell you that I'm completely bald. I suffer from a nervous complaint and don't have a single hair on my body." "No problem," he replies.
Another letter arrives soon after and in this she says, "I think you should also know that I don't have any arms; I write by putting the pen between my toes."
A little startled to receive this news, he still tells her to come, but by return of post she writes that she meant to tell him she only has one eye in the middle of her forehead.
It's too late for him to back out, so he writes to say he's looking forward to seeing her and could she wear a carnation in her buttonhole so that he will be able to recognize her.

★ ★ ★

Overheard on the top deck of a bus:
"Do you know, Jack, if girls are made of sugar and spice and all that's nice, how come they taste like fish?"

★ ★ ★

The wife of the Head of State was accompanying a visiting VIP through the streets of the capital in a horse-drawn carriage. Suddenly, one of the horses gave a rip-roaring fart.

"Oh, I do apologise!" she said to her guest.

"That's all right," he replied. "In fact, I thought it was the horse."

★ ★ ★

They've just come up with a novel way to stop you smoking. When you buy a new packet of cigarettes, stick the first one up a mate's backside, filter first, then put it back in the packet and mix them all up. You'd have to be pretty brave to pick one out and smoke it after that.

★ ★ ★

Did you hear about Santa Claus going to the psychiatrist?
He didn't believe in himself.

★ ★ ★

It's Christmas time and the dustman knocks at the door for his Christmas tip. The door opens and a beautiful shapely blonde invites him in, takes him upstairs, strips off and makes mad passionate love to him for the next two hours. They then go back downstairs, have some breakfast and before he leaves she give him £1.

The astonished dustman asks her what the £1 is for and the woman replies, "When I asked my husband if I should give you a £10 tip for Christmas he replied, 'Fuck the dustman and give him £1'. The breakfast was my idea."

★ ★ ★

The mystery in life that's never been solved is why, when men get drunk, someone creeps into their bedroom in the dead of night, pees in the wardrobe and pukes in their shoes.

★ ★ ★

The King was due to set off for the crusade and knew he would be away for more than a year. Not trusting the knights who would be left behind, he had a special chastity belt made for the queen containing a little guillotine.

A year passed and when the King returned, he asked the knights to bare all and every single one of them, except one, had lost their manhood.

The King turned to the knight who was still intact, saying, "You are the only one who has remained loyal to me. You may pick their punishment. Why don't you speak up – have you lost your tongue?"

★ ★ ★

PARENTHOOD

A man rushed into a newspaper office saying, "I hope I'm not too late to put an announcement in the paper – my wife has just given birth to a baby girl after 10 years of trying."

"Of course, sir," replied the clerk. "How many insertions?"

"Oh, I can't remember – bloody thousands!"

★ ★ ★

A man is loading his kids into the car, five squeezed in the back and two in the front. As he gets in himself he's heard to mutter, "Wow, I almost screwed myself out of a seat!"

★ ★ ★

Did you know there's no chance of a cock-up if you use artificial insemination?

★ ★ ★

A simple-minded couple go to the doctor's because the wife is pregnant again with the fifth child in as many years.

"Why didn't you use the condoms that I instructed you to wear?" asked the doctor.

"I'm sorry, doc," they replied, "but we don't have an organ, so we put it over the flute instead."

★ ★ ★

A very ugly couple were walking along the road with two beautiful children when they overheard a passer-by express amazement at the fact that two such ugly people could have such lovely children. They turned to the passer-by and said, "You imbecile, we didn't make them with our faces!"

★ ★ ★

Doreen was absolutely amazed. She was nearly 50 and her husband was 75 and the doctor had told her she was pregnant. She couldn't wait to tell her husband and rang him up immediately.

"Henry, wonderful news; I'm pregnant. You're going to be a father."

"Well, that's terrific," said Henry proudly, "and who is that speaking?"

★ ★ ★

A male and female astronaut landed on an undiscovered planet and soon met up with some of the inhabitants. These inhabitants showed them many things, including a baby machine which produced the new offspring. On seeing this, the astronauts were asked how their little ones were made. Rather than explain, they stripped off and gave a full and satisfying demonstration. The inhabitants looked puzzled.

"But where are the new ones?"

"Oh, that won't happen for another nine months," they replied.

"Goodness me, if it takes that long, why were you rushing so much at the end?"

★ ★ ★

On seeing her friend pregnant, the woman offered congratulations but added sadly, "We've been trying for years but with no luck."

"Well, do as I did," replied the happy woman. "Go to a faith healer," and then lowering her voice she murmured, "but go on your own."

★ ★ ★

A husband and wife and their six children sat down in the restaurant and called over the waiter to order their meal. It was obvious that the six children were three sets of twins and the waiter couldn't help but remark, "I hope you don't mind my asking, but do you always have twins?"

"Oh no," replied the wife without thinking. "Sometimes we don't get anything."

★ ★ ★

Did you hear about the woman who had a hard time breastfeeding her baby? She couldn't get her husband out of the way.

★ ★ ★

What's the similarity between toys and women's breasts?
They were both intended for kids but it's the dads who keep playing with them.

★ ★ ★

Two women talking:
"My first pregnancy resulted in triplets and that only happens once every 250,000 times."
"Wow!" said her friend. "I'm surprised you ever had time to do any housework."

★ ★ ★

It was decided to add sex education to the school curriculum and the parents were asked how they felt about this.
The majority were in agreement with one proviso – no graphic demonstrations, just keep it oral.

★ ★ ★

Yes, parenthood changes everything. But parenthood also changes with each baby. Here, a couple of the ways having a second and third child differs from having your first:
Your Clothes – 1st baby: you begin wearing maternity clothes as soon as your OB/GYN confirms your pregnancy. 2nd baby: you wear your regular clothes for as long as possible. 3rd baby: your maternity clothes are your regular clothes.
The Baby's Name – 1st baby: you pore over baby-name books and practise pronouncing and writing combinations of all your favourites. 2nd baby: someone has to name their kid after your great-aunt Mavis, right? It might as well be you. 3rd baby: you open a name book, close your eyes and see where your finger falls. Bimaldo? Perfect!

★ ★ ★

"Good gracious," said Flo's friend, putting down the newspaper. "It says here that there are 19 women in the village all expecting a baby on the same day – June 23. Your baby's not due until July, is it?"
"No, it's not, but then I didn't go on the Mothers' Union trip to Weymouth."

★ ★ ★

A kindly old curate happened upon three young girls crying in the deserted old graveyard. Taking pity on their distress, he invited them into the rectory for a cup of tea and a slice of cake. In the warmth of the kitchen and comforted by the smell of freshly baked cakes, the three girls cheered up.
"Now," he said, smiling as he brought over the tea tray, "who's going to be mother?" and they all burst into tears again.

★ ★ ★

"John, your dad's not very good at these things, so I wonder if you'd tell your brother about the birds and the bees," said Mum.
John sought out his brother and said, "Hey, Bill, d'you remember what we did last night?"
"Sure, we went down the Palais, picked up a couple of birds, had a dance, then took them round the back of the bus station for a good 'one two'. Why do you ask?"
"Mum just wanted you to know that what you did last night is the same for the birds and the bees."

★ ★ ★

Poor old Sammy. He was a Caesarean baby and even now, 20 years later, he still goes out of the house through the skylight.

★ ★ ★

Two husbands are in hospital anxiously awaiting for their wives to give birth. One of them is so nervous, the other tries to comfort him. "It'll be all right, mate, I've been through this before."

The nervous man asks a lot of questions, finally saying, "Can you tell me how long it will be before I can have sex with my wife again?"
"Are you private or NHS?"
"NHS."
"In that case, you'll have to wait until you get home."

★ ★ ★

"Doctor, I've only got three weeks to go before my baby is born, can you advise me on the best position for delivering it?" she asked.
"Well, the most common way is exactly the same position as when you conceived."
"Oh goodness, you mean in the dark under the stairs, standing on an orange box!"

★ ★ ★

Bob and Sheila had a small flat in the city and decided the only way they could have a Sunday afternoon 'quickie' was to send their 10-year-old son out on the balcony and ask him to report on the neighbourhood activities. It was sure to distract him for an hour. The boy began his commentary as the parents got down to business.
"An ambulance has just stopped at old Mrs Jenkins' place, Mr Wales is walking his dog, Matt and Jenny are on their bikes and the Davidsons are having sex."
Mum and Dad sat up in bed astonished.
"What do you mean?" said dad. "How do you know?" he spluttered.
"Their kid is standing out on the balcony with binoculars too," replied the son.

★ ★ ★

"Daddy, what's telepathy?" "It's when two people are thinking the same thought at the same time." "Like you and mommy?" "No, son, when mommy and I are thinking the same thought, that's called coincidence."

★ ★ ★

A young boy at school called Tommy is always in trouble. Stealing, pinching, bullying, his misdemeanours are endless. Then one day, the head teacher calls his mother in to tell her that they will have no choice but to expel the boy if he doesn't stop. This time he's been found wanking in the classroom.

"You know it's a big problem," says the head teacher. "You've got to stop him from doing it."

"How?" she asks.

"Well, tell him he'll go blind if he carries on like that."

When they get home, mum insists that dad goes upstairs and has a word with him.

"Go and explain what will happen," she says.

So dad goes up to his son's bedroom and starts to talk to him.

"Hold on a minute, dad," says the little boy. "I'm over here."

★ ★ ★

Grandpa takes his grandson to Blackpool for the day and they go on every ride in the fair except for the big dipper. But the boy's not satisfied, he wants more.

"Oh please, Grandpa, please, please let's go on the big dipper."

After ten minutes of constant pestering, Grandpa relents and they go on three times.

"Can I have an ice cream now, Grandpa, please, please can I have an ice cream?"

Grandpa knows his mother has said, 'No,' but it's anything for a quiet life, so he buys the boy a cornet. In the afternoon, they go down on to the beach and the boy has a donkey ride. He loves it. In fact, he loves it so much, he wants Grandpa to buy the donkey.

"No, no, no," says Grandpa, but the boy screams and yells and pesters him so much that he eventually buys the donkey for £50.

"What are you going to call it?" he asks.

"Tosser," said the boy, "because he kicks a lot and is always tossing people off his back."

Later on, at three in the morning, Grandpa is woken up by the little boy because the donkey has broken his leash and disappeared.

"Grandpa, Grandpa!" cried the boy. "Tosser's off."

"Now look here, boy, I've taken you to Blackpool, you've had a good time at the fair, filled yourself with ice cream, bought a donkey. Don't you think I've done enough for one day?"

★ ★ ★

A little girl goes to the barber shop with her father. She stands directly next to the barber's chair, while her dad gets his haircut, eating her snack cake. The barber says to her, "Sweetheart, you're gonna get hair on your Twinkie."

She says, "I know. I'm gonna get boobs too."

★ ★ ★

A woman was pregnant with twins, and shortly before they were due, she had an accident and went into a coma. Her husband was away on business and could not be reached.

While in the coma, she gave birth to her twins, and the only person around to name her children was her brother.

When the mother came out of her coma to find that her brother had named the twins, she became very worried because he wasn't a very bright guy.

When she saw him she asked him about the twins.

He said, "The first one was a girl."

The mother: "What did you name her?!?"

Brother: "Denise!"

The Mom: "Oh, wow, that's not too bad! What about the second one?"

Brother: "The second one was a boy."

The Mom: "Oh, and what did you name him?"

Brother: "Denephew!"

★ ★ ★

The children and grand children of an elderly Jewish woman decided to send grandma on a cruise. Grandma boarded the ship and showed her ticket to the purser.

He looked at it and said, "Oh, I see you have U.D."

She replied, "U.D.? Voss is U.D.?"

He said, "U.D. is Upper Deck."

She then went to the upper deck and showed her ticket to the purser there and he said, "I see, that in addition to U.D., you also have O.C."

Grandma replied, "O.C.? Voss is O.C.?"

The purser said, "O.C. is Outside Cabin."

Grandma, needless to say, was delighted. She then showed her ticket to the cabin boy and he said, "Oh, I see that you also have B.I.B."

"B.I.B.? Voss is B.I.B.?" asked grandma.

The cabin boy answered, "B.I.B. is Breakfast In Bed."

"Oh," she said. "Mine children and grandchildren are vonderful."

Well, the next morning, bright and early, the staff came right into her room with trays of food for her breakfast in bed and she said, "F.U.C.K."

Shocked, they said, "F.U.C.K.? What do you mean F.U.C.K.?," to which she replied, "Yes, F.U.C.K. First U Could Knock!"

★ ★ ★

PINK

How many gays does it take to screw in a light bulb?
One, if he takes it slowly and uses special lubricating jelly.

★ ★ ★

Have you heard? There are now special pool tables in lesbian bars –
no balls.

★ ★ ★

Police were called today to break up a fight at the drag races.
Two gays arrived wearing the same dress.

★ ★ ★

In the gay shop down the road they're selling a strong kind of condom.
It's called seal-a-meal.

★ ★ ★

A young man was introduced to the Queen as the new royal
photographer. "How amazing!" she said. "My uncle is a photographer."
"Well, that is a coincidence," he replied. "My uncle's an old Queen."

★ ★ ★

The social climber confided to her friend over a cup of coffee.
"It's awful, my son's just told me he's gay…"
"Oh well, at least his boyfriend's a judge."

★ ★ ★

Percy and Alan had a tiff at the funfair, so Alan went off on his own to
the Tunnel of Love. Suddenly there was a huge explosion and the
tunnel collapsed. Percy rushed over, beside himself with worry, and
scrambled through the debris until he found Alan.
"Alan, Alan, are you all right?"
"No, I'm not," said Alan. "I went round three times and you didn't
wave once."

★ ★ ★

Do you know the difference between a general rodeo and a gay rodeo?
At a general rodeo they all shout, "Ride that sucker!"

★ ★ ★

In a smoky old night-club the pianist leant over to a man on the front table and said, "You see, I told you I could make you forget about that girl."
"You sure did," he replied. "Play with it again, Sam."

★ ★ ★

Remember, if you are a bisexual, it doubles your chances of a date on a Saturday night.

★ ★ ★

Did you hear about the woman who married a bisexual?
She didn't know which way to turn.

★ ★ ★

Apology from the latecomer:
"Sorry, I'm late. I met a man on a narrow path and didn't know whether to toss him off or let him block my passage."

★ ★ ★

A very small guy walks into a bar and finds himself standing next to a huge man.
The man turns to him and says, "Hi, I'm 6ft 6in, 345lbs, 22in penis, 3.5lb left testicle, 3.5lb right testicle, Turner Brown."
The small guy immediately faints.
When he comes around he is being helped to a chair by the big man, who asks, "What's wrong with you, man?"
"I'm sorry, can you repeat what you said before?"
"Sure, 6ft 6in, 345lbs, 22in penis, 3.5lb left testicle, 3.5lb right testicle, Turner Brown."

The small guy sighs with relief.
"Oh, wow, I thought you said turn around."

★ ★ ★

Four gay guys walked into a pub but there was only one barstool.
It was no problem, though, they turned it upside down.

★ ★ ★

Two men talking over a pint of beer:
"How's your son getting on?" one asked.
"Very well, thank you. He's just been given a seat on the board, and because it means he's going to be so busy all the time, he's given his deluxe cruiser away. Such a kind-hearted boy."
"Mmm, that sounds a bit like my boy," replied the second man. "He's just successfully floated his company on the stockmarket and as a gesture of goodwill gave away his BMW sports car."
Just then a third man joined them.
"We were just talking about our sons. How's yours doing?"
"Funny you should ask," he said. "We've just found out he's a homosexual, but he's made some very good friends. One's given him a beautiful boat and the other's given him a car."

★ ★ ★

A gay man walks into a club holding a very small paper bag.
"If anyone can guess what is in this bag, they can come home with me tonight."
A wisecracking Hell's Angel replies, "Yeah, you've got an old Triumph 500 in there."
Everyone starts to laugh as the gay man takes a peek in the bag and he replies, "Yep, we have a winner."

★ ★ ★

"Doctor, doctor, I've got a pain up my backside."

"Bend over, let's have a look. Oh yes, I can see what the trouble is, you've got a dozen red roses stuck up it."

"Oh really," said the man happily. "Is there a message on them? Does it say who they're from?"

★ ★ ★

Superman's cruising around, looking for some fun when he suddenly sees Superwoman lying flat out on her back, absolutely naked, in her garden.

Now he's a bit of a cheeky bugger and he thinks to himself, at my speed I could go down, have my way with her and then fly off before she realizes what went on.

So he dives down, does the business and is away at the speed of light.

"Bloody hell, what was that?" says Superwoman.

"I don't know," says the Invisible Man, "but it bloody hurt."

★ ★ ★

Advice to prison inmates – never volunteer to play the female role in the Christmas panto.

★ ★ ★

After a disastrous love affair, the young man decided to get away from it all and took a cabin up in the woods, miles from civilization. All went well for a few weeks, but then he started to get bored, so he was delighted to see a man coming up the road one day towards his cabin.

"Hi," said the newcomer. "My name's Bob. Just heard you've moved here, so there's a party in your honour tomorrow night."

"That's great," said the young man, thinking how friendly people were. Bob continued, "Yep, there'll be singing, dancing, lots of beer and plenty of sex."

"I'll be there," said the young man. "What shall I wear?"

"Oh, come as you are, there'll only be you and me."

★ ★ ★

A man goes into the local deli and asks for a pound of German sausage. The shopkeeper is just about to place it in the slicing machine when the man shouts, "Don't do that... my arse isn't a money box, you know!"

★ ★ ★

After travelling for some hours, the motorist realized he was completely lost, so it was with a sigh of relief that he saw a little village nestling in the valley. Arriving on the main street, he knocked at the door of the first house.
"Excuse me, sir, can you tell me the name of this village?"
"Of course, you're in Little Poofsville."
"That's a strange name. Why's it called that?"
"I don't know, I'll just call the wife. Hey, Bob, why's it...?"

★ ★ ★

It was very late at night when the man pulled up at the only hotel in town and asked for a room. "I'm sorry, sir, all the rooms are taken, there's a county fair here tomorrow."
Horrified at the thought of having to travel further, he pleaded with the man for somewhere to stay.
"Well...," said the owner, "we do have a spare bed, but it means you'll have to share a twin room with one of our local residents and he snores so badly you'll never get any sleep."
"Don't worry, I'll sort it," said the man and off to the room he went.
Next morning, the man came down to pay his bill, looking well rested.
"Everything all right, sir, you weren't disturbed too much?"
"Oh no, not at all. Before I went to sleep, I went over to the other man who was still awake, gave him a kiss on the forehead and wished him, 'Pleasant dreams, darling'. He stayed awake all night watching me."

★ ★ ★

"Doctor, doctor, I think I might be gay," said the young man.
"What makes you think that?"

"My father was gay, my grandfather was gay, my two uncles and my older brother were gay."

"Good gracious," said the doctor. "Is there no one in your family who likes women?"

"Yes, my sister does."

★ ★ ★

What did one Lesbian say to the other?
Your face or mine.

★ ★ ★

What do you call a lesbian dinosaur?
A lickalotapus.

★ ★ ★

A Lesbian goes to the gynaecologist and after being examined, he says, "Well, this is meticulously well kept."

"Oh yes," she replies, "I have a woman in three times a week."

★ ★ ★

"Dad, now that I'm 15, can I wear a bra and suspender belt?"
"No, you can't, John."

★ ★ ★

Is a Lesbian a pansy without a stalk?

★ ★ ★

A gay guy walks into a barber shop.

He says to the barber. "Sir, how can I make hair grow on my chest?"

The barber replies, "Go home and put Vaseline on your chest real thick…"

That night the young man does as the barber told him. His partner climbs into bed and reaches over to hold him and feels the slime on his chest. He says, "What the hell is this?"

The other man replies, "The barber told me that if I put Vaseline on my chest hair would grow..."

His partner replies, "You stupid son of a bitch, if that were the case you would have a damn pony tail hanging out of your ass."

★ ★ ★

PROTECTION

A man goes into a chemist's and asks the lady assistant for a packet of condoms, but he's not sure what size he needs.

"That's no problem," replies the lady. "Just pop into the back where we have a board with a number of different holes and that way we'll know your size."

The man does as he's told and sticks his willy in the different holes, not knowing that each time he does so the lady assistant, hidden on the other side, is fondling him.

Eventually he discovers his size and returns to the shop.

"Did you find your size?" she asks.

"Oh, yes, but bugger the condoms, how much do you want for that board?" he replies.

★ ★ ★

The local doctor was asked to give a talk on sex education to the girls at the local high school but, knowing his wife was a bit of a prude, told her he was speaking on hot-air ballooning.

Some days later the headmistress met the doctor's wife in the street.

"Please tell the doctor again how much we enjoyed his talk. I think the girls learnt a lot from him."

"Well, I am surprised," exclaimed the wife.

"As far as I know he's only done it twice and the second time he couldn't get it to rise properly."

★ ★ ★

Have you heard about the man who put a condom on inside out... and went?

My girlfriend is fanatical about practising safe sex. She even makes me use dental floss after it.

★ ★ ★

A young man out for a good time pops into the local chemist's to stock up. The shop is empty.

"Anyone there?" he shouts and from the back room comes the

chemist's wife, a bitter and unhappy woman.

"Four French Letters, please, Miss."

"Don't you Miss me," she replies.

"Oh, sorry, make that five then, please."

★ ★ ★

What's the difference between 365 days in a year and 365 condoms?
One's a good year and the other's a fucking good year.

★ ★ ★

What do a man and a packet of condoms have in common?
They both come in three sizes; small, medium and liars.

★ ★ ★

Two friends meet in casualty:

"Hello, John, how did you break your ankle?"

"I pulled out to avoid a child," he said angrily, "and fell off the bloody bed."

★ ★ ★

A local nymphomaniac is out walking in the country when she spies two brothers harvesting the wheat. Now the two boys are ideal specimens of manhood but not very worldly.

"Hi, boys, why don't you take a break from work and we can all have a good time. But you'll have to wear these condoms because I don't want to get pregnant."

The boys are entranced by her and immediately agree to anything she suggests.

A year goes by and one day one of the brothers says, "Our Jack, do you remember the time we met that girl in the cornfield?"

"I do that," he replied dreamily.

"Well, do you care if she gets pregnant?"

"No, not anymore."

"Nor me. Let's take these things off now."

★ ★ ★

Chemist to young man:
"Sir, I would recommend these condoms; they're guaranteed by the makers."
"Ah, but what if they break."
"Then, sir, the guarantee runs out."

★ ★ ★

A man walked into a chemist's shop complaining angrily.
"I bought a gross of condoms here on Friday, but it turned out to be only 130."
"I'm so very sorry, sir," apologised the chemist, and he immediately wrapped up another 14, adding sarcastically, "I hope it didn't spoil your weekend."

★ ★ ★

The CO walks into a chemist's and inquires about the price of a condom. "Well, we don't usually sell them singly, but it would be 30p," says the assistant.
"And how much would it cost for one to be repaired?"
"Oh, sir, it wouldn't be worthwhile, there's so much work involved – it would cost at least £20."
The man leaves and returns the next day.
"I've had a word with the men, we'll buy a new one."

★ ★ ★

A man rang the vet in some distress.
"It's an emergency! My dog has swallowed a condom! What shall I do?"
"No need to get too alarmed, just keep him in and I'll get back to you at the end of surgery."

Half an hour later, the vet rang back. "How's it going?"
"Oh, it's all right now, we found another condom in my wife's handbag."

★ ★ ★

"What's wrong, Jack, you look a bit down in the dumps this morning. Is the wife giving you a lot of lip?"
"Dead right she is. She's just had a coil fitted – it picks up the local CB radio, so now I'm getting hassle at both ends!"

★ ★ ★

A new film is being premiered in London next week, about the dangers of having casual sex. It's called *Germs of Endearment*.

★ ★ ★

QUICK REPARTEE

How do you say 'screw you' in agent talk?"
"Trust me."

★ ★ ★

What is the first thing elephants do before they make love?
They remove their trunks.

★ ★ ★

"Drink makes you look beautiful and very sexy."
"But I haven't been drinking." "No, but I have."

★ ★ ★

An ornithological meteorologist is a man who looks at birds and can tell whether...

★ ★ ★

Why doesn't Father Christmas have any children?
He only comes once a year and then it's down the chimney.

★ ★ ★

Have you ever had Chinese beer?It doesn't get you drunk, but after a few pints you get the urge to take your clothes off and iron them.

★ ★ ★

I went to this discussion group on premature ejaculation.
In fact, I was five minutes early, but it was all over.

★ ★ ★

"You've got to hand it to Bob when it comes to petting."
"Why, is he that lazy?"

★ ★ ★

She was only an architect's daughter but she let the borough surveyor.

* * *

What happens when you eat onions and beans?
Tear gas.

* * *

You know John, as soon as I get home I'm going to tear the wife's bra off – the elastic's killing me.

* * *

What did the art critic say to the flasher?
"Well hung, sir, good show."

* * *

What is the greatest test of courage?
Two cannibals having oral sex.

* * *

What's the difference between a virgin and a light bulb?
You can unscrew a light bulb.

* * *

The man was so fat he used to rock himself to sleep trying to get up.

* * *

And maybe the unluckiest person alive would be the man who fell into a pool of tits and came up sucking his own thumb.

* * *

Do you know the definition of a hen-pecked man?
One who is sterile but daren't tell his pregnant wife.

★ ★ ★

What's pink and moist and split in the middle?
A grapefruit.

★ ★ ★

He's not only unlucky, he's also very short.
Yesterday he walked under a black cat.

★ ★ ★

I wish I hadn't bought that cheap suit.
Yesterday I went out. It was only cloudy but it shrank three inches.

★ ★ ★

Why do bald men have holes in their pockets?
They like to run their hands through their hair.

★ ★ ★

Do you know why pubic hair is curly?
If it wasn't it would blind you.

★ ★ ★

How do you get rid of unwanted pubic hair?
Spit it out.

★ ★ ★

"Hey, Jack, what do you grow in your garden?"
"Tired."

★ ★ ★

What do you call a man with a one-inch willy?
Justin.

★ ★ ★

Why is the Irish pound called the punt?
Because it rhymes with bank manager.

★ ★ ★

What is a woman's belly button for?
It's somewhere to put your chewing gum on the way down.

★ ★ ★

Is it true that a man who goes to sleep with a sex problem on his mind
will wake up in the morning with the answer in his hand?

★ ★ ★

I know a man who has submarine hands.
You never know where they'll turn up next.

★ ★ ★

Which one is the odd one out?
Luncheon meat, soya bean or a vibrator?
Luncheon meat, because the other two are meat substitutes.

★ ★ ★

There's one thing wrong with oral sex – the view.

★ ★ ★

A brassiere is a device for making mountains out of molehills.

★ ★ ★

A lady is a woman who doesn't smoke or drink and only swears when it slips out.

★ ★ ★

He was so lazy he preferred masturbation to regular sex because he didn't have to get up in the middle of the night to drive his hand home.

★ ★ ★

What do video games and *Men Only* have in common?
They both improve hand-to-eye co-ordination.

★ ★ ★

Why do men prefer big tits and tight pussies?
Because they have big mouths and little willies.

★ ★ ★

What does an ugly girl put behind her ears to make her more attractive? Her legs.

★ ★ ★

What's the definition of indefinitely? When your balls are bouncing off her arse, that's when you're in – definitely.

★ ★ ★

Have you noticed the difference between men and women when they fill the car up with petrol?
The men always give the hose a few shakes when they're finished.

★ ★ ★

What do you get when you turn three blondes upside down?
Two brunettes.

★ ★ ★

What do you say to a girl who can suck a marble through a hose pipe?
Will you marry me?

★ ★ ★

Why is a nymphomaniac like a door knob?
Everyone gets a turn.

★ ★ ★

What have ugly girls and mopeds got in common?
They're both fun to ride as long as no one sees you.

★ ★ ★

Why is virginity like a balloon?
One prick and it's gone.

★ ★ ★

What did the fat woman say to the fat man?
Thanks for the tip.

★ ★ ★

Disappointed party agent to friend a week before the General Election. "I'm having trouble getting my member in."
"Oh dear," replied friend. "Have you tried Vaseline?"

★ ★ ★

What are the two words men don't like to hear?
'Stop' and 'don't'.

★ ★ ★

Did you hear about the girl who went out with the undertaker?
He only wanted her for her body.

★ ★ ★

Adam came first. But then men always do.

★ ★ ★

Have you heard about the man who's so lazy, instead of taking his teeth out at night he sleeps in a six-inch-deep glass of water?

★ ★ ★

What do you do if a bird shits on your car?
Never take her out again.

★ ★ ★

How do you know if a man's a bachelor?
He comes to work every morning from a different direction.

★ ★ ★

What is the difference between men and Opal Fruits?
Men don't come in four refreshing fruit flavours.

★ ★ ★

Did you hear about the girl who came second in a beauty contest?
She was the only entrant.

★ ★ ★

Office boy to new secretary: "You may use my dictaphone."
"No, thanks, I'll use my finger, just like everyone else."

★ ★ ★

What's the similarity between nymphomaniacs and turtles?
When they're on their backs, they're screwed.

★ ★ ★

What lives in a hole and only comes out for food and sex? Your tongue.

★ ★ ★

What's the difference between a skunk and an estate agent both lying dead in the middle of the road?
There are skid marks in front of the skunk.

★ ★ ★

Why are men like snowfalls?
You don't know when they're coming, how many inches you'll get or how long they'll stay.

★ ★ ★

Old proverb: A regularly serviced relationship is like a car.
It'll give you trouble-free rides for many years.

★ ★ ★

And don't forget – if you shake it more than three times, you're playing with it.

★ ★ ★

Have you noticed how cars only break down on the way home and never when you're going to work?

★ ★ ★

What's the difference between a nymphomaniac and butter?
Butter is difficult to spread.

★ ★ ★

What's the similarity between cabbage and pubic hair?
You push them both to one side and continue eating.

★ ★ ★

Do you know why it's called sex?
Because it's easier to spell than Ahhhhm ooohmm, uggghh, eeeeee....

★ ★ ★

The unhappy atheist had no one to talk to during orgasm.

★ ★ ★

What's pink and hard first thing in the morning?
The *Financial Times* crossword.

★ ★ ★

What do you get if you cross a rooster with a disobedient dog?
A cock that doesn't come!

★ ★ ★

Did you hear about the nymphomaniac who when asked how many husbands she'd had, replied, "Shall I count my own?"

★ ★ ★

Did you hear about the poor old spinster who dreamt she'd got married but when she woke up there was nothing in it?

★ ★ ★

Have you heard about the 'good time' girl in the newsagent's? When asked if she kept stationery she replied, "I do up to the last ten seconds and then I go absolutely mad."

★ ★ ★

Did you hear about the miserly man who enjoyed being constipated?
He hated to part with anything.

★ ★ ★

The man was so unlucky – one day when he approached a prostitute she said she had a headache.

★ ★ ★

Do you know there are only two kinds of people who know how to govern this country? Hairdressers and taxi drivers.

★ ★ ★

Why can't you be an estate agent if you've been circumcised?
You have to be a complete prick to be an estate agent.

★ ★ ★

Why is sex with an SAS man so unsatisfactory?
He slips in and out unnoticed.

★ ★ ★

What's the difference between a bumpy road and Marilyn Monroe?
One knackers your tyres…

★ ★ ★

What do you get if you cross a nymphomaniac with a dictionary?
A fucking know-it-all.

★ ★ ★

Did you hear about the man who had five dicks?
His trousers fitted like a glove.

★ ★ ★

How many fish do you get in a pair of tights?
Two soles, two eels and a wet plaice.

★ ★ ★

Did you hear about the drug addict?
He started on heroin, went on to curry, progressed to Madras, then Vindaloo, and now he's in a Korma!

★ ★ ★

Why do MPs' wives always get on top?
Because MPs always fuck up.

★ ★ ★

Why does a poor butcher remind you of pathetic manhood?
Neither of them have any meat worth bothering about.

★ ★ ★

What's the similarity between Guy Fawkes and a 'poor excuse for a man'?
They both have a limp fuse when it comes to a blow job.

★ ★ ★

What's the similarity between a man and a stamp?
One lick and they stick to you.

★ ★ ★

What's the similarity between a Hepatitis B injection and sex with a useless man?
A quick, short prick in the bum and it's all over.

★ ★ ★

What's seven inches long and buzzes?
A mobile telephone.

★ ★ ★

Did you know? The last person to catch AIDS is a wanker.

★ ★ ★

What's the difference between Ohh... and Agh?
Four inches.

★ ★ ★

Did you hear about the lady who had trouble getting up in the mornings?
She had a velcro nightdress.

★ ★ ★

What is the similarity between your dick and a Rubik's cube?
The longer you play with it, the harder it gets.

★ ★ ★

What do you get if you merge Xerox with Wurlitzer?
A company that makes reproductive organs.

★ ★ ★

What's the similarity between a bank account and sex?
After a withdrawal you lose interest.

★ ★ ★

Did you hear about Bob?
He lost his Christmas list, so he has no idea who his friends are.

★ ★ ★

A man goes up to a girl he fancies and says, "Excuse me, but I don't think your hand and my leg have been introduced."

★ ★ ★

Why do women rub their eyes when they get out of bed in the morning? They don't have balls to scratch.

★ ★ ★

What's better than roses on your piano? Tulips on your organ.

★ ★ ★

Vaseline makes the coming easy, and the going back.

★ ★ ★

What's the similarity between a soldier and a carthorse?
One darts into the fray and the other…

★ ★ ★

What's got four legs and an arm? A rotweiler.

★ ★ ★

A group of chess enthusiasts checked into a hotel and were standing in the lobby discussing their recent tournament victories. After about an hour, the manager came out of the office and asked them to disperse. "But why?" they asked, as they moved off. "Because," he said, "I can't stand chess nuts boasting in an open foyer."

★ ★ ★

A woman has twins and gives them up for adoption. One of them goes to a family in Egypt and is named "Ahmal". The other goes to a family in Spain; they name him "Juan". Years later, Juan sends a picture of himself to his birth mother. Upon receiving the picture, she tells her husband that she wishes she also had a picture of Ahmal. Her husband responds, "They're twins! If you've seen Juan, you've seen Ahmal."

★ ★ ★

449

These friars were behind on their belfry payments, so they opened up a small florist shop to raise funds. Since everyone liked to buy flowers from the men of God, a rival florist across town thought the competition was unfair. He asked the good fathers to close down, but they would not. He went back and begged the friars to close. They ignored him. So, the rival florist hired Hugh MacTaggart, the roughest and most vicious thug in town, to "persuade" them to close. Hugh beat up the friars and trashed their store, saying he'd be back if they didn't shut up shop. Terrified, they did so, thereby proving that Hugh, and only Hugh, can prevent florist friars.

★ ★ ★

Mahatma Gandhi, as you know, walked barefoot most of the time, which produced an impressive set of calluses on his feet. He also ate very little, which made him rather frail and, with his odd diet, he suffered from bad breath. This made him a super-calloused fragile mystic hexed by halitosis. [with profound apologies to Mary Poppins]

★ ★ ★

And finally, there was the person who sent ten different puns to friends, with the hope that at least one of the puns would make them laugh. Unfortunately, no pun in ten did.

★ ★ ★

RIP

It was Bob's funeral. His wife and three children were sitting in the front row listening to the vicar as he spoke enthusiastically about the man's life.

"He was a wonderful father, a hard-working man and a great asset to the community…"

At this point, the widow suddenly jumped up flustered and shooed her children out of the door.

"Oh dear, I think I must have got the wrong time, this surely can't be Bob's funeral."

★ ★ ★

The devil tells a man who's just arrived in hell that he must choose one of three doors to enter and in the room beyond he will spend eternity. The man is very worried that he will choose the wrong door, so eventually persuades the devil to let him have a quick look behind the doors before making his choice. Behind the first door he sees everyone standing on their head on a wooden floor. He doesn't fancy doing that for eternity but the second door is even worse. Everyone is standing on their head on a stone floor.

However, in the third room everyone is standing around drinking tea, ankle deep in manure. Oh well, thought the man, at least I'm not standing on my head, so he tells the devil his choice is room 3. He goes into room 3 and just as the door slams shut behind him he hears the devil shout out, "OK, everyone, break's over! Get back on your heads."

★ ★ ★

Two neighbours, one upright and a pillar of the church, the other a drinker and fornicator. Eventually, the wicked one dies from his excesses. A few years later the other one dies, goes up to heaven and is astonished to see the wicked one with a large barrel of beer and a naked angel on his lap.

The upright man is outraged and complains to St Peter. "I denied myself all the good things in life so that I could come to heaven and when I get here I see him enjoying himself when he should be rotting in hell."

"Don't worry, he is in hell. The barrel's got a hole in it and the angel hasn't."

★ ★ ★

A woman returns from her husband's cremation and tips his ashes on to the kitchen table. She then says to them, "You see this beautiful fur coat which I always asked for and never got. Well, I've bought it myself. And you see this pearl necklace I always longed for. Well, I've bought that too. And you see these exclusive leather boots, the one's I always wanted – I've also bought these."
Then she stands up, leans over the table and blows all her husband's ashes on the floor saying, "And this is the blow job you always wanted and never got."

★ ★ ★

Did you hear about the suicide club that held a special meeting?
They never held another one.

★ ★ ★

A man was up before the judge accused of making love to his wife after she died. In his defence the husband said he didn't know she was dead: she had been like that for years.

★ ★ ★

Did you hear about the wife who couldn't afford a headstone for her husband? She left his head out.

★ ★ ★

Two men are walking through a graveyard when they stop to read the writing on one of the headstones which says, "Not dead, just sleeping." One man turns to the other and says, "He ain't fooling nobody, only himself."

★ ★ ★

"I'm sorry to hear you buried Jack yesterday," said the neighbour.
"Had to," replied Joan. "He was dead, you know."

★ ★ ★

A man goes to a fortune teller because he fears he's going to die.
"Don't be silly," replies Gypsy Rose. "You'll live to the ripe old age of
95." "But I am 95," he replies. "There, you see, I'm always right."

★ ★ ★

Did you hear about 'good time Sal'?
When she died they had to bury her in a Y-shaped coffin.

★ ★ ★

Three nuns at the pearly gates were being questioned by St Peter
before being allowed to enter.
He said to the first nun, "Who was the first man?"
"Adam," she replied, the gates opened and in she went.
To the second nun he asked, "What was the name of the first woman?"
"Eve," came the reply and in she went.
Then to the third he said, "What were the first words spoken by
Eve to Adam?"
"Wow, that's a hard one!" replied the nun and at that the gates opened
and she disappeared inside.

★ ★ ★

Did you hear about the woman who wore black garters?
To commemorate those who passed beyond.

★ ★ ★

A woman died, went to heaven and asked if she could be reunited with
her husband.
"What's his name?" asked the angel.
"Smith."

"Oh dear, we have thousands of Smiths. Is there anything you can tell me about him that would make him easier to find?"

"Well, not really," she replied, "except that he did say just before he died that if I was unfaithful to him, he'd turn in his grave."

"Ah yes," said the angel. "You'll be wanting revolving Smith."

★ ★ ★

A man died with a full erection and no matter how hard the undertakers tried to put the coffin lid down, it would not close. Eventually they rang up the wife and told her their problem.

"I'll tell you what to do" she said. "Cut it off and stick it up his backside."

The day of the funeral came and as the wife passed the open coffin she looked down at the pained expression on his face and hissed, "There you are, you bugger, you wouldn't believe me when I said how much it hurts."

★ ★ ★

A new group of men had arrived in heaven and were told to get into two lines. One was for henpecked men, the other for independent, liberated men. However, only one man stood in this second line and when asked why, he replied, "Because my wife told me I had to."

★ ★ ★

A man arrived in heaven and had to answer a few questions before he was allowed to stay.

"Have you ever done anything good in your life?" asked the angel.

"Well, um… I once gave a blind beggar 5p."

"Anything else?"

"I put 15p in the charity box when they were collecting for the local hospital."

At this the angel turned to the gatekeeper and said, "Give him his 20p back and tell him to go to hell."

★ ★ ★

Dorothy is very upset as her husband Albert had just passed away. She goes to the mortuary and the instant she sees him she starts wailing and crying. One of the attendants rushes up to comfort her. Through her tears she explains that she is upset because Albert is wearing a black suit and that it was his dying wish to be buried in a blue suit. The attendant apologizes and explains that they always put the bodies in a black suit, but he'll see what he can do. The next day Dorothy returns to the mortuary to have one last moment with Albert. When the attendant pulls back the curtain, Dorothy smiles through her tears as Albert is now wearing a blue suit. She asks the attendant, "How did you manage to get hold of that beautiful blue suit?"

"Well, yesterday afternoon after you left, a man about your husband's size was brought in and he was wearing a blue suit. His wife explained that she was very upset as he had always wanted to be buried in a black suit," the attendant replied. He continued, "After that it was simply a matter of swapping the heads over."

★ ★ ★

A lawyer and the Pope die on the same day and arrive in heaven together. St Peter takes the Pope to his room which is quite small, poorly furnished and only has a skylight. He then takes the lawyer to his quarters, which are five-star in comfort and outside is his own swimming pool set in landscaped gardens. "Wow, I can't believe it!" he gasps. "Why have I got this when the Pope has so little?"

"It's like this; we have many popes up here and it gets a little boring, but we've never had a lawyer before."

★ ★ ★

At the funeral of his wife, Bob was distraught. The vicar thought he'd better go and comfort the poor man, so went over, put his arms around his shoulders and said, "Come on, Bobby, time will help heal the loss and who knows, maybe one day you'll meet someone new."

"So what?" cried Bob. "But where will I get a fuck tonight?"

★ ★ ★

Two men arrive at the gates of heaven together and get asked some questions by the gatekeeper.

"Right, Mr White. I see from your records that you've lived an exemplary life. You've done a lot for your community, you've been a good husband and a loving father. Just one question, have you ever been unfaithful?"

"Never," replied the man.

"In that case, I grant you a BMW and free petrol to get you around heaven."

The gatekeeper then turned to the second man.

"Well, Mr Black, I see you've not had a bad life, you've been good to your parents, you've worked hard and lived fairly modestly, but just one question, have you ever been unfaithful?"

Mr Black had to admit that he'd been unfaithful on four occasions.

"In that case, I grant you a mini for your transport around heaven."

Some days went by and the two men happened to meet up. Mr White was sitting dejectedly at the wheel of his car.

"What's wrong?" asked Mr Black. "You've got a lovely car, free petrol, why are you looking so down in the mouth?"

He replied, sadly, "I've just seen my wife riding around on a bicycle."

★ ★ ★

An old couple in their eighties die and both go to heaven on the same day when they are met by one of the angels.

After signing in, the couple are shown to their new house. It is magnificent – wonderful views, plush interior, all mod cons and push button controls, plus a limousine in the garage outside. The old man turns to his wife and says, "Bloody hell, Flo, if you hadn't made us stop smoking, we'd have been here enjoying this years ago."

★ ★ ★

One of the world's best wicket keepers had just taken his place on the field when he was struck by a bolt of lightning and died instantly. When he got to heaven he was met by St Peter, who showed him to his new quarters saying, "If you look out of your back window, you'll see our cricket pitch being prepared for a very important game tomorrow against Hell. It would make us winners of the ashes."

"That's amazing," said the wicket keeper. "I didn't know there was cricket up here."

"Of course there is, why do you think we sent for you!"

★ ★ ★

A woman asked her friend at work if she would look after her budgie while she was away on holiday. Unfortunately, the bird was quite old and died within a couple of days.

Arriving back at work, the woman asked how her budgie was and her friend replied bluntly, "It's dead, dropped off its perch and that was that."

The poor woman collapsed in floods of tears. "You could have broken it more gently to me; you could have said one minute he was singing his heart out and then all of a sudden he lay quietly down and went to sleep with a smile on his face. At least I could have imagined he died happy. Anyway, I bet my mum next door was sad to hear the news as well."

"Yes, the day after it happened she was singing merrily in the garden when all of a sudden..."

★ ★ ★

Flo goes along to the local seance to try and get in touch with her late husband.

She's in luck and it's not long before she's asking him how he spends his time in heaven. "Well, I get up in the morning, have something to eat, do a bit of bonking, take a nap, have something to eat, do a bit more bonking, go for a walk, eat, bonk, eat again and then go to bed," he said.

"But, Alf, you were never like that down here," said Flo, quite amazed.

"No, but I wasn't a rabbit then."

★ ★ ★

"Doctor, doctor, was the operation successful?"
"Sorry, I'm not the doctor, I'm the Angel Gabriel."

★ ★ ★

The funeral was halfway through when the vicar got up to talk.
"Come on, someone must have something nice to say about our departed brother" he said.
Silence.
"He must have done something good during his life, can't anyone remember?"
Still there was silence.
"Perhaps he once helped an old lady across the street... or put some money in a collecting box. Come on, someone say something," he pleaded.
All of a sudden, a man stood up at the back and said, "His brother was worse!"

★ ★ ★

An old fellow in Yorkshire died of a bad chest and on the day of the funeral, they got him into the coffin and took him up to the cemetery at the top of the hill. Unfortunately, just as they got there the hearse doors opened and the coffin slipped out back down the hill, across the main road and smashed through the door of the chemist's shop. It hit the counter and the top burst open.
"What's going on?" asked the lady in the shop.
The old man in the coffin sat up and said, "Can you give me something to stop me coughin'?"

★ ★ ★

The chairman of a leading travel agency dies and finds himself sitting alone on a cloud. Along comes an angel and says, "Hello, we're having trouble deciding where you should go, whether it should be heaven or hell. So we've decided you can choose for yourself from these brochures."

The angel gives the man some brochures containing pictures and descriptions of both places. Heaven looks very nice and peaceful with lots of lovely scenery and people sitting around reading or listening to music. Hell looks a lot more lively. Scantily clad girls are frolicking in pools; there are pictures of tables sagging under the weight of sumptuous food; there's dancing, drinking and generally 'a good time' feel. It doesn't take long for the chairman to decide he'd like to go to hell and with that he's whisked away. A month goes by and the angel happens to be passing Hell's gateway when he sees the chairman chained to a rock with a pair of bellows in his hand, frantically keeping the flames of Hell burning. He spots the angel and says bitterly, "This is nothing like I thought it was going to be."

"Ah, well," said the angel. "You of all people should know better than to believe all it says in the brochures."

★ ★ ★

While they were visiting Jerusalem, George's mother-in-law died. With death certificate in hand, George went to the American Consulate to make arrangements to send the body home. The Consul told George that sending the body back for burial could cost as much as $5,000. To bury the body locally would only be $150.00. George answers, "I don't care how much it will cost to send the body back; that's what I want to do." The Consul says, "You must have loved your mother-in-law very much." "No, it's not that," says George. "You see, I know of a case years ago of a person that was buried here in Jerusalem. On the third day he arose from the dead! I just can't take that chance."

★ ★ ★

Some time after Bernie died, his widow, Rachel, was finally able to speak about what a thoughtful, considerate and wonderful man her late husband had been. "My Bernie thought of everything", she told them. "Just before he died, he called me to his bedside. He handed me three envelopes. 'Rachel', he told me. 'I have put all my last wishes in these three envelopes. After I am gone, please open them and do exactly as I have instructed. Knowing you'll do this, I can rest in peace'."

"What was in the envelopes?" her friends asked.

"The first envelope contained £5,000 with a note, 'Please use this money to buy a nice casket.' So I bought a beautiful mahogany casket with such a comfortable lining that I know Bernie is resting very comfortably.

"The second envelope contained £10,000 with a note, 'Please use this for a nice funeral.' I made Bernie a very dignified funeral and bought all his favourite foods for the wake."

"And the third envelope?" asked her friends.

"The third envelope contained £25,000 with a note, 'Please use this to buy a nice stone.'"

At that point, Rachel held up her hand and pointed to her ring finger, on which was a gorgeous ten-carat diamond ring.

"So?" said Rachel. "You like my stone?"

★ ★ ★

When Beethoven passed away, he was buried in a churchyard. A couple of days later, the town drunk was walking through the cemetery and heard strange noises coming from the area where Beethoven was buried. Terrified, the drunk ran and got the priest to come and listen. The priest bent close to the grave and heard faint, unrecognizable music coming from the grave. Frightened, the priest ran and got the town magistrate. When the magistrate arrived, he bent his ear to the grave, listened for a moment and said, "Ah, yes, that's Beethoven's Ninth Symphony, being played backwards."

He listened a while longer, and said, "There's the Eighth Symphony, and it's backwards, too. Most puzzling." The magistrate kept listening, "There's the Seventh... the Sixth... the Fifth..."

Suddenly the realization of what was happening dawned on the magistrate. He stood up and announced to the crowd that had gathered in the cemetery, "My fellow citizens, there's nothing to worry about. It's just Beethoven decomposing."

★ ★ ★

462

A couple had been debating the purchase of a new car for weeks. He wanted a new truck. She wanted a fast little sports car so she could zip through traffic around town. He would probably have settled on any beat up old truck, but everything she seemed to like was way out of their price range.

"Look!" she said. "I want something that goes from 0 to 200 in four seconds or less. And my birthday is coming up. You could surprise me."

So, for her birthday, he bought her brand-new bathroom scales.

* The service will be at Downing Funeral Home on Monday the 12th. Due to the condition of the body, this will be a closed casket service. Please send your donations to the "Think Before You Say Things To Your Wife Foundation", Dallas, Texas.

★ ★ ★

Three men die in a car accident on Christmas Eve. They all find themselves at the Pearly Gates waiting to enter Heaven. On entering they must present something relating to or associated with Christmas. The first man searches in his pocket, and finds some mistletoe, so he is allowed in.

The second man presents a cracker, so he is also allowed in.

The third man pulls out a pair of stockings.

Confused at this last gesture, St Peter asks, "How on earth do these represent Christmas?"

"They're Carol's."

★ ★ ★

A wonderful funeral was in progress and the country preacher talked at length of the traits of the deceased, what an honest man he was, and what a loving husband and kind father he had been. Finally, the widow leaned over and whispered to one of her children, "Go up there and take a look in the coffin and see if that's really your pa.'

★ ★ ★

Little Tim was in the garden filling in a hole when his neighbour peered over the fence. Interested in what the cheeky-faced youngster was up to, he politely asked, "What are you up to there, Tim?"

"My goldfish died," replied Tim tearfully, without looking up, "and I've just buried him."

The neighbour was concerned. "That's an awfully big hole for a goldfish, isn't it?"

Tim patted down the last heap of earth then replied, "That's because he's inside your stupid cat."

★ ★ ★

TOMBSTONE HUMOUR

Harry Edsel Smith of Albany, New York:
Born 1903–Died 1942.
Looked up the elevator shaft to see if the
car was on the way down. It was.

In a Thurmont, Maryland, cemetery:
Here lies an Atheist, all dressed up and no
place to go.

On Agrave in East Dalhousie Cemetery, Nova Scotia:
Here lies Ezekial Aikle, Age 102. Only The Good Die Young.

In a London cemetery:
Here lies Ann Mann, Who lived an old maid
but died an old Mann. Dec 8, 1767

In a Ribbesford, England, cemetery:
Anna Wallace
The children of Israel wanted bread, And
the Lord sent them manna. Clark Wallace
wanted a wife, And the Devil sent him Anna.

In a Ruidoso, New Mexico, cemetery:
Here lies Johnny Yeast... Pardon me
for not rising.

In a Uniontown, Pennsylvania, cemetery:
Here lies the body of Jonathan Blake.
Stepped on the gas instead of the brake.

In a Silver City, Nevada, cemetery:
Here lays The Kid.
We planted him raw.
He was quick on the trigger
But slow on the draw.

John Penny's epitaph in Wimborne, England:
Reader, if cash thou art in want of any,
Dig 6 feet deep and thou wilt find a Penny.

In a cemetery in Hartscombe, England :
On the 22nd of June, Jonathan Fiddle went
out of tune.

Anna Hopewell's grave in Enosburg Falls, Vermont:
Here lies the body of our Anna,
Done to death by a banana.
It wasn't the fruit that laid her low,
But the skin of the thing that made her go.

On a grave from the 1880s in Nantucket, Massachusetts:
Under the sod and under the trees,
Lies the body of Jonathan Pease.
He is not here, there's only the pod.
Pease shelled out and went to God

★ ★ ★

A funeral service is being held in a church for a woman who has just passed away. At the end of the service, the pall-bearers are carrying the casket out when they accidentally bump into a wall, jarring the casket. They hear a faint moan.

They open the casket and find that the woman is actually still alive. She lives for ten more years and then dies.

A ceremony is again held at the same church and at the end of the ceremony, the pall bearers are again carrying out the casket. As they set off, the husband cries out, "Watch out for that wall!"

★ ★ ★

A man was leaving a convenience store with his morning coffee when he noticed a most unusual funeral procession approaching the nearby cemetery. A long black hearse was followed by a second long black hearse about 50 feet behind the first one.

Behind the second hearse was a solitary man walking a dog on a leash. Behind him, a short distance back, were about 200 men walking in single file.

The man couldn't restrain his curiosity. He respectfully approached the man walking the dog and said, "I am so sorry for your loss, and I know now is a bad time to disturb you, but I've never seen a funeral like this. Whose funeral is it?"

"My wife's."

"What happened to her?"

The man replied, "My dog attacked and killed her." He inquired further, "But who is in the second hearse?"

The man answered, "My mother-in-law. She was trying to help my wife when the dog turned on her."

A poignant and thoughtful moment of silence passed between the two men.

"Can I borrow the dog?"

"Get in line."

★ ★ ★

A passenger in a taxi leaned over to ask the driver a question and tapped him on the shoulder.

The driver screamed, lost control of the cab, nearly hit a bus, drove up over the kerb and stopped just inches from a large plate-glass window. For a few moments everything was silent in the cab, and then the still shaking driver said, "I'm sorry, but you scared the living daylights out of me."

The frightened passenger apologized to the driver and said he didn't realize a mere tap on the shoulder could frighten him so much.

The driver replied, "No, no, I'm sorry, it's entirely my fault. Today is my first day driving a cab… I've been driving a hearse for the last 25 years."

★ ★ ★

A man placed some flowers on the grave of his dearly departed mother and had started back toward his car when his attention was diverted to another man kneeling at a grave. The man seemed to be praying with profound intensity and kept repeating, "Why did you have to die? Why did you have to die?"

The first man approached him and said, "Sir, I don't wish to intrude on your private grief, but this demonstration of pain is more than I've ever seen before. For whom do you mourn so deeply? A child? A parent?" The mourner took a moment to collect himself, then replied, "My wife's first husband."

★ ★ ★

A new business was opening and one of the owner's friends wanted to send him flowers for the occasion. They arrived at the new business site and the owner read the card, "Rest in Peace".

The owner was angry and called the florist to complain.

After he had told the florist of the obvious mistake and how angry he was, the florist replied, "Sir, I'm really sorry for the mistake, but rather than getting angry, you should imagine this: somewhere there is a funeral taking place today, and they have flowers with a note saying, 'Congratulations on your new location.'"

★ ★ ★

A woman goes into the local newspaper office to see that the obituary for her recently deceased husband is published. After the editor informs her that the fee for the obituary is 50 cents a word, she pauses, reflects and then says, "Well, then, let it read, 'Fred Brown died.'" Surprised at the woman's thrift, the editor stammers that there is a seven-word minimum for all obituaries. The woman pauses again, counts on her fingers and replies, "In that case, 'Fred Brown died: 1983 Pick-up for sale.'"

★ ★ ★

A man was lying on his death bed, time was running out and his family were standing round about.

"Joe, Joe," whispered his wife, "is there anything I can do for you? Do you have a last wish?"

Joe lifted his head slowly from the pillow and sniffed the air. He could smell his wife's baking in the oven.

"Can I have just a last slice of the wonderful cake you're baking?" he croaked.

"I'm afraid not, Joe, that's for the funeral."

★ ★ ★

The two men had just reached the 10th hole when a funeral procession went slowly by. The first man stopped playing, took his hat off and bowed his head.

"That was very good of you," said the second man.

"Well, it's only right. We were married 27 years and she was a good wife to me," he replied.

★ ★ ★

One of Ireland's greatest footballers died and went to Heaven where he was met by an angel at the Pearly Gates.

"Is there any reason why you think you should not be allowed in?" asked the angel.

The footballer thought for a moment and then replied, "Actually there was an international match that I played in, Ireland against England, and I dived in the penalty area so that we were awarded a penalty. It helped us to beat England 2–1."

"Well, it's not the most serious mistake I've ever heard so you may come in."

"Oh that's wonderful, I've always regretted that moment… thank you so much, St Peter."

"Think nothing of it," said the angel. "Incidentally, I'm not St Peter; it's his day off. I'm St Patrick."

★ ★ ★

A very successful businessman was lying on his death bed. Just before the end he whispered, "Beryl, are you there?"

"Yes, Jack, I'm here."

"Tom, are you there?"

"Yes, dad, I'm here."

"Richard are you there?"

"Yes, dad," he sobbed. "I'm here."

Suddenly Jack jerked himself up and shouted angrily, "So who's minding the business then?"

★ ★ ★

An old woman had been going to the same doctor for over 50 years and during that time had made his life a living hell by constantly complaining about one thing after another.

Eventually, however, she died and was buried in the local churchyard, but it was less than a month later that the doctor also died and was buried in the next plot to her.

For a few minutes after the mourners had gone all was quiet and then the doctor heard tapping on the side of his coffin.

"What is it now, Mrs Mowner?" he sighed.

"Can you give me something for worms, doctor?"

★ ★ ★

Two Scotsmen were talking in the pub and one turns to the other saying, "Now, Sandy, if I should die first, will you pour a bottle of the finest malt whisky over my grave?"

"That I will," says Jock, "but do you mind if it goes through my kidneys first?"

★ ★ ★

The beautiful young girl was sitting on the park bench, crying her eyes out. When Matthew saw her unhappiness, he went over and sat down, asking what was wrong.

"Everything," she wailed. "I've just lost my job so I can't pay the mortgage and I'm going to be evicted. Then this morning I discovered I had a fatal hereditary disease which means I'll die in middle age."

"Oh dear," he said kindly, "why don't I try to cheer you up. How about coming out to dinner with me on Friday night?"

"I can't," she sniffed. "I'm going to kill myself on Friday night."

"Well, all right then. How about Thursday night instead?""

★ ★ ★

"Please come in and sit down, Mr Morton," said the doctor, looking grave. "I'm afraid your test results have come back and it's very bad news. You only have a year to live."

Mr Morton put his head in his hands and gasped, "Oh no, oh no, what shall I do?"

"Well, if I were you," replied the doctor. "I'd move out into the country, to a very quiet place, and marry an ugly, nagging woman. I assure you, it'll be the longest year of your life."

★ ★ ★

"It was a dreadful shock to us all," sobbed Mrs. Maggs. "Poor old dad!"

"Please don't upset yourself too much," comforted the vicar. "We'll make sure he has a memorable send-off. How old was he, by the way?"

"98," she replied.

"98!" exclaimed the vicar. "So why were you all so shocked?"

"We didn't know he had a bad heart till he went bungee jumping yesterday."

★ ★ ★

A teacher, a garbage man and a lawyer wound up together at the Pearly Gates.

St Peter informed them that in order to get into Heaven, they would each have to answer one question.

St Peter asked the teacher, "What was the name of the ship that crashed into the iceberg? They just made a movie about it."

The teacher answered quickly, "That would be the *Titanic*." St Peter let him through the gate.

St Peter turned to the garbage man and, figuring Heaven didn't need all the odours that this guy would bring with him, decided to make the question a little harder. "How many people died on the ship?"

Fortunately for him, the trash man had just seen the movie, and answered, "1,228."

"That's right! You may enter."

St Peter then turned to the lawyer. "Name them."

★ ★ ★

"Hello, children," said the new teacher. "Let's get to know each other better. Tell me what your fathers do for a living."

"My dad's a greengrocer," said Matthew.

"Mine's a doctor," said Jane.

"My dad works in an office," said Becky.

"And what about your father, Simon?"

"My dad's dead, miss," came the reply.

"Oh dear. What did he do before he died?"

"He grabbed his chest, groaned a lot and then fell on to the floor, miss."

★ ★ ★

As the wife watched her husband's coffin disappear into the ground, she turned to her friend and said, "You know, Ethel, I blame myself for his death."

"Oh, why's that then?"

"Because I shot him," she replied.

★ ★ ★

A 'diddle' of antique dealers are tragically killed in a plane crash and the group of 10 find themselves outside the Pearly Gates. "Mmmm," said St Peter, scratching his head, "we don't usually let in such a lot of antique dealers at the same time. I'll have to go and ask God."

So Peter went off and found God in his office. "There's a group of antique dealers at the gates, shall we let them in?" he asked.

"Just this once," replied God, "if there's so many of them, they'll be too bothered about each other to cause havoc anywhere else."

St Peter went back to the entrance but returned moments later in a panic. "They've gone!" he exclaimed breathlessly.

"What? The antique dealers?"

"No," replied Peter, "the Pearly Gates."

★ ★ ★

"Number 11, legs eleven," shouted the bingo caller.

"Bingo!" came the reply, and as the balls were set up for the next game, the caller recognized old Flo sitting miserably in the corner. He walked over and said, "Hello, Flo. What's up? You've got a face like a wet weekend."

"Hello, Ron," she replied. "My husband died three days ago."

"Oh, I'm so sorry," he said. "So have you come here on your own?"

"I have," she replied, "and the worst thing is that no one can pick me up till much later today, after the funeral is over."

★ ★ ★

An old man and woman were married for years even though they hated each other. When they had a fight, screams and yelling could be heard all over the neighbourhood and deep into the night.

Neighbours often heard the man uttering the following terrible threat: "When I die I will dig my way up and out of the grave to come back and haunt you for the rest of your life!"

They believed he practised black magic and was responsible for all missing cats and dogs in the area.

In the end the man died abruptly under strange circumstances and the funeral had a closed casket.

After the burial, the wife went straight to the local bar and began to party as if there were no tomorrow. Her celebrations were so over the top that her neighbours approached in a group to ask her whether she was feeling okay. "Are you not afraid/concerned/worried that this man who practised black magic would come back for you? After all, he stated that when he died he would dig his way up and out of the grave to come back and haunt you for the rest of your life?"

The wife put down her drink and said, "Nah... let the old man dig. I had him buried upside down!"

★ ★ ★

Three men who all died on the same day were at the entrance to Heaven when God announced that only one of the men would make it in. That would be the person who died the worst death.

God asks the first man how he died and he replies, "Well, for the last three weeks I have suspected that my wife has been cheating on me so I came home early to catch her in the act. When I arrived home I heard the shower running so I searched the house for him. I checked every room. Eventually I went out on to the verandah, then I saw him hanging from the ledge by his fingertips so I jumped up and down on his hands – he still held on. So I got the hammer and slammed his fingers. He let go and fell. He survived so I got the fridge (which weighs a ton) and lobbed it over the edge crushing him. Then I felt so bad that I killed him I got my gun and shot myself. That is how I died."

The second man recounts his story. "Well, it was the afternoon and I was doing my exercises on my verandah on the 12th floor when I slipped and fell off the balcony. Luckily, I only fell three floors and managed to grab the ledge of a balcony. I was hanging on when some idiot started jumping on my fingers. Then the fool got a hammer and bashed my fingers until the bones broke so I fell. I could not believe my luck when I landed in a bush surviving the fall – the last thing I remember is this fridge hurtling at me. That is how I died."

The third man explains how he died, "Picture this: I'm hiding naked in a fridge…"

★ ★ ★

One day, an engineer died and went to Heaven. But, St Peter said, "I can't let you in because your name is not on the list."

So the engineer went down to Hell and was let in. He stayed there for a couple of days and then decided that it was too hot and lacked a few amenities. So he installed flushing toilets, air-conditioning, running water and a lot of other things.

One day God calls down and says to Satan, "So Satan, how's it down there in hell?" and Satan says, "Well, it's great. I've got an engineer down here and he has built air-conditioning, running water, flushing toilets, and I don't know what else he's gonna build next."

Then God says, "You've got an engineer down there? That's a big mistake, send him up here right now!" and Satan replies, "No way. This is the best thing that's ever happened to hell."

So God says, "Send him up or I'll sue!!" and Satan says smirking, "Now just where are you gonna get a lawyer?"

★ ★ ★

Three men die in car accident and wind up in Heaven. An angel asks, "When you are in your casket and your friends and family are mourning you, what would you like to hear them say about you?"

The first guy says, "I would like them to say that I was a great doctor and a loving family man." The second guy says, "I would like them to say that I was a schoolteacher who made a huge difference to kids." The last guy says, "I would like them to say – LOOK, he's moving!"

★ ★ ★

During a funeral for a woman who had henpecked her husband, drove her kids half nuts, scrapped with the neighbors at the slightest opportunity, and even made neurotics of their cat and dog with her explosive temper. As the casket was lowered into the grave, a violent thunderstorm broke, and the pastor's benediction was interrupted by a blinding flash of lightning, followed by terrific thunder. "Well, at least we know she got there all right," commented her husband.

★ ★ ★

A man dies and goes to Heaven. He gets to meet God and asks God if he can ask him a few questions. "Sure," God says. "Go right ahead."
"OK," the man says. "Why did you make women so pretty?"
God says, "So you would like them."
"OK," the guy says. "But how come you made them so beautiful?"
"So you would love them," God replies.
The man ponders a moment and then asks, "But why did you make them such airheads?"
God says, "So they would love you!"

★ ★ ★

One day a guy dies and finds himself in hell. As he is wallowing in despair, he has his first meeting with the devil...
Satan: "Why so glum?"
Guy: "What do you think? I'm in hell!"
Satan: "Hell's not so bad. We actually have a lot of fun down here. Are you a drinking man?"
Guy: "Sure, I love to drink."
Satan: "Well, you're gonna love Mondays then. On Mondays that's all we do is drink. Whisky, tequila, Guinness, wine coolers, vodka and tonic, diet Coke and colas. We drink until we throw up and then we drink some more! And you don't have to worry about getting a hangover because you're dead anyway."
Guy: "Gee, that sounds great!"
Satan: "You a smoker?"

Guy: "You better believe it!"

Satan: "All right! You're gonna love Tuesdays. We get the finest cigars from all over the world and smoke our lungs out. If you get cancer no biggie, you're already dead, remember?"

Guy: "Wow… that's awesome!"

Satan: "I bet you like to gamble."

Guy: "Why yes, as a matter of fact I do."

Satan: "Because Wednesdays you can gamble all you want. Craps, Blackjack, Roulette, Poker, Slots. If you go bankrupt… you're dead anyhow."

Satan: "Do you do drugs?"

Guy: "Are you kidding? Love drugs! You don't mean…"

Satan: "That's right! Thursday is drug day. Help yourself to a great big bowl of crack, or smack. Smoke a doobie the size of a submarine. You can do all the drugs you want… you're dead, who cares."

Guy: "WOW! I never realized Hell was such a cool place!"

Satan: "You gay?"

Guy: "No… why?"

Satan: "Ooooh. You're gonna hate Fridays."

★ ★ ★

A lady dies and goes to heaven. She arrives at the Pearly Gates and is greeted by Saint Peter. There are just a few people waiting, so she strikes up a conversation with him. Just then, she hears a blood-curdling scream!

"What was that?" she asks.

"Oh, don't worry about that," says Saint Peter. "It's just someone getting a hole drilled in their head so they can be fitted for their halo."

A few seconds later, she hears another agonized scream, this one even more terrible than the one before.

"What was that?!" she asked anxiously.

"Oh, don't worry," says Saint Peter soothingly. "It's just someone getting holes drilled in their back so they can be fitted for their wings."

The lady starts to back away.

"Where are you going?" asks Saint Peter.

"I think I'll go downstairs if it's all the same to you," says the lady.

"But you can't go there," says the saint. "You'll be raped and sodomized!"

"It's OK," says the lady. "I've already got the holes for that."

★ ★ ★

A guy is strolling along a sandy beach one day when he comes across a very old bottle. He's just dusting it off when two rather tired-looking genies pop out. "Two genies!" he exclaims. "That must mean six wishes!"

"Sorry, buddy, it's three or nuthin," say the genies, "and hurry up."

The guy makes his three wishes and races off home to see if they've been granted. He gets home and runs into his bedroom, where he finds the most gorgeous girl he has ever seen waiting for him.

After hours of mad, passionate sex, he stumbles out of bed and walks into the living room where he is knee deep in $1,000 bills.

The guy can hardly believe his luck.

Just then there is a knock at the door. He rushes over to open it, when two hooded KKK members throw a rope around his neck and string him up naked until he is dead.

The two then take off their white hoods to reveal that they are, in fact, the two genies, both looking rather puzzled.

The first genie turns to the second and says, "I can understand the beautiful woman and all the money in the world, by why on earth would you want to be hung like a black man?"

★ ★ ★

When Mr. Wilkins answered the door late in the evening one day after he'd lost his wife in a scuba diving incident in Monterey Bay, he was greeted by two grim-faced police officers.

"We're sorry to call on you at this late hour, Mr Wilkins, but we have some information about your wife."

"Well, tell me!" he demanded.

One of the officers said: "We have some bad news, some pretty good

news and some really great news. Which do you want to hear first?"
Fearing the worst, Mr Wilkins said, "Give me the bad news first."
So the police officer says, "I'm sorry to have to tell you this, sir, but we found your wife's body this morning in Monterey Bay."
"OH MY GOD!" said Mr Wilkins, overcome with emotion.
Then, remembering what the officer had said, he asked, "What's the good news?"
"Well…" said the officer. "When we pulled her up, she had two five-pound lobsters and a dozen good size Dungeness crabs on her."
"Huh?" he said, not understanding. "So, what's the great news?"
The officer smiled, licking his chops, and said, "We're going to pull her up again tomorrow morning."

★ ★ ★

A train hits a busload of nuns and they all perish. They are all in heaven trying to enter the pearly gates controlled by St Peter.
He asks the first nun, sister Karen, "Have you ever had any contact with a penis?"
The nun giggles and shyly replies, "Well, once I touched the head of one with the tip of my finger."
St Peter says, "OK, dip the tip of your finger in the holy water and pass through the gate."
St Peter asks the next nun the same question, "Sister Elizabeth, have you ever had any contact with a penis?"
The nun is a little reluctant to reply but she says, "Well, once I fondled and stroked one."
St Peter says, "OK, dip your whole hand in the holy water and pass through the gate."
All of a sudden there is a lot of commotion in the line of nuns: one nun is pushing her way to the front of the line. When she reaches the front of the line, St Peter says, "Sister, sister, what seems to be the rush?"
The nun replies, "If I'm going to have to gargle that holy water, I want to go before sister Mary sticks her ass in it!"

★ ★ ★

SPORT

The steward at the local cross-country race asked one of the competitors what time he pulled out.
"I didn't," replied the runner," and now I'm really worried."

★ ★ ★

A world-class gymnast, away from home at an athletics meeting, spends a night of passion with one of her fellow athletes. On returning home she's overcome with guilt and goes off to confession.
When the priest gives her absolution she's so relieved she comes out of church doing handstands and double somersaults just as Mrs O'Neil is going in.
"Oh, no," murmurs the woman.
"What a day to do that as the penance and me with no knickers on."

★ ★ ★

My girlfriend is a real athlete.
Always ready to play ball with me.

★ ★ ★

Jack had just played a gruelling game of tennis down at his local club when he looked at his watch and realized he was going to be late for his mother's cocktail party.
"Damn," he muttered to himself as he hastily changed and rushed off home forgetting about the two tennis balls that he'd put in his pocket. In fact he didn't realize anything was wrong until he started getting very odd looks from a lovely young girl.
Blushing madly, he stammered, "Oh, er…. they're just my tennis balls."
"Golly," she replied. "I bet that's even more painful than tennis elbow."

★ ★ ★

A devout church woman happened to see a scruffy-looking man sitting on a park bench and as she went past him she pressed £5 into the palm of his hand, saying, "Have faith, young man, have faith."

Two days later, she walked through the park again and sitting on the bench was the same scruffy man. When he saw her, his eyes lit up and he ran to meet her.

"Here you are, Ma'am, Have Faith came in at 10–1," and with that he stuck a wad of notes in her hand.

★ ★ ★

Two blokes meet up on the river bank to do a day's fishing. One turns to the other and says, "Haven't seen you around for a while; have you been away?"

"Yes," says the man looking glum. "I've been on my honeymoon."

"Congratulations. Is she pretty, your wife?"

"No, she's plug ugly, she can't cook and she's bad in bed."

"Then why on earth did you marry her?"

"She's got worms."

★ ★ ★

Did you hear about the world's worst boxer?

He had advertising on the bottom of his boots. He eventually gave up when he saw a face in the third row that he recognized and after two minutes realized it was his own!

★ ★ ★

A man goes skydiving for the first time. After listening to the instructor for what seems like days, he is ready to go. Excited, he jumps out of the airplane.

About five seconds later, he pulls the ripcord. Nothing happens. He tries again.

Still nothing. He starts to panic, but remembers his back-up chute. He pulls that cord. Nothing happens. He frantically begins pulling both cords, but to no avail.

Suddenly, he looks down and he can't believe his eyes. Another man is in the air with him, but this guy is going "up"! Just as the other guy passes by, the skydiver – by this time scared out of his wits – yells,

"Hey, do you know anything about skydiving?"
The other guy yells back, "Fuck no! Do you know anything about lighting gas stoves?"

★ ★ ★

Standing at the edge of the lake, a man saw a woman flailing about in the deep water. Unable to swim, the man screamed for help. A trout fisherman ran up. The man said, "My wife is drowning and I can't swim. Please save her. I'll give you a hundred dollars."
The fisherman dived into the water. In ten powerful strokes, he reached the woman, put his arm around her and swam back to shore. Depositing her at the feet of the man, the fisherman said, "Okay, where's my hundred?"
The man said, "Look, when I saw her going down for the third time, I thought it was my wife. But this is my mother-in-law."
The fisherman reached into his pocket and said, "Just my luck. How much do I owe you?"

★ ★ ★

CRICKET

Three cricket managers meet up to talk over the previous cricket season and as they are strolling back to their hotel they notice a sign saying, 'Come and find out what the future has in store for you – Speak now to Mystical May.' They've had a bit to drink, so decide to go in and have some fun.
"We'd like to know if God's a cricket fan, and if so, can he tell us how our teams will do in the future?" says one of them, winking at the other two.
But Mystical May takes them very seriously and asks them which teams they manage and what they want to ask.
The first says, "When will Somerset win a major trophy?"

After a moment's silence, a loud voice is heard, "2040."
"Damn, I'll have gone by then."
The second man asks the same question for Lancashire and the voice says, "2038."
"Oh no, I won't be here either."
Then the third man, one of the England Selectors, asks, "When will England win the Ashes?"
This time, there is an even longer silence before the voice booms out, "Bloody hell, I won't be around either."

★ ★ ★

A man found himself hurtling to earth after his parachute failed to open. Thinking this was the end, he was suddenly amazed to see a group of men standing in a circle shouting to him, "Don't worry, you'll be all right, we'll catch you!"
Unable to believe his luck, he was just about to relax when looking down again he realized they were the English cricket team.

★ ★ ★

He was the laziest boy in the class. Only yesterday, the children were asked to produce an account of a cricket match. All the others spent an hour writing, while he took 30 seconds.
When the teacher saw it later she read, "Rain stopped play."

★ ★ ★

A very famous cricketer who could play right-handed or left-handed was asked how he decided which way to play that day. The man explained.
"If my wife is lying on her left side, I play left-handed and if she's lying on her right side, then I play right-handed."
"Ah, but what if she's lying on her back?"
"In that case, I ring up and tell them I'll be late that morning."

★ ★ ★

A passer-by happened to see a coffin being brought out of the church, with a cricket bat and pads on its lid. He turned to one of the mourners and said, "Like his cricket, did he?"

"He still does... he's straight off to a match after this, once they've cremated his wife."

★ ★ ★

Did you hear about the fanatical cricket fan?

On the day his pregnant wife was rushed to hospital, he was to be found in the waiting room listening to the test match on a radio. Suddenly, his anxious mother in-law arrived and asked him for the latest news.

"It's going well," he replied enthusiastically. "They've got five out and there's only two to go."

At that she fainted.

★ ★ ★

The cricketer was talking to his dumb blonde girl friend.

"Have you heard of WG Grace?"

"Heard of him? I had lunch with him the other day."

"Don't be silly. He's been dead for seventy years."

"I thought he was quiet."

★ ★ ★

"You're looking miserable."

"The wife's gone off with the milkman."

"I'm sorry to hear that."

"Yes. Now we'll be one batsman short on Sunday."

★ ★ ★

Two commuters were talking on the train. "I was going to go to the Test Match on Saturday," said one, "but you know how crowded the trains get, then there's the struggle to get in, and there's always the chance it might rain and..."

"I know," said the other. "I've got to go shopping with the wife, too!"

★ ★ ★

DEFINITION OF CRICKET

You have two sides, one out in the field and one in. Each man that's in the side that's in goes out, and when he's out he comes in and the next man goes in until he's out. When they are all out, the side that's out comes in and the side thats been in goes out and tries to get those coming in, out.

Sometimes you get men still in and not out. When a man goes out to go in, the men who are out try to get him out, and when he is out he goes in and the next man in goes out and goes in.

There are two men called umpires who stay all out all the time and they decide when the men who are in are out. When both sides have been in and all the men have out, and both sides have been out twice after all the men have been in, including those who are not out, that is the end of the game!

★ ★ ★

No rain had fallen for months and the group of Indians were faced with a long drought. Suddenly, one spoke up. "When I was in England I saw something that might work. What happens is that two men in white coats go into a field and hammer six poles into the ground, then another two men with clubs appear and stand in front of the poles. Then eleven men, also in white, come out holding a ball, and then, just when they are all spread round the field, that's when the rain comes pouring down!"

★ ★ ★

The two rival cricketers were talking. "The local team wants me to play for them very badly." "Well, you're just the man for the job."

★ ★ ★

The finest batsman the county had ever had was killed in a bad car crash and one of the substitute cricketers thought it was time he showed what he could do.

"Listen, boss, how about me taking his place?" he asked.

"Well, I'm not sure," replied the manager. "We'll have to see what the undertakers say first."

★ ★ ★

Why did the battered wife decide to live with the English cricket team? They never beat anybody.

★ ★ ★

Two men were down in Hell, stoking the fires as they had done for the past twenty years. Then one day, to their astonishment, it began to snow. And the snow got heavier and heavier until eventually the fire went out and the icy wind blew.

"Bloody hell," said one, "what's going on?"

"It looks as if England have won the Ashes," replied the other.

★ ★ ★

A horse was walking by the village green when he spotted a game of cricket in progress. He went over to the Captain and asked, "Any chance of a game?"

The Captain looked dumbfounded when he heard the horse talk but it so happened that one of his team had just retired injured so he agreed to put him in at number 7. The horse was sensational. He hit a four or a six off every ball in the over and the crowd were going wild. However, when the bowler changed ends, batsman 6 hit a single.

"Run," he shouted to the horse, "run, quick." But the horse didn't move an inch and the batsman was run out.

"Why didn't you run?" he demanded, as he left the field.

"Listen," said the horse angrily. "If I could run I'd be at the racecourse now, not stuck in some bloody village cricket team."

★ ★ ★

FOOTBALL

Why are football managers like nappies?
They're always on someone's arse and full of crap.

★ ★ ★

This Glasgow Celtic fan was such a fanatic even the house was painted green and white.
His wife said, "I'm pissed off, you think more of Celtic than you do of me."
"Christ Almighty, woman," he said. "I think more of fucking Rangers than I do of you."

★ ★ ★

What do the fans on the football terraces of Borussia Moenchengladbach dread to hear?
Someone standing up and shouting, "Give us a B…"

★ ★ ★

A block of flats is on fire and a woman with a baby is trapped on the eighth floor. She is leaning out of the window, screaming for help.
Below her on the pavement, the crowd are urging her to throw down the baby, saying they will catch it, but she is afraid it might be dropped. Then along comes a world-famous goalkeeper who persuades her that the baby will be safe in his hands. So at last convinced all will be well she throws down the baby and to much cheering and clapping he catches the baby… bounces it twice and boots it up the street.

★ ★ ★

On holiday, Bob was amazed when he went to see the local football team and halfway through the match they all suddenly stood stock-still except one, who put the ball behind his back.

"What's going on?" he asked the supporter next to him.
"They're just posing for this week's 'Spot The Ball' competition."

★ ★ ★

Did you hear about the disappointed nymphomaniac?
She volunteered to put up some of the men from the visiting football club. Six of them should have arrived after the match, but one called Dix injured himself during the game and had to go to hospital.
On hearing the doorbell, she opened the door and greeted them enthusiastically.
"So how many do I get?" she said.
"There are five of us here without Dix," they replied.
And she slammed the door in their faces.

★ ★ ★

A professional footballer was out on a first date and after the pubs closed he invited her back to his place. Removing his jacket, she noticed "UMBRO" tattooed on both arms and he explained it was part of an advertising campaign and he received £1,000 for each arm. When he saw how impressed she was he removed his shirt and there across his chest was the word "PUMA".
"I got £1,500 for this," he said. "And £800 each for these…" With that, he dropped his trousers to show her the word "KAPPA" tattooed on both ankles.
"But this is easily the best," he laughed and with that he showed her his penis.
"Oh," she exclaimed. "Why 'SLAG'?"
"No, no," he replied. "I got £8,000 for this and if you stay around a while you'll see it says 'SLAZENGER'."

★ ★ ★

Who says girls can't make the football team?
Suzie did! She's so athletic, she'll play ball with anyone.

★ ★ ★

"I'm transferring you to North Nogoland," said the boss to his salesman.

"But, sir, all you ever get there are whores and footballers."

"My wife comes from there!"

"Really, what position did she play?"

★ ★ ★

"Football, football, football! I'm sick of it. If you took me out on Saturday afternoon instead of going to the match I think I'd die of shock."

"Now, now, dear," said her husband. "It's no good trying to bribe me."

★ ★ ★

Definition of a good referee: 1) Must be fair 2) Must be consistent 3) Must be able to stay in control 4) Must award your team at least two penalties and give out two red cards to opposition players

★ ★ ★

It was the women's football league final and a large crowd had turned out to watch. But 10 minutes into the game, the goalkeeper was thrown against the post and knocked to the ground. Immediately, all the linesmen and officials rushed over to give her help but after five minutes and no sign of recovery, the referee walked over to find out what was going on.

"We're trying to give her the kiss of life," explained one of the officials, "but she keeps trying to get up and walk away."

★ ★ ★

"Hey, ref, are you blind or what?" shouted a very angry man in the crowd as he saw another player on the opposing team get away with a foul. The ref walked over to the heckler and shouted, "What did you say?"

"Bloody hell," replied the man. "He's deaf as well."

★ ★ ★

Did you hear what happened when two men went to watch the worst football team in the league? When they handed over £10 and asked for "Two, please", the ticket seller replied, "What will that be, defenders, midfielders or strikers?"

★ ★ ★

A man walks into the local pub with a parrot on his shoulder to watch England playing Brazil on Sky Sports. The match soon starts to go Brazil's way and after 10 minutes they score from a free-kick. All of a sudden, the parrot starts to make awful moaning noises.

"Sorry," says the man, "he's a fanatical England supporter, so he's obviously quite upset."

The score remains the same until half-time, but Brazil score a second goal only five minutes into the second half. This time the parrot is beside himself with anguish – moaning, stomping up and down and burying his head in his feathers. When a third Brazilian goal is scored, there's absolute chaos. The bird starts pulling out all his feathers until there is a pile of them on the floor.

"Heavens," says the barman, "if he reacts so frantically when they lose, what's he like when they win?"

"I don't know, I've only had him a couple of years."

★ ★ ★

"Now listen, son, we can't afford for you to get injured before the Cup match next week, so I'll put you on for the first 45 minutes and pull you off at half-time."

"Wow, thanks, boss, all I got at my old club was a slice of orange at half-time."

★ ★ ★

Bob received a free ticket to the FA Cup Final from his company. Unfortunately, when Bob arrived at the stadium he realized the seat was in the last row in the corner of the stadium. He was closer to the Goodyear Blimp than the field!

About halfway through the first half, Bob noticed an empty seat 10 rows from the halfway line. He decided to take a chance and made his way through the stadium and around the security guards to the empty seat. As he sat down, he asked the gentleman sitting next to him, "Excuse me, is anyone sitting here?"

The man said, "No."

Very excited to be in such a great seat for the game, Bob said to the man next to him, "This is incredible! Who in their right mind would have a seat like this at the FA Cup Final and not use it?!"

The man replied, "Well, actually, the seat belongs to me. I was supposed to come with my wife, but she passed away. This is the first Cup Final we haven't been to together since we got married in 1967."

"That's really sad," said Bob. "But still, couldn't you find someone to take the seat? A relative or a close friend?"

"No," the man replied. "They're all at the funeral."

★ ★ ★

Two men are changing in the dressing rooms after playing football. After showering, one of them puts on bra and pants.

"Hey, what's going on here?" asks his mate. "How long have you been wearing these?"

"Ever since my wife found them in my car," he replies.

★ ★ ★

David Beckham is celebrating wildly: "43 days, 43 days!" he shouts happily. Posh asks him why he's going so crazy.

He answers, "Well, Honey, I've done this jigsaw in only 43 days."

"And that's good?" asks Posh.

"You bet, Hon" says David. "It says 3 to 6 years on the box."

★ ★ ★

Sir Alex Ferguson is queuing in his local building society, when a gunman bursts in through the door demanding money. Ferguson attempts to tackle the raider, but gets knocked over... as he falls, his head smashes the counter and Sir Alex is out cold. The robber escapes and the cashier tries to revive Ferguson. After a few minutes he comes round and looks bewildered. His first words are: "Where the hell am I?" The Cashier replies, "Don't worry, it's ok, you're in the Nationwide." Ferguson replies, "F**k me, is it May already?"

★ ★ ★

Q: How many Man United fans does it take to change a light bulb?
A: 560,001. (That is one to change it, 60,000 to say they've been changing it for years and 500,000 to buy the replica kit.)

★ ★ ★

Q: What's the difference between Sir Alex Ferguson and God?
A: God doesn't think he's Alex Ferguson.

★ ★ ★

Q: Why can't you get a cup of tea at Old Trafford?
A: All the mugs are on the field and all the cups are at Highbury.

★ ★ ★

Q: What do you call an Arsenal fan in a suit?
A: The accused.

★ ★ ★

Two men are fishing on a river bank in a remote area of the River Thames on a Saturday afternoon miles away from any radio or TV.
Suddenly one man turns to the other and says, "Tottenham have lost again."
The other man was flabbergasted and said, "How in the name of God do you know that?"
The other man replied, "It's ten to five."

★ ★ ★

The seven dwarfs are down in the mines when there is a cave-in.
Snow White runs to the entrance and yells down to them.
In the distance a voice shouts out, "Arsenal are good enough to win the Champions League."
Snow White says, "Well, at least Dopey's alive!"

★ ★ ★

Newcastle have moved quickly to halt rumours of a rift between Sir Bobby Robson and Alan Shearer.
A club spokesman said, "It's ridiculous to suggest that there is a personality clash between the two – everybody at the club knows that Shearer hasn't got one."

★ ★ ★

Why do Geordie supporters have moustaches?
A: So they can look like their mothers.

★ ★ ★

Quasimodo asks Esmeralda, "Am I really the ugliest b**tard in the world?" "Why don't you go upstairs to the Magic Mirror and ask?" says Esmeralda.
Quasimodo goes upstairs to the mirror and returns a few minutes later. As he hobbles in Esmeralda asks, "Well, what did the mirror say?"
To which Quasimodo replies, "Who's Peter Beardsley...?"

★ ★ ★

Two Manchester United fans are walking along the street when one of them sees a mirror on the ground.
He picks it up and says, "Hey, I recognize that bloke."
The other man takes it from him and replies, "Of course you do, you prat, it's me."

★ ★ ★

A Plymouth Argyle fan is walking through the park one day when he stumbles over an old lamp. A genie pops out and tells him he has just one wish – what would he like? The man looks down at his dog and tells the genie he would like his dog to win the Crufts Dog Show to become supreme champion.

"You've got to be joking!" replies the genie. "Just look at him. He must be on his last legs, he's a fleabitten old mongrel with half a tail."

"OK," sighs the man, "in that case can you make Plymouth win the FA Cup?"

The genie looks at him for a moment and then says, "Let's have another look at this dog then."

★ ★ ★

A motorist is stopped for going through a red light and is asked to take a breathalyzer test.

"I can't blow," says the man, "I suffer from asthma," and he shows the policeman his asthmatic's card.

"OK, then we'll have to take you down to the station for a blood test."

"I can't. I'm a haemophiliac," and he produces a doctor's card.

"In that case, it'll have to be a urine test."

Once again, the man produces a card from his wallet. It reads, 'Leicester City Supporters Club – please don't take the piss'.

★ ★ ★

Coventry CIty suffered a break-in recently when thieves stole the entire contents of the trophy room. Police are looking for a man carrying a roll of sky-blue carpet.

★ ★ ★

"Did you notice the football team ogling that girl as she walked by?" the wife asked her husband.

"What football team?" came the reply.

★ ★ ★

495

Two football fans were down at the front of the crowd when some hooligans towards the back started to throw beer cans.

One of the fans got very agitated and couldn't concentrate on the game properly. "Don't worry," said his mate. "It's like the war, if it's got your name on it…"

"That's the trouble," interrupted the other. "My name's Foster."

★ ★ ★

The Manchester United players are all in the dressing room ten minutes before kick-off when Roy Keane comes limping in, looking in pain. "Sorry, boss, it's my back," he says to a worried Alex Ferguson. "I pulled a muscle in training yesterday, and I won't be able to play unless I get a cortisone injection."

"Hey!" says David Beckham, "if he's getting a new car then I want one as well!"

★ ★ ★

GOLF

"What happened to you?" exclaimed his mates, as Jack walked into the bar with a black eye.

"I got it playing golf," he said rather sheepishly, "and before you ask, it wasn't a golf ball it was a club."

Laughing into their beer, his mates insisted on hearing the full story.

"Well, I hit a bad shot and my golf ball landed in a field of cows. When I went to retrieve it, one of the women golfers was in there also looking for a lost ball. Luckily, I found mine quite quickly and was about to leave when I noticed one of the cows frantically flipping its tail. I walked over, lifted the cow's tail and saw a golf ball wedged in its crack. So I called the lady over, raised the tail and said, 'This looks like yours'."

That's when she hit me with the club."

★ ★ ★

When a US oil tycoon appeared at a local British golf course, followed by a servant pulling a foam-cushioned chaise-longue, his opponents thought that this was taking things too far. "JR, are you going to make that poor caddie lug that couch all over the course after you?" he was asked. "Caddie, my eye," explained JR. "That's my psychiatrist."

★ ★ ★

An Englishman, a Scotsman and an Arab were talking about their families. "I have 10 children" said the Englishman. "One more, and I'll have my own football team."
"I have 14 children. One more, and I'll have my own rugby team," replied the Scotsman.
"Well, I have 17 wives," said the Arab. "One more and I'll have my own golf course."

★ ★ ★

Why do golfers always carry two pairs of trousers with them ?
Just in case they get a hole in one.

★ ★ ★

For more than six months a woman had been having golf lessons, but still couldn't hit the ball more than a few yards down the fairway.
Unable to take it any longer, her coach shouted, "You're not holding the club properly. Hold it like you hold your husband's willy."
So the woman did and the ball flew through the air landing on the green.
"That's terrific," said the stunned coach. "You can take the club out of your mouth now."

★ ★ ★

Did you hear about the world's worst golfer?
He stood on a rake and yelled, "That was the best two balls I've hit today."

★ ★ ★

A young couple meet on holiday and after a whirlwind romance decide to get married.

"I must warn you," says the man, "that I'm golf crazy. I like to play everyday, you'll hardly ever see me."

"Don't worry," she says. "I have something to confess as well. I'm a hooker."

"That's OK," he says. "You're probably not keeping your wrists straight."

★ ★ ★

It was competition day at the local golf club and the retired colonel found himself paired up with the bishop.

They set off and it wasn't long before the colonel forgot who he was playing with and, on missing a short putt, exclaimed, "Bugger, I missed!"

The bishop shook his head reproachfully.

A little later, the same happened again, and the colonel missed an easy putt.

"Bugger, I missed!" he shouted loudly, at which point the bishop was forced to tell him that the Almighty would not be pleased with his language and that something dreadful might happen to him.

But almost immediately on the next hole the Colonel went and missed his drive and was so incensed he shouted and swore for a good half minute.

All of a sudden the skies opened, there was a terrible clap of thunder, and lightning struck the Bishop dead.

After a short pause a voice was heard from above, "Bugger, I missed!"

★ ★ ★

Each week the vicar and the retired colonel played a round of golf and no matter how well he did, the vicar was never able to beat him.

After one very close defeat the colonel turned to him and said, "Don't worry, Vicar, you will win in the end. You'll be burying me in the not too distant future."

"That's true," said the vicar dispiritedly. "But even then it's your hole."

★ ★ ★

A group of men, who were very competitive when it came to golf, were arguing on the ninth tee. When the captain arrived and asked what was wrong they replied.

"See my partner, Bob, over there lying in the bunker? He's just died of a stroke and these buggers want to add it to my score."

★ ★ ★

Colin Moanalot was drinking in the club bar and complaining about his morning's round.

"I only hit four balls properly this morning," he moaned.

"Aye," came a voice from the other end of the bar, "and two of those were when you stepped on the garden rake."

★ ★ ★

It is the honeymoon night and the happy couple strip off as quickly as possible and jump into bed.

But just before they start, she whispers to him, "Before we start, I feel I must tell you that one of my previous lovers was the captain of our local golf club."

"Listen, love," he replies. "Whatever went on before doesn't matter; we're married now so let's get down to it."

And for the next 30 minutes they vigorously do the business. Afterwards the husband lights a cigarette and picks up the phone.

"What are you doing?" she asks.

"I'm going to get us some smoked salmon and pink champagne – we deserve it," he says smiling.

"Oh no," she says, "the captain of the golf club would have made love to me again."

So once again they have 30 minutes of unbridled passion and then once again he calls for room service.

"No, no," she cries, "he would have done it a third time."

Again, they do it, but by this time the husband is feeling knackered. He reaches for the phone and before she can say anything, he says wearily, "I'm just ringing the golf captain to find out what the par for the hole is."

★ ★ ★

"Molly, would you get married again if I died?" asked her husband.
"Probably," she replied.
"And would you share with him all the little things we did together?"
"I expect so," she said.
"And would you let him have my prize golf clubs?"
"Oh no," she replied, "he's left handed."

★ ★ ★

A local golf club was being built for the less well off in the district and it was agreed that the women's team would practise once the men had finished and they would share the same equipment. That night, once the men had gone, the ladies walked out to the first hole when they suddenly heard an anguished voice behind them.
"Hold on," shouted Doreen. "I've got the clubs, but the men have gone home and taken their balls with them!"

★ ★ ★

An old man knocked at the door of the solicitors' offices and asked one of the partners if his grandson, an articled clerk, could have the afternoon off to accompany him to the last day of the Open at Wentworth.
"I'm afraid you're out of luck. He's taken the afternoon off to go to your funeral," came the reply.

★ ★ ★

Every Sunday afternoon when her husband was away on the local golf course, the wife would entertain her lover on the sofa. The two were humping away so passionately one afternoon that they didn't notice how bad the weather had got until they heard her husband walking up the garden path. In blind panic, the man jumped off and hid behind the sofa as he walked in.

"Couldn't play in that weather," he complained. "Can't see a yard in front of you." And with that he settled down to read the newspaper. An hour passed and the man behind the sofa had such bad cramp he couldn't take it any more. He stood up, picked up the husband's clubs and strode confidently to the door, remarking, "Bloody weather, you didn't happen to see a ball coming this way?" And with that, he was gone.

★ ★ ★

The local golf club was having an 'Open Day' to attract new members and one man from the wrong side of town asked the official, "Is this where the changing rooms are at?"

"My, dear, sir, you do not finish a sentence with a proposition, I'll have you know."

"OK, by me" replied the man. "Is this where the changing rooms are at, fuck face?"

★ ★ ★

A man joined the local golf club and before taking a walk round the greens, he decided to have a couple of drinks in the bar. When he tried to pay he was told,

"That's all right, sir, it's on the house for new members."

He then decided to have lunch and again they refused his money.

Feeling well pleased with himself, the new member decided he'd have a go at a few practice shots so he went to the club shop for some new golf balls.

"That'll be £5 each – £30 please, sir."

"Goodness" commented the man, "they've really got you by the balls round here."

★ ★ ★

For a whole week, the golfing instructor has been giving lessons to a new female member of the club and at the end of the session he invites her out for a drink. She accepts and they go off into town. After a couple of drinks, he invites her to dinner, then to a club and finally back to his place.

"Look, Ron," she says as they sit close together on his sofa, "I think I ought to tell you that I'm not really a woman, I'm a transvestite."

"Why you awful, you dreadful, you… you… immoral…"

"Come on, Ron, we are living in a more tolerant society."

"But it's unforgivable. You've been playing off the women's tee all week!"

★ ★ ★

On his tour of the world's best golf courses, a man ends up on a course in Africa. As he sets off for the first hole, he is accompanied by a caddie who carries a shotgun.

"Surely we don't need that," he says.

"Believe me, we do," replies the caddie.

All goes well until they get to the 7th hole and the man's tee shot lands in the bunker. As he steps into the sand a huge cobra suddenly looms up and as quick as a flash, the caddie aims his gun and shoots the snake dead.

"Bloody hell, I see what you mean," says the golfer, sweating profusely.

Then at the 12th hole, the ball lands in the rough and as the golfer goes over to hit it, a lion appears unexpectedly. Again, the caddie immediately takes aim and frightens the lion off with a gun blast. The rest of the holes are played without interruption, but on the 18th the golfer finds he's hit the ball close to the water. As he steps up to take the shot a crocodile rears up out of the lake and grabs hold of him.

"Quick, man, do something!" he yells at the caddie.

"Sorry, sir, I can't give you a shot at this hole."

★ ★ ★

Two skinflints decided to put a small wager on their game of golf. £1 to the winner was agreed and they set off. By the end of the sixth tee, they were level, but then Clive hooked his ball into the rough. Try as they might, there was no sign of his ball, and it would mean that Clive would drop at least two strokes. Thinking of the wager they'd put on the game, he waited for Gerald to turn his back, then took out a second ball, dropped it on the grass and shouted in triumph.

"Ah, found it at last, here it is."

"Clive, you're a bloody cheat," said Malcolm angrily. "That's not your ball; there's nothing you won't do to win the bet."

"Now look here," blustered Clive. "How do you know it's not my ball?"

"Because I've been standing on it for the past five minutes," replied Malcolm indignantly.

★ ★ ★

"My doctor has told me I must give up golf."

"Oh, I see he's played with you too!"

★ ★ ★

Jack and his wife were playing a round of golf, but on the seventh tee, Jack's ball landed behind the maintenance shed.

"Don't worry," said his wife. "There's no need to take a penalty shot, if we open both doors and take out the mowers you can drive straight through."

They did as she suggested and he gave the ball a mighty hit. Unfortunately, he missed the far opening and the ball ricocheted back and hit his wife in the head, killing her stone dead.

A couple of days later he was playing a round of golf with his friend and to his astonishment, ended up in a similar position.

"No need to take a penalty shot," said his friend, "just open the doors at either end of the shed and hit the ball through."

"Not bloody likely," replied the man. "I tried that a couple of days ago and ended up with a double bogey."

★ ★ ★

An irritable old man was taking a short cut across the golf course when he got struck by a golf ball.

"I'm terribly sorry," said the player, running up to him.

"That's not good enough. I've got a weak heart, anything could have happened. I demand £500 in compensation." "But I said, 'Fore'!" exclaimed the player. "OK, done," replied the man.

★ ★ ★

"I really want to give this my best shot," said Jack to his mate. "My mother-in-law is watching from the clubhouse balcony."
"Oh, get away!" replied his friend. "It's too far away, you couldn't possibly hit her from here."

★ ★ ★

Beryl had been moaning at Jack for ages because he wouldn't teach her golf. Eventually it got him down so much he gave in and took her out one Monday afternoon.
After spending some time explaining the finer points of the game they stepped up to the first tee and Beryl hit a mighty drive which landed straight on the green and disappeared into the hole.
"OK," said Jack. "I'll take a practice shot too, and then we'll begin."

★ ★ ★

The men were talking in the Clubhouse bar after spending a day on the greens. Each was recounting their golfing experiences.
One said, "If I'm going round on my own, the dog comes to keep me company and if I go one over par on a hole he somersaults backwards."
"That's incredible!" responded the others.
Warming to the subject, the man continued.
"Yes, and if I go two over par at a hole, he does a double somersault backwards."
"Amazing," came the response, "that's quite a feat, how does he do it?"
"Oh, I kick him twice."

★ ★ ★

"What's wrong, Beryl?" asked Joan, seeing her friend in floods of tears.
"It's Jack, he's left me."

"Oh get away, he's always walking out on you."
"No, no, you don't understand. This time it's for good, he's taken his golf clubs."

★ ★ ★

Two blokes were in the Clubhouse having drinks. One turned to the other and said, "I say, did you hear about poor old Malcolm? Pressure got to him, you know. Went berserk yesterday and beat his wife to death with a golf club." "Poor show," replied Gerald, "but just for the record, how many strokes?"

★ ★ ★

Maurice wakes up one morning feeling lousy. "Becky," he shouts. "I'm feeling terrible, I'm sore all over, what should I do?"
"So go see Doctor Myers," she replies.
After a thorough examination Doctor Myers says, "I am sorry to have to tell you this Maurice, but I have bad news for you. You're very ill and in my opinion you don't have very long to live – anything from a few days to three months. I suggest you go home and make the necessary arrangements."
Maurice is devastated. Later that evening, after the crying is over, Maurice tells Becky that as he is a devoted golfer, he would like to be buried with his golf clubs. If there's a golf course in heaven, he would then have his clubs to play with.
But Becky says, "Maurice, as neither of us knows if there is a golf club in heaven, I think you should go see Rabbi Levy and ask his opinion."
Maurice goes to see Levy. "Rabbi, is there a golf course in heaven?"
Rabbi Levy says, "I'll speak to God for you. Come back in a few days' time."
Two days later, Maurice returns. "Rabbi, have you got any news?"
Rabbi Levy says, "Yes, Maurice, I have spoken to God and I have some good news and some bad news for you. The good news is that God says there is the most wonderful golf course you could imagine in heaven. The sun shines every day, 365 days a year and you can play the game to your heart's content."

Maurice says, "That's wonderful news, Rabbi, but what's the bad news?"

Rabbi Levy replies, "Tomorrow morning, 8 o'clock – you tee off."

★ ★ ★

A woman was out golfing one day when she hit the ball into the woods. She went into the woods to look for it and found a frog in a trap. The frog said to her, "If you release me from this trap, I will grant you three wishes." The woman freed the frog and the frog said, "Thank you, but I failed to mention that there was a condition to your wishes – that whatever you wish for, your husband will get 10 times more or better!"

The woman said, "That will be okay," and for her first wish, she asked to be the most beautiful woman in the world.

The frog warned her, "You do realize that this wish will also make your husband the most handsome man in the world, an Adonis, that women will flock to."

The woman replied, "That will be okay because I will be the most beautiful woman and he will only have eyes for me."

So, KAZAM, she's the most beautiful woman in the world!

For her second wish, she wanted to be the richest woman in the world. The frog said, "That will make your husband the richest man in the world and he will be ten times richer than you."

The woman said, "That will be okay because what is mine is his and what is his is mine."

So, KAZAM, she's the richest woman in the world!

The frog then inquired about her third wish, and she answered, "I'd like a mild heart attack."

★ ★ ★

STATE OF HEALTH

Did you hear about the woman who went to the doctor for exhaustion and was told to stay out of bed for a few days?

★ ★ ★

When they buried Jack the hypochondriac, the words on his headstone read, "There, you see – I told you I was ill."

★ ★ ★

Old Jack hadn't been feeling too well, but had to go out to collect his pension. All went well until he set off for home when suddenly he felt an eruption in his stomach and knew he had to get to the toilet as soon as possible. He wasn't too far from the public toilets, which was lucky really because all hell was about to break loose. He raced into the cubicle backwards to save time, pulling his trousers down as he did, sat down and relaxed... But as he looked down, he saw two pairs of shoes.

"Bugger me!" he cursed, jumping up quickly. "Sorry mate, I didn't see you there, I didn't mean to shit all over you, it was an emergency."

"Oh that's quite alright," replied the man. "It's a good thing I saw you coming and pulled your trousers up before you sat down."

★ ★ ★

"Alcohol is a dreadful thing," said Bob. "It's bad for the health. Do you know, it killed my first wife?"

"No, how dreadful!" said Fred. "Alcoholic, was she?"

"Oh no, I came home pissed and shot her."

★ ★ ★

A fitness fanatic was doing his regular 100 press-ups in the park when along came a drunk. After watching him for a few moments the drunk doubled over in hysterics.

"What are you laughing at?" demanded the man.

"See here, mister, I don't want to upset you but somebody's stolen your gal."

★ ★ ★

With a few hours to kill before the pubs open, a man limps into a faith healing meeting and finds a seat on the front row. After the 30-minute service, the faith healer comes down from the platform and starts to touch some of the people. To the first one he puts his hands over the woman's eyes and she jumps up shouting, "I can see, I can see!"

He then lays his hands on a man who cannot walk and to everyone's delight he gets up out of his wheelchair and begins to dance. And so it goes on, people are being healed left, right and centre. Suddenly, the healer is standing in front of the newcomer and is just about to put out his hands when he shouts, "No, no, don't touch me! I've waited weeks for the orange disability stickers for my car, and they only came this morning."

★ ★ ★

A man went into the pharmacy to see if they had anything for a permanent erection. He felt highly embarrassed when he realised the shop was owned by two women but it was too late to walk out, so he said, "I've got this permanent erection, it won't go down and I wondered what you could give me for it."

"Just one moment, sir," and the two women went to the back of the shop to confer.

They came back smiling.

"We can offer you the shop and £100 in cash."

★ ★ ★

A woman was so dreadfully upset about being flat-chested that she travelled to deepest Africa to see a witch doctor. When she told him of her plight he gave her a simple spell to make and told her that when she returned home her boobs would grow every time a man said 'Pardon' to her.

A few days later, she was shopping in the High Street when a man came up to her and said, "Pardon me, Miss, could you tell me the way to the Post Office?"

After she had directed him she noticed with delight that her boobs had grown an inch. The following week she was coming out of the bank when a man bumped into her.

"Pardon me, Miss," he said.

Again her boobs grew an inch and she was very pleased with the way things were turning out.

The next night, she and her mates went for an Indian and as the waiter was serving up their meal, he tripped and dropped some madras curry on her clothes.

"Oh Miss, I am so sorry, a thousand pardons to you."

Sadly the restaurant was cleared due to an obstruction.

★ ★ ★

An old spinster, ill in bed and not wearing her glasses, was visited by what she thought was the vicar. After he had gone she said to her next-door neighbour, "Wasn't it nice of the vicar to come visiting?"

"That wasn't the vicar, it was the doctor."

"Oh dear," replied the spinster downheartedly. "I thought he was rather familiar."

★ ★ ★

Did you hear about the alcoholic who was staggering home with a bottle of whisky in his pocket?

He slipped over and, feeling something wet running down his leg, prayed to God it was blood.

★ ★ ★

Did you hear about the hypochondriac who received a Valentine's Card and thought it must be from his cardiologist?

★ ★ ★

How do patients in a burns unit pick their noses?

From a catalogue.

★ ★ ★

Did you hear about the unlucky man who had a wet dream and had to go to the VD clinic?

★ ★ ★

Do you know how Alcoholics Anonymous practises Russian Roulette? They pass round six glasses of tonic water – but one of them is a gin and tonic.

★ ★ ★

There's one definite way of giving a person amnesia.
Lend them money.

★ ★ ★

A London man had an awful time last week when he didn't realise the difference between fixative and laxative.
His teeth have been stuck on the lavatory for three days.

★ ★ ★

Did you hear about the gynaecologist who papered his hall through the front door letterbox?

★ ★ ★

"Hey, haven't we met somewhere before?"
"Yes, I'm the nurse at the VD clinic."

★ ★ ★

Young nurse in nurses' home knocks on matron's door while she's having a bath.
"Yes, who is it?" asks the matron.
"I have Mr Thompson to see you."
"Come come, nurse", responds matron. "I'm naked in the bath."
The nurse continues, "Mr Thompson, the blind man."

"OK, bring him in," says matron.
The door opens and the nurse and Mr Thompson enter the bathroom. Looking at the matron, Mr Thompson says, "Fair pair of tits matron. Now where do you want these blinds?"

★ ★ ★

Said the plain nurse to the pretty nurse, "When I gave the man in bed five a bed-bath yesterday, I noticed he had LUDO tattooed on his er... thing."
"That's not LUDO," replied the pretty nurse. "That's Llandudno."

★ ★ ★

A young nurse is walking along the corridor with one of her boobs hanging out of her uniform. Matron appears and on seeing this is outraged. She asks for an immediate explanation. The nurse, with a resigned air, replies, "Sorry, Matron, it's these young house doctors. They never put anything back where they found it."

★ ★ ★

Talk about the cutbacks in the NHS!
One hospital has just installed coin-operated bed pans.

★ ★ ★

Two nurses, locked out of the nurses' home late at night, shinned up the drainpipe and climbed in through an open window. The first nurse turned to her friend and said, "Doing this makes me feel like a burglar."
"And me," said the second, "but where will we find two burglars at this time of night?"

★ ★ ★

A woman is visiting her sick aunt in hospital and as she's leaving, she notices a ward completely enclosed by glass.

"Excuse me, nurse, what's that for?" she asks.

"That's the Isolation Ward. The man in there has got distemper, the plague, hepatitis and AIDS."

As they look, they see a man going towards the glass pushing a trolley. "Is that his lunch?"

"Yes, he has Ryvita, After-Eight chocolates and dried sheets of lasagne."

"Goodness, will that make him better?"

"No," replied the nurse, "but it's the only thing that we can slide under the door."

★ ★ ★

An unscrupulous young man decided to embarrass the new student nurse, so when she came round to make his bed, he asked, "Excuse me nurse, where does a woman's hair grow blackest and thickest and curliest?"

The poor nurse turned scarlet and went off to find the Sister.

A little later, Sister came over to the young man's bed and said, "Mr Jenkins, I hear you've been upsetting one of our nurses. Just exactly what did you say to her?"

"All I asked was where does a woman's hair grow blackest, thickest and curliest, Sister."

"Indeed, and where might that be?" she said, glaring at him.

"Why, in Africa of course."

★ ★ ★

"Doctor, we have had to buy three new operating tables this month alone. Will you please try not to cut so deeply?"

★ ★ ★

She must be the unluckiest person in the world.
She's just had a kidney transplant from a bed wetter.

★ ★ ★

A very rich young man, hearing about the amazing advances in body part transplants, decided he would like a new brain. He went to the specialist to find out what was on offer.

"Well, at the moment we have a computer analyst for £10,000; a university professor for £15,000 and a high court judge for £20,000."

"Money is no object," said the young man. "Tell me, what is the best and most expensive brain you have?"

"Well," said the specialist, "We do have an MP's on offer at £50,000."

"I don't understand; why is that so much more expensive?"

"That's simple," said the specialist. "It's hardly ever used."

★ ★ ★

A man went into hospital to have a penis transplant, having lost his own in an industrial accident. After the operation, he immediately asked the surgeon how it went.

"Well," hesitated the surgeon, "mixed results really. The transplant was a success. I think you'll agree it's an impressive member, but unfortunately your hand has rejected it."

★ ★ ★

A worried wife sent her rugby-mad husband to see a psychiatrist. What she didn't know was that the psychiatrist was also a fanatical supporter of the game.

"Now Mr Owen, let's try some word association. What do you think of if I describe something as smooth, curvy and sometimes difficult to handle?"

"A rugby ball," came the reply.

"Good. Now what about the act of coming up behind someone who is bending down and putting your arms round their waist?"

"A scrum."

"Excellent. And lastly – firm, athletic thighs?"

"A top class rugby player."

"Well, Mr Owen, I can see no problem there. Your reactions are absolutely normal considering some of the silly answers I get in here."

★ ★ ★

"Hello, is this the right number for the Downside Psychiatric Hospital?"
"That's right."
"May I speak to the man in Room Four?"
"I'm sorry, sir, there is no man in Room Four."
"Hooray, I've escaped, I'm free."

★ ★ ★

A man walks into a bar, orders a pint, drinks it and then wets himself, leaving a puddle all over the floor. The landlord is livid, but the man is so embarrassed and so apologetic, he allows him to stay. But after another pint the man does it again – pisses all down his leg. That's it, the landlord throws him out of the pub, telling him never to come back. A month later, however, he sees the man walk through the door.

"You're banned," he bellows across the room and the poor man is so embarrassed he rushes out sobbing. Six months go by and one lunchtime the same man appears again.

"Hold on landlord, everything's sorted out now. It was a nervous affliction."

"Well, OK," says the landlord who could see that the man had changed, and he serves him a pint of beer. No sooner had he drunk it than he weed all down his leg onto the carpet.

"You bloody twat," roars the landlord. "You told me you had it sorted."

"I do," smiles the man. "I went to a psychiatrist and he has taught me not to be embarrassed and upset about it. I'm quite confident now, in fact I feel proud."

★ ★ ★

"I think I know what's wrong with you," said the psychiatrist to his patient. "You're feeling all screwed up."

"Yes, that's right, how did you know?" replied the patient.

"Well, ever since you walked in, you've been trying to get into the wastepaper basket."

★ ★ ★

516

Did you hear about the psychiatrist who was so busy, instead of a couch he used bunk beds?

★ ★ ★

A man goes to the psychiatrist. The psychiatrist says, "You're mad."
The man says, "I want a second opinion."
"OK," answers the psychiatrist. "You're ugly too."

★ ★ ★

A therapist is trying to find out if there is any link between the number of times people have sex and the way they live their lives. He gathers together a group of people and asks, "How many have sex four times a week?"
Half the class put their hands up.
"How many have sex four times a month?"
Ten hands go up.
"Four times a year?"
Two hands go up.
"And once a year?"
Up pops a hand at the back of the group, belonging to a man who is jumping up and down and smiling all over his face."
"Well," says the therapist, "You're very happy considering you only have sex once a year."
"I am, I am," he cries, "tonight's the night!"

★ ★ ★

A man goes to see a sex psychologist because he has a fetish about eggs.
"Just look at this, doc," he says, pulling an egg out of his jacket pocket.
"Look at these beautiful curves, the smoothness of the shell, the beautiful colour..."
The psychologist is amazed.
"Do you really believe all this?"

517

The man whispers quietly to him, "No, not really, but you've got to say these things if you want it to go to bed with you!"

★ ★ ★

A plastic surgeon was complaining to his colleague about one of his regular patients.
"I'm being sued by Cynthia Prighorse. I told her she was unwise to have so many facelifts."
"Why, what happened?" asked the colleague.
"She's got a beard."

★ ★ ★

A young man goes to a plastic surgeon because he's got a very small dick. The surgeon tells him he could be helped but it would mean implanting part of a baby elephant's trunk. The man agrees and the operation is a great success.
A few days later, he decides to celebrate and takes out an old girlfriend for a romantic meal to tell her how everything could be different between them now.
Suddenly, his new appendage flies out of his trousers, grabs a bread roll and disappears.
"Wow, that's quite a trick!" says the girl. "Do it again."
But the young man, with a pained look on his face, replies, "I'm not sure if my arse could stand another bread roll."

★ ★ ★

A wife's face was so badly injured in an accident it required plastic surgery.
"We can do it," the surgeon said to her husband, "but it will cost you £2,000 and we will need to take skin off your backside."
The man agreed and the operation was a great success. His wife was even more beautiful. A few days later the plastic surgeon rang the husband to tell him he had paid £500 too much.
"Oh no," said the husband, "the extra is for the extra pleasure I get

everytime I see my mother-in-law kiss my arse."

★ ★ ★

A flat-chested woman tells her husband that she wants to go and see a plastic surgeon.

The husband replies, "Well, before you go, try this first. Rub some toilet paper on your nipples four or five times a day."

"Will that make my breasts get bigger?"

"Well, look what it did for your rear end."

★ ★ ★

A man went back to the plastic surgeon to complain about a new hand he'd had grafted on after his own hand had been smashed up in an accident.

"Well, it looks alright to me," said the plastic surgeon.

"It is, most of the time. Trouble is, you gave me a female hand and every time I go for a slash, it won't let go."

★ ★ ★

A man went into the chiropodist's and, taking his dick out, laid it on the table.

"But that's not a foot," said the chiropodist.

"I know," the man said proudly, "but it's a good ten inches."

★ ★ ★

A man went to the optician's to replace his glasses, because the others were broken.

"But you only had a new pair last week," said the optician. "We can't just replace them like that, without a good explanation. What were you doing?"

"I was kissing my girlfriend," he said.

"Well, that shouldn't have broken them."

"She crossed her legs," he replied.

★ ★ ★

"You don't have to open your mouth that far, madam," said the dentist. "I expect to stay outside while extracting your teeth."

★ ★ ★

A very nervous woman walked into the dental surgery, saying, "I'd rather have a baby than a tooth out."
The dentist replied, "I hope you're sure about that, because I'll have to adjust the chair."

★ ★ ★

A woman goes to the doctor to tell him she wants a baby but she doesn't want a relationship with a man.
The doctor tells her it's no problem: she should just take her clothes off, lie on the couch with legs wide apart and he'll go and get a bottle of semen.
However, coming back from the storeroom he catches sight of her on the table, and is overcome by her beauty and stunning body. He leaves the bottle behind, drops his trousers around his ankles and comes back into the room saying, "Sorry, but we're out of bottles. You'll have to have draught."

★ ★ ★

Three of the top scientists in the country decide, for posterity, to make a donation to the national sperm bank. The first goes in, the nurse does her business, and out he comes. The second scientist goes in, again the nurse sees to him, and out he comes. The third then goes in and the other two decide to take a peek, but when they pull the curtain aside they see the nurse on her knees giving him a blow job.
"Hey!" they cry out in dismay. "Why are you using your mouth when you only used your hands on us?"
"Ah," the nurse replies, "but he's got private health insurance."

★ ★ ★

A man went to a sperm bank but found the whole atmosphere of the place made it impossible for him to perform. So he asked one of the young nurses who was new to the clinic if she would help him.

Some time later, he emerged with a very small sample and was asked by the doctor why he had been so long.

"Sorry, doc," he replied. "I would have been out sooner but it took ages to get your nurse to cough it back up."

★ ★ ★

Of all the sperm that lived in Jack's body, one was fitter and more active than the rest. It was determined that when the time came, it would fertilise the egg and make the woman pregnant.

Some time later, all the signs showed that the moment was coming and off they raced, the fittest one out front. But suddenly, it stopped dead, turned round and tried desperately to swim back the other way.

"What's wrong?" they shouted.

"Quick, get back! It's a blow job."

★ ★ ★

A woman went to the doctor's because she was feeling tired and listless. He asked her to strip off and noticing she was somewhat overweight said, "Why don't you diet?"

She looked down and replied, "Do you think so? What colour do you suggest?"

★ ★ ★

Mum was so worried about the small size of her son's penis, she took him to the doctor. Knowing she would only be satisfied if he gave her son something for it, the doctor told her that Marmite on toast would soon cure the problem.

Next morning at breakfast there was a huge pile of Marmite on toast sitting on the table.

"But Mum, I can't eat all that," protested the son.

"Don't be daft," replied Mum. "Three are for you, the rest is for your father."

★ ★ ★

She told the doctor that every time she sneezed she experienced an orgasm.
"Are you taking anything for it?" he asked.
"Yes, pepper," she replied.

★ ★ ★

"Mr Jones, your health is very poor," said the doctor. "Try going on a healthier diet: eat more fruit."
"But, doctor, I have three olives in every martini."

★ ★ ★

A girl goes to the doctor's because she's found two green marks on the inside of her thighs. After examining her, the doctor asks a few questions.
"You're not a prostitute, are you?"
"How dare you? No I am not," she says.
"Do you have a boyfriend?"
"I am engaged."
"Ah, would he happen to be a gypsy?"
"Yes, he is."
"Then just tell him that his earrings aren't real gold."

★ ★ ★

"Doctor, doctor, there's something wrong with me. I can't stop farting, but they don't smell."
"Really?" said the doctor, waving his hand in the air and opening a window. "I think you may need an operation."
"Oh no, on my insides?"
"No, on your nose."

★ ★ ★

"Doctor, doctor, I've got a penis growing on my forehead, what can I do?" said the distraught young man.

"I'm afraid there's not much that can be done. It would be too risky to surgically remove it."

"Does that mean that every time I look in the mirror I'm going to see a penis staring back at me?"

"Well, er... no," said the doctor hesitatingly, as he didn't like giving bad news to his patients. "You won't see the penis because you'll have a pair of bollocks hanging over your eyes."

★ ★ ★

A man goes into the doctor's, takes his dick out and lays it on the table. After looking at it for a few minutes, the doctor says, "Well, it looks alright to me."

The man smiles, "Yes, it's good isn't it?"

★ ★ ★

The doctor pointed to a jar on the shelf in his surgery and said, "I want you to fill that."

"What!" gasped the patient. "From here?"

★ ★ ★

"Just go over to the window and stick your tongue out," said the doctor to his patient.

"Why?"

"Because I don't like the person who lives opposite."

★ ★ ★

A woman goes into the doctor's surgery.

"Say 'aah'," said the doctor. "Good, that seems alright, but what's with the postage stamp on your tongue?"

"So that's where I left it!"

★ ★ ★

The doctor's trainee assistant was always getting things round the wrong way, and it was hard to find jobs for her to do that she wouldn't cock up. One day a man arrived for a blood test. It seemed a straightforward job, so he asked his assistant to do it for him. However after 30 minutes, she hadn't returned, so he went looking for her and, on opening the door, stopped dead in his tracks.

"You silly bitch!" he cried. "I said prick his finger."

★ ★ ★

A very small woman went to the doctor's complaining that her fanny was painful. After a complete examination, the puzzled doctor could find nothing wrong.

"Do you have this pain all the time?" he asked.

"No, only when it's wet outside."

"OK, well next time it's wet, come and see me," he suggested.

The following week it had rained heavily and the woman appeared once more at the surgery. Again the doctor examined her and immediately discovered the problem.

"Just lie there a moment," he said, "while I find some scissors."

A moment later she sighed with relief.

"Oh doctor, the pain's gone. It's wonderful, what did you do?"

"Oh, quite simple really. I just trimmed an inch off the top of your wellingtons."

★ ★ ★

A man takes a girl back to his flat but after some heavy petting, he suddenly stops and says, "It's no good, I'm so frightened of getting AIDS, would you mind if I used my toe?"

She doesn't mind, so he sticks his toe up and she sits astride him.

A few days later, he notices something wrong with his toe, so he goes to the doctor.

"My goodness, I'm getting some odd cases at the moment," says the doctor. "You've got thrush on your toe and only yesterday I had a woman in who had athlete's foot in a most unusual place."

★ ★ ★

A man went to the doctor because he could not get an erection. Some weeks passed but none of the treatments worked so finally the doctor gave him an ancient remedy which involved injecting him in his member.

It was such a success that the man had a permanent erection, so he went back to the doctor to ask if it could be reduced.

"I'm sorry, it's impossible," said the doctor.

"But surely you can do something. All drugs have antidotes."

"I agree," said the doctor, "but this injection was not a drug. Just three of sand to one of cement!"

★ ★ ★

"It's incredible," said the doctor to the man. "You're pregnant! This will make medical history."

"Oh no," said the man, "I'm not married. What will the neighbours say?"

★ ★ ★

A man went to the doctor's covered in blood and bruises.

"What happened?" asked the doctor.

"It's my wife; she had another nightmare."

"But surely she couldn't have done this."

"Listen doctor, she shouted out, 'Get out quick, my husband's coming home!' and being only half awake, I jumped out of the window."

★ ★ ★

A woman goes to the doctor feeling very unwell. He takes some tests and tells her to come back in a week for the results.

The following week her husband comes to collect the results because she is too ill to leave the house. "Her name is Jane Smith," he says.

Unfortunately, the doctor has two Jane Smiths on his books and tests for both of them have just come back.

"Oh dear," says the doctor, having read both results. "Your wife either has VD or Alzheimer's disease."

"Oh no, what shall I do?" says the distraught husband.

The doctor replies, "Take her on a long journey, changing trains and buses at least four times, then leave her there and see if she finds her way home. If she does get back on her own, then don't fuck her!"

⋆ ⋆ ⋆

A man goes to his doctor because he has not been able to have an erection for five years. The doctor tells him that after such a long time the condition has become very serious, and there's only one pill that can help. But beware, the pill is so powerful that once taken, the man will have three huge erections and that will be it for the rest of his life. He also tells him that the pill is voice-activated and will only work when the man says, "ding dong". Once the man has had his erection, it will return to normal by saying, "ding dong" again.

It's a hard decision to make, knowing that these three erections will be the last he ever has, but he reasons it's better than not at all, so he takes the pill.

On the way home, he starts to have doubts as to whether it works, so he decides to try it out.

"Ding dong," he says, and this huge todger comes hurtling out of his trousers.

"Blimey!" says the man and quickly says "ding dong" to return to normal.

Now full of anticipation, the man races home and crosses the road without looking properly.

"Ding dong," goes the ice-cream van and once again this huge appendage appears, frightening the passers-by.

"Ding dong," and it goes back to normal.

Thankfully he gets home without any mishap, knowing he's only got one left. He rushes into the house, pushes his beautiful but frustrated wife to the floor, tears her clothes off and says, "Darling, darling, I love you so much, ding dong."

"What's the ding dong for?" asks his wife.

⋆ ⋆ ⋆

A man goes to the doctor and tells him he swallowed three 10p pieces four weeks ago. "Can you get them out?" he asks.

The doctor looks at him, puzzled.

"You swallowed the money four weeks ago and it's only now you're coming to see me?"

"That's right," replies the man. "I didn't need the money then."

★ ★ ★

The man was so boring, when he masturbated, his hand fell asleep.

★ ★ ★

A man goes to the doctor with a most unusual complaint. His penis is so big it drags his vocal chords down and causes him to stutter. The doctor tells him he can be cured but it will mean an operation to take away eight inches from his very large member. The man agrees and the operation is a complete success.

However, some weeks go by and the man misses his extra long penis – after all, it made him quite a celebrity. So he goes back to the doctor to ask if it can be put back on.

"I'mmm sorrrry thaaat's nooot posssiible."

★ ★ ★

A woman went to the doctor to tell him that every time she went to the toilet, pennies, 10 and 50 pence pieces came out.

"Don't worry," said the doctor. "You're just going through your change."

★ ★ ★

A man had over a hundred dogs in his house. The doctor told him to stop whistling in his sleep.

★ ★ ★

A buxom young lady goes to the doctor and he asks her to undress. When she's completely naked, he starts to feel her thighs.

"Do you know what I'm doing?" he asks.

"Yes, you're checking to see if there are any abnormalities."

Then he starts to fondle her breasts.

"Do you know what I'm doing now?"

"Yes, you're checking to see if there are any strange lumps."

Then the doctor lays her down on the table, jumps on top of her and starts making love.

"Now do you know what I'm doing?" he asks.

"Yes," she replies. "You're getting VD."

★ ★ ★

A woman goes to the doctor to get her husband's test results, only to learn that he has a very serious illness and will be dead by the following morning. In a most terrible state of shock and crying uncontrollably, she returns home determined to make his last night on earth the best he's ever had. That night, she wears her sexiest black lacy underwear and makes love to him passionately for five hours without a break. The husband is over the moon at his wife's incredible performance and after an hour's rest asks her if they can do it again... and again... and again. Another two hours of lovemaking take place until the wife lies back completely exhausted.

"Just once more, please," begs the husband, and at that, the wife turns to him with a spark of anger.

"OK, OK, it's alright for you, you don't have to get up in the morning."

★ ★ ★

A man went to the doctor complaining of a severe migraine-like headache and constant ringing noises in his ears. After a very thorough examination, the doctor told him that his symptoms were caused by an infection in his testicles and the only cure was to have them removed.

The man was aghast at the news and insisted on a second, third and even fourth opinion, but all the doctors agreed that having his testicles removed was the only cure.

At first, the man thought he would try to live with his afflictions, but it became unbearable, so he agreed to the operation. A little later, on leaving hospital and feeling very low, he decided to pop into the local gentlemen's outfitters and cheer himself up by buying a new suit. The tailor took one look at him and said, "Yes, you'll need a 36" waist, a 35" inside leg and a 15" collar. Chest size is 44"."

"That's amazing," said the man. "How do you know all that?"

"After 40 years in the trade I'm an expert at all men's sizes. For instance, I also know you take a size 11 shoe, an 8" hat and medium-sized underpants."

"Absolutely spot on," replied the man, "except that I take a small size in underpants."

"Oh no, sir, no," said the tailor. "If you wore a small size in underpants it could make you sterile; you'd certainly suffer from severe headaches and ringing noises in your ears."

★ ★ ★

The doctor told the old deaf man he needed a sample of his urine, a stool specimen and a sperm specimen.

"What's he saying?" said the old man to his wife.

"He wants you to leave your underpants here."

★ ★ ★

"You've got to cut down on your smoking, drinking and sex life, otherwise your heart is going to give out on you," said the doctor to his 70-year-old patient. "Only two cigarettes a day and one pint of beer."

"What about sex?" asked the man.

"Only with your wife," replied the doctor. "You mustn't get excited."

★ ★ ★

"Doctor, doctor, my balls have turned green."

"Well, you've heard of cauliflower ears. Those are brothel sprouts."

★ ★ ★

"Doctor, every bone in my body hurts."
"Then be thankful you're not a kipper."

★ ★ ★

A doctor is the only man who can tell a woman to take all her clothes off and then send her husband the bill.

★ ★ ★

I have a great doctor. If you can't afford the operation, he touches up the x-rays.

★ ★ ★

A man goes to the doctor, upset because every night he has the same dream where two gorgeous women are trying to get into bed with him but he keeps pushing them away.
The doctor asks what the man would like him to do and the patient replies, "Break my arms."

★ ★ ★

The old woman advises her next-door neighbour, who she knows is suffering from piles, "Put some tea leaves up there. It's a good remedy."
So she does, but it's no better. In fact, it gets worse, so she goes to the doctor. As she's bending over, she says to him, "Can you see anything?"
The doctor replies, "No, but you're going to meet a tall, dark, handsome man on Monday."

★ ★ ★

A man was asked to send a sample of his urine to the surgery before the doctor could complete his examination. Unfortunately, the man had to go to work, so asked the young boy next door to drop it in for him. On the way, however, the boy spilled most of it and, fearing trouble, topped it up with a cow's in a nearby field. It wasn't long before the doctor called for the man to come to the surgery as soon as possible, and when he returned home later he was in a raging anger. "So much for trying all your fancy positions," he said to his wife. "You would have to try on top, and now I'm going to have a baby."

★ ★ ★

A woman goes to her doctor complaining that she is exhausted all the time. After the diagnostic tests showed nothing, the doctor gets around to asking her how often she has intercourse.
"Every Monday, Wednesday, and Saturday," she says.
The doctor advises her to cut out Wednesday.
"I can't," says the woman. "That's the only night I'm home with my husband."

★ ★ ★

"I am very sorry to say that I have two pieces of bad news for you," said the doctor to his patient.
"Oh dear, what is it?" asked the patient.
"You have only 24 hours to live," came the reply.
"Oh no, what other piece of bad news could there be?"
"I tried to get you on the phone all day yesterday."

★ ★ ★

A man went to the doctor complaining of a sharp pain in his willy.
"And what about sex?" asked the doctor. "How often do you perform?"
"About twice a week," he replied.
"Does it burn after intercourse?"
"I don't know, doctor, I've never put a match to it."

★ ★ ★

A man went to the doctor and said he couldn't stop farting. It was dreadful. He just couldn't stop.
The doctor went away and came back with a huge long pole.

"Oh no," said the man.

"It's alright," replied the doctor, "I'm only going to open the window."

★ ★ ★

A young wife went to the doctor's complaining that her husband never made love to her. She wanted to know if it was her fault. After a complete examination, the doctor concluded it was not her – it must be her husband.

"Give him two of these pills every morning, and by evening you should be happily satisfied. But let me know how it goes because these pills are still experimental."

Only one day had passed before she stormed back into the surgery.

"I am so angry," she said. "One minute we were sipping tea, the next moment he lunged at me, lifted my dress, pulled down my knickers and took me on the table there and then."

"But isn't that what you wanted?" puzzled the doctor.

"Yes, but not in the middle of the coffee shop; I'll never be able to show my face in there again."

★ ★ ★

"Doctor, I'm so overweight, I've tried hundreds of different diets but nothing seems to work. Can you help me?" asked the fat man.

The doctor gave him some pills and told him to come back in a month. This he did, having lost over a stone in weight.

"It's wonderful," said the man. "Every night I'd take a pill and then all night I dream of being stranded on this desert island with twenty beautiful girls, each one of them demanding sexual satisfaction. No wonder I've lost weight."

"That'll be £40 then," said the doctor, and the man went away very happy. Now this man had a friend, a miserly sort of fellow who was also having trouble losing weight so he was recommended to go along and see the same doctor and get similar treatment. However, after a month had gone by he returned in a very disgruntled mood even though he had lost a stone in weight as well.

"What's wrong, the pills have worked, haven't they?" asked the doctor. "Oh sure, every night when I went to sleep I dreamt I was in the jungle being chased by wild savages brandishing machetes. Every morning I was knackered. But how come I get this nightmare and my mate is surrounded by beautiful women?"

"Well, what did you expect?" said the doctor. "You insisted you have it on the NHS."

★ ★ ★

"Doctor, I want to get married but I think my cock's too small. What shall I do?"

He replied, "Go and stay down on the local farm, dip your cock in fresh milk every day and have it sucked by a calf."

Some weeks later, they met in the street and the doctor asked him how his marriage was going.

"Oh, I didn't bother in the end. I bought the calf instead."

★ ★ ★

Said the doctor to his woman patient, "You have acute appendicitis."

"Thank you, and you have a real neat bum," she replied.

★ ★ ★

A middle-aged couple go to the doctor's and ask him if he would mind watching them have sexual intercourse. It's an odd request, but the doctor agrees and charges them £40. They come back a second week and request the same thing even though the doctor tells them they're doing nothing wrong. However, they insist and he charges them another £40.

After the third visit, the doctor asks them why they are doing this and the man replies, "Well, she's married, so we can't go to her house. I live with my mother, so we can't go there, and hotels are so expensive. But here I can get half the cost back on my private health insurance."

★ ★ ★

A man took his wife to the doctor's complaining about her sex drive. It was non-stop; whatever time of the day, whatever place, she was always hankering after sex.

"I'll see what I can do," said the doctor and he asked her to go into the consulting room and strip off. As soon as he started to examine her, she began to make little groaning noises, and tempt him forward with her open legs. It was too much for him, and in no time at all he was astride her.

But all the noise attracted the attention of the husband waiting outside, so he opened the door to find out what was happening.

"What the hell's going on here?" he shouted.

"Oh er... nothing to worry about, I'm taking your wife's temperature," said the sweating doctor.

"Really?" said the man, taking a flick knife out of his pocket. "When that thing comes out, it better have numbers on it."

★ ★ ★

"Doctor, it's my husband – he thinks he's a chicken."

"Good gracious," replied the doctor. "Why didn't you tell me sooner?"

"Well, we needed the eggs."

★ ★ ★

"How did you get on at the doctor's, Pete?" asked his mate George.

"Well, he thinks he can do something for me," replied Pete. "He's told me to drink a glass of this medicine after a hot bath."

"So do you feel any different?"

"Not yet, I've only managed to drink half the bath water up to now."

★ ★ ★

"The doctor said he would have me on my feet in two weeks."

"And did he?"

"Yes, I had to sell the car to pay the bill."

★ ★ ★

TEN THINGS YOU DON'T WANT TO HEAR IN SURGERY

1. Don't worry. I think it is sharp enough.

2. Nurse, did this patient sign the organs donation card?

3. Damn. Page 84 of the manual is missing.

4. Everybody stand back! I lost a contact lens.

5. Hand me that... uh... that uh... thingie...

6. Better save that. We'll need it for the autopsy.

7. "Accept this sacrifice, O Great Lord of Darkness"

8. Wait a minute, if this is his spleen, then what's that?

9. "Y'know, there's big money in kidneys. Hell, he's got two of 'em.

10. What do you mean, "You want a divorce"?

★ ★ ★

The doctor and his wife were having a heated argument at breakfast. As he stormed out of the house, the man angrily yelled to his wife, "You aren't that good in bed either!"
By mid-morning, he decided he'd better make amends, and phoned home. After many rings, his wife, clearly out of breath, answered the phone.
"What took you so long to answer and why are you panting?"
"I was in bed."
"What in the world are you doing in bed at this hour?"
"Getting a second opinion."

★ ★ ★

A college physics professor was explaining a particularly complicated concept to his class when a medical student interrupted him.

"Why do we have to learn this stuff?" one young man blurted out.

"To save lives," the professor responded before continuing the lecture.

A few minutes later the student spoke up again. "So how does physics save lives?"

The professor stared at the student for a long time without saying a word. Finally, he replied. "Physics saves lives," he said, "because it keeps the idiots out of medical school."

★ ★ ★

"It's no good Mabel, I can't find anything wrong with you. It must be the effects of drinking," said the doctor.

"Well, in that case, I'll come back when you're sober!" exclaimed Mabel.

★ ★ ★

There are only two men in the doctor's waiting room. One has his arm bandaged up and the second is covered in food – potatoes in his hair, a lamb chop sticking out of his pocket, gravy running down his trousers and peas up his nose. The second man turns to the first and asks him what happened.

"Oh, it's my own fault," he replied. "I was looking at this beautiful girl instead of watching where I was going. I tripped over a step and I think I might have broken my arm. What about you?"

"Oh, it's nothing much, I'm just not eating properly."

★ ★ ★

A woman took her son to the doctor's surgery.

"Doctor, tell me please, can a boy of 13 take out his own appendix?" she demanded.

"Indeed not," said the doctor.

"There you are, I told you so!" she yelled at her son. "Now put it back immediately."

★ ★ ★

A simple old woman fell and badly hurt her leg.

"You'll have to rest for a few days," said the doctor, after he'd bandaged it up, "and please don't use the stairs until I give you permission."

The following week, the old woman returned to the surgery for a check-up.

"Very good," said the doctor, "your leg is almost healed. You can start using the stairs again."

"Oh, thank goodness for that," she replied happily. "Shinning up the drainpipe was wearing me out."

★ ★ ★

"Every time I look in the mirror, I see an old man, tired and haggard."

"Well at least your eyesight's perfect," replied the doctor.

★ ★ ★

There were only two people in the doctor's waiting room. Robert had come for a blood test and was sitting opposite a man who was constantly mumbling to himself, "Please let me be ill, please, please let me be ill."

Unable to contain his curiosity any longer, Robert asked the man, "I'm sorry, I couldn't help but overhear you say you hoped you were sick. Why is that?"

The man replied sadly, "I'd hate to be well and feel like this!"

★ ★ ★

The great consultant looked down his nose at the scruffy man who shuffled into the room. After a quick examination, he asked, "Have you been to see anyone else before coming to see me?"

"Yes, Dr Peek," he replied warily.

"Dr Peek! That charlatan!" exclaimed the consultant, "and I suppose he fed you lots of useless pills and doled out some pathetic advice?"

"I don't know, he told me to come and see you."

★ ★ ★

"Oh, doctor," said the distraught patient. "Why do so many people take an instant dislike to me?"

"Saves time," came the reply.

★ ★ ★

"Come in, Mr Burton," said the doctor solemnly. "I've had the results of your tests and I've got some good news and some bad news."

"What's the bad news?" asked the man anxiously.

"I'm afraid you have a rare illness picked up from your expeditions into the jungle. There's no cure. In fact, within the next 24 hours, you'll go into a coma and die."

The man gasped in pain. "Then what the hell's the good news?" he asked.

The doctor's face lit up with anticipation.

"You know my new receptionist, the blonde one? I've just asked her out and she said yes!"

★ ★ ★

An old woman goes to the doctor's to get the results of her tests.

"Sit down, Mrs Chivers," says the doctor kindly, "I'm afraid the news isn't very good."

"Tell me the worst," she replies.

"Well, there are two things. First you have cancer..."

"Oh no," she gasps.

"...and secondly, you have Alzheimer's disease."

"Oh, thank goodness for that," she says, smiling. "For a moment I thought you were going to tell me I had cancer."

★ ★ ★

Which is worse, Alzheimer's disease or Parkinson's disease?

Parkinson's; I'd rather forget a beer than spill one.

★ ★ ★

Two simple lads were working in the sawmill when Jack accidentally cut his arm off. As quick as lightning, his mate Pete put it in a plastic bag and rushed them both to hospital. After four hours, the brilliant surgeon had sewn the arm back on and within three months, Jack was as good as new. That winter, Jack was so cold that his concentration slipped and he cut off his right leg. Quick as a flash, Pete wrapped up the leg in a plastic bag and rushed them to hospital. Although the operation was more difficult, the surgeon, once again, miraculously attached the leg back to Jack's body and after six months he had fully recovered. The months went by until, one day, Jack fell asleep at work and cut his head off. Ready for every emergency, Pete got the head in a plastic bag and rushed them to hospital.

"This is a very difficult operation," said the surgeon. "It's touch and go." He told Pete to come back the following morning to see how things were progressing. The next day, Pete arrived at the hospital and met a very serious looking surgeon.

"I'm sorry, your friend didn't make it."

Grief-stricken, Pete replied, "I know you did all you could Doc, and you did warn me it might not work."

"Oh, it wasn't the operation," said the surgeon, "that was successful; Jack suffocated in the plastic bag."

★ ★ ★

The man came into work, one arm in a sling, a bandage round his head, two black eyes and a painful limp.

"And what time do you call this?" asked his boss. "You're very late."

"I'm sorry sir, I tripped over the garden step," said the poor man.

"Oh yeah, and it took a whole hour to do that, did it?" replied the boss scornfully.

★ ★ ★

Three surgeons were relaxing in the bar after a conference and the first one said, "I had a pretty easy time last week. I had to operate on a computer analyst and when I opened him up, all the parts were filed and labelled and the retrieval system was very competent."

"Well, my week was even easier," said the second surgeon. "I had to operate on an electronics expert, and all the different systems were colour-coded so you could see what was wrong immediately."

"Yes, that sounds good," said the third surgeon. "But I had the easiest of all. I had to operate on an estate agent. They've only got two moving parts – the mouth and the arsehole – and they're both used for the same thing."

★ ★ ★

Simple Sam is the local odd-job man in the village, not too bright but always willing to have a go. One day, he hears there are vacancies going in the local sawmill, so he goes along in the hope of getting a job. Reluctantly, the boss takes him on, emphasising how dangerous the job is and how he must always think 'safety.' However, only two hours into the job and Sam stumbles over a plank of wood, puts his hands out to save himself and gets all his fingers and thumbs sawn off by a giant blade. There's no one else about, so he runs off in shock to the local hospital, where he faints on the doorstep. Later, as he regains consciousness, he hears the doctor's voice.

"Sam, Sam, if only you'd brought your fingers in with you we might have been able to sew them on before it was too late."

"I would have," he cried, "but I couldn't pick them up."

★ ★ ★

A young, rich lawyer had a very bad car crash. The car was a write-off but even worse, the lawyer's arm had been severed. When the paramedics arrived, they heard him whimpering, "My BMW, oh no, my BMW."

"Sir," said one of the helpers, "I think you should be more concerned about your arm."

The lawyer looked round and seeing just his shoulder, exclaimed, "Oh no, my Rolex, my Rolex."

★ ★ ★

A woman went to the doctor complaining of terrible knee pains. After the diagnostic tests showed nothing, the doctor questioned her, "There must be something you're doing that you haven't told me about. Can you think of anything that might be doing this to your knees?"

"Well," the woman said a little sheepishly, "my husband and I have sex doggy-style on the floor every night."

"That's got to be it," said the doctor. "There are plenty of other positions and ways to have sex, you know."

"Not if you're going to watch television, there ain't!" she replied.

★ ★ ★

Three old men are talking about their aches, pains and bodily functions.

The 70-year-old man says, "I have this problem. I wake up every morning at seven, and it takes me twenty minutes to pee."

The 80-year-old man says, "My case is worse. I get up at eight and I sit there and grunt and groan for half an hour before I finally have a bowel movement."

The 90-year-old man says, "At seven I pee like a horse, and at eight I crap like a cow."

"So what's your problem?" ask the others.

"I don't wake up until nine!"

★ ★ ★

A young couple got married and were having sex all the time during their honeymoon. When the honeymoon was over, they had to adjust their sex schedule to their work schedule. So every day the husband would get home at five o'clock, and every day they would go to bed at 5:15. In the door at 5, in the sack at 5:15.

This went on for months, never missing a day until the wife came down with the 'flu and went to the doctor to get a 'flu shot. The shot killed all the germs inside her except for three. These three germs were huddled together inside her body, talking over their survival

541

strategies. One germ said, "I am going to hide between two toes on her left foot. I don't think the antibiotics will find me there."

The second exclaimed, "I am going to hide behind her right ear. I don't think they'll find me there."

The last germ said, "I don't know about you guys, but when that 5:15 pulls out tonight, I'm gonna be on it!"

★ ★ ★

How do two psychiatrists greet each other?
You are fine. How am I?

★ ★ ★

How many psychiatrists does it take to change a light bulb?
Only one, but the light bulb has to want to change.

★ ★ ★

How do crazy people go through the forest?
They take the psycho path.

★ ★ ★

The dentist looked at his patient and gave his verdict.

"For the very best results, your treatment will cost about £5,000 – but," he added hastily, "you will have perfect teeth for the rest of your life."

"Oh dear!" exclaimed the patient. "That's an awful lot of money. I couldn't pay it all in one go."

"No, no, I quite understand. We could arrange monthly payments."

"I see. I suppose it would be a bit like buying a luxury item, like a yacht," mused the man.

"That's right," replied the dentist. "I am."

★ ★ ★

"Come in, Donald," said the dentist, "and take a seat. Now, I wonder if you'll do something for me. Before we start, would you mind screaming very loudly?"

Donald looked puzzled. "Well, I suppose so," he replied, "but can you tell me why?"

"By all means," replied the dentist. "My team's got through to the FA Cup Final, and I'm never going to get there if I don't get rid of that lot out there."

★ ★ ★

"I wish you hadn't left it for so long before coming to see me," said the dentist to his patient. "Your teeth are way past being saved, so I'll have to take them all out and make you a set of false ones."

The terrified patient gasped, "I can't – I just can't stand the pain."

"Come now," said the dentist impatiently. "Just imagine how nice it will be to be able to eat your food properly again. And I can assure you there'll be very little pain."

The man still didn't look convinced.

"I'll tell you what," said the dentist, who'd just had an idea. "Why don't you talk to Mr Taylor. He lives down your street and I did the same for him not so long ago. If you ask him about the pain, I'm positive he'll reassure you."

So later in the week, the man contacted Mr Taylor and asked him about the pain.

"Mmm," mused Mr Taylor, "let me put it this way. I had my teeth done four months ago and last week I was repairing our garden gate when I accidentally hammered a nail into my hand. And that was the first time in four months my teeth didn't hurt!"

★ ★ ★

"Kate, listen to me," pleaded her dentist. "We've got to stop this. It'll only end in tears."

"But why?" she asked. "We've had a great relationship for over a year and my husband's never found out. He's not even suspicious."

"But he will be soon. Don't you realise you've only got one tooth left in your mouth?"

★ ★ ★

"Thanks for seeing us so quickly," said the grateful man to the dentist. "As I said on the phone, it's a bit of an emergency because this toothache's come just as we were flying out to the Bahamas at six o'clock tonight. Please take it out as quickly as possible. Don't worry about painkillers or anything like that, just yank it out."

"Well, I think I ought to warn you that it will be very painful if I don't use anything."

"Not to worry. Just get a move on."

"OK. I think you're very brave. Just pop up into the chair for me please."

The man turned to his wife and said, "You heard what he said, Ruth, sit up in the chair."

★ ★ ★

"I'm not paying this outrageous bill," yelled the man. "You've charged me four times over."

"Maybe so," replied the dentist calmly, "but you made so much noise during your treatment that the other three patients in the waiting room cancelled their appointments."

★ ★ ★

A man comes to his doctor and tells him that his wife has refused to have sex with him for the past seven months. The doctor tells the man to bring his wife in so he can talk to her. Presently, the wife comes into the doctor's office, and the doctor asks her what's wrong.

The wife explains, "For the last seven months, I have taken a cab to work every morning. I don't have any money, so the cab driver asks me, "So are you going to pay today or what?" so I take an "or what". When I get to work, I'm late, so the boss asks me, "So are we going to write this down in the book or what?" so I take an "or what".

After work, I take the cab and again I don't have any money, so the cab driver asks me again, "So are you going to pay this time or what?" so again I take an "or what". So you see, doc, when I get home I'm all tired out, and I don't want it any more."

544

The doctor thinks for a second, and then turns to the wife and says, "So are we going to tell your husband or what?"

★ ★ ★

A young man goes to a doctor for a physical examination. When he gets into the room, the man strips for his exam. He has a dick the size of a child's little finger. A nurse standing in the room sees his little dick, and begins to laugh hysterically.

The young man gives her a stern look and says, "You shouldn't laugh, it's been swollen like that for two weeks now!"

★ ★ ★

An elderly woman went into the doctor's office. When the doctor asked why she was there, she replied, "I'd like to have some birth control pills."

Taken aback, the doctor thought for a minute and then said, "Excuse me, Mrs Smith, but you're 75 years old. What possible use could you have for birth control pills?"

The woman responded, "They help me sleep better."

The doctor thought some more but, still perplexed, continued, "How in the world do birth control pills help you to sleep?"

The woman said, "I put them in my granddaughter's orange juice and I sleep better at night."

★ ★ ★

The old family doctor, being away on holiday, entrusted his practice to his son – a recently graduated medical student. When the old man returned, the youngster told him, amongst other things, that he cured Miss Ferguson, an aged and wealthy spinster, of her chronic indigestion.

"My boy," said the old doctor, "I'm proud of you, but Miss Ferguson's indigestion is what put you through medical school."

★ ★ ★

A man is talking to the family doctor. "Doc, I think my wife's going deaf."
The doctor answers, "Well, here's something you can try on her to test her hearing. Stand some distance away from her, and ask her a question. If she doesn't answer, move a little closer and ask again. Keep repeating this until she answers. Then you'll be able to tell just how hard of hearing she really is."
The man goes home and tries it out. He walks in the door and says, "Honey, what's for dinner?" He doesn't get an answer, so he moves closer to her.
"Honey, what's for dinner?" Still no answer.
He repeats this several times, until he's standing just a few feet away from her. Finally, she answers, "For the eleventh time, I said we're having MEATLOAF!"

★ ★ ★

A pipe burst in a doctor's house. He called a plumber. The plumber arrived, unpacked his tools, did mysterious plumber-type things for a while, and handed the doctor a bill for £600.
The doctor exclaimed, "This is ridiculous! I don't even make that much as a doctor!"
The plumber waited for him to finish and quietly said, "Neither did I when I was a doctor."

★ ★ ★

A man who thought he was John the Baptist was disturbing the neighbourhood, so for public safety, he was committed.
He was put into a room with another patient, and immediately began his routine, "I am John The Baptist! Jesus Christ has sent me!"
The other guy looked at him and declared, "I did not!"

★ ★ ★

To assess Bob's state of mind, the psychiatrist told him he was going to make some random marks on the paper and Bob was to tell him what he saw.

After the first mark Bob replied, "That's Madonna in the nude."
For the second mark he said, "That's my next door neighbour stark naked."
For the third mark, "That's the whole of my wife's knitting circle with no clothes on."
The psychiatrist looked up exasperated. "The trouble with you, Bob, is that you're obsessed with sex."
"Get off!" retorted Bob angrily. "You're the one drawing the dirty pictures."

★ ★ ★

Did you hear about the psychiatrist who kept his wife under the bed? He thought she was a little potty.

★ ★ ★

"I'm very disappointed," said the psychiatrist to his patient. "If you're committed to curing this nervous problem, you must come and see me on a regular basis. Yet it's nearly a month since you missed your last appointment."
The man replied, "I was only doing what you said."
"What's that supposed to mean? What did I say?"
"You told me to keep away from anyone who got on my nerves."

★ ★ ★

"What's up, Jack?" asked his mate.
"It's the wife. She introduced me to her psychiatrist this morning. She said, 'This is Jack, my husband, one of the men I was telling you about.'"

★ ★ ★

The woman went for her weekly appointment with the psychiatrist.
"So, Mrs Freelot, what have your dreams been about this week?"
"I haven't had any," she replied.
"Oh dear," he said, sighing deeply. "How can I help you if you won't do your homework?"

★ ★ ★

"Doctor, doctor!" cried the man in anguish. "When I woke up this morning I thought I was a horse. Now all I can do is eat oats and graze on the grass in my garden."

"Really!" replied the psychiatrist. "Now that's interesting. Would you like to graze round at my house? Only my roses could do with the manure."

★ ★ ★

A 70-year-old man goes to the doctor's for a physical.

The doctor runs some tests and says to the man, "Well, everything seems to be in top condition physically, but what about mentally? How is your connection with God?"

And the man says, "Oh, me and God? We're tight. We have a real bond, he's good to me. Every night when I have to get up to go to the bathroom, he turns on the light for me, and then, when I leave, he turns it back off."

Well, upon hearing this, the doctor was astonished. He called the man's wife and said, "I'd like to speak to you about your husband's connection with God. He claims that every night when he needs to use the bathroom, God turns on the light for him and turns it off for him again when he leaves. Is this true?"

And she says, "The old fool's been peeing in the fridge again!"

★ ★ ★

After an annual check-up, the doctor came out to tell his patient the good news.

"You had a great check-up – no health problems at all. Is there anything that you'd like to talk about or ask me?"

"Well," he said, "I was thinking about getting a vasectomy."

"That's a pretty big decision. Have you talked it over with your family?"

"Yeah, and they're in favour 15 to 2."

★ ★ ★

Man: Doctor, me leg keeps talkin' to me.
Doc: Don't be ridiculous!
Leg: Lend us a fiver!
Man: Told ya.
Leg: Giz a tenner!
Doc: My God!
Leg: Doc, can you spare 20 quid?
Doc: I know your problem. Your leg's broke!

★ ★ ★

Q: Should I have a baby after 35?
A: No, 35 children is enough.

Q: I'm two months pregnant now. When will my baby move?
A: With any luck, right after he finishes college.

Q: What is the most common pregnancy craving?
A: For men to be the ones who get pregnant.

Q: What is the most reliable method to determine a baby's sex?
A: Childbirth.

Q: The more pregnant I get, the more often strangers smile at me. Why?
A: 'Cause you're fatter than they are.

Q: My wife is five months pregnant and so moody that sometimes she's borderline irrational.
A: So what's your question?

Q: My childbirth instructor says it's not pain I'll feel during labour, but pressure. Is she right?
A: Yes, in the same way that a tornado might be called an air current.

Q: When is the best time to get an epidural?
A: Right after you find out you're pregnant.

Q: Is there any reason I have to be in the delivery room while my wife is in labour?

A: Not unless the word "alimony" means anything to you.

Q: Is there anything I should avoid while recovering from childbirth?

A: Yes, pregnancy.

Q: Do I have to have a baby shower?

A: Not if you change the baby's nappy very quickly.

Q: Our baby was born last week. When will my wife begin to feel and act normal again?

A: When the kids are in college.

★ ★ ★

A woman went to her new doctor for a check-up. He turned out to be extremely handsome. He told her he was going to put his hand on her back and he wanted her to say 'Eighty-eight.'

"Eighty-eight," she purred.

"Good. Now I'm going to put my hand on your throat and I want you to again say 'Eighty-eight.' "

"Eighhty... eighhhhtttt."

"Fine. Now I'm going to put my hand on your chest and I want you once more to say 'Eighty-eight.' "

"One, two, three, four, five..."

★ ★ ★

A cardiac specialist died, and at his funeral, the coffin was placed in front of a huge mock-up of a heart, made up of flowers. When the pastor finished with the sermon and eulogy, and after everyone said their goodbyes, the heart opened, the coffin rolled inside and the heart closed. Just then one of the mourners burst into laughter.

The guy next to him asked, "Why are you laughing?"

"I was thinking about my own funeral," the man replied.

"What's so funny about that?"

"I'm a gynaecologist."

★ ★ ★

A psychiatrist visited a California mental institution and asked a patient, "How did you get here? What was the nature of your illness?" He got this reply:

"Well, it all started when I got married, and I guess I should never have done it. I got hitched to a widow with a grown daughter, who then became my stepdaughter. My daddy came to visit us, fell in love with my lovely stepdaughter, then married her. And so my stepdaughter was now my stepmother. Soon, my wife had a son who was, of course, my daddy's brother-in-law since he is the half-brother of my stepdaughter, who is now, of course, my daddy's wife. So, as I told you, when my stepdaughter married my daddy, she was at once my stepmother! Now, since my new son is brother to my stepmother, he also became my uncle. As you know, my wife is my step-grandmother since she is my stepmother's mother. Don't forget that my stepmother is my stepdaughter. Remember, too, that I am my wife's grandson. But hold on just a few minutes more. You see, since I'm married to my step-grandmother, I am not only the wife's grandson and her hubby, but I am also my own grandfather. Now can you understand how I got put in this place?"

★ ★ ★

The old man takes the old lady to the doctor for a check-up.

The doctor wants to have some fun with the old man, so after the check-up he tells him that the problem is serious: the old lady's health is deteriorating, and the only cure is sex.

The old man says, "Sex?"

"Yes," the doctor repeated, "sex – you know."

"How many times she must have sex?" he asked, concerned.

The doctor says, "Three times a week."

"And on which days?" the old man says.

"Well," said the doctor, "let's say Tuesday, Thursday and Saturday."

The old man mulled this over. "Well, doctor, Tuesday and Thursday I can do. But on Saturday I have plans; I can't bring her to you."

★ ★ ★

Jack is involved in a terrible car accident, which causes him to lose one of his eyes. The doctor explains to him that he can get a fake eye to replace it. He agrees and chooses the least expensive option, a wooden eye.

Some months pass and Jack's friends, concerned for the dispirited fellow, persuade him to join them at a party.

On arrival, self-conscious Jack finds a seat in the corner until he spots a beautiful woman across the room. Plucking up the courage to approach, he notices she has a hair lip. "What a pair we would make!" thought he. "My wooden eye and her hair lip!"

On reaching her, Jack asks if she would like to dance, and the woman replies eagerly, "Would I!"

Affronted, he points right back at her and says, "Hair lip!"

★ ★ ★

Stephanie's husband had been slipping in and out of a coma for several months, yet she had stayed by his bedside each and every day. One day, when he came to, he motioned for her to come nearer.

As she sat by him, he whispered, eyes full of tears, "You know what? You have been with me all through the bad times. When I got fired, you were there to support me. When my business failed, you were there. When I got shot, you were by my side. When we lost the house, you stayed right here. When my health started failing, you were still by my side. You know what?"

"What, dear?" Stephanie gently asked, smiling as her heart began to fill with warmth.

"I think you're bad luck!"

★ ★ ★

A dentist was getting ready to clean an elderly lady's teeth. He noticed that she was a little nervous, so he began to tell her a story as he was putting on his surgical gloves.

"Do you know how they make these rubber gloves?"

"No?" she replied.

"Well," he spoofed, "down in Mexico, they have this big building set up with a large tank of latex, and the workers are all picked according to hand size. Each individual walks up to the tank, dips their hands in, and then walk around for a bit while the latex sets up and dries right onto their hands! Then they peel off the gloves and throw them into the big 'Finished Goods Crate' and start the process all over again."

Upon hearing this explanation the woman sat in silence, not laughing in the slightest.

A few minutes later, during the procedure, he had to stop cleaning her teeth because she burst out laughing.

The dentist was baffled, and asked her what was so funny.

The woman blushed and exclaimed, "I just suddenly thought about how they must make condoms!"

★ ★ ★

The other day, while I was seeing my psychiatrist, he asked me what I looked for in a woman.

Naturally I replied, "Big tits."

He said, "No, I meant for a serious relationship."

So I said, "Oh, seriously big tits."

"No, no, no. I mean what do you look for in the one woman you want to spend the rest of your life with?"

He looked at me, baffled, as I just sat there on his couch, laughing until my stomach hurt.

"Spend the rest of my life with one woman? No woman's tits are that big."

★ ★ ★

An optician was instructing a new employee on how to charge a customer.

"As you are fitting his glasses, if he asks how much they cost, you say £75. If his eyes don't flutter, say... 'For the frames. The lenses will be £50.' If his eyes still don't flutter, you add... 'Each.' "

★ ★ ★

A man staggers into casualty with concussion, multiple bruises, two black eyes and a five iron wrapped tightly around his throat.

Naturally, the doctor asks him what happened.

"Well," said the man, "I was playing a quiet round of golf with my wife, when on a difficult hole, we both sliced our balls into a cow pasture. While we were looking for our balls, I noticed one of the cows had something in its rear end. I walked over and lifted the tail, and sure enough, there was a golf ball with my wife's monogram on it – stuck right in the middle of the cow's backside. That's when I made my big mistake."

"What did you do?" asks the doctor.

"Well, I was lifting the cow's tail and shouted to my wife, 'Hey, this looks like yours!' "

★ ★ ★

A man went into the proctologist's office for his first examination.

The nurse told him to have a seat in the examination room, and that the doctor would be with him in just a few minutes.

When the man sat down and began observing the tools, he noticed there were three items on a stand next to the doctor's desk.

1. A tube of K-Y jelly
2. A rubber glove
3. A beer

When the doctor finally came in, the man said, "Look, Doc, I'm a little confused. This is my first exam. I know what the K-Y is for, and I know what the glove is for, but what about the beer?"

At that the doctor became noticeably outraged and stormed to the door, flung it open and yelled, "Damnit, nurse! I said a BUTT light!"

★ ★ ★

In the hospital, the relatives gathered in the waiting room, where their family member lay gravely ill. Finally, the doctor came in looking tired and sombre.

"I'm afraid I'm the bearer of bad news," he said as he surveyed the worried faces. "The only hope left for your loved one at this time is a brain transplant. It's an experimental procedure, a risky one, and you will have to pay for the brain yourselves."

The family members sat silently as they absorbed the news. Some time later, someone asked, "Well, how much does a brain cost?"

The doctor quickly responded, "£5,000 for a male brain, and £200 for a female brain."

The moment turned awkward. Men in the room tried not to smile, avoiding eye contact with the women, but some actually smirked. A man, unable to control his curiosity, blurted out the question everyone wanted to ask. "Why is the male brain so much more?"

The doctor smiled at the childish innocence and so to the entire group said, "It's just standard pricing procedure. We have to mark down the price of the female brains, because they've been used."

★ ★ ★

An Irish surgeon who had couched a cataract and restored the sight of a poor woman in Dublin, observed in her case what he deemed a phenomenon in optics. He called together his professional brethren, declaring himself unequal to the solution.

He stated to them that the sight of his patient was so perfectly restored, that she could see to thread the smallest needle, or to perform any other operation, which required particular accuracy of vision; but that when he presented her with a book, she was not capable of distinguishing one letter from another!

This very singular case excited the ingenuity of all the gentlemen present, and various solutions were offered, but none could command the general assent.

Doubt crowded on doubt, and the problem grew darker from every explanation, when at length, by a question put by the servant who attended, it was discovered that the woman had never learned to read.

★ ★ ★

A young doctor had moved out to a small community to replace a doctor who was retiring.

The older gent suggested the young one accompany him on his rounds, so the community could become used to a new doctor. At the first house, a woman complained, "I've been a little sick to my stomach."

The older doctor said, "Well, you've probably been overdoing the fresh fruit. Why not cut back on the amount you've been eating and see if that does the trick?"

As they left the younger man said, "You didn't even examine that woman. How'd you come to your diagnosis so quickly?"

"I didn't have to. You noticed I dropped my stethoscope on the floor in there? When I bent over to pick it up, I noticed half a dozen banana peels in the bin. That was what was probably making her sick."

"Huh," the younger doctor said. "Pretty clever. I think I'll try that at the next house."

Arriving at the next house, they spent several minutes talking with an elderly woman. She complained that she just didn't have the energy she once did. "I'm feeling terribly run down lately."

"You've probably been doing too much work for the church," the younger doctor told her. "Perhaps you should cut back a bit and see if that helps."

As they left, the elder doctor said, "Your diagnosis is almost certainly correct, but how did you arrive at it?"

"Well, just like you at the last house, I dropped my stethoscope. When I bent down to retrieve it, I noticed the vicar under the bed."

★ ★ ★

A woman went to doctor's office. She was seen by one of the new doctors, but after about four minutes in the examination room, she burst out, screaming as she ran down the hall. An older doctor stopped and asked her what the problem was, and she explained. He had her sit down and relax in another room.

He then marched back to the first and demanded, "What's the matter with you? Mrs Terry is 63 years old, she has four grown children and seven grandchildren, and you told her she was pregnant?"

The new doctor smiled smugly as he continued to write on his clipboard.

"Cured her hiccoughs though, didn't it?"

★ ★ ★

Two doctors opened an office in a small town and put up a sign reading, "Dr Smith and Dr Jones, Psychiatry and Proctology."

The town fathers were not too happy with the sign, and they proposed "Hysteria and Posteriors."

The doctors didn't find it acceptable, so they suggested "Schizoids and Haemorrhoids."

The town didn't like that either, and countered with "Catatonics and High Colonics."

Thumbs down again. By now the story was in the papers, and suggestions began rolling in:

"Manic-depressives and Anal-retentives."

"Minds and Behinds."

"Lost Souls and Arseholes."

"Analysis and Anal Cysts."

"Queers and Rears."

"Nuts and Butts."

"Freaks and Cheeks."

"Loons and Moons."

None of these satisfied one side or the other, but they finally settled on "Dr Smith and Dr Jones, Odds and Ends."

★ ★ ★

Dr Parker, the biology teacher at a posh suburban girl's junior college, said during class, "Miss Smith, would you please name the organ of the human body, which under the appropriate conditions, expands to six times its normal size, and define the conditions."

Miss Smith gasped, blushed deeply, then said freezingly, "Dr Parker, I do not think that is a proper question to ask me, you should be asking a boy. And I assure you my parents will hear of this." With that she sat down, very red-faced.

Unperturbed, Dr Parker called on Miss Johnson and asked the same question. Miss Johnson, with composure, replied, "The pupil of the eye, in dim light."

"Correct," said Dr Parker. "And now, Miss Smith, I have three things to say to you. One, you have not studied your lesson. Two, you have a dirty mind. And three, you will one day be faced with a dreadful disappointment."

★ ★ ★

Four women were playing golf. The first teed off and watched in horror as her ball headed directly toward a foursome of men. One of the men immediately grabbed his crotch and fell to the ground in agony. The woman rushed over to the man and began to apologize.

"Please allow me to help," she begged. "I'm a professional physiotherapist, and I can quickly relieve your pain."

"No, I'll be OK, just give me a minute," he said, as he rolled on the ground in the fetal position, still clasping his hands over his crotch.

The woman persisted and insisted she could help, so the man finally agreed.

She gently took his hands away from his crotch. Then, she loosened his trousers and began to gently massage his privates.

"Does that feel better?" she asked.

"It feels great," he said, "but my thumb still hurts like crazy."

★ ★ ★

One morning a female punk rocker walked into the emergency department in the hospital. This young woman had purple hair styled into a Mohawk, a variety of tattoos and strange clothing. It was determined that the patient had acute appendicitis and she was scheduled for immediate surgery.

When she was completely disrobed on the operating table, the staff found that her pubic hair had been dyed green and above it was a tattoo reading, "Keep off the grass."

After operating, the surgeon added a small note to the dressing, which said, "Sorry, had to mow the lawn."

★ ★ ★

Two doctors in practice in a small country clinic had to hire a new nurse, after the one they had won the lottery and quit. They interviewed Nurse Nancy and decided to hire her. She had only worked two days when one doctor called the other to his office and said that they would have to let Nurse Nancy go.
"Why? We only just hired her!"
"Well, I think she is dyslexic and gets things backwards. I told her to give Mr Smith two shots of morphine every 24 hours, but she gave him 24 shots in two hours and it almost killed him. I told her to give Mrs Jones an enema every 12 hours and she gave her 12 in one hour."
The doctor had barely finished his reasons when the other doctor rushed out of the room. "Where are you going in such a hurry?" the doctor asked.
"To see Nurse Nancy. I just instructed her to prick Mr Hill's boil!"

★ ★ ★

In a mental institution, a nurse walks into a room and sees a patient acting like he's driving a car.
The nurse asks him, "Charlie, what are you doing?"
Charlie replies, "Driving to Chicago!"
The nurse wishes him a good trip, and leaves the room.
The next day, the nurse enters Charlie's room just as he stops driving his imaginary car and asks, "Well Charlie, how you doing?"
Charlie says, "I just got into Chicago."
"Great," replied the nurse.
The nurse leaves Charlie's room and goes across the hall into Bob's room to find Bob sitting on his bed, masturbating vigorously.
With surprise she asks, "Bob, what on earth are you doing?"
Bob says, "I'm screwing Charlie's wife while he's in Chicago."

★ ★ ★

When the doctor says: "One of several things could cause your symptoms."
What the doctor means: "I haven't the foggiest idea what's wrong with you."

When the doctor says: "Are you certain you haven't had this before?"
What the doctor means: "Because now you've got it again."

When the doctor says: "I'd like to run that last test again."
What the doctor means: "The lab lost your sample."

When the doctor says: "This prescription has a few side effects."
What the doctor means: "You may experience sudden hair growth on your palms."

When the doctor says: "Let's go over your symptoms once more."
What the doctor means: "I can't remember who you are."

When the doctor says: "How long have you had these symptoms?"
What the doctor means: "How do you feel about living with them for the rest of your life?"

When the doctor says: "It looks like bursitis."
What the doctor means: "Does the name 'Quasimodo' ring a bell?"

When the doctor says: "This won't hurt much."
What the doctor means: "Did you bring a bullet to bite?"

When the doctor says:"'"There's a lot of this going around."
What the doctor means: "And we'll give it a name as soon as we figure out what it is."

When the doctor says: "We'll just remove this ingrown toenail."
What the doctor means: "A cane and orthopaedic shoes should help."

★ ★ ★

A woman starts dating a doctor. Before too long, she becomes pregnant and they don't know what to do.
About nine months later, just about the time she is going to give birth,

a priest goes into the hospital for a prostate gland infection. The doctor says to the woman, "I know what we'll do. After I've operated on the priest, I'll give the baby to him and tell him it was a miracle."

"Do you think it will work?" she asks the doctor.

"It's worth a try," he says.

So, the doctor delivers the baby and then operates on the priest. After the operation he goes in to the priest and says, "Father, you're not going to believe this."

"What?" says the priest. "What happened?"

"You gave birth to a child."

"But that's impossible!"

"I just did the operation," insists the doctor. "It's a miracle! Here's your baby."

About fifteen years go by, and the priest realizes he must tell his son the truth. One day he sits the boy down and says, "Son, I have something to tell you. I'm not your father."

The son says, "What do you mean, you're not my father?"

The priest replies, "I'm your mother. The archbishop is your father."

★ ★ ★

You might be a nurse if...

When using a public toilet, you wash your hands with soap for a full minute and turn off the faucets with your elbows.

When you tell a man you meet for the first time you're a nurse, you're expected to laugh hysterically when he asks you for a sponge bath, as if it was the most original and wittiest thing you've ever heard.

Your favourite dream is the one where you leave a mess at a patient's bedside and tell a doctor to clean it up.

Men assume you must be great in bed because of the 9 billion porn movies about nurses.

Everyone, including complete strangers, tells you about each and every ache and pain they have.

You want to put your foot through the TV screen every time you see a nurse on a soap opera doing nothing but talking on the phone and flirting with doctors.

You can almost SEE the germs on doorknobs and telephones.

You can watch the goriest movie and eat anything afterwards, even spaghetti with lots of tomato sauce.

You use a plastic 30cc medicine cup for a shotglass.

★ ★ ★

TOP TEN THINGS YOU NEED TO KNOW TO BE A NURSE

10. If it's wet, make it dry.

9. If it's dry, make it wet.

8. Always ask for on-call pay before agreeing to overtime.

7. Never tell management what you are really thinking.

6. Never finish a report with, "You have an easy assignment".

5. Never say, "This looks like a easy assignment".

4. Don't expect nurses aids to do their job.

3. Don't expect doctors to believe anything you tell them.

2. If you don't have enough time to do everything, take about 30 minutes to complain about it.

1. If it moves, rattles, shakes, falls down, or won't stay in place: tape it.

★ ★ ★

A mother and her daughter were at the gynaecologist's office. The mother asked the doctor to examine her daughter. "She has been having some strange symptoms and I'm worried about her," the mother said.

The doctor examined the daughter carefully and then announced, "Madam, I believe your daughter is pregnant."

The mother gasped, "That's nonsense! Why, my little girl has nothing whatsoever to do with men." She turned to the girl. "You don't, do you, dear?"

"No, mumsy," said the girl. "Why, you know that I have never so much as kissed a man!" The doctor looked from mother to daughter, and back again. Then, silently he stood up and walked to the window, staring out.

He continued staring until the mother felt compelled to ask, "Doctor, is there something wrong out there?"

"No, Madam," said the doctor. "It's just that the last time anything like this happened, a star appeared in the East and I was looking to see if another one was going to show up."

★ ★ ★

A guy out on the golf course takes a high speed ball right in the crotch. Writhing in agony, he falls to the ground. He finally gets himself to the doctor. He says, "How bad is it doc? I'm going on my honeymoon next week and my fiancée is still a virgin in every way."

The doc said, "I'll have to put your penis in a splint to let it heal and keep it straight. It should be OK next week." So he took four tongue depressors and formed a neat little 4-sided bandage and wired it all together. It was an impressive work of art.

The guy mentions none of this to his girlfriend. They marry and on their honeymoon night in the hotel room, she rips open her blouse to reveal a gorgeous set of breasts. This was the first time he ever saw them. She says, "You are the first, no one has ever touched these breasts."

He pulls down his pants, whips it out and says, "Look at this, it's still in the crate!"

★ ★ ★

A young doctor was just setting up his first office when his secretary told him there was a man to see him. The doctor wanted to make a good first impression by having the man think he was successful and very busy. He told his secretary to show the man in.

At that moment, the doctor picked up the telephone and pretended to be having a conversation with a patient. The man waited until the 'conversation' was over. Then, the doctor put the telephone down and asked, "Can I help you?"

To which the man replied, "No, I'm just here to connect your telephone."

★ ★ ★

A man walked into a therapist's office looking very depressed.

"Doc, you've got to help me. I can't go on like this."

"What's the problem?" the doctor inquired.

"Well, I'm 35 years old and I still have no luck with the ladies. No matter how hard I try, I just seem to scare them away."

"My friend, this is not a serious problem. You just need to work on your self-esteem. Each morning, I want you to get up and run to the bathroom mirror. Tell yourself that you are a good person, a fun person, and an attractive person. But say it with real conviction. Within a week you'll have women buzzing all around you."

The man seemed content with this advice and walked out of the office a bit excited. Three weeks later, though, he returned with the same downtrodden expression on his face.

"Did my advice not work?" asked the doctor.

"It worked alright. For the past several weeks I've enjoyed some of the best moments in my life with the most fabulous looking women."

"So, what's your problem?"

"I don't have a problem," the man replied. "My wife does."

★ ★ ★

The doctor took Dan into the room and said, "Dan, I have some good news and some bad news."

Dan said, "Give me the good news."

"They're going to name a disease after you."

★ ★ ★

One day, in line at the office canteen, Jack says to Mike behind him, "My elbow hurts like hell. I guess I should see a doctor."

"Listen, you don't have to bother with getting an appointment," Mike replies. "There's a diagnostic computer at the chemist's on the corner. Just give it a urine sample and the computer will tell you what's wrong and what to do about it. It only takes 10 seconds."

So Jack deposits a urine sample in a jar and takes it to the chemist. He puts in his money and the computer lights up and asks for the urine sample. He pours the sample into the slot and waits. Ten seconds later the computer ejects a printout:

You have tennis elbow. Soak your arm in warm water and avoid heavy activity. It will improve in two weeks.

That evening, while thinking how amazing this new technology was, Jack began wondering if the computer could be fooled. He mixed some tap water, a stool sample from his dog, urine samples from his wife and daughter, and masturbated into the mixture for good measure. Jack hurries back to the drugstore, eager to check the results. He deposits his money, pours in his concoction, and awaits the results. The computer prints the following:

1. Your tap water is too hard. Get a water softener.

2. Your dog has ringworm. Bathe him with anti-fungal shampoo.

3. Your daughter has a cocaine habit. Get her into rehab.

4. Your wife is pregnant. Twin girls. They aren't yours. Get a lawyer.

5. If you don't stop playing with yourself, your elbow will never get better.

★ ★ ★

A man with two badly burned ears went to casualty for medical treatment.
"What happened?" asked the doctor.
"Well, my wife was ironing while I was watching the football game on TV," began the man. "She put the hot iron near the telephone and when the phone rang, I answered the iron."
The doctor nodded. "But what happened to the other ear?"
"Well, no sooner had I hung up," said the man, "than the same guy called again."

★ ★ ★

Three men met at a party, and it wasn't long until the conversation got around to their line of work and what kind of cars they drove. "I'm a veterinarian," said the first fellow. "So, naturally, I drive a white 'Vet.' "
As they smiled and nodded, the second man said, "I own a sign company, so I drive a purple Neon."
Now the third guy was suddenly quiet until he was egged on by the other two.
"Well," he finally said, "I'm a proctologist... and I have a brown Probe."

★ ★ ★

Two elderly couples were enjoying friendly conversation when one of the men asked the other, "Fred, how was the memory clinic you went to last month?"
"Outstanding," Fred replied. "They taught us all the latest psychological techniques: visualization, association, all those sorts of thing. It was great."
"That's great! And what was the name of the clinic?"
Fred went blank. He thought and thought, but couldn't remember. Then a smile broke across his face and he asked, "What do you call that flower with the long stem and thorns?"
"You mean a rose?"
"Yes, that's it!" Turning to his wife, he said, "Rose, what was the name of that memory clinic?"

★ ★ ★

In a murder trial, the defence attorney was cross-examining a pathologist. Here's what happened:

Attorney: Before you signed the death certificate, had you taken the pulse?

Coroner: No.

Attorney: Did you listen to the heart?

Coroner: No.

Attorney: Did you check for breathing?

Coroner: No.

Attorney: So, when you signed the death certificate, you weren't sure the man was dead, were you?

Coroner: Well, let me put it this way. The man's brain was sitting in a jar on my desk. But I guess it's possible he could be out there practicing law somewhere.

★ ★ ★

Josh goes to the doctor's, complaining of not feeling well.

The doctor runs some test on him and in a few minutes comes back in.

The doctor says, "Josh, sit down. I'm afraid I've got some bad news. You don't have much time to live."

Josh is obviously upset about this, but asks, "How much longer do I have, doc?"

The doctor says, "10."

Josh says, "10 what? 10 weeks... 10 months... 10 years?"

The doctor replies, "9... 8... 7..."

★ ★ ★

A doctor had just finished a marathon sex session with one of his patients. He was resting afterwards and was feeling a bit guilty because he thought it wasn't really ethical to screw one of his patients.

However, a little voice in his head said, "Lots of other doctors have sex with their patients, so it's not like you're the first..."

This made the doctor feel a little bit better, until still another voice in his head said, "...but they probably weren't veterinarians."

★ ★ ★

An 80-year-old couple were having problems remembering things, so they decided to go to their doctor to get checked out. When they arrived, they explained to the doctor about the memory problems they were having. After checking the couple out, the doctor told them that they were physically fine, but might want to start writing things down and make notes to help them remember things.

The couple thanked the doctor and left.

Later that night while watching TV, the man got up from his chair and his wife asked, "Where are you going?"

He replied, "To the kitchen."

She asked, "Will you get me a bowl of ice-cream?"

He replied, "Sure."

"Don't you think you should write it down so you can remember it?"

He said, "No, I can remember that."

She then said, "Well I would also like some strawberries on top. You had better write that down because I know you'll forget that."

He said, "I can remember that, you want a bowl of ice-cream with strawberries."

She added, "Well, I also would like whipped cream on top. I know you will forget that so you better write it down."

With irritation in his voice, he said, "I don't need to write that down! I can remember it." He stormed into the kitchen.

After about 20 minutes, he returned from the kitchen and handed her a plate of bacon and eggs. She stared at the plate for a moment and said angrily, "I TOLD you to write it down! You forgot my toast!"

★ ★ ★

"How did it happen?" the doctor asked the middle-aged farmhand as he set the man's broken leg.

"Well, doc, 25 years ago..."

"Never mind the past. Tell me how you broke your leg this morning."

"Like I was saying... 25 years ago, when I first started working on the farm, that night, right after I'd gone to bed, the farmer's beautiful daughter came into my room. She asked me if there was anything I wanted. I said, 'No, everything is fine.'

" 'Are you sure?' she asked.

" 'I'm sure,' I said.

" 'Isn't there anything I can do for you?' she wanted to know.

" 'I reckon not,' I replied."

"Excuse me," said the doctor, "but what does this story have to do with your leg?"

"Well, this morning," the farmhand explained, "when it dawned on me what she meant, I fell off the roof!"

★ ★ ★

A woman goes to her doctor and says she wants an operation because her vagina lips are much too large. She asks the doctor to keep the operation a secret as she is embarrassed and does not want anyone to find out. The doctor agrees.

She wakes up from the operation and finds three roses carefully placed on her nightstand. Outraged, she immediately calls the doctor and says, "I told you not to tell anyone!"

The doctor replies, "Don't worry, I didn't tell a soul!"

When the woman enquires about the roses the doctor says, "Oh, those! The first rose is from me. I felt bad because you went through this all by yourself. The second rose is from my nurse. She assisted me with your operation and has been through this procedure herself, so she understands what you're going through. And the third rose is from the guy upstairs in the burn unit. He wanted to thank you for his new ears."

★ ★ ★

Morris the loud-mouth mechanic was removing the cylinder heads from the motor of a car when he spotted the famous heart surgeon, Dr

Michael DeBakey, who was standing off to the side, waiting for the service manager to come take a look at his Mercedes.

Morris shouted across the garage, "Hey, DeBakey! Is dat you? Come on ova' here a minute."

The famous surgeon, a bit surprised, walked over to where Morris was working on the car. Morris straightened up, wiped his hands on a rag and asked argumentatively, "So, Mr Fancy Doctor, look at dis here work. I also open hearts, take valves out, grind 'em, put in new parts, and when I finish dis baby will purr like a kitten. So how come you get da big bucks, when you an' me is doing basically da same work?"

Dr DeBakey leaned over and whispered to Morris the loud-mouth mechanic.

"Try doing it with the engine running."

★ ★ ★

A man walks into a pharmacy and asks for a pack of condoms. As soon as he has paid for them, he starts laughing and walks out. The next day, the same performance, with the man walking out, laughing. The pharmacist thinks this odd and asks his assistant, if the man returns, to follow him.

Sure enough, he returns the next day, repeating his actions once more. The assistant duly follows. Half an hour later, he returns.

"So did you follow him?"

"I did."

"And... where did he go?"

"Over to your house..."

★ ★ ★

A husband and wife were playing on the ninth green when she collapsed from a heart attack. "Please dear, I need help," she said.

The husband ran off saying, "I'll go get some help."

A little while later he returned, picked up his club and began to line up his shot on the green.

His wife, on the ground, raised up her head and said, "I may be dying, and you're putting?"

"Don't worry dear. I found a doctor on the second hole who said he'll come and help."

"The second hole? When in the hell is he coming?"

"Hey! I told you not to worry," he said, practice-stroking his putt. "Everyone's already agreed to let him play through."

★ ★ ★

One night a man and a woman are both at a bar knocking back a few beers. They start talking and come to realize that they're both doctors. After about an hour, the man says to the woman, "Hey. How about if we sleep together tonight? No strings attached. It'll just be one night of fun." The woman doctor agrees to it.

So they go back to her place and he goes in the bedroom. She goes in the bathroom and starts scrubbing up like she's about to go into the operating room, taking a good ten minutes over it.

Finally she goes in the bedroom and they have sex for an hour or so. Afterwards, the man says to the woman, "You're a surgeon, aren't you?"

"Yeah, how did you know?"

The man says, "I could tell by the way you scrubbed up before we started."

"Oh, that makes sense," says the woman. "You're an anaesthetist, aren't you?"

"Yeah," says the man, a bit surprised. "How did you know?"

The woman answers, "Because I slept through most of it and didn't feel a thing."

★ ★ ★

Three woman and their children were outside their psychiatrist's office. The wily old doctor was able to diagnose any complaint after asking the patient a few questions.

The first woman went in and the doctor asked her a few questions and proclaimed: "Madam, all you ever think is food! That is why you named you daughter Candy!"

"Why," exclaimed the woman, "you're absolutely right, doctor!"

Then it was the second woman's turn. She got the same treatment and the doctor pronounced: "Madam, you're obsessed with the thought of money. That is why you named you daughter Penny!"

"You're right, doctor!" exclaimed the second woman and left.

The third woman, who had been listening to all this, got up indignantly and said, "What rubbish! I don't believe a single word you said. Obsessions indeed!"

Then, waving to her little son to follow her, she said, "Let's go home now, Dick."

★ ★ ★

An 80-year-old man got up and was putting on his coat.

His wife said, "Where are you going?"

He said, "I'm going to the doctor."

And she said, "Why? Are you sick?"

"No," he said, "I'm going to get me some of those new Viagra pills."

So his wife got up out of her rocker, and started to put on her sweater, at which her husband asked, "Where are you going?"

She said, "I'm going to the doctor, too."

"Why?" he asked.

"If you're going to start using that rusty old thing again, I'm going to get a tetanus shot!"

★ ★ ★

At a big cocktail party, an obstetrician's wife noticed that another guest – a big, oversexed blonde – was making overtures at her husband. But it was a large, informal gathering, so she tried to laugh it off, until she saw them disappear into a bedroom together.

At once, she rushed into the room, pulled the two apart and screamed, "Look, lady! My husband only delivers babies, he doesn't install them!"

★ ★ ★

A guy stops by to visit his friend who is paralyzed from the waist down. They talk for a while, and then the friend asks, "My feet are cold. Would you be so kind as to go get me my sneakers please?"

The guest obliges and goes upstairs. There he sees his friend's daughters, both very good-looking. Being the adventurous and quick-thinking type, he says, "Hi, ladies! Your daddy sent me here to have sex with you!"

They stare at him and say, "That can't be!"

He replies, "OK, let's check!"

He shouts down the stairs to his friend, "Both of them?"

"Yes, both of them!"

★ ★ ★

A little old lady goes to the doctor and says, "Doctor, I have this problem with gas, but it really doesn't bother me too much. My farts never smell and are always silent. As a matter of fact, I've farted at least twenty times since I've been here in your office. You didn't know I was farting because they don't smell and are silent."

The doctor says, "I see. Well, take these pills and come back to see me next week."

The next week the lady comes back. "Doctor," she says, "I don't know what the hell you gave me, but now my farts, although still silent, stink terribly."

The doctor says, "Good. Now that we've cleared up your sinuses, let's work on your hearing."

★ ★ ★

A professor is giving the first year medical students their first lecture on autopsies, and decides to give them a few basics before starting.

"You must be capable of two things to do an autopsy. The first thing is that you must have no sense of fear." At this point, the lecturer sticks his finger into the dead man's anus, and then licks it.

He asks all the students to do the same thing with the corpses in front of them. After a couple of minutes' silence, they follow suit.

"The second thing is that you must have an acute sense of observation. I stuck my middle finger into the corpse's anus, but I licked my index."

★ ★ ★

A man goes to visit his 85-year-old grandfather in hospital.

"How are you, grandpa?" he asks.

"Feeling fine," says the old man.

"What's the food like?" asks his grandson.

"Terrific, wonderful menus."

"And the nursing?"

"Just couldn't be better. These young nurses really take care of you."

"What about sleeping? Do you sleep OK?"

"No problem at all. Nine hours solid every night. At ten o'clock, they bring me a cup of hot chocolate and a Viagra tablet... and that's it. I go out like a light."

The grandson is puzzled and a little alarmed by this, so he rushes off to question the nurse in charge.

"What are you people doing?" he says, "I'm told you're giving an 85-year-old man Viagra on a daily basis. Surely that can't be true?"

"Oh, yes," replies the nurse. "Every night at ten o'clock, we give him a cup of chocolate and a Viagra tablet. It works wonderfully well. The chocolate makes him sleep, and the Viagra stops him from rolling out of bed."

★ ★ ★

A man was having problems with premature ejaculation, so he decided to go to the doctor. He asked the doctor what he could do to cure his problem. The doctor suggested that, when he was getting ready to ejaculate, he should try startling himself.

The same day, the man went to the store and bought himself a starter pistol. All excited to try this suggestion, he ran home to his wife. At home, he found his wife was in bed, naked and waiting.

As the two began, they found themselves in the 69 position. Moments later, the man felt the urge to ejaculate and fired the starter pistol.

The next day, the man went back to the doctor. The doctor asked how things went.

The man answered, "Not that well... When I fired the pistol, my wife crapped on my face, bit three inches off my penis and my neighbour came out of the closet with his hands up in the air."

★ ★ ★

A man entered a doctor's office.

"How may I help, sir?" asked the doctor.

He answered, "Well, doc, I have a problem. My dick seems to have turned orange."

"Well, let's see our little problem," replied the doctor.

The man whipped down his trousers to show his problem to the astonished doctor.

"What on earth do you do all day?" asked the doctor.

He answered, "All I do is sit on my ass, eat Cheetos, and watch porno all day."

★ ★ ★

A man walks into a doctor's office and says, "I have a problem with my dick."

The icy receptionist says, "Sir, we do not say words like that at the doctor's office. Now please leave and come back and replace 'dick' with some other body part like 'ear'.

The man does as he's told, and comes back in and says, "I have a problem with my ear."

The lady says, "What is that?"

To which the man replies, "I can't piss out of it!"

★ ★ ★

A man goes into a pharmacy to buy condoms.

The pharmacist says, "What size?"

The man says, "Goodness, I don't know."

The pharmacist replies, "Go see Sophie in aisle four."

He goes over to see Sophie; she grabs him in the crotch and yells, "Medium!" The man is mortified; he hurries over to pay and get out of the store.

Another man comes in to buy condoms, the pharmacist asks the size, and again sends him over to Sophie in aisle four. Sophie grabs him and yells, "Large!".

The guy struts over to the register, pays and leaves.

A college boy comes in to buy condoms.

The pharmacist asks, "What size?"

The boy, highly embarrassed, stutters, "I've never done this before. I don't know what size."

The clerk sends him over to Sophie in aisle four. She grabs him and yells, "Clean up in aisle four!"

★ ★ ★

Two good friends are out driving on Route 66 and one guy has to take a pee. Being in the middle of nowhere, they pull over by some shrubbery and the guy goes to relieve himself. Suddenly, he screams, "Aaagh! A rattler bit my cock!"

"Relax!" says his friend, "I'll go find a pay phone and call a doctor."

So his friend drives off and finds a pay phone, calls a doctor and asks what he should do.

"Well," says the doctor, "you must cut crosses in the wound and suck out the poison."

"Is that the only way, Doc?" asks the man.

"Yes, you must do that or he'll die."

He finally gets back to his friend who asks, "So, what did the doctor say?"

"You're gonna die, buddy. You're gonna die."

★ ★ ★

Bob Smith gets home from work one day and finds his wife has been crying. "What's wrong?" he asks.

"John, promise you won't get mad, but I went to see the new doctor

576

today and he told me I've got a pretty pussy."

"What?" he shouts, enraged. With that, he grabs a baseball bat from the cupboard and storms down to the doctor's office and through the reception area.

Without knocking, he bursts into the doctor's office. The doctor is in the process of giving an old lady a breast examination. She screams and tries to cover herself. Without waiting, Mr Smith charges up to the doctor, smashes the baseball bat down on the desk and says, "You flaming pervert! How dare you say my wife has a pretty pussy!"

The doctor replies, "I'm sorry Mr Smith, but there has been a misunderstanding. I only told your wife that she has acute angina."

★ ★ ★

A guy goes into a bar and sees a beautiful woman. After an hour of gathering up his courage, he finally goes over to her and asks, tentatively, "Um, would you mind if I chatted with you for a while?"

She yells, "No, I won't sleep with you tonight!"

Everyone in the bar is now staring at them. Naturally, the guy is hopelessly and completely embarrassed, and he slinks back to his table.

After a few minutes, the woman walks over to him and apologizes. She smiles at him and says, "I'm sorry if I embarrassed you. You see, I'm a graduate student in psychology, and I'm studying how people respond to embarrassing situations."

To which he responds, at the top of his lungs, "What do you mean, £200?"

★ ★ ★

An 80-year-old man is having his annual check-up. The doctor asks him how he's feeling.

"I've never been better!" he replies. "I've got an 18-year-old bride who's pregnant and having my child! What do you think about that?"

The doctor considers this for a moment, then says, "Well, let me tell you a story. I know a guy who's an avid hunter. He never misses a season. But one day he's in a bit of a hurry and he accidentally grabs his umbrella instead of his gun. So, he's in the woods, and suddenly a

577

grizzly bear appears in front of him. He raises up his umbrella, points it at the bear, and squeezes the handle. The bear drops dead in front of him."

The old man exclaims, "That's impossible! Someone else must have shot that bear."

"Exactly."

★ ★ ★

One day, a man went to the doctor because he was getting a burning sensation every time that he defecated. The doctor told him he'd need to clean out his colon once a week for the next month. He gave the man a cleaning rod and shoved it up his butt for the first cleaning.

The man took the rod home and, a week later, tried to do the cleaning himself. However, he couldn't get it in at the right angle by himself, so he called in his wife. She sympathetically shoved it up and cleaned his colon for him, when he let out a sudden gasp.

"What is it, sweetheart?" asked his wife.

"I just realized," answered the man, "that when the doctor did it, he had both hands on my shoulders!"

★ ★ ★

An 80-year-old man walks into a hospital and says, "I'd like to donate some sperm."

So the nurse gives him a jar and tells him to come back tomorrow with the sperm. The next day he comes back, but the jar was empty.

So the nurse asks, "What happened? Where's the sperm?"

Well, he replies, "I went home and I tried so hard. I used my right hand, and then my left hand. Then my wife tried. She used her right hand and then she tried her left hand. Then she used her mouth, once using her teeth and once without. Then we asked our neighbour to come over, and she tried with her left hand, and then her right hand. Then she tried with her mouth, once with her teeth and once without."

The nurse gasps. "Oh dear! You even asked your neighbour!"

The man replies, "Yes, and we still couldn't get the jar open!"

★ ★ ★

A man walks into a pharmacy and asks the pharmacist where the tampons are. The pharmacist directs him to aisle four. A few minutes later, the man returns with some toilet paper and some cotton balls.

Curious, the pharmacist asks, "Excuse me, it's none of my business, but you asked where the tampons were, and now you come to me with toilet paper and cotton balls. Why?"

The man responds, "Well, last night I sent the old lady to the store for a carton of cigarettes, and she brought me a tin of tobacco and some papers. Tonight, she can roll her own!"

★ ★ ★

Three desperately ill men met with their doctor one day to discuss their options. One was an alcoholic, one was a chain-smoker, and one was a homosexual sex addict.

The doctor, addressing all three of them, said, "If any of you indulge in your vices one more time, you will surely die."

The men left the doctor's office, each convinced that he would never again indulge himself in his vice.

While walking toward the subway for their return trip to the suburbs, they passed a bar. The alcoholic, hearing the loud music and seeing the lights, could not stop himself. His buddies accompanied him into the bar, where he had a shot of whiskey. No sooner had he replaced the shot glass on the bar, he fell off his stool, stone-cold dead.

His companions, somewhat shaken up, left the bar, realizing how seriously they must take the doctor's words.

As they walked along, they came upon a cigarette butt lying on the ground, still burning. The homosexual looked at the chain-smoker and said, "If you bend over to pick that up, we're both dead."

★ ★ ★

Hello. Welcome to the Psychiatric Hotline.

If you are obsessive-compulsive, please press 1 repeatedly.

If you are co-dependent, please ask someone to press 2.

If you have multiple personalities, please press 3, 4, 5, and 6.

If you are paranoid-delusional, we know who you are and what you want. Just stay on the line so we can trace the call.

If you are schizophrenic, listen carefully and a little voice will tell you which number to press.

If you are manic-depressive, it doesn't matter which number you press. No one will answer.

If you are anxious, just start pressing numbers at random.

If you are phobic, don't press anything.

If you are anally retentive, please hold.

★ ★ ★

A 90-year-old woman is distraught after the death of her warm, caring, faithful husband of seventy years. She can't live without him and decides that the best way to do herself in is to stab herself in her pitifully broken heart. Still, she doesn't want to linger, so she calls a doctor to find out exactly where the heart is.
He tells her to put her first two fingers together, hold them horizontally, and place the tip of the first finger just below her left nipple. The heart, he says, is immediately below the first knuckle on her second finger.
Later that day, the doctor is called to casualty to put 14 stitches in the elderly woman's left thigh.

★ ★ ★

The Queen was visiting one of Canada's top hospitals, and during her tour of the floors she passed a room where a male patient was masturbating.

"Oh my goodness," said the Queen, "that is disgraceful. What is the meaning of this?"

The doctor replied, "That man has a very serious condition where the testicles rapidly fill with semen. If he doesn't do that five times a day, they would explode, and he would die instantly."

"Oh, I am sorry," said the Queen.

On the next floor they passed a room where a young nurse was giving a patient oral sex.

"Oh my goodness," said the Queen, "What's happening in there?"

The doctor replied, "Same problem, better health plan."

★ ★ ★

A couple went to the hospital to have a baby. The doctor told them that he had invented a new machine that would automatically transfer a portion of the mother's labour pain to the father.

He asked if the husband was willing to try it out. Both the husband and wife were very much in favour of it.

The doctor set the knob at 10% to start with, explaining that even 10% was probably more pain than the father had ever experienced before. But, as labour progressed, the doctor then adjusted the machine to 20% pain transfer.

The husband was still feeling fine. The doctor checked the husband's blood pressure and pulse, and was amazed at how well he was doing. At this, they decided to try for 50%. The husband continued to feel quite well.

Since it was obviously helping out his wife considerably, he encouraged the doctor to transfer all the pain to him. Finally, the wife delivered a healthy baby with virtually no pain. She and her husband were ecstatic.

When they got home, they found the milkman dead on the porch.

★ ★ ★

A ranch woman takes her three sons to the doctor for physicals for the first time in their lives.

The doctor examines the boys and tells the woman that they are healthy but that she needs to give them iron supplements. She goes home and wonders exactly what iron supplements are. Finally, she goes to the hardware store and buys iron ball bearings and mixes them into their food.

Several days later, the youngest son comes to her and tells her that he is pissing ball bearings. She tells him that it is normal because she had put them in his food.

Later, the middle son comes to her and says that he is crapping ball bearings. Again, she says that it is OK.

That evening, the eldest son comes in very upset. He says, "Ma, you won't believe what happened."

She says, "I know. You're passing ball bearings."

"No," he says. "I was out behind the barn jacking off and I shot the dog."

★ ★ ★

A man goes to the doctor and says, "Doc, you have to help me!"

The doctor asks, "What's your problem?"

The man says, "Every morning I wake up with my 'morning flagpole', give the wife a quick one, and then go to work. On the way to work, I carpool with the next door neighbour's wife who gives me a blow job during the ride to work. Once I get there, I do some work, and then at morning tea-time, I go into the photocopy room and crank one out with one of the young office girls. At lunch, I take my secretary out to a hotel and give her a good boning. For afternoon tea, I give the boss's wife a good servicing. Then, I go home and slip the maid a few inches. Then, at night, I give the wife another screw."

"So...?" asked the perplexed doctor. "What's your problem?"

The guy says, "Well, it hurts when I masturbate!"

★ ★ ★

Because of a bad case of haemorrhoids, a gay man goes to his doctor. The physician prescribes suppositories, but when it comes time to use them, the young man is afraid he will do it wrong. So he goes into the bathroom and bends over, and looks through his legs into the mirror to line up the target. All of a sudden, his penis becomes stiff, blocking his view.

"Oh, stop it," the young man scolds his organ, "it's only me."

★ ★ ★

A man comes into the maternity ward and yells, "My wife's going to have her baby in the cab!"

A young doctor grabs his stuff, rushed out to the cab, lifts the lady's dress, and begins to take off her underwear. Suddenly he notices that there are several cabs, and he is in the wrong one.

★ ★ ★

The following psychological test was developed by a thinktank of top U.S. and European psychologists. The results are incredibly accurate in describing your personality with one simple question:

Which is your favourite Teletubby:

A. Yellow
B. Purple
C. Green
D. Red

Profile for women:

A. You chose the Yellow Teletubby. You are bubbly and cheerful. People come to you when troubled because you always make them feel better about themselves. You are apt to clash with Red Teletubby people.

B. You chose the Purple Teletubby. You are active and erratic. You have many ideas and set high standards for yourselves and others. Stay away from Green Teletubby people, who tend to bring you down.

C. You chose the Green Teletubby. You are calm and reliable. Family plays a major role in your life and you often sacrifice your needs to please others. Yellow Teletubby people are a good match for you.

D. You chose the Red Teletubby. You are bold and emotional. You are fierce in your opinions and quick to anger, but stick by your friends through thick and thin. Purple and Red Teletubby people are an explosive combination.

Profile for men:

A. You chose the Yellow Teletubby. You are gay.

B. You chose the Purple Teletubby. You are gay.

C. You chose the Green Teletubby. You are gay.

D. You chose the Red Teletubby. You are gay.

★ ★ ★

A wife went in to see a therapist and said, "I've got a big problem, doctor. Every time we're in bed and my husband climaxes, he lets out this earsplitting yell."
"My dear," the doctor said reassuringly, "that's completely natural. I don't see what the problem is."
"The problem is," she complained, "it wakes me up!"

★ ★ ★

A businessman, feeling unwell one day, goes to see the doctor about it. The doctor says to him, "Well, it must be your diet. What sort of greens do you eat?"
The man replies, "Well, actually, I only eat peas. I hate all other green foods."
The doctor was quite shocked at this, and says, "Well man, that's your problem. All those peas will be clogging up your system – you'll have

584

to give them up!"

The man says, "But how long for? I mean, I really like peas..."

The doctor replies, "Forever, I'm afraid."

The man is dismayed by this, but he gives it a go, and sure enough, his condition improves, so he decides that he will never eat a pea again.

One night, years later, he's at a convention for his employer and getting quite sloshed, when one of his colleagues says, "Well, ashully, I'd love a cigarette, coz I avint ad a smoke in four years, I gave it up."

On hearing this, the barman puts in, "Really? I haven't had a game of golf in three years, because it cost me my first marriage, so I gave it up!"

The businessman says, "Thas nuvving, I haven't ad a pea in 6 years."

The barman jumps up, bellowing, "OK, everyone who can't swim, grab a table..."

★ ★ ★

Dr Jones goes to the retirement home for his monthly rounds.

He sees Joe and asks him, "Joe, how much is three times three?"

Joe responds "59."

The doctor goes over to Tom and asks, "Tom, how much is three times three?"

Tom responds, "Wednesday."

He finally goes over to John and asks, "John, how much is three times three?"

"Nine," replies John.

Delighted, the doctor responds, "That's right! Now how did you come to that answer?"

"It was easy," replied John. "I just subtracted 59 from Wednesday."

★ ★ ★

Having lunch one day, a sex therapist said to her friend, "According to a survey we just completed, ninety per cent of all people masturbate in the shower. Only ten per cent of them sing."

585

"Really?" asked the friend.

The therapist nodded her head and proceeded to ask, "And do you know what song they sing?"

The friend shook her head and replied, "No."

The therapist replied, "I didn't think so."

★ ★ ★

A woman accompanied her husband to the doctor's office. After his check-up, the doctor called the wife into his office alone.

"Your husband is suffering from a very severe disease, combined with horrible stress. If you don't do the following, your husband will surely die."

The woman gasped and listened attentively.

"Each morning, fix him a healthy breakfast. Be pleasant, and make sure he is in a good mood. For lunch, make him a nutritious meal. For dinner, prepare an especially nice meal for him. Don't burden him with chores, as he probably had a hard day. Don't discuss your problems with him, it will only make his stress worse. And most importantly, make love with your husband several times a week and satisfy his every whim. If you can do this for the next ten months or a year, I think your husband will regain his health completely."

On the way home, the husband asked his wife, "What did the doctor say?"

She looked him straight in the eye and replied, "You're going to die."

★ ★ ★

An attractive young lady, chaperoned by an ugly old woman, entered the doctor's office. "We have come for an examination," said the young lady.

"Alright," said the doctor. "Go behind that curtain and take your clothes off."

"No, not me," said the girl. "It's my old aunt here."

"Very well... Madam, put your tongue out."

★ ★ ★

Patient: Doctor, should I file my nails?
Doctor: No, throw them away like everybody else.

★ ★ ★

A woman told her doctor that she was really worried because every part of her body hurt.
The doctor looked concerned, and said, "Show me where."
The woman touched her own arm and screamed, "Ouch!"
Then she touched her leg and screamed, "Ouch!"
She touched her nose and cried, "Ouch!"
She looked at her doctor and said, "See? It hurts everywhere!"
The doctor nodded and said, "Don't worry, it's not serious. You've just got a broken finger."

★ ★ ★

A guy walks into the psychiatrist's office wearing only Clingfilm for shorts. The shrink says, "Well, I can see you're nuts."

★ ★ ★

A son and father went to see a doctor, since the father was getting very ill. The doctor told the father and son that the father was dying from cancer. The father turned to his son and said, "Son, even on this gloomy day, it's our tradition to drink to health as it is in death; so let's go to the pub and celebrate my demise."
Reluctantly, the son followed his father to the local pub. There, while enjoying their ale, the father saw some old friends and told them he was dying from AIDS.
Shocked, the son turned to his father and said, "Father, it is not AIDS you are dying from. It is cancer. Why on earth did you lie to those men?"
The father replied, "Aye, my son, you are right, but I don't want those guys sleeping with your mother when I'm gone."

★ ★ ★

A doctor and a lawyer were talking at a party, but were constantly interrupted by people asking the doctor for free medical advice. After an hour, the exasperated doctor asked the lawyer, "What do you do to stop people from asking you for legal advice when you're off duty?"
"I give it to them," replied the lawyer, "and then I send them a bill."
The doctor was shocked, but agreed to give it a try. The next day, still feeling slightly guilty, the doctor prepared the bills. When he went to place them in his mailbox, he found a bill from the lawyer.

★   ★   ★

One day, vistor at the mental asylum asked the director what the criterion was which defined whether a patient should be institutionalised. "Well," said the director, "we fill up a bathtub, then we offer a teaspoon, a teacup and a bucket to the patient and ask him or her to empty the bathtub."
"Oh, I understand," said the visitor. "A normal person would use the bucket, because it's bigger than the spoon or the teacup."
"No," said the director. "A normal person would pull the plug. Do you want a room with or without a view?"

★   ★   ★

Doctor: "Good morning. What can I do for you?"
Patient: "Aaaargh!"
Doctor: "I see, that sounds very painful."
Patient: *(in considerable pain)* "Eeeeeee!"
Doctor: "Have you taken anything for it?"
Patient: *(getting impatient)* "Aye!"
Doctor: "Well, I really don't see what I can do for you."
Patient: *(now exasperated)* "Oooooh!"
Doctor: "If you can't describe any other symptoms, I may not be able to help."
Patient *(reaching the end of his tether)*: "YOOOUU!"
Doctor: "Well, I think the problem is Irritable Vowel Syndrome."

★   ★   ★

STATE OF WEALTH

An old spinster was walking home one night when she was accosted by a mugger.

"Hand over your money," he demanded.

She said she hadn't got any money, but he didn't believe her and started to search her. He frisked her up and down, put his hands inside her bra and also inside her pants. Satisfied there was no money, he was just about to go when she said, "Hold on a minute. Keep trying. I can always write you a cheque."

★ ★ ★

A woman rings her husband up at work to tell him she's won the jackpot on the lottery and that he'd better start packing.

"Darling, that's wonderful!" he shouts with glee. "Where are we going?"

"I'm not bothered," she replies. "Just make sure you're gone by the time I get home."

★ ★ ★

A smart-talking man who thought he could charm the birds off the trees met his match one night. The man had just learned that his father only had days to live, after which he would inherit over half a million pounds. Overjoyed at the promised wealth, he celebrated at the local wine bar, where he saw a ravishing long-legged blonde. He couldn't wait to brag to her, and indeed she was so interested in him that they went back to his house together. The next day, she became his stepmother.

★ ★ ★

A girl went into the local police station to report a theft.

"He stole £50 I had pinned inside my knickers," she said.

"Did you put up a fight?" asked the policeman.

"No," she replied. "I didn't know he was after my money."

★ ★ ★

Bob suggested to his wife that a good way to save money would be to put £1 in the money box every time they made love. A year went by, and Bob decided to empty the money box and see how much money had been saved. He couldn't believe his eyes when he found not only £1 coins, but lots of £5, £10 and £20 notes as well.

"How come we've got all these notes?" he asked, amazed.

"Well, not everyone's as stingy as you," she retorted.

★ ★ ★

As it was very windy, the lady held onto her hat and took no notice of the fact that her skirt was flying up around her thighs. Realising she was getting funny looks from some of the passing men, she said, "Look lads, this hat cost a fortune and is brand new. What you're looking at is 40 years old."

★ ★ ★

Down at his local social club, Jack was amazed to see a girl lean over the table exposing her bare bum. Not only that, but on each buttock was tattooed the number 6. Jack immediately felt it was a sign he was going to be lucky, so he went over to the Treasurer and bought ticket 66 for the prize draw the next night. It was a bonus prize of £1,000.

The following night, Jack arrived after the draw had taken place, and he turned to his mate at the bar, saying, "Was the winning ticket 66?"

"No, sorry mate, but you were almost right. It was 606."

★ ★ ★

A man went round to his mate's house, and the wife answered the door.

"Is he in?"

"No," she said.

"I fancy you."

"Go away."

"How about a quick one?"

"Piss off."

"I'll give you £300."

"Alright, come in."

Later her husband comes home. "Did Jack come round?" he asked.

"Yes."

"Did he drop my wage packet off?"

★ ★ ★

Legend has it that when a person is born they are kissed on the part of their anatomy that will bring them fame and fortune.

There are a lot of men who make excellent Chairmen – I wonder where the angel kissed them.

★ ★ ★

A man receives a letter ordering him to attend the local tax office for an interview about his last year's earnings. Unsure of what to wear, he asks his mate, who tells him to look very smart, wear a suit and a good pair of shoes to show that he's an honest man.

Later on in the pub he meets another mate, tells him about his impending interview and that he's off to buy a good pair of shoes. But his mate disagrees, telling him he should wear old clothes, and look very poor, so that they will feel sorry for him. By this time, the man is very confused, so on the way home he calls in at his cousin's house for advice. His cousin is a wealthy businessman.

"Well, my advice to you is the same as I gave my daughter, Marlene, when she asked me what she should wear on her wedding night – a long bri-nylon nightie or a short skimpy baby-doll nightie. My answer to you both is it doesn't matter what you wear, because either way you're going to get fucked."

★ ★ ★

A man walked into a bank with a large sack of coins.

"Did you hoard all this yourself?" asks the bankteller.

"No," came the reply. "My wife whored, I pimped."

★ ★ ★

"It's no good, sir," said the DSS man to his interviewee. "It's no good saying you feel like 65 – you have to be 65."

★ ★ ★

A rich couple lost all their money, so the husband turned to his wife and said, "If you learn to cook, we can get rid of the housekeeper." And she retorted, "If you were better in bed, we could get rid of the gardener."

★ ★ ★

Two friends on a walking tour of Dartmoor get lost in the mist and, after many hours of wandering about, finally come across a cottage. A widow lives in the cottage and, after hearing their sorry story, she welcomes them in and gives them some supper and a glass of beer. She tells them she only has two bedrooms, so one can sleep in the spare room and one with her. The two men toss a coin and Jack ends up sleeping with the widow. He has a wonderful night, and in the morning after breakfast, they depart. After a few minutes, Bob asks Jack how it went.

"What a night, mate. It was great, but this morning she asked for my name and address so I gave her yours – you know what my wife's like." Bob was so incensed by this that it broke up their friendship and they didn't see each other again for nine months. When the widow died, Bob said, "Hello Jack, you remember that widow? Well, I've had a letter from her solicitor and she's—"

Jack hastily interrupted, "Look, I'm sorry Bob, but my wife would have strung me up by the balls."

"Let me finish," said Bob. "The solicitor's letter said she'd died and left me £1 million."

★ ★ ★

Did you hear about the debutante who wrote home from the States to say she had a beautiful fur coat and it only cost her 200 bucks? She never could spell!

★ ★ ★

On the way home to her flat, a young couple passed a jeweller's store. The man stopped and said, "If you're very nice to me tonight I'll buy you that diamond ring."

The girl, who loved material possessions, agreed immediately.

The next day, after a night of passion, the couple passed the shop and went in. But instead of buying her a beautiful diamond ring, he bought her a cheap brooch instead.

Later that day she visited her mother and, between the sobs, told her what had happened.

"My darling," replied her mother. "One thing you must learn – when they're hard, they're soft, and when they're soft, they're hard."

★ ★ ★

Two men are sitting on a park bench reading newspapers. Suddenly one of them puts down his paper and bursts into uncontrollable tears.

"Excuse me," says the other, "I can't help but notice you're very upset about something. Can I help?"

"I've just read that the richest man in the whole world has died."

"I'm sorry. Were you related to him?"

"No," sobbed the man, "that's why I'm crying."

★ ★ ★

A randy old financier was bonking his secretary up against his desk, when there was a knock at the door. The timing couldn't have been worse. She rushed back to her room and, in haste, he stuck his dick in the desk drawer. As the door opened the newcomer commented, "Why, Mr Large, you're looking pleased with yourself."

"Yes," he replied, "I've just come into some stocks and shares."

★ ★ ★

What is green and takes an hour to drink?
The family allowance cheque.

★ ★ ★

A jackpot-winner on the lottery was asked what he was going to do with his new-found wealth.

"I'm going to travel around the world, visit all the racecourses, spend time in Las Vegas, enjoy myself with the girls, drink lots and buy a super, top of the range sports car."

"And what will you do with any money left over?"

"Oh, I don't know, probably just squander it."

★ ★ ★

"He'll be alright soon," reassured the doctor. "He's just suffering from shock after seeing all of his numbers come up on this week's lottery."

"Oh, thank you, doctor," replied the wife. "Just one thing – how long should I leave it before I tell him I didn't put a lottery ticket on this week?"

★ ★ ★

Flo's husband dies and because he was such a popular fellow, she decides to put an announcement in the paper. But not having a lot of money, she tells the local newspaper she wants to keep it as short as possible. "Just put 'Ben Potts dead'."

"Actually, Madam, you can have up to six words for the same price. Is there anything you would like to add?"

Flo thinks for a while, and then says, "Yes, OK, can you add 'Ferret for sale'?"

★ ★ ★

A man was always thinking up ways of making easy money, and one day he thought he was on to a certainty. He taught his parrot to say the 23rd Psalm, and then took it down to the local pub.

"I bet anyone £5 that my parrot can recite the 23rd Psalm, from beginning to end," he said.

Quite a lot of interest was shown, and the money laid on the bar.

"Go on then, parrot, recite the psalm."

But the parrot remained completely dumb, and eventually the man took it home, having lost quite a lot of money.

"Why the bloody hell didn't you do as I taught you, you scrawny old bird?"

"Now hold on," said the parrot. "Think what the odds will be tomorrow when we go back."

★ ★ ★

What's the difference between a bank investor and a seagull?
A seagull can still put down a deposit on a BMW.

★ ★ ★

A group of students were being taught good business practice by a guest speaker from a thriving international company.

"Now, here's a tricky problem you may come across. One of your best customers comes in to settle his bill. He pays by cash with £50 notes, but two of the notes have stuck together, so he's paid too much. Now, the question is – should you tell your partner?"

★ ★ ★

Was it love at first sight?
No, second. The first time, I didn't know he had so much money.

★ ★ ★

At a party to celebrate her 21st birthday, the daughter put all her presents on display, including a cheque from her father to buy a new car. During the evening the guests would wander over to take a look at the presents, and on one occasion a man was standing at the table looking at the cheque, doubled up with laughter.

"Mum," whispered the birthday girl, "who is that man?"
"Oh him, he's your dad's bank manager."

★ ★ ★

A lawyer and a blonde are sitting next to each other on a long haul flight. The lawyer leans over to her and asks if she would like to play a fun game. The blonde just wants to take a nap, so she politely declines and rolls over to the window to catch a few winks.

The lawyer persists and explains that the game is really easy and a lot of fun. "I ask you a question, and if you don't know the answer, you pay me £5, and visa-versa."

Again, she politely declines and tries to get some sleep.

The lawyer, confident in outsmarting her, says, "OK, if you don't know the answer you pay me £5, and if I don't know the answer, I will pay you £50!" This catches the blonde's attention and, resigning herself, agrees to play.

The lawyer asks the first question. "What's the distance from the earth to the moon?" The blonde doesn't say a word, reaches in to her purse, pulls out a fiver, and hands it to the lawyer.

Now it's the blonde's turn. She asks the lawyer, "What goes up a hill with three legs, and comes down with four?"

The lawyer looks at her with a puzzled look. He takes out his laptop and searches all his references. He taps into the airphone with his modem and searches the internet. Frustrated, he sends emails to all his colleagues. All this to no avail: after over an hour, he wakes the blonde and hands her £50. The blonde politely takes the £50 and turns away to get back to sleep.

The lawyer, more than a little miffed, wakes the blonde and asks, "So come on, what's the answer?"

Without a word, the blonde reaches into her purse, hands the lawyer £5, and goes back to sleep.

★ ★ ★

"Mr Smith, I have reviewed this case very carefully," the divorce court judge said, "and I've decided to give your wife £275 a week."

"That's very kind, Your Honour," the husband said. "And every now and then I'll try to send her a few quid, myself."

★ ★ ★

Santa Claus, the tooth fairy, an honest lawyer and an old drunk are walking down the street together when they simultaneously spot a fifty pound note. Who gets it?

The old drunk, of course. None of the other three are real.

★ ★ ★

A man walks into a toy shop to get a Barbie doll for his daughter. He asks the sales assistant how much it would cost him.

"Well," she says, "we have Barbie Goes to the Gym for £19.99, Barbie Goes to the Ball for £19.99, Barbie Goes Shopping for £19.99, Barbie Goes to the Beach for £19.99, Barbie Goes Nightclubbing for £19.99, and Divorced Barbie for £299.99."

"Hang on a minute," interjects the puzzled man. "Why is Divorced Barbie £299.99 when all the others are only £19.99?"

"Ah, well, it's simple, sir," came the reply. "Divorced Barbie comes with Ken's house, Ken's car, Ken's boat, Ken's furniture..."

★ ★ ★

A man was walking down the street one day when he saw a woman with the most perfect breasts he had ever seen.

He walked up to her and said, "Excuse me, Ma'am. You have perfect breasts, and I will pay you £100 to bite them." The woman was horrified and began to walk away.

The man caught up with her and said, "Alright, I'll pay you £1,000 to bite your breasts." Still horrified, the woman began to run away.

The man caught up with her again and said, "Fine. I'll pay you £10,000 to bite your breasts, and not a penny more." The woman decided that £10,000 would be worth it, so she finally agreed.

They went into a deserted alley away from the city action. The woman revealed her perfect breasts and the man began to touch, squeeze, fondle and poke the woman's breasts – everything except biting them.

The woman then said, "Well, are you going to bite them or not?"

The man replied, "Nah, too expensive."

★ ★ ★

A woman and her husband were participating in a blood drive, and as part of the pre-screening process, an elderly volunteer was asking some questions.

"Have you ever paid for sex?" the volunteer asked the husband sweetly.

He glanced wearily over at his wife, who was trying to calm a new baby and tend to several other children milling around her. "Oh yes," he sighed, "every time."

★ ★ ★

Why does the Law Society prohibit sex between lawyers and their clients?
To prevent clients from being billed twice for the same service.

★ ★ ★

TRAVELS

A taxi driver had an attractive female passenger in the back when suddenly the engine failed. He got out and lifted the bonnet to see what was wrong. The girl got out too, and came over to see what he was doing.

"Do you want a screwdriver?" she asked.

"In a moment, Miss. I'll just finish up here first."

★ ★ ★

"Fasten your seatbelts, please, ladies and gentlemen. We'll be landing in New York in less than ten minutes," said the pilot of Concorde over the intercom. Unfortunately, he forgot to turn the intercom off, and the passengers overheard him telling his co-pilot what he would do when they landed.

"First, I'm going to have a bloody good crap... I'm in agony... and then I'm going to give that sexy new air stewardess a right good rogering." The new air stewardess, on hearing what the pilot said, blushed deeply and ran up the aisle to warn him, but halfway up she tripped and fell.

An old lady sitting in the aisle seat near her leant over and said, "Don't worry dear, there's no need to rush. He said he was going to have a crap first."

★ ★ ★

When in Madrid, a man is recommended to go to a special local restaurant that serves the testicles of the slain bull from the local bull fight. When he gets there, he sees written up outside the restaurant, "After the killing in the ring, the testicles are on your plate within 30 minutes."

Sitting at the table, the man orders the hot testicles, but when they arrive he is slightly disgruntled at what looks like two pickled walnuts covered with tomato sauce.

"This is very disappointing," he says to the waiter. "I have seen bulls' knackers and they are huge."

The waiter smiles and says, "Ah yes, sir, but sometimes the bull wins."

★ ★ ★

A pretty American girl on holiday in Scotland asked a man wearing a kilt, "I've often wondered what you have under your kilt."
He replied, "I'm a man of few words. Give me your hand."

★ ★ ★

A jumbo jet full to capacity is flying across the Atlantic when the pilot suddenly makes an announcement.
"I must apologise, ladies and gentlemen, one of our engines has failed. We've got three others, so we'll reach our destination, but it will be a little later than scheduled."
Some time passes, and then he makes another announcement.
"I'm sorry for the inconvenience; we've lost another engine, so we'll be an hour late getting to our destination."
Then some minutes later, he announces the loss of another engine and tells his passengers that the delay in landing will be two hours.
At this point, one of the passengers turns to the person next to him and says, "Bloody hell, if we lose another engine, we'll be up here all night."

★ ★ ★

Three men are sitting in the same railway carriage when suddenly a phone rings. The first man puts his thumb to his mouth and forefinger up to his ear and carries on a conversation, explaining afterwards that he's got microchips implanted in both digits, so he doesn't need to carry around a phone. Some weeks go by and the three men find themselves in the same carriage again. A phone rings and this time, the second man starts to talk seemingly to nothing. Afterwards he explains he has two microchips, one in his ear and the other in his mouth – even better than using the finger and thumb technique. Suddenly, the third man gets up, groans slightly and bends over with his legs apart.
"Excuse me," he says. "I think a fax is just coming through."

★ ★ ★

Two cab drivers met. "Hey," asked one, "why did you paint one side of your cab red and the other side blue?"

"Well," the other responded, "when I get into an accident, you should see how all the witnesses contradict each other."

★ ★ ★

Two strangers are in a train compartment, a biologist and a young woman. As they travel through the countryside, they pass field after field of animals, many of them doing what comes naturally.

The young lady starts to get hot under the collar and, turning to the man, asks him if he could tell her what attracts the animals to each other.

"It would be a pleasure," he says. "At certain times in the year, the female gives off an odour attracting the male to her and heightening his sexual awareness."

At last they reach their destination and, on parting, the man says he hopes they'll meet again one day.

"Only if your head cold is better," she replies.

★ ★ ★

A businessman visited a very upmarket restaurant in Paris and ordered moules marinières, duck à l'orange and a sorbet ice-cream. When the first two courses were served, he noticed the man had his thumb stuck in the dishes, but not when he brought out the dessert.

"Garçon, tell me please, why did you have your thumb in the first two courses of my meal, but not when you brought out the ice-cream?"

"Certainly, sir. I have bad rheumatism in my thumb, and something warm helps relieve the pain."

At this, the businessman was outraged. "It is appalling that in such a restaurant as this, customers have to put up with these disgusting habits. Go shove it up your bum."

Unperturbed, the waiter replied, "I only do that in the kitchen."

★ ★ ★

An American seaman working on a trawler around the Far East takes shore leave, and spends the whole week having sex everything in sight. Alas, he picks up a very serious strain of VD, and is forced to go along to an American doctor.

"I'm afraid there is not much we can do for you," says the doctor. "We'll have to cut your penis off or you may die."

The man is dumbfounded but, determined to get a second opinion, he visits a European doctor. The diagnosis is exactly the same.

Dismayed beyond belief, he goes to see a local doctor tucked away in the backstreets of the city. The doctor tells him there is no need for the operation, it is just a way for these foreign doctors to make more money. The man is overjoyed.

"You mean I don't have to have it cut off."

"No," replied the doctor. "Just wait a few days and your cock will fall off by itself."

★ ★ ★

Three men were captured by savages in the depths of the jungle. They were told to go out and collect one type of fruit and bring it back to the camp. Two returned quickly. The first had gathered cherries, and as a torture, he had to put them up his backside. Watching this, the second man looked on aghast, as he had gathered oranges. But just then, the third man arrived back and the second man started to smile. "What is it?" said the first. "Aren't you worried? Look at the size of those oranges."

"No," replied the man. "I've just seen Bob return and he's got melons."

★ ★ ★

"I'm a little stiff from rugby."

"That's OK, it doesn't matter where you come from."

★ ★ ★

Stranded miles from home after an all-night party, Good Time Lil flags down a passing taxi and says to the driver, "Look mate, I'm out of money, but if you'll take me back to Brighton, we can do the business on the back seat."

The unscrupulous driver agrees, takes her home and then gets into the back seat with her. He takes down his trousers, she takes off her knickers and sits astride him, when he suddenly complains.

"You haven't got anything smaller by any chance?"

★ ★ ★

Three men are captured by savages in the deepest part of the jungle, and are told they have one last wish before being killed. The first man asks for a crate of bourbon, which he drinks until he collapses unconscious on the ground. The savages then kill him and eat him, but keep his skin to make a canoe.

The second man asks for a dozen women, all of whom he screws in turn until he collapses, exhausted. The savages then do the same to this man.

Finally, it's the turn of the third man to pick a wish and he asks for a knife, with which he starts stabbing himself all over his body. Puzzled, the savages ask him what he is doing.

Came the reply, "No bugger is going to make a canoe out of me."

★ ★ ★

An elderly couple went away on a weekend break, but couldn't find anywhere to stay. As a kindly gesture, the manager of a four star hotel offered to let them stay in the bridal suite.

"What the heck do we want that for?" asked the irritable old man. "I'm 75 years old."

"Excuse me sir, but I've allowed people to stay in the snooker room before now without expecting them to play snooker all night."

★ ★ ★

"I've just had the most fabulous holiday in St Tropez," said the office girl to her friends. "I met this dishy masseur."

"You mean monsieur, don't you?" said Doreen. "A masseur is someone

who gets you to strip and rubs you all over..."
 "So this dishy masseur...."

* * *

A couple were staying overnight at a country hotel, but were unable to get to sleep because of the loud noise coming from downstairs. Eventually, the man could stand it no longer and rang down to reception.

"What the hell's going on? The noise is deafening."

"My apologies, sir, they're holding the Policeman's Ball."

"Well, for fuck's sake, tell them to leave it alone."

* * *

A woman from the city stops overnight at a B&B in the heart of the countryside. The toilet is at the bottom of the garden, and after using it she comes back in and complains to the owner.

"There's no lock on that toilet."

"No need," he says. "Who'd want to steal a pail of shit?"

* * *

The leader of the Western world and a monkey were sent up to space to look for life on other planets. They eventually landed many light years away on an unfamiliar world. Each had an envelope with a set of instructions. The monkey opened his envelope, which told him to study the terrain, take readings of the air pressure, rocks and minerals and make contact with any alien inhabitants. The leader of the Western world opened his envelope and read, "Feed the monkey."

* * *

Bob was so excited. He'd never been up in a plane before, but today he was having a special trip in a two-seater. At 3 o'clock, they took off and were soon travelling high up in the sky when, all of a sudden, the pilot collapsed and died of a heart attack. Bob was petrified. After some minutes of total panic he found the radio.

"Mayday, mayday! Somebody help me – the pilot's dead and I'm up here on my own."

"Receiving you loud and clear," came a voice from the control room. "Try to keep calm; can you tell me where you are?"

"I don't know!" he yelled. "But we're flying upside down."

"And how do you know that?"

"Because crap's running out of my collar."

★ ★ ★

Flying for the first time, an old man was having trouble with his ears, so the stewardess brought him some chewing gum. As he was leaving, he turned to her and said, "Thanks for the chewing gum, but how do I get it out of my ears?"

★ ★ ★

The man was angry.

"Look, I booked a room with ensuite facilities."

"But this isn't your room, sir, this is the lift."

★ ★ ★

A van driver picks up a young female hitchhiker and after they've travelled some distance he propositions her. She agrees and suggests they get into the back of the van, but he tells her it's full of plumbing equipment.

"I know," he says. "Let's do it on the bonnet." So, throwing all caution to the wind, they climb aboard and start bonking away. The passion is getting stronger and stronger, the van is swaying from side to side and at the crucial moment he flings himself away and hits his back on the aerial. The next day, it's still very painful so he goes along to the doctor's.

"Mmm... that's the worse case of Van Aerial disease I've ever seen."

★ ★ ★

A man stopped overnight at an hotel and rang down to reception asking for one of their local girls.

"How disgusting," said the owner's wife. "Go and tell him we don't allow that sort of thing here."

But the husband thought she was making a lot of fuss about nothing.

"OK, I'll go and tell him," she said and off she stormed upstairs.

Half an hour passed and the man appeared downstairs. He said to the owner, "The girls round here are a bit feisty aren't they? The one you sent me was a real tough one but I got her in the end."

★ ★ ★

A group of ladies are travelling in a railway carriage that has no toilet facilities. As it pulls into one of the stations, a drunk climbs aboard, sits himself in the corner and immediately falls asleep. Some time later he wakes up dying for a pee.

"Excuse me, ladies, this is a bit of an emergency. Would you mind if I peed out of the window?"

The women are broad-minded enough and tell him to go ahead. However, a little further on he needs another one, so he asks the ladies again.

"Go ahead," said the spokeslady, "but I think we would all prefer it if this time you peed in the carriage and got rid of your fart out of the window."

★ ★ ★

A car breaks down along the motorway one day, so the driver eases it over onto the hard shoulder. He jumps out of the car, opens the boot and pulls out two men in trenchcoats.

The men stand behind the car, open up their coats and start exposing themselves to the oncoming traffic. One of the worst pile-ups in history occurs.

When questioned by police why he put two deviates along the side of the road, the man replied, "I broke down and was just using my emergency flashers!"

★ ★ ★

NEWS ITEMS FROM AROUND THE WORLD

1. When his .38-calibre revolver failed to fire at its intended victim during a hold-up in Long Beach, California, robber James Elliot did something that can only inspire wonder: he peered down the barrel and tried the trigger again. Happily for most concerned, this time it worked.

2. Labourer Alexander Robinson of Mobile, Alabama, redefined the limits of tactlessness when he opened his eyes after surgery to restore his sight and said agreeably to his wife, "Boy, you sure have got fat in four years."

3. The chef at a hotel in Switzerland lost a finger in a meat-cutting machine and, after a little hopping around, submitted a claim to his insurance company.
    The company, suspecting negligence, sent out one of its men to have a look for himself. He tried the machine out and lost a finger. The chef's claim was approved.

4. Mourners at the funeral of Anna Bochinsky in Moinesti, Romania, were naturally somewhat taken aback when she abruptly leapt from her coffin as it was being carried to the grave. Before they could react to this unexpected outburst, the woman bounded into the nearest road, where she was run over and killed by a passing car.

5. An American tourist in South America had the misfortune to be attacked by killer bees as he stood on the bank of the Amazon. Seeking refuge, he leapt into the river – and was devoured by piranha fish.

6. A Malaysian monkey that had been trained to gather coconuts from trees demonstrated a pressing need for a refresher course when it leapt onto the shoulders of a passer-by in Kuala Lumpur and tried to twist his head off. The passer-by was treated at a local hospital for a sprained neck.

7. In Fort Lauderdale, Florida, a 16-year-old youth was charged with

beating up his 15-year-old wife after the latter hid the caps to his toy pistol.

8. A man who shovelled snow for an hour to clear a space for his car during a blizzard in Chicago returned with his vehicle to find a woman had taken the space.
   Understandably, he shot her dead.

9. One of the criteria by which Miss Nude USA was chosen in 1979 was "taste in clothing".

10. After stopping for drinks at an illegal bar, a Zimbabwean bus driver found that the 20 mental patients he was supposed to be transporting from Harare to Bulawayo had escaped. Not wanting to admit his incompetence, the driver went to a nearby bus-stop and offered everyone in the queue a free ride. He then delivered the passengers to the mental hospital, telling staff that the patients were very excitable and prone to bizarre fantasies. The deception wasn't discovered for three days.

★ ★ ★

The year is 2222 and Mike and Maureen land on Mars after accumulating enough frequent flier miles.

They meet a Martian couple and are talking about all sorts of things.

Mike asks if Mars has a stockmarket, if they have laptop computers, how they make money, etc.

Finally, Maureen brings up the subject of sex.

"Just how do you guys do it?" asks Maureen.

"Pretty much the way you do," responds the Martian.

Discussion ensues, and finally the couples decide to swap partners for the night to experience one another.

Maureen and the male Martian go off to a bedroom where the Martian strips. He's got only a teeny, weeny member about half an inch long and just a quarter inch thick.

"I don't think this is going to work," says Maureen.

"Why not?" he asks. "What's the matter?"

"Well," she replies, "it's just not long enough to reach me."

"No problem," he says, and proceeds to slap his forehead with his palm. With each slap of his forehead, his member grows until it's quite impressively long.

"Well," she says, "that's quite impressive, but it's still pretty narrow..."

"No problem," he says, and starts pulling his ears.

With each pull, his member grows wider and wider until the entire measurement is extremely exciting to the woman.

"Wow!" she exclaims, as they fall into bed and make mad, passionate love.

The next day the couples rejoin their normal partners and go their separate ways.

As they walk along, Mike asks, "Well, was it any good?"

"I hate to say it," says Maureen, "but it was pretty wonderful. How about you?"

"It was horrible," he replies. "All I got was a headache. All she kept doing the whole time was slapping my forehead and pulling my ears."

★ ★ ★

A couple went on holiday to a fishing resort. The husband liked to fish at the crack of dawn; his wife preferred to read.

One morning, the husband returned after several hours of fishing and decided to take a nap.

The wife, to escape her snoring husband, decided to take the boat out. Since she was not familiar with the lake, she rowed out to the middle, anchored the boat, and started reading her book.

Along came the sheriff in his boat. He pulled up alongside and said, "Good morning, ma'am. What are you doing here?"

"Reading a book," she replied, thinking, "Is this guy blind or what?"

"You're in a restricted fishing area," he informed her.

"But, Officer, I'm not fishing. You can see that, surely."

"But you have all the equipment, ma'am. I'll have to write you up."

"If you do that, I will charge you with rape," returned the irate woman.

"But I haven't even touched you," the sheriff objected.

"That's true, but you have all the equipment."

★ ★ ★

A man is driving home late one night on a lonely road, and is feeling very horny. As he passes a pumpkin patch by the roadside, his mind starts to wander.

He thinks to himself, 'Well, y'know, a pumpkin is soft and squishy inside, and there's noone around for miles."

So he pulls over to the side of the road, picks up a nice juicy-looking pumpkin, cuts the appropriate sized hole in it, and begins to do his business.

In no time at all he gets so carried away that he fails to notice the police car that has pulled up beside him.

The policeman walks over and says, "Excuse me sir, but do you realize that you are screwing a pumpkin?"

In horror, the guy looks at the pumpkin, and, thinking fast, says, "A pumpkin? Oh my god, is it midnight already?"

★ ★ ★

UNFAITHFULNESS

After partying through most of the night, a young couple woke up the next day with awful hangovers.

"I'm sorry, love," said the husband, "but was it you I made love to last night in the spare bedroom?"

"I don't know," she replied. "About what time would that be?"

★ ★ ★

"What the bloody hell do you think you're doing?" said the angry husband when he caught his wife in bed with another man.

The wife turned to her lover and said, "You see, I told you he was stupid."

★ ★ ★

A duke and duchess were not getting on very well; in fact, the duchess believed her husband to be having an affair with the housemaid, so she decided to test her theory.

The duchess sent the housemaid away for the night and when her husband made an excuse to leave his bed, she rushed down the back stairs and got into her housemaid's bed. Lo and behold, in he came and had his wicked way before she turned the lights on.

"You didn't expect to find me here, did you?" said the Duchess.

"Indeed not, madam," replied the Butler.

★ ★ ★

A man turns to his friend and asks him why he's looking so puzzled. He replies, "I've received this letter today and it's from a man who says he'll beat me if I don't stay away from his wife."

"So what's puzzling you?"

"Well, he hasn't signed it."

★ ★ ★

When a man arrives home from work one evening he's greeted by his wife, who's holding a bottle of hair conditioner in her hand.

"What's that for?" he asks. "My hair's just fine."
"Yours maybe, but this is for your girlfriend whose hair keeps coming out all over your shoulders!"

★ ★ ★

After a night of unbridled passion with his beautiful young secretary, the unfaithful husband was afraid to face up to his wife.
"Don't worry," said the secretary. "Just put this piece of chalk behind your ear and tell her the truth."
When the man got home he crept quietly upstairs, but she was sitting up in bed waiting for him.
"Where have you been 'til this time?" she yelled.
"I've been enjoying a night of passion with a beautiful young girl," he replied.
"You bloody liar, you've been playing pool with your mates all night, I can see the chalk behind your ear."

★ ★ ★

A man came home early from work to find his wife in bed with a strange man.
"Let me explain," she said. "He came to the door looking for something to eat, so I gave him the breakfast you didn't want this morning. Then he asked if there were any clothes I didn't want, so I gave him your old blue suit that was going to the jumble sale. At that point he asked if there was anything else you didn't use."

★ ★ ★

"You never make a sound when you have an orgasm," said the disappointed husband to his wife.
"How would you know?" she retorted. "You're never there."

★ ★ ★

A good-looking young man goes into the chiropodist's and enquires how many customers are before him.

"Well I've got one corn, two bunions and one with toenails to clip."

The young man leaves and doesn't return. On the following three days the same man comes in and asks the same question. Each time there are about four or five customers before him, and each time the man leaves again. The chiropodist is so intrigued he sends his receptionist out to follow him.

"I don't know what's going on," replies the receptionist on her return. "He just goes straight round to your house."

★ ★ ★

"Did you sleep with my husband last night?"

"No, not a wink."

★ ★ ★

The inevitable happened. A man came home from work early, and as his wife heard the key in the door, the lover jumped out of bed, grabbed his jacket and leapt into the wardrobe.

The husband, seeing his wife in bed, shouted, "I know there's a man here somewhere. Come on, where is he?"

He looked under the bed, "No, he's not here." He looked out of the window. "No, he's not here." And he looked in the wardrobe. But seeing a man holding a gun, he shouted, "And he's not here either."

★ ★ ★

"Do you talk to your wife when you're making love?"

"Only if she rings up."

★ ★ ★

"How many wives have you had?" asks Jack to Rob.

"Mmmm, about 50, but only one was my own."

★ ★ ★

"Do you like my new Italian suit?" said John to his mate.

"I do. Where did you get it from?"

"I didn't get it, my wife did. It was a surprise – I came home early from work and it was hanging on the end of the bed!"

★ ★ ★

A jealous wife suspected her husband of being unfaithful, so when they were both invited to a fancy-dress party she feigned a headache and told him to go on his own. So off he went in his spacesuit costume, and an hour later she followed in her own masked outfit. When she got there, she spied her husband chatting up every female at the party, so after a while propositioned him herself to see what the response would be. Lo and behold, he had her outside quicker than you could say Jack Robinson, and screwed her against the tree. Not long after, she left, and the next morning at breakfast was ready to confront him with his supposed unfaithfulness.

"How was the party?" she asked.

"Not really my scene," he replied. "I went up to the den to play poker with the boys, and lent my spacesuit costume to Freddie Parker."

★ ★ ★

A man comes home to find his wife in bed with his best friend. The shocked husband says to his friend, "I have to... but you?"

★ ★ ★

Two men are getting dressed in the changing room. One puts on a girdle. "Since when have you been wearing a girdle?" the other asks. "Since my wife found it in the glove compartment," he replies.

★ ★ ★

What is a vindictive pregnancy?

Someone who's had it in for you while you've been away.

★ ★ ★

My best friend ran away with my wife, and do you know – I miss him.

★ ★ ★

A businessman away for the week at a conference sends a telegram to his wife saying he'll be home Friday night and is bringing a colleague with him. Friday night comes and he arrives home only to find his wife in bed with a stranger. The man goes completely berserk, threatening to kill them both, but his colleague eventually manages to calm him down by saying there's probably some explanation and they'll sort it out in the morning. Sure enough, the next morning the colleague says to his friend, "You see, there was a good explanation. She's just told me there was a postal strike on Friday, so she didn't get the message."

★ ★ ★

A man comes home early from work to find his wife in bed. He's immediately suspicious and opens the wardrobe to find her lover hiding amongst the clothes, stark naked.
"What are you doing in there?" demands the angry husband.
"I'm the local pest controller," stumbles the man, "and we've heard there's a plague of moths about..."
"Well bugger me!" replies the man in amazement as he looks down at his body. "The bastards!"

★ ★ ★

"When I came home from work last night, I found my wife in bed with another man. How can I stop this from happening again?"
"Work more overtime."

★ ★ ★

"I want to divorce my husband," said the shapely brunette to her solicitor.
"On what grounds?"
"Infidelity. He's not the father of my child."

★ ★ ★

A man and a woman were having dinner in a fine restaurant. Their waitress, taking another order at another table, noticed that the man was slowly sliding down his chair and under the table, with the woman acting unconcerned.

The waitress watched as the man slid all the way down his chair and out of sight under the table. Still, the woman appeared calm and unruffled, apparently unaware that her dining companion had disappeared.

After the waitress finished taking the order, she came over to the table and said to the woman, "Pardon me, ma'am, but I think your husband just slid under the table."

The woman calmly looked up at her and replied firmly, "No he didn't. He just walked in the door."

★ ★ ★

Two men in the barber's, a colonel and a sergeant.

"Shall I put some aftershave on, sir?" asked the barber of the colonel.

"Good gracious man, no. My wife would think I smelled like a brothel."

The barber turned to the sergeant, "What about you, sir?"

"Certainly, my wife doesn't know what a brothel smells like."

★ ★ ★

Coming back from work one day, a husband sees his wife wearing a stunning diamond ring. When he asks her where she got it, she tells him she's won it in a raffle. In the following two weeks his wife is also seen wearing a beautiful fur coat and carrying a crocodile handbag. Again, she tells him she won them in a raffle. The following Thursday she informs her husband that she's going out again and asks if he would be kind enough to turn the shower on for her.

"Oh, I don't think so," he said. "You don't want to get your raffle ticket wet."

★ ★ ★

In the back seat of a car, a couple are having it away, time and time again. Every time he finishes, she asks for more. Eventually he tells her he's just got to go outside for a breather. While he's standing there, he sees a man looking in a shop window at some car stereos.

"Listen, mate," he says. "I've got a spare radio which you can have for free if you'll do me a favour. I've got a girl in the back seat of my car who's sex mad. She wants it time and time again, and you'd be doing me a favour if you took over for a while."

The man agrees and gets into the car. A little while later a policeman comes along, shines his torch through the car window and asks what's going on.

"I'm making love to my wife," he replies.

"Well, can't you do it at home?" asks the policeman.

"Until you shone that light in, I didn't realize it was my wife!"

★ ★ ★

Two men talking in a bar. "Listen, Jack, we've been mates a long time. I'd like you to do something for me. I've got to go out of town for a few days and I'd like you to keep a close eye on my wife. I have suspicions that she's up to something."

A few days pass and they meet up again in the pub.

"I watched your wife carefully, Bob," said Jack. "On the second evening a man knocked on the door and she opened it in a see-through night-dress. They kissed passionately and then went upstairs to the bedroom, where I saw him put his hand between her legs – but then they closed the curtains and I saw no more."

"Oh dear," said Bob. "You see, the doubt remains."

★ ★ ★

"You'll never believe this," said the man when he got home that night. "I saw the paperboy this morning and he boasts he's slept with every woman on the street except one."

"Oh, I bet that's her at Number Eight," replied the wife.

★ ★ ★

A man walked into a bar and ordered a double Scotch, drank it down in one gulp and immediately ordered another.

"You don't look so good," remarked the bartender. "Is it bad news?"

"Yes," replied the man. "I just found my wife in bed with my best friend."

"Oh no," said the bartender. "Here, have the next one on me. What did you do?"

"I told her to pack her bags, get out and never come back."

"And what about your best friend?"

"I went right up to him and said 'Bad dog!' "

★ ★ ★

Two men are talking in a bar. One says, "I've got such a clever wife. Why, she's even found a burglar-proof way of protecting her clothes. Sometimes when I come home from work, there's a man in the wardrobe looking after them."

★ ★ ★

Jack lived his life to a strict routine and would go out for a pint every Monday, Wednesday and Friday. However, one Friday night he didn't feel very well, so decided to stay in and watch television with his wife. Halfway through the evening, the phone rang and his wife heard him say, "Why the hell are you ringing me? Ask the Met Office!" and he slammed down the phone.

"Who was that?" she asked.

"Some silly bugger asking me if the coast was clear."

★ ★ ★

Said Jack to his mate at the pub, "Do you know, she loves me so much. Last week I was off sick. Every morning she was so glad to have me home, she'd run out into the street when the milkman or postman arrived, shrieking, "My husband's here, my husband's at home!"

★ ★ ★

A wife was forever finding herself at home on her own, because her husband worked late at the office.

For her birthday, she insisted they go out to the best club in town. She was determined he wouldn't get out of it, so that night he was duly dragged along. At the door, the bouncer greeted her husband in a familiar way.

"Hello, Bob, nice to see you."

Quickly, Bob explained that the bouncer worked in his office during the day and he worked at night for some extra money. In they went and left their coats in the cloakroom, at which point the girl in charge also greeted Bob in a familiar way.

"Hello, Bob, how are you tonight?"

Again, he remarked that the girl used to work in his office before changing jobs. However, it all went horribly wrong when the stripper also greeted him.

"That's it!" roared the wife as she stormed out and hailed down a taxi. "I could just about accept the explanations about the bouncer and cloakroom attendant, but you'll never convince me that the stripper works as a secretary through the day. No, no, no, definitely not!" she screamed.

Hearing this, the taxi driver turned round and said, "By Jove, you've got a difficult one tonight, Bob."

★ ★ ★

Jack and Bill are in the urinals, and on seeing Bill's prick, Jack exclaims, "How the heck did you get such a huge prick? It's a real stonker."

"Oh, that's easy," replies Bill proudly. "Every night before I get into bed I knock it five times on the bottom of the bed."

That night, Jack decides to do the same, and before getting into bed knocks his prick on the bottom of the bed five times.

Awakened by the noise, his wife whispers, "Is that you, Bill?"

★ ★ ★

Why did the unfaithful man buy a dog?

If his wife overheard him saying, "Lie down, roll over, give it to me and I'll give you a bone", she'd think it was the dog he was talking to.

★ ★ ★

What does the unfaithful man say to his wife after having sex?
"Sweetheart, I'll be home in half an hour."

★ ★ ★

A wife hears the shattering news that she's pregnant and immediately rings her husband.
"I'm pregnant, you bastard, why didn't you wear a condom?" she yells.
"Now, hold on a minute," he replies. "I always wear a condom. Anyway, who is this?"

★ ★ ★

Jack Carter, chairman of an international company, is outraged one morning when he sees that someone has peed in the snow outside his office window. Not just peed but formed the words, "Fuck the wanker Jack."
He immediately calls in his private secretary and demands that the culprits be discovered.
Later, the secretary returns and rather nervously gives him the news.
"Sir, the urine belongs to the deputy chairman, but... er..."
"But what? Come on, but what?"
"Well, sir, the handwriting belongs to your wife."

★ ★ ★

Betty's walking down the street when she comes upon her hated neighbour, Doreen.
"Hey bitch, how dare you say my John's got a wart on the end of his dick?"
"I said no such thing," replied Doreen. "I said it just felt like he had a wart on the end of his dick."

★ ★ ★

Husband comes home from the office and sees his wife in the garden. "Sarah, I have some good news and some bad news to tell you. I'm leaving you for Molly."
"I see," says the wife, "and what's the bad news?"

★ ★ ★

"That was a wonderful weekend we spent in Paris," said the director to his secretary. "Will you ever be able to forget it?"
"I don't know," she replied. "What's it worth?"

★ ★ ★

Drowsing contentedly after an afternoon of bonking in bed, suddenly there's the sound of a car pulling up outside. Dreamily, the girl whispers, "Oh, quick, get moving, that's my husband."
Quick as a flash, the man jumps out of bed, rushes to the window and suddenly stops dead.
"What d'ya mean?" he bellows. "I am your husband!"

★ ★ ★

A couple are having it away on the sofa when the phone rings. After answering it, she replaces the receiver and turns to her lover, saying, "It was only my husband."
"Oh, no," replies the man. "I'd better get out of here."
"Don't worry, he won't be home for hours. He's playing pool with you and two other mates."

★ ★ ★

Bob was off on his usual three day inspection of garden centres when he realised he'd left the house without his new seed catalogue. Returning quietly, he saw his wife in the kitchen, bending over, looking inside the fridge. Unable to resist, he crept up behind her, lifted her flimsy nightdress and was just about to do the business when she said, "Only six eggs this week Jack. Bob's away till Friday."

★ ★ ★

When a husband found his wife in bed with another man, he was so angry he knocked the man unconscious, tied him up and took him down to the garden shed. On regaining consciousness, the man realised his offending member was chained to the floor and the husband was standing over him with a machete."
"Bloody hell, you're not going to cut it off, are you?"
"No" said the husband, handing him the knife. "You can do that, while I set fire to the shed."

★ ★ ★

The chief executive of an international company pulled up in his Rolls outside a pub where two men were drinking.
"Hey, Jack, you see that man in the Rolls? He was trying to get me for months."
"Really?" said Jack. "Whose company were you with at the time?"
"His wife's."

★ ★ ★

Jack and Bill spent the night drinking heavily in the pub and got so drunk that Jack missed his bus home.
"Never mind," slurped Bill. "Come on home with me."
They staggered back to Bill's house and went inside.
"I'll just show you where everything is," he said. "There's the kitchen and if we go upstairs... there's the bathroom, you can kip down in here and this is my bedroom."
Bill opened his bedroom door. "And there's my wife and the man next to her is me!"

★ ★ ★

A man partners up with a new member of the golf club, and they've played nine holes when he comments, "I see you've got a club in a special leather case, but you haven't used it yet."

"Oh no, that's not a club," explains the man. "I'm a freelance hitman, so I carry my gun around with me at all times in case someone needs my services."

They continue playing another two holes when suddenly the man turns to him urgently. "I've been thinking of what you've been saying and I'd like to hire your services. Do you see that house across the 15th fairway? That's my house, and if I'm not mistaken my wife is having it off with the next- door neighbour."

"Let me have a look," says the hit man and he gets out the rifle, adjusts the telescopic sight and aims at the bedroom window.

"Does the man have red hair and a moustache?"

"Yes, yes, that's him," he says excitedly. "Shoot them both. Take away my wife's good looks – the cause of all my misery, and get him right in the balls – the bastard."

"Hold on a minute," says the hit man, "I think I'm going to be able to save you a bullet."

★ ★ ★

Guns don't kill people; it's husbands that come home early.

★ ★ ★

Overheard on the top deck of a bus:
"I hear your old man's in hospital, Flo. I hope it's nothing too serious."
"Just his knee. I found a blonde sitting on it."

★ ★ ★

Did you hear about the unfaithful film star who, when a flash of lightning lit up his bedroom, jumped out of bed shouting, "I'll pay for the negatives!"?

★ ★ ★

"Mum, Dad, I have something to tell you. I'm getting married to Julie from the post office – she's agreed to be my wife."

"That's wonderful news," says Mum.

"Er... yes ..." says Dad, a little hesitantly.

Later, when they are on their own, Dad confesses to his son that during his marriage he did have one teeny weeny extra marital affair and that Julie is in fact his half-sister. The boy is devastated. He breaks off the engagement but it takes over two years before he can ever look at another girl. Then one day, he comes home again.

"Mum, Dad, I've asked Tracy to marry me and she's accepted."

Mum's delighted, she's been so worried about her poor boy, but once again Dad doesn't say much until later.

"I'm sorry son, I did have one other fling and I'm afraid Tracy is also your half-sister."

The boy collapses in despair, but then a fierce anger takes over and he decides to tell his Mum all the dreadful details.

"Don't you worry about your father," she says. "Go ahead and marry Tracy. What he doesn't know is that he's not really your dad."

★ ★ ★

An angry wife went round to the house of her husband's lover and confronted her with the evidence of their liaison.

"Look at these photographs," she said, "taken by a private detective over the past month. This is you and my husband swimming naked in the pool; here's one of you and my husband canoodling in the woods; and here's one of you both stark naked on the bed upstairs. What have you got to say?"

"Mmm..." pondered the lover. "I think I'll take one of those and half a dozen of that last picture."

★ ★ ★

Waking up half-asleep because he needed a pee, a man saw three pairs of feet sticking out of the bottom of the bed. He dug his wife in the ribs, saying, "Hey, Winnie, there's three pairs of feet at the bottom of our bed."

"Don't be silly," she said, "you're dreaming. Go and count them."

"Sorry love, there are only two, and don't my nails need cutting!"

★ ★ ★

A couple has a male friend who's visiting from out of town, when an unexpected blizzard blows in and keeps him from travelling. Since the couple has no guest room, he states his intention to find a nearby hotel, and be on his way in the morning.

"Nonsense," says the wife. "Our bed is big enough for all three of us, and we're all friends here." The husband concurs, and before long they're settled in: husband in the middle, wife on his left, friend on his right.

After a while, the husband begins snoring, and the wife sneaks over to the friend's side of the bed, and invites him to have sex with her. Naturally, he'd like to, but he's reluctant. "We're in the same bed as your husband! He'll wake up, and he'll kill me."

"Don't worry about it," she says, "he's such a sound sleeper, he'll never notice. If you don't believe me, just yank a hair off his asshole. He won't even wake up."

So the friend yanks a hair off the husband's anus, and sure enough, she's right.

Her husband sleeps right through having a hair yanked out of his ass.

So, she and the friend have sex, and then she goes back to her side of the bed.

After about twenty minutes, though, she's back on his side of the bed, asking him to do it again. The same argument follows, another hair is yanked from the husband's asshole, and again they have sex. This keeps up for about half the night, until after about the sixth time, when the wife goes back to her side.

Then the husband rolls over, and whispers to his friend, "I don't mind that you're shagging my wife, but do you really have to use my asshole as your scoreboard?"

★ ★ ★

While away at a convention, an executive happened to meet a young woman who was pretty and intelligent. When he persuaded her to disrobe in his hotel room, he found out she had a superb body as well. Unfortunately, the executive found himself unable to perform.

On his first night home, the executive walked from the shower into the bedroom to find his wife covered in a rumpled bathrobe, her hair curled, her face creamed, munching candy loudly while she pored through a movie magazine.

Then, without warning, he felt the onset of a magnificent erection.

Looking down at this, he snarled, "Why you ungrateful, mixed-up son of a bitch. Now I know why they call you a prick!"

★ ★ ★

UNIFORM

A fireman comes home from work with a new idea to spice up his sex life. He tells his wife, "Tonight when we go to bed I'll shout 'First Bell' and you take all your clothes off. Then I'll shout 'Second Bell' and you jump into bed, and then on the shout of 'Third Bell' we'll make love all night."

So the following day, the fireman comes home from work, shouts 'First Bell' and she strips off, 'Second Bell' into bed, 'Third Bell' and away they go. But five minutes later, the wife calls out, "Fourth Bell."

"What's that mean?" asks her puzzled husband.

She replies, "It means more hose; you haven't got to the fire yet."

★ ★ ★

Passengers are boarding the plane for Los Angeles and sitting in first class is a blonde girl.

"I'm sorry, Miss," says the air hostess, "but your seat is at the back of the plane. This area is for people with first class tickets only."

But the blonde refuses to move. "I'm young, I'm beautiful – I deserve to be in first class."

The air hostess goes and gets the co-pilot, who also asks her to move, but again she replies, "I'm young, I'm beautiful – I deserve to be in first class."

The plane is filling up fast and it's crucial the crew get the problem sorted out, so they call for the pilot and tell him the situation. He immediately goes up to the girl, whispers something in her ear and she leaves the first class area straight away.

"What did you say to her?" asks the co-pilot.

"I simply told her the front half of the plane wasn't going as far as Los Angeles."

★ ★ ★

A lady got stopped for speeding for the umpteenth time, and knew that if she was given another ticket she would be banned from driving. Thinking quickly of something to say to the policeman when he came up to the car, she joked, "Have you come to ask me to the Policeman's

Ball?"

Without thinking, he said, "Policemen don't have balls."

There was an embarrassed silence, and he walked away.

★ ★ ★

The policeman came across a car that had wrapped itself around a tree. Sitting in the front seat was a young man, still in his seat belt, but screaming with agony.

"Now, now, sir, help is on its way. It's a good thing you had your seat belt on, otherwise you might have gone straight through the window like your girlfriend."

"Aaargh!" came the reply. "Have you seen what's in her hand?"

★ ★ ★

Walking along the street, a policeman came across a young man kicking an older man and he stepped in to break it up.

"It's OK, Officer, I asked him to do it," said the older man. "Many years ago, I was in the flat of this beautiful young girl when she suddenly removed her dress saying she was feeling hot. So I turned the fire off. Then she stripped off completely, so I thought I'd better leave. As I walked out of the door, she said that one day I'd remember this and then ask the first person I saw to kick me. Well I've just realised what she meant."

"Keep kicking," said the policeman.

★ ★ ★

An old army colonel was awaiting news of the imminent arrival of his son at the exclusive Harley Street Clinic.

"How do you know it will be a son?" asked the doctor.

"Of course it will be. Family tradition, man." And in fact, it was a son. On hearing the news, the colonel asked for him to be circumcised.

"Family tradition," he said.

Later, the doctor called to say the baby was ailing.

"Give it some brandy. Don't argue, just do it."

Some time later, the doctor rang again to say the baby was no better. "I'm coming over," said the colonel. "Meanwhile, put him on the breast."

By the time the colonel arrived, the baby was doing well.

"Excellent!" he chortled. "You see, this is a real father's son. Mouth full of tit, belly full of brandy, and a sore cock."

★ ★ ★

A colonel was posted to the Far East and after three months, his wife came to join him. On the first morning she decided to stay in bed, still feeling tired from the flight, but at ten o'clock the colonel's manservant appeared unannounced, and threw back the bedclothes, saying, "Come on, Miss, time's up, go get yourself some breakfast and then be on your way."

★ ★ ★

A unit of soldiers returned to base after spending four months in the war zone. The base also had a squad of women soldiers and the colonel in charge of the men took the leader of the women aside and warned her to keep her ladies under lock and key, as his men hadn't seen a woman for months. The women replied, "It's all right, there'll be no trouble," and, tapping her head, she continued, "My girls have it up here."

The colonel retorted, "I don't care where they have it. If my men start looking, they'll find it."

★ ★ ★

A new sergeant major had just arrived at the foreign legion outpost and decided to tour the base immediately. In one small shed he found a camel and, when asked why it was there, the private replied hesitantly, "It's for the men to use if their carnal desires get the better of them, sir."

The sergeant major was outraged.

"Get rid of it immediately, from now on, nothing like that goes on here."

However, six months later and painfully missing the fairer sex, the sergeant major asked his private if the camel had indeed gone.

"Well, no sir, I'm sorry," came the reply.

"Then let me go and have another look." The sergeant major went back to the shed, dropped his trousers, stood on a bucket and gave the camel a right seeing-to.

Afterwards he said to the private, panting, "Is that how the men do it?" Embarrassed, he replied, "Well, no, sir, actually the men ride the camel to the nearest brothel."

★ ★ ★

An army unit was crossing the desert when one of the camels stopped and refused to move, so it and its rider were left behind. They were stuck there for four hours and nothing the soldier did would move him.

Eventually along came an ATS driver, who listened to the problem and said, "Don't worry, leave it to me."

She put her hand beneath the camel's belly and within seconds he jumped up and disappeared at a rate of knots.

"That's amazing, Miss. What did you do?"

"I just tickled its balls."

"Gracious, then you'd better tickle mine, I've got to catch the bugger."

★ ★ ★

Two old colonels were talking over their port about one of their colleagues.

"I say, did you know old Smithers has started living in sin with a monkey?"

"By Jove!" replied the other. "Is it a male or female monkey?"

"Now steady on, a female monkey of course, there's nothing unnatural about Smithers."

★ ★ ★

Two retired colonels were bemoaning the younger generation over drinks at their gentlemen's club.

"You'll never believe this," said the first colonel. "When I told my granddaughter that her great-grandfather was killed at Waterloo, she wanted to know on what platform it happened!"

"Oh, how ridiculous," replied the second colonel. "As if it mattered what platform he was on."

★ ★ ★

A new sergeant major arrived at the base and the retiring sergeant major, who had one more week to go, said to him, "If you've any problems just come and see me."

The next morning, a man was brought to him on a charge of homosexuality.

The new sergeant major, not sure what to do, popped in to see the old sergeant major and asked, "Sir, what do you give for cock-sucking?"

"Oh, £2 or £2.50," he replied.

★ ★ ★

The conductor told a man off for smoking on the Tube.

"Can't you see that No Smoking sign on the wall?" he said.

"Yes, I can," he replied. "But it's not easy keeping all your rules. That one over there says 'Wear a WonderBra!' "

★ ★ ★

A young man sits down next to a nun in the park and they strike up a conversation. Some time passes, and the young man confesses to the nun that her habit really turns him on and that he would dearly like to make love to her.

"Are you a Catholic?" she asks.

"Yes," he replies.

"OK, let's go behind those bushes."

They do as she suggests and the nun satisfies him with a blow job. Afterwards, feeling very guilty, the man tells the nun that in fact he isn't a Catholic.

She replies, "Well, I have something to tell you as well. My name is Bob and I'm on my way to a fancy dress party."

★ ★ ★

A very drunk man walked into the police station complaining that someone had stolen his horse.

Sighing wearily, the officer on duty asked, "And what colour was the horse, sir?"

"Er... don't know," he replied, "but it was female."

The officer repeated, "It was female. And how do you know that, sir?"

"Well, I was riding along the pavement when I heard this voice say 'Look at that cunt on the horse.'"

★ ★ ★

The plane is about to taxi down the runway when passengers see the pilot and co-pilot walking up towards the cockpit. Both look as if they are virtually blind, carrying white sticks and bumping into everyone.

At first, the full plane of passengers cannot believe what they have just seen, but as the plane taxis to the end of the runway and turns to pick up speed, a slight panic begins. By the time it's hurtling down the runway, there is ever increasing panic and as the plane lifts into the air an earth shattering scream goes up from the cabins. This sudden change in pitch is followed by the plane rising into the sky.

"Ah, thank goodness," says the pilot to his colleague. "Safe again. You know, one day the passengers aren't going to scream and then we're really done for."

★ ★ ★

The man staggered along the street and opened the door of his car just as the police were passing.

"One moment, sir," said the policeman. "I hope you weren't thinking of driving?"

"I sure am," he slurred. "I'm in no condition to walk."

★ ★ ★

In a distant outpost of the Foreign Legion, one of the more recent recruits confides to his sergeant that the lack of female company is driving him round the twist.

"No need to let that worry you, son. Here, let me show you. See that barrel over there, the one with the hole in the side? You'll find that will help relieve the pressure. You're free to use it on Tuesday through to Sunday."

"That's great, thanks. But er... What's wrong with Monday?"

"Well, you have to be fair; if you're using it six days a week, then on Monday, it's your turn inside the barrel."

★ ★ ★

In one of the remotest parts of Outer Mongolia, high up in the mountains, is an outpost of an old regiment. The men have been on duty for six months without a break and only themselves for company. A new recruit joins them and he's only been there for a few weeks when a sudden roar goes up from the look-out.

"Hurry, they're coming!" he shouts.

A might roar goes up and all the troops desert their posts and charge out of the gates. The newcomer turns to his mate and says, "What's going on? It's only a herd of goats. What's all the fuss about?"

"If you'd been out here for six months without a break, and without female company, you'd know alright," replies his mate.

"But why all the rush? There seems to be plenty to go around."

"Oh yes, but no one wants to get lumbered with an ugly one!"

★ ★ ★

A motorist is stopped for going through a red light and is asked to take a breathaliser test.

"I can't blow," says the man. "I suffer from asthma," and he shows the policeman his asthmatic's card.

"OK, then we'll have to take you down to the station for a blood test."

"I can't. I'm a haemophiliac," and he produces a doctor's card.

"In that case, it'll have to be a urine test."

Once again, the man produces a card from his wallet. This time, it's a Manchester City Supporters Club membership card and as he shows it to the policeman he says, "Please don't take the piss."

★ ★ ★

A man driving along in a car hits the kerb and the roundabout.
"You're drunk," says the policeman.
"Oh thank you very much, I thought the steering had gone," he replies.

★ ★ ★

"Excuse me, Sir, where do you think you're going at this time of night?" said the policeman to the staggering drunk.
"I'm going to a lecture."
"Now? Hardly. Who's giving a lecture at this time of night?"
"My wife."

★ ★ ★

The young leader could hardly believe his eyes when he saw ten of his best fighters running away down the street being chased by a copper wielding a baton.
"What the fuck's going on?" he said. "There's only one of them."
"We know," they yelled, "but we don't know which one of us he's after!"

★ ★ ★

The situation looked bad. The platoon had suffered many fatalities and the men were very dispirited. The commanding officer felt it was time to give them a pep talk.
"Right, chaps, listen to me. You've done a sterling job, couldn't have asked for better but we have been outnumbered. But we'll fight on, for King and country, until the very last bullet has been fired. When that happens, you have my permission to make a run for it. Oh, by the way, I've got a bad knee, so I'd better set off now."

★ ★ ★

A drunk man was walking down the street, one foot on the pavement and one in the gutter, when he was stopped by a policeman.

"I'm going to have to take you in for being drunk," he said.

"Are you sure I'm drunk?"

"Oh yes, completely, you've one foot on the pavement and one in the gutter."

"Oh, thank goodness for that. I thought I'd lost part of my leg."

★ ★ ★

An overbearing, pompous Sergeant Major spends the night with a German prostitute and the next morning he turns arrogantly to the girl and says, "My dear, after last night, you'll have a baby in nine months' time and you can call it Toby, after me."

She replies, "In two days' time, you'll have a rash and you can call it German measles."

★ ★ ★

A man walked into a police station to report that his wife was missing.

"She went out about four hours ago and she hasn't been back to cook my dinner, so I know there must be something wrong."

"OK, sir, let's not panic. I'll just take down some details. Can you describe your wife or what she was wearing when she left the house?"

"No, but I did see her walking down the road with our next-door neighbour, and she's not back either."

"I don't suppose you can give us a description of her?"

"Oh yes, she's about 5'6", black shoulder-length curly hair, 36–24–36, wearing a red miniskirt and a red and white jacket."

★ ★ ★

This particular evening, the policeman was determined to crack down on drunk and disorderly drivers. He parked near one of the toughest, noisiest and rowdiest bars in town, sat back and waited. A little later, a man staggered out of the bar, tripped over and then attempted to open three cars before he eventually found his own. The man got in and immediately fell asleep. Feeling very pleased with himself, the officer waited all evening until everyone left the bar, got into their cars and drove away. Finally, the sleeper woke up, started the engine and began to pull away.

"Got you," said the police officer to himself and he pulled the driver over and administered a breathaliser test. He was astonished to find the man passed with a zero blood alcohol reading.

"But how can that be?" he said.

"Well, officer," said the man, "tonight I'm the designated decoy."

★ ★ ★

A fireman looked out of the firehouse window and noticed a little boy playing on the pavement.

He had small ladders hung on the side of his little red wagon, and a garden hose coiled up in it. He was wearing a fireman's hat. He had the wagon tied to his dog, so that the dog could pull the wagon.

The fireman thought this was really cute, so he went out and told the little boy what a great-looking fire engine he had. As he did, he noticed that the dog was tied to the wagon by his testicles.

The fireman said, "Son, I don't want to tell you how to run your fire company or anything, but I think if you tied that rope around the dog's neck you would go faster."

"Maybe so," said the little boy, "but then I'd lose my siren!"

★ ★ ★

A retired general ran into his former orderly, also retired, in a Manhattan bar, and spent the rest of the evening persuading him to come work for him as his valet. "Your duties will be exactly the same as they were in the army," the general said. "Nothing to it – you'll catch on again in no time."

Next morning, promptly at eight o'clock, the ex-orderly entered the general's bedroom, pulled open the drapes, gave the general a gentle shake, strode around the other side of the bed, spanked his employer's wife on her bottom and said, "OK, sweetheart, it's back to the village for you."

★ ★ ★

VANITY

A woman has no luck finding a husband, so she decides to put an ad in the local newspaper, under 'Personal'.

'Wanted a man with view to marriage, must be loyal, rich and a good lover.'

Some days go by and then one morning there's a ring on the doorbell. To her amazement, when she opens the door there's a man in a wheelchair. He has no arms or legs.

"I've come about the ad in the paper," he says.

"Oh, well er… are you loyal?"

"Sure am. I was in the army, stationed in Northern Ireland when we came under fire. I ran back to rescue one of my men when there was a loud explosion and I ended up like this."

"Well, are you rich?"

"You bet. I took over the family business and have now built it into an international concern."

"But are you a good lover?" she demanded.

"How do you think I rang the doorbell?"

★ ★ ★

After leading him on for a while, the girlfriend suddenly moves away, telling him, "If you want to go all the way with me, you'll have to have a sports car and a ten-inch dick."

"OK, but I'll be back," he tells her.

And indeed he arrives on her doorstep the following week in a gleaming white sports car. She is very impressed.

"And that's not all," he says "As far as my dick's concerned, my doctor says he can cut it down to any size you want."

★ ★ ★

The professor of physiology turned to a young student in his class and asked her what part of the body becomes 10 times its normal size when under emotional stress. The young girl blushed profusely and said she'd rather not answer. At this point the young student next to her volunteered the answer – it was of course the pupil of the eye.

"That's right," said the professor and turning to the young girl he said, "My dear, your refusal to answer tells me three things. First you haven't studied your homework, second you have a one-track mind and, third, I'm afraid you're going to be sadly disappointed."

★ ★ ★

"Wow!" said the man looking at his naked body in the mirror. "If I was five centimetres longer I'd be a king."

"Mmm," said his wife, unimpressed. "If you were five centimetres shorter you'd be a queen."

★ ★ ★

"Darling," said the blushing bride on her honeymoon night. "What is a penis?"

Her husband, joyful that she showed such innocence, dropped his trousers to show her.

"Oh that," she said disappointed. "It's just like a prick, only smaller."

★ ★ ★

A man and his domineering wife went into the tailor's to order him some new trousers. When asked if he would like a 5in or 10in zip the man replied quickly, "20in please."

After they left the shop she turned to him scornfully and said, "You remind me of our next-door neighbour. Every morning he opens the huge double doors of his garage and wheels out his bicycle."

★ ★ ★

At the Tuesday coffee morning the ladies got into a heated argument about which of their husbands had the biggest member. The Mayor's wife said it was her husband and was so insistent that in the end she was told she had to prove it. On arriving home she told her husband, who looked aghast.

"Dorothy, you know mine is only small. What are we going to do?"

Fortunately, they had a friend whose member was enormous and they asked him if he would do them a favour.

"Don't worry, no one will know because you'll be hidden behind a screen and you'll put it through a hole."

The day came and the friend stuck his enormous member through the hole. The Mayor's wife smiled smugly, sure she had won. However, suddenly a woman's voice was heard to say, "Hold on, that's not the Mayor's, that's the vicar's. I recognize the wart on the end."

★ ★ ★

Man boasting to his mate:
"What has 250 teeth and guards a monster?
My trouser flies."

★ ★ ★

A tactful girl is one who makes a slow man think he's a wolf.

★ ★ ★

A very pompous self-made man decided to pay for his son to go to private school and the whole family went up to visit the headmaster.

"I'm Sir Dunwell Bates, this is my wife Lady Bates, my daughter Miss Bates and my son Master Bates."

"Don't worry," replied the headmaster. "We'll soon put that right."

★ ★ ★

Did you hear about the man who had an audition with the Chippendales?
He was put on their short list.

★ ★ ★

Have you heard of John Little, the nudist who stuck a magnifying glass to his fig leaf and reflected great credit upon himself?

★ ★ ★

Always marry a girl with small hands – it makes your dick look bigger.

★ ★ ★

A rather arrogant social climber liked to impress her friends and relations by putting on sumptuous dinner parties. One night, however, as they were all sitting around the table her stomach took a turn for the worse, and she was unable to contain a fart. Without turning a hair, she immediately said, "Jeeves, please stop that!" But Jeeves replied immediately, "Of course, madam, which way did it go?"

★ ★ ★

A body builder went down to the local antique shop to find a mirror to hang on the back of the bathroom door, so that in the mornings after a shower he could admire his fine physique.
"There are plenty of mirrors to choose from," said the shop owner, "but don't have that one – it's evil."
Well, nothing would satisfy him until he had bought the evil mirror which he took home and hung behind the door. Next morning he looked at himself and realized he wasn't as well endowed as he would like. Knowing the mirror had magic powers, he said, "Mirror, mirror, on the wall, make my tool touch the floor." And his legs fell off.

★ ★ ★

A girl and boy out on only their second date had never done anything more than kiss and cuddle all night because the boy was embarrassed by the size of his penis.
However, this night he decided to take the bull by the horns and placed it in her hands.
"No, thanks," she said. "I don't smoke."

★ ★ ★

Out on their first date, an arrogant man took the girl back to his flat for coffee.
" don't talk much," she said.

At that he dropped his trousers and proudly said, "This does all my talking for me."

"Well, that doesn't have much to say either," she retorted.

★ ★ ★

A man dyes his hair jet black because it had been going grey and is so pleased with the results that, when he's buying a paper in the newsagent's, asks the shopkeeper how old he thinks he is.

"Oh, about 32," he says.

"No, I'm 40," laughs the man, very pleased.

Then he goes into the chip shop to buy some fish and asks the woman behind the counter how old she thinks he is.

"Oh, about 34."

"No, I'm 40," comes the smug reply.

Later, he sees an old woman at the bus stop.

"How old do you think I am?" he says.

"Well," says the old woman. "I'll have to feel your willy before I can tell you."

"What!" gasps the man.

"That's the only way I can tell," she says.

"OK then." He unzips his flies and she puts her hand in.

"Ooohooh," she says. "You're 40."

"How can you tell?" he says.

"Ah, I was standing behind you in the chip shop."

★ ★ ★

A vain man who thought he had a body "to die for" gave his girlfriend a photograph of himself, posing in the nude.

"What are you going to do with that?" he boasted.

"Mmm," she replied. "I think I'll get it enlarged."

★ ★ ★

Did you hear about the vain man who was trying to impress his new girlfriend? When he stood in front of the mirror admiring himself, he

said, "I had to fight hard to get this body."
"Really," she replied. "I'm sorry you lost."

★ ★ ★

Or how about the chap who read a sign saying, "Wet floor" – so he did.

★ ★ ★

The vain young man lay back contentedly on the bed after making love to his new girlfriend. "How was it for you?" he asked.
"Oh, pretty painless," she replied. "I never felt a thing."

★ ★ ★

Some of the guys out west are so mighty they can run in the three-legged race without a partner.

★ ★ ★

"What are you doing?" he asked excitedly as she put her hand down his trousers.
"Oh nothing," she said. "I thought it might have been the start of something big."

★ ★ ★

Two young men go on holiday together to Spain and spend all day on the beach and go clubbing at night. By the time they leave the beach each day, Bob has usually made a date with one of the many pretty girls round about, but Des never has any luck.
"What am I going to do. Why can't I score?" he asks Bob.
His mate looks at him critically – he is rather a poor example of manhood – and says, "Tomorrow, when you come to the beach, stick an orange down your swimming trunks."
The following day, Bob is late in joining Des and it's not until lunchtime that they meet up.
"Hi, Des, how's it going?"

"Still not pulled anyone," he replies dejectedly.

Bob takes another good look at him and whispers, "Next time, Des, put the orange down the front of your trunks."

★ ★ ★

As he stood at the mirror yet again, admiring his good looks and muscular body, he turned to his long-suffering wife and said, "There can't be that many men who are so well endowed."

"One less than you think," came the mumbled reply.

★ ★ ★

It was the day of the works outing and the boss had arranged for a bus to pick up the employees and their spouses and take them to Blackpool for the day. And what a day they had. The weather was good, the food was great and the booze flowed endlessly. By the time they got back in the bus to go home there was a great deal of merriment. However, an hour into the journey and most of the men needed a pee – they'd swilled down so much beer it was inevitable.

"You'll have to stop the bus, we're busting back here!" shouted a voice.

"There aren't any services for miles!" he shouted back. "But if it's a real emergency, I'll stop in the next lay-by."

Soon, twenty desperate and drunk men staggered off the bus and were so relieved to pee they didn't care who was watching. In bed that night, Doreen turned to Bill and said, "Men! You're disgusting, exposing yourself to all us women on the bus... still," she smiled, hugging him, "ours was grand."

★ ★ ★

Three 'social climber' women met up at a school reunion twenty years after they had last seen each other, and the conversation quickly turned to husbands.

"My husband is a regional sales director, responsible for a huge area in the Midlands," said the first.

"Well, mine is a top scientist working in the laboratories of a large international company," said the next without a second's hesitation.

"My husband works on the dustcarts, but he has such a big tool. Four pigeons can stand on it at one go."

As the evening progressed and the drinks had a relaxing effect upon the women, they all confessed to having exaggerated a bit.

"My husband's really only a salesman," said the first.

"Well, my husband's not quite a scientist, he's a lab technician," said the second.

"I boasted a little too," admitted the third. "Only three pigeons can stand on my husband's dick at the same time... mind, a fourth could get on if it stood on one leg."

★ ★ ★

An extraordinarily handsome man decided he had the God-given responsibility to marry the perfect woman so they could produce children beyond comparison. With that as his mission he began searching for the perfect woman. After a diligent, but fruitless, search up and down the east coast, he started to head west.

Shortly thereafter he met a farmer who had three stunning, gorgeous daughters that positively took his breath away. So he explained his mission to the farmer, asking for permission to marry one of them.

The farmer simply replied, "They're all looking to get married, so you came to the right place. Look them over and select the one you want."

The man dated the first daughter. The next day the farmer asked for the man's opinion.

"Well," said the man, "she's just a weeeee bit, not that you could hardly tell, but pigeon-toed."

The farmer nodded and suggested the man date one of the other girls. So the man went out with the second daughter. The next day, the farmer again asked how things went.

"Well," the man replied, "she's just a weeeee bit, not that you can hardly tell, cross-eyed."

The farmer nodded and suggested he date the third girl to see if things might be better. So he did. The next morning the man rushed in exclaiming, "She's perfect, just perfect! She's the one I want to marry!" So they were wed right away.

Months later the baby was born. When the man visited nursery he was horrified: the baby was the ugliest, most pathetic human specimen you can imagine.

He rushed to his father-in-law asking how such a thing could happen considering the parents.

"Well," explained the farmer, "she was just a weeeee bit, not that you could hardly tell, pregnant when you met her."

★ ★ ★

Monica Lewinsky was walking on the beach when she found a lantern washed up on the shore. She started to rub it and out popped a genie. "Oh goodie, now I will get three wishes!" she exclaimed.

"No," said the genie. "You have been very bad this year, and because of this, I can only give you one wish."

"Let's see," says Monica. "I don't need fame, because I have plenty of that due to all of the media coverage.

"And I don't need money, because after I write my book and do all my interviews, I'll have all the money I could ever want. I would like to get rid of these love handles, though.

"Yes, that's it, for my one wish, I would like my love handles removed." Poof!!!!

And just like that… her ears were gone.

★ ★ ★

I love looking in the mirror admiring my looks, do you think that's vanity?

No, just a vivid imagination

★ ★ ★

Do you notice how my voice fills the hall?

Yes, and did you notice how many people left to make way for it?

★ ★ ★

★ VANITY ★

I can play piano by ear.
And I can fiddle with my toes.

★ ★ ★

When I was a sailor I sailed across the Atlantic both ways without even
taking a bath.
I always said you were a dirty double-crosser.

★ ★ ★

How do you find my breath?
Offensive, it's keeping you alive.

★ ★ ★

He's good at everything he does.
And as far as I can see he usually does nothing.

★ ★ ★

Boys fall in love with me at first sight.
Bet they change their minds when they look again, though.

★ ★ ★

We should try and fight air pollution.
You could start by stopping breathing.

★ ★ ★

Do you find me entertaining?
I'd say you were too dim to entertain a thought.

★ ★ ★

Shall I put the TV on?
Well, it would certainly improve the view in here.

★ ★ ★

WORKING DAY

An unemployed man got a new job at the zoo. He had to dress up in a gorilla's skin and pretend to be a gorilla so the crowds would keep rolling in to the zoo.

On his first day in the job, the man puts on the skin and goes into the cage. The people all cheer to see him. He starts really putting on a show, jumping around, beating his chest and roaring.

During one acrobatic attempt, though, he loses his balance and crashes through some safety netting, landing square in the middle of the lion cage! As he lies there stunned, the lion roars. The man's terrified and starts screaming, "Help, Help!"

The lion races over to him, places his paws on his chest and hisses, "Shut up or we'll both lose our jobs!"

★ ★ ★

One day the zookeeper noticed that the orang-utang was reading two books – the Bible and Darwin's *Origin of Species*. In surprise he asked the ape, "Why are you reading both those books?"

"Well," said the orang-utang. "I just wanted to know if I was my brother's keeper or my keeper's brother."

★ ★ ★

A salesman was amazed to see a lot of very expensive cars in the hotel car park and commented on it to the hotel owner, a beautiful blonde, as he was signing in. He asked her who owned all the cars, and she replied, "Actually, they are all mine." "Gosh, you must have a very successful business to afford all those cars." "Not necessarily," she said, "I've won them all in bets I've had with the men who've stayed here. You see, I bet them that they can't do what my eight-year-old nephew can do." "Well, of course I can," he replied. "Any man could do what an eight-year-old boy can do." So the bet was agreed with the car and the hotel as the stake. First the blonde called the boy over, took out one of her ample breasts and asked him to kiss it. The boy did as she asked and then the amazed man did

659

the same. Then she dropped her panties and asked the boy to kiss her down below. He did and the man followed. At this point the man thought he had won the bet and gleefully asked for the key to the motel. "Oh no, wait a minute," she said, and she turned to her nephew. "Just one more thing, bend your willy in half and ask the gentleman for his car keys."

★ ★ ★

A plumber was giving advice to his apprentice.

"Tact is very important in this job. For instance, when I walked into a bathroom to mend a pipe there was a naked woman, so I quickly said, 'Excuse me, sir,' and came out. Now that's tact."

Later on the two were called out to a house on an emergency and the plumber asked his apprentice to check the water tank upstairs. A few minutes later he came back down with a black eye.

"What happened?" asked the plumber.

"It's all your fault and your silly tact!" said the boy.

"I walked into one of the bedrooms and saw a couple stark naked on the bed and I said, 'Excuse me, gentlemen'!"

★ ★ ★

Bill, the local barber, had a secret remedy to restore hair and on the odd occasion he would pass it on to his very special customers.

One such customer came in and asked Bill to give him the remedy for £1,000. After some thought Bill agreed and told him all he needed do to restore hair to his bald patch was apply some female secretions.

"But how do I know it works?" replied the customer. "You've still got a bald patch on your head."

"Maybe," said Bill. "But have you ever seen a finer moustache?"

★ ★ ★

The office boy was obsessed with the secretary's breasts; it was all he could think about at work, so eventually he plucked up his courage to ask her if she would let him fondle them for 10 minutes for £250. The secretary agreed and they disappeared into the backroom where he enjoyed an orgy of fondling her breasts and sucking her tits, all the time murmuring to himself, "I can't, I can't, I just can't fathom it." At last the girl turned to him and said, "What can't you fathom?" "I just can't fathom out how I'm going to pay you."

★ ★ ★

Have you heard about the local flasher who was going to retire? He decided to stick it out for another year.

★ ★ ★

Three men were working on a building site when one fell off the scaffolding into the cement mixer. The police were immediately called and the mixer was emptied, revealing bits of bone, flesh and blood. "Do you know who he was?" asked the police. "Sure, it was Jack." "Well, it's going to be very difficult to make a formal identification. Did he have any distinguishing marks?" One of the men thought for a moment and then said, "Yeah, he did. He had two rectums." The police looked puzzled at this so the man explained. "Last time we went down the pub with him I heard the landlord say – Jack's just come in with the two arseholes."

★ ★ ★

"Can you paint me in the nude?" said a beautiful girl to the artist. "Certainly," he replied, "but I'll have to keep my socks on. I must have somewhere for the brushes."

★ ★ ★

A scientist invented a new piece of confectionery and asked for volunteers to taste it. They were amazed – each side tasted different: chocolate, liquorice, nuts, spearmint and fruity boiled sweets.

Then the voice of a leering old man at the back shouted out, "You should make one that tastes of pussy."
"Well, try this," replied the scientist.
"Ugh, it tastes of crap."
"Sorry, try the other side."

★ ★ ★

I have a boss at work who's really strict on punctuality. One day his assistant came in – broken nose, blood streaming down his face and his arm in a sling. His boss said, "Hey, where do you think you've been? You're an hour late." "I fell down the stairs," he replied. "What, and it took you a whole hour!"

★ ★ ★

An artist had his wicked way with a beautiful young model in his studio. He said, "You're the first model I've ever made love to."
"Oh yeah," she replied scornfully. "Who were your other models?"
"Well," he said, "there was a bowl of fruit, a brace of ducks and the River Thames."

★ ★ ★

Did you hear about the nuclear scientist who was always so preoccupied with formulating yet more amazing experiments that one day he unbuttoned his jacket, took out his tie and pissed himself.

★ ★ ★

An old woman was handling all the meat on the butcher's slab but not buying anything. Eventually the butcher lost his patience with her and said, "Listen, madam, it's not like your Jack; it doesn't get bigger the longer you handle it."

★ ★ ★

What is professional courtesy? It's when a shark comes towards a solicitor swimming in the water and then veers away.

★ ★ ★

This man was married to the prettiest girl in the office and was the envy of his workmates. One man in particular said to him, "I'll give you £250 to smack your wife's pretty bottom."

The husband was furious, but when he told his wife she said, "Come on! We've got lots of bills, what's a few smacks on the bottom?"

Next day in their bedroom the wife removed her knickers and bent over... the workmate gently stroked her and said, "What curves, what dimples," eventually producing a camera and taking a photo. The husband was besides himself with rage. "Get on with it or the deal's off."

"Oh no," said the workmate, "I could never smack such a beautiful bottom, besides it would cost me £250 if I did."

★ ★ ★

The local bank was held up by masked gunmen, and customers and staff were ordered to lie face down on the floor. Everyone did as they were told except one young girl who lay down on her back.

"Don't be silly, lay down the other way, this is a bank robbery not the office party," whispered her friend.

★ ★ ★

The woman was having her house painted and each night when her husband came home from work she would show him how much had been done. On this particular night he accidentally put his hand on the banister and left an ugly mark. So the next morning she said to the decorator, "Would you mind coming upstairs a minute so that I can show you where my husband put his hand?"

He replied, "If it's all the same to you madam, a cup of tea will do."

★ ★ ★

A very enterprising young man was determined to be the best salesman for the Higgins Dental Mouthwash Company. And indeed after one month his sales figures had soared off the top of the graph. "How did you manage it?" asked one of his colleagues.

"Oh, it was quite simple. I set up a stall at the local bus station, selling a new special pate. I ask them to try it and afterwards when they ask me for the ingredients I tell them it's pork, spices and seagull shit. That's when they try to spit it out and that's when I ask them if they'd like some antiseptic mouthwash."

★ ★ ★

The sleazy young salesman said to his customer, a voluptuous blonde, "If you are keen to have the car we could arrange very easy credit terms with no down payment."
"How do you mean?" she asked.
"Nothing down but your knickers."

★ ★ ★

The phone rings and it's a man asking to speak to Bob Wankbreak.
"No, I don't think we've got anyone here by that name, just a mo... I'll ask. Is there a Wankbreak here?"
"You gotta be joking," came the reply. "We haven't even got time for a tea break!"

★ ★ ★

Driving through a remote part of the country on a very hot day, an unscrupulous salesman came across a hiker who had collapsed in the heat.
"Water, please, water," he croaked.
"Now, sir, this is your lucky day. Here in my case I have a never-before-seen range of ties and you can have one at a 25% discount."
"Water, please, water," croaked the man again.
"Now, come on, sir, you'll never get an offer like this again. For as little as £10 you can have a beautiful silk tie."
"Water, please, water."

After a few more minutes, the salesman realized he wasn't going to get a sale. "OK, if it's water you want, the local golf club is just round the next bend. They'll be able to help you."

The hiker made one last effort to crawl round the corner and up the drive to the front door where he was met once again by the salesman.

"Water, please, water," begged the hiker.

"Of course, sir, we have all types of water, but you can't come in without a tie on."

★ ★ ★

The salesman's eyes lit up when he saw the young man walk into the showroom looking for a new car. But after 30 minutes, it was obvious the sale wasn't going to be as easy as he hoped.

The young man was insistent on buying a four-door saloon, whereas the salesman was trying to persuade him to purchase the more expensive two-door coupe. Suddenly, he had an idea.

"Sir, how many tits does a cow have?"

"Four," answered the puzzled man.

"And how many tits does Madonna have?"

"Two".

"Now, sir, which gives the better ride?"

★ ★ ★

A Japanese man went for a job on a building site.

"What are you good at?" he was asked.

"I'm no good at bricklaying, carpentry or painting. I worked in a car factory," he said.

"OK, I'll put you in charge of supplies over there in the shed."

Time went by and two days later there was still no sign at all of the Japanese man.

"Where the hell's he got to?" asked the boss.

As they started to walk towards the shed, out popped the man shouting, 'Surplies, surplies!"

★ ★ ★

A window cleaner was doing the upstairs windows of a semi-detached when he noticed a beautiful girl lying seductively on the bed, wearing only a sheer nightie.

"Hello," he said. "You're the second pregnant girl I've met this morning."

"But I'm not pregnant," she said.

"I haven't cleaned all the windows yet."

★ ★ ★

One afternoon, a casting director was auditioning an extra for a forthcoming commercial. On meeting, the director looked at him closely and said, "I'm sure we've met before. I never forget a face. You weren't at the last Isle of Wight Festival wearing a long sheepskin coat and dark glasses?"

"No," replied the man.

But the director persisted. "You weren't celebrating New Year's Eve in Trafalgar Square, five years ago, and dived into the fountain?"

"No," replied the man.

"Well, I can't understand it," said the director, "faces are my business. I always remember them."

A moment of silence went by when suddenly the director jumped up shouting, "You weren't playing the fruit machine in the Kings Arms twenty minutes ago?"

"Yes, I was," he replied.

"There, I told you, I never forget a face."

★ ★ ★

Three surgeons were relaxing in the bar after a conference and the first one said, "I had a pretty easy time last week. I had to operate on a computer analyst and when I opened him up, all the parts were filed and labelled and the retrieval system was very competent."

"Well, my week was even easier," said the second surgeon. "I had to operate on an electronics expert, all the different systems were colour-coded so you could see what was wrong immediately."

"Yes, that sounds good," said the third surgeon. "But I had the easiest job of all. I had to operate on an estate agent. They've only got two moving parts – the mouth and the arsehole – and they're both used for the same thing."

★ ★ ★

"Excuse me, sir, may I have tomorrow afternoon off. The wife wants me to go shopping with her."
"Certainly not."
"Thank you, sir, I knew you'd understand."

★ ★ ★

Two men were up a pylon repairing damage caused by bad weather. One was at the top and the other, a dimwitted sort of fellow, was halfway down.
"Pass me up the spanner!" shouted the man at the top.
"No thanks, I've had my dinner."
"I said pass me a spanner."
"What did you say, a hammer?"
"No, you prat, I said a spanner."
The fella halfway down finally got the message and threw up a spanner. Unfortunately, it hit the other man on the head, knocked him off his perch and he fell to the ground, dead on impact. A few days later, an inquest was held and the coroner asked for any information that might throw some light on the accident.
His mate got up and said, "I think it had something to do with sex, Your Honourship."
"Sex? What do you mean?"
"Well, as he was passing me I heard him shout, 'Cunt!'"

★ ★ ★

"Hey, Jack, quick, come over here mate," shouted a man on the scaffolding of a new building.
Jack put down his trowel, moved the pile of bricks and headed off

towards the scaffolding. Unfortunately, on the way he slipped and fell down one of the trenches spraining his ankle, and then in struggling to get out he pulled the cement mixer over on top of him. Feeling quite badly battered and bruised, and hobbling painfully, he eventually got to the scaffolding. Looking up, he shouted, "Yes, Reg, what is it?"
"I just wanted to tell you I could see your house from here!"

★ ★ ★

An artist had been working on a nude portrait for a long time. Every day, he was up early and worked late – bringing perfection with every stroke of his paint brush.
After a month, the artist had become very weary from this non-stop effort and decided to take it easy for the day. Since his model had already shown up, he suggested they merely have a glass of wine and talk – normally he preferred to do his painting in silence.
They talked for a few hours, getting to know each other better. Then as they were sipping their claret, the artist heard a car arriving outside. He jumped up and said, "Oh no! It's my wife! Quick, take off your clothes!"

★ ★ ★

Artist Pablo Picasso surprised a burglar in his new chateau. The intruder got away, but Picasso did a rough sketch of what he looked like. On the basis of his drawing, the police arrested a mother superior, the minister of finance, a washing machine and the Eiffel tower.

★ ★ ★

A market researcher called at a house and his knock was answered by a young woman with three small children. He asked her if she knew his company, Cheeseborough-Ponds. When she said no, he mentioned that among their many products was Vaseline and she certainly knew of that product. When asked if she used it, the answer was "Yes". Asked how she used it, she said, "To assist sexual intercourse." The interviewer was amazed. He said, "I always ask that question because everyone uses our product and they always say they use it for the child's bicycle chain, or the gate hinge; but I know that most use it for sexual intercourse. Since you've been so frank, could you tell me exactly how you use it?"

"Yes, we put it on the doorknob to keep the kids out."

★ ★ ★

A Texas business man went over to Japan for a meeting. Once there, his boss sent him a key for a motel room, and a girl to have sex with.

That night when they had sex, the girl kept saying, "Sanwa! Sanwa!" The man thought she was saying, "Good! Good!"

The next day after the meeting, the boss and his executive and the Texan had a game of golf. After the executive made a hole in one the Texan was there screaming, "Sanwa Sanwa," and the executive said, "What do you mean wrong hole?!"

★ ★ ★

A flight attendant was stationed at the departure gate to check tickets. As a man approached, she extended her hand for the ticket and he opened his trench coat and flashed her.

Without missing a beat she said, "Sir, I asked to see your ticket, not your stub."

★ ★ ★

A cleaning woman was applying for a new position. When asked why she left her last employment, she replied, "Yes sir, they paid good wages, but it was the most ridiculous place I ever worked. They played a game called Bridge, and last night lots of folks were there.

"As I was about to bring in the refreshments, I heard a man say, 'Lay down and let's see what you've got.'

"Another man said, 'I've got strength but no length.'

"Another man said to a lady, 'Take your hand off my trick.' I pretty near dropped dead just then when the lady answered, 'You jumped me twice when you didn't have the strength for one raise.'

"Another lady was talking about protecting her honour, and two other ladies said, 'Now it's time for me to play with your husband and you can play with mine.'

"Well, I just got my hat and coat and as I was leaving, I hope to die if I didn't hear someone say, 'Well, I guess we'll go home now, that was the last rubber.'"

★ ★ ★

There was a farmer who grew watermelons. He was disturbed by some local kids who would sneak into his watermelon patch at night and eat watermelons.

After some careful thought he came up with a clever idea that he thought would scare the kids away for sure. So he made up a sign and posted it in the field. The next day the kids show up and they see this sign, it says, "Warning!! One of the watermelons in this field has been injected with cyanide."

So the kids run off, make up their own sign and post it next to the sign that the farmer made. The farmer shows up the next week and when he looks over the field he notices that no watermelons are missing, but he notices a new sign next to his. He drives up to the sign which reads, "Now there are two."

★ ★ ★

A farm boy was drafted. On his first trip home, his father asked him what he thought of army life.

"It's pretty good, Pa. The food's not bad, the work's easy, but best of all they let ya sleep real late in the morning."

★ ★ ★

In a long line of people waiting for a bank teller, one guy suddenly started massaging the back of the person in front of him.

Surprised, the man in front turned and snarled, "Just what the hell are you doing?" "Well," said the guy, "you see, I'm a massage therapist and I could see that you were tense, so I had to massage

670

your back. Sometimes I just can't help practising my art!" "That's the stupidest thing I've ever heard!" the guy replied. "I work for the IRS. Do you see me screwing the guy in front of me?"

★ ★ ★

A guy starts a new job, and the boss says, "If you marry my daughter, I'll make you a partner, give you an expense account, a Mercedes and a million-dollar annual salary."

The guy says, "What exactly's wrong with her?"

The boss shows him a picture, and she's hideous. The boss says, "It's only fair to tell you, she's not only ugly, she's as dumb as a wall."

The guy says, "I don't care what you offer me, it ain't worth it."

The boss says, "I'll give you a five-million-dollar salary and build you a mansion on Long Island."

The guy accepts, figuring he can put a bag over her head when they have sex.

About a year later, the guy buys an original Van Gogh and he's about to hang it on the wall. He climbs a ladder and yells to his wife, "Bring me a hammer."

She mumbles, "Get the hammer. Get the hammer," and she fetches the hammer.

The guy says, "Get me some nails."

She mumbles, "Get the nails. Get the nails," and she gets him some nails. The guys starts hammering a nail into the wall, he hits his thumb, and he yells, "Fuck!"

She mumbles, "Get the bag. Get the bag."

★ ★ ★

Bob called home one afternoon to see what his wife was making for dinner.

"Hello?" said a little girl's voice.

"Hi, honey, it's Daddy," said Bob. "Is Mommy near the phone?"

"No, Daddy. She's upstairs in the bedroom with uncle Frank."

After a pause, Bob said, "But you don't have an Uncle Frank, honey!"

671

"Yes, I do. He's upstairs in the bedroom with Mommy!"

"Okay, then. Here's what I want you to do. Put down the phone, run upstairs, knock on the bedroom door and shout in to Mommy and Uncle Frank that my car just pulled up outside the house."

"Okay, Daddy!"

A few minutes later, the little girl came back to the phone. "Well, I did what you said, Daddy."

"And what happened?"

"Well, Mommy jumped out of bed with no clothes on and ran around screaming, then she tripped over the rug and went out the front window and now she's all dead."

"Oh my god! What about Uncle Frank?"

"He jumped out of bed with no clothes on too and he was all scared and he jumped out the back window into the swimming pool, but he must have forgot that you took out all the water last week to clean it, so he hit the bottom of the swimming pool, and now he's dead too."

There was a long pause, then Bob said, "Swimming pool? Is this 555-7039?"

★ ★ ★